*Kwasi Sarkodie-Mensah*
*Editor*

# Reference Services for the Adult Learner: Challenging Issues for the Traditional and Technological Era

*Reference Services for the Adult Learner: Challenging Issues for the Traditional and Technological Era* has been co-published simultaneously as *The Reference Librarian*, Numbers 69/70 2000.

*More advance*
*REVIEWS, COMMENTARIES, EVALUATIONS . . .*

"**R**eference Services for the Adult Learner covers a broad spectrum of concerns of adult students, including library anxiety, special circumstances (e.g., time limitations, often working full-time, being out of school for several years), and other issues that they have in common with traditional students (e.g., disabilities, international students). Andragogy, the art of helping adults to learn, is different from helping traditional students. The authors pay particular attention to delineating the learning styles of adult students and provide effective approaches to developing their library skills and easing their distress. Included are descriptions of several specific programs for adult students that have been successfully implemented.

While the book is ostensibly about reference services, the line between reference and instruction is even more difficult to discern with adult learners, and several authors describe the interactions with adult students as being individual instruction sessions, often quite extensive. *Reference Services for the Adult Learner* provides useful guidelines and helpful approaches for reference

and instruction librarians who deal with this growing segment of academic library users."

**Lynda Leahy, MA MLS**
*Associate Librarian of Harvard College for Research & Instruction,*
*Harvard University, MA*

*More advance*
*REVIEWS, COMMENTARIES, EVALUATIONS . . .*

"**K**waski Sarkodie-Mensah and colleagues have put together a dynamic resource for today's reference and instruction librarians. The wealth of information for the adult learner is analyzed by practitioners with tremendous knowledge on this subject nationally and internationally. A a library administrator who continues to work at the reference desk I was amazed on the impact of technostress and technophobia on library users and who reference librarians can do to help. One author notes that "The challenge to Academic librarians is to teach users to make more efficient use of electronic databases," this is exactly what the information explosion is about.

In my opinion the most intriguing essay was "The Information Explosion and The Adult Learner: Implications for Reference Librarians," which describes the various levels of development among adult learners

In the remaining chapter every facet of the adult learner is addressed followed by suggestions as to what should be done to alleviate fears."

**Joyce C. Wright, AM, LS, CAS**
*Director of Undergraduate Library*
*Associate Professor*
*of Library Administration*
*University of Illinois*
*at Urbana-Champaign*

# Reference Services
# for the Adult Learner:
# Challenging Issues
# for the Traditional
# and Technological Era

*Reference Services for the Adult Learner: Challenging Issues for the Traditional and Technological Era* has been co-published simultaneously as *The Reference Librarian*, Numbers 69/70 2000.

# The *Reference Librarian* Monographic "Separates"

Below is a list of "separates," which in serials librarianship means a special issue simultaneously published as a special journal issue or double-issue *and* as a "separate" hardbound monograph. (This is a format which we also call a "DocuSerial.")

"Separates" are published because specialized libraries or professionals may wish to purchase a specific thematic issue by itself in a format which can be separately cataloged and shelved, as opposed to purchasing the journal on an on-going basis. Faculty members may also more easily consider a "separate" for classroom adoption.

"Separates" are carefully classified separately with the major book jobbers so that the journal tie-in can be noted on new book order slips to avoid duplicate purchasing.

You may wish to visit Haworth's website at . . .

## http://www.HaworthPress.com

. . . to search our online catalog for complete tables of contents of these separates and related publications.

You may also call 1-800-HAWORTH (outside US/Canada: 607-722-5857), or Fax 1-800-895-0582 (outside US/Canada: 607-771-0012), or e-mail at:

## getinfo@haworthpressinc.com

---

*Reference Services for the Adult Learner: Challenging Issues for the Traditional and Technological Era,* edited by Kwasi Sarkodie-Mensah, PhD (No. 69/70, 2000). *Containing research from librarians and adult learners from the United States, Canada, and Australia, this comprehensive guide offers you strategies for teaching adult patrons that will enable them to properly use and easily locate all of the materials in your library.*

*Library Outreach, Partnership, and Distance Education: Reference Librarians at the Gateway,* edited by Wendi Arant and Pixey Anne Mosley (No. 67/68, 1999). *Focuses on community outreach in libraries toward a broader public by extending services based on recent developments in information technology.*

*From Past-Present to Future-Perfect: A Tribute to Charles A. Bunge and the Challenges of Contemporary Reference Service,* edited by Chris D. Ferguson, PhD (No. 66, 1999). *Explore reprints of selected articles by Charles Bunge, bibliographies of his published work, and original articles that draw on Bunge's values and ideas in assessing the present and shaping the future of reference service.*

*Reference Services and Media,* edited by Martha Merrill, PhD (No. 65, 1999). *Gives you valuable information about various aspects of reference services and media, including changes, planning issues, and the use and impact of new technologies.*

*Coming of Age in Reference Services: A Case History of the Washington State University Libraries,* edited by Christy Zlatos, MSLS (No. 64, 1999). *A celebration of the perserverance, ingenuity, and talent of the librarians who have served, past and present, at the Holland Library reference desk.*

*Document Delivery Services: Contrasting Views,* edited by Robin Kinder, MLS (No. 63, 1999). *Reviews the planning and process of implementing document delivery in four university libraries–Miami University, University of Colorado at Denver, University of Montana at Missoula, and Purdue University Libraries.*

*The Holocaust: Memories, Research, Reference,* edited by Robert Hauptman, PhD, and Susan Hubbs Motin (No. 61/62, 1998). *"A wonderful resource for reference librarians, students, and teachers . . . on how to present this painful, historical event." (Ephraim Kaye, PhD, The International School for Holocaust Studies, Yad Vashem, Jerusalem)*

***Electronic Resources: Use and User Behavior,*** edited by Hemalata Iyer, PhD (No. 60, 1998). *Covers electronic resources and their use in libraries, with emphasis on the Internet and the Geographic Information Systems (GIS).*

***Philosophies of Reference Service,*** edited by Celia Hales Mabry (No. 59, 1997). *"Recommended reading for any manager responsible for managing reference services and hiring reference librarians in any type of library." (Charles R. Anderson, MLS, Associate Director for Public Services, King County Library System, Bellevue, Washington)*

***Business Reference Services and Sources: How End Users and Librarians Work Together,*** edited by Katherine M. Shelfer (No. 58, 1997). *"This is an important collection of papers suitable for all business librarians. . . . Highly recommended!" (Lucy Heckman, MLS, MBA, Business and Economics Reference Librarian, St. John's University, Jamaica, New York)*

***Reference Sources on the Internet: Off the Shelf and onto the Web,*** edited by Karen R. Diaz (No. 57, 1997). *Surf off the library shelves and onto the Internet and cut your research time in half!*

***Reference Services for Archives and Manuscripts,*** edited by Laura B. Cohen (No. 56, 1997). *"Features stimulating and interesting essays on security in archives, ethics in the archival profession, and electronic records." ("The Year's Best Professional Reading" (1998), Library Journal)*

***Career Planning and Job Searching in the Information Age,*** edited by Elizabeth A. Lorenzen, MLS (No. 55, 1996). *"Offers stimulating background for dealing with the issues of technology and service. . . . A reference tool to be looked at often." (The One-Person Library)*

***The Roles of Reference Librarians: Today and Tomorrow,*** edited by Kathleen Low, MLS (No. 54, 1996). *"A great asset to all reference collections. . . . Presents important, valuable information for reference librarians as well as other library users." (Library Times International)*

***Reference Services for the Unserved,*** edited by Fay Zipkowitz, MSLS, DA (No. 53, 1996). *"A useful tool in developing strategies to provide services to all patrons." (Science Books & Films)*

***Library Instruction Revisited: Bibliographic Instruction Comes of Age,*** edited by Lyn Elizabeth M. Martin, MLS (No. 51/52, 1995). *"A powerful collection authored by respected practitioners who have stormed the bibliographic instruction (BI) trenches and, luckily for us, have recounted their successes and shortcomings." (The Journal of Academic Librarianship)*

***Library Users and Reference Services,*** edited by Jo Bell Whitlatch, PhD (No. 49/50, 1995). *"Well-planned, balanced, and informative. . . . Both new and seasoned professionals will find material for service attitude formation and practical advice for the front lines of service." (Anna M. Donnelly, MS, MA, Associate Professor and Reference Librarian, St. John's University Library)*

***Social Science Reference Services,*** edited by Pam Baxter, MLS (No. 48, 1995). *"Offers practical guidance to the reference librarian. . . . a valuable source of information about specific literatures within the social sciences and the skills and techniques needed to provide access to those literatures." (Nancy P. O'Brien, MLS, Head, Education and Social Science Library, and Professor of Library Administration, University of Illinois at Urbana-Champaign)*

***Reference Services in the Humanities,*** edited by Judy Reynolds, MLS (No. 47, 1994). *"A well-chosen collection of situations and challenges encountered by reference librarians in the humanities." (College Research Library News)*

***Racial and Ethnic Diversity in Academic Libraries: Multicultural Issues,*** edited by Deborah A. Curry, MLS, MA, Susan Griswold Blandy, MEd, and Lyn Elizabeth M. Martin, MLS (No. 45/46, 1994). *"The useful techniques and attractive strategies presented here will provide the incentive for fellow professionals in academic libraries around the country to go and do likewise in their own institutions." (David Cohen, Adjunct Professor of Library Science, School of Library and Information Science, Queens College; Director, EMIE (Ethnic Materials Information Exchange); Editor, EMIE Bulletin)*

***School Library Reference Services in the 90s: Where We Are, Where We're Heading,*** edited by Carol Truett, PhD (No. 44, 1994). *"Unique and valuable to the the teacher-librarian as well as* *students of librarianship. . . . The overall work successfully interweaves the concept of the continuously changing role of the teacher-librarian." (Emergency Librarian)*

**Reference Services Planning in the 90s,** edited by Gail Z. Eckwright, MLS, and Lori M. Keenan, MLS (No. 43, 1994). *"This monograph is well-researched and definitive, encompassing reference service as practices by library and information scientists. . . . it should be required reading for all professional librarian trainees." (Feliciter)*

**Librarians on the Internet: Impact on Reference Services,** edited by Robin Kinder, MLS (No. 41/42, 1994). *"Succeeds in demonstrating that the Internet is becoming increasingly a challenging but practical and manageable tool in the reference librarian's ever-expanding armory." (Reference Reviews)*

**Reference Service Expertise,** edited by Bill Katz (No. 40, 1993). *This important volume presents a wealth of practical ideas for improving the art of reference librarianship.*

**Modern Library Technology and Reference Services,** edited by Samuel T. Huang, MLS, MS (No. 39, 1993). *"This book packs a surprising amount of information into a relatively few number of pages. . . . This book will answer many questions." (Science Books and Films)*

**Assessment and Accountability in Reference Work,** edited by Susan Griswold Blandy, Lyn M. Martin, and Mary L. Strife (No. 38, 1992). *"An important collection of well-written, real-world chapters addressing the central questions that surround performance and services in all libraries." (Library Times International)*

**The Reference Librarian and Implications of Mediation,** edited by M. Keith Ewing, MLS, and Robert Hauptman, MLS (No. 37, 1992). *"An excellent and thorough analysis of reference mediation. . . . well worth reading by anyone involved in the delivery of reference services." (Fred Batt, MLS, Associate University Librarian for Public Services, California State University, Sacramento)*

**Library Services for Career Planning, Job Searching and Employment Opportunities,** edited by Byron Anderson, MA, MLS (No. 36, 1992). *"An interesting book which tells professional libraries how to set up career information centers. . . . Clearly valuable reading for anyone establishing a career library." (Career Opportunities News)*

**In the Spirit of 1992: Access to Western European Libraries and Literature,** edited by Mary M. Huston, PhD, and Maureen Pastine, MLS (No. 35, 1992). *"A valuable and practical [collection] which every subject specialist in the field would do well to consult." (Western European Specialists Section Newsletter)*

**Access Services: The Convergence of Reference and Technical Services,** edited by Gillian M. McCombs, ALA (No. 34, 1992). *"Deserves a wide readership among both technical and public services librarians. . . . highly recommended for any librarian interested in how reference and technical services roles may be combined." (Library Resources & Technical Services)*

**Opportunities for Reference Services: The Bright Side of Reference Services in the 1990s,** edited by Bill Katz (No. 33, 1991). *"A well-deserved look at the brighter side of reference services. . . . Should be read by reference librarians and their administrators in all types of libraries." (Library Times International)*

**Government Documents and Reference Services,** edited by Robin Kinder, MLS (No. 32, 1991). *Discusses access possibilities and policies with regard to government information, covering such important topics as new and impending legislation, information on most frequently used and requested sources, and grant writing.*

**The Reference Library User: Problems and Solutions,** edited by Bill Katz (No. 31, 1991). *"Valuable information and tangible suggestions that will help us as a profession look critically at our users and decide how they are best served." (Information Technology and Libraries)*

**Continuing Education of Reference Librarians,** edited by Bill Katz (No. 30/31, 1990). *"Has something for everyone interested in this field. . . . Library trainers and library school teachers may well find stimulus in some of the programs outlined here." (Library Association Record)*

*Weeding and Maintenance of Reference Collections,* edited by Sydney J. Pierce, PhD, MLS (No. 29, 1990). *"This volume may spur you on to planned activity before lack of space dictates 'ad hoc' solutions." (New Library World)*

*Serials and Reference Services,* edited by Robin Kinder, MLS, and Bill Katz (No. 27/28, 1990). *"The concerns and problems discussed are those of serials and reference librarians everywhere. . . . The writing is of a high standard and the book is useful and entertaining. . . . This book can be recommended." (Library Association Record)*

*Rothstein on Reference: . . . with some help from friends,* edited by Bill Katz and Charles Bunge, PhD, MLS (No. 25/26, 1990). *"An important and stimulating collection of essays on reference librarianship. . . . Highly recommended!" (Richard W. Grefrath, MA, MLS, Reference Librarian, University of Nevada Library)* Dedicated to the work of Sam Rothstein, one of the world's most respected teachers of reference librarians, this special volume features his writings as well as articles written about him and his teachings by other professionals in the field.

*Integrating Library Use Skills Into the General Education Curriculum,* edited by Maureen Pastine, MLS, and Bill Katz (No. 24, 1989). *"All contributions are written and presented to a high standard with excellent references at the end of each. . . . One of the best summaries I have seen on this topic." (Australian Library Review)*

*Expert Systems in Reference Services,* edited by Christine Roysdon, MLS, and Howard D. White, PhD, MLS (No. 23, 1989). *"The single most comprehensive work on the subject of expert systems in reference service." (Information Processing and Management)*

*Information Brokers and Reference Services,* edited by Bill Katz and Robin Kinder, MLS (No. 22, 1989). *"An excellent tool for reference librarians and indispensable for anyone seriously considering their own information-brokering service." (Booklist)*

*Information and Referral in Reference Services*, edited by Marcia Stucklen Middleton, MLS and Bill Katz (No. 21, 1988). *Investigates a wide variety of situations and models which fall under the umbrella of information and referral.*

*Reference Services and Public Policy,* edited by Richard Irving, MLS, and Bill Katz (No. 20, 1988). *Looks at the relationship between public policy and information and reports ways in which libraries respond to the need for public policy information.*

*Finance, Budget, and Management for Reference Services,* edited by Ruth A. Fraley, MLS, MBA, and Bill Katz (No. 19, 1989). *"Interesting and relevant to the current state of financial needs in reference service. . . . A must for anyone new to or already working in the reference service area." (Riverina Library Review)*

*Current Trends in Information: Research and Theory,* edited by Bill Katz and Robin Kinder, MLS (No. 18, 1984). *"Practical direction to improve reference services and does so in a variety of ways ranging from humorous and clever metaphoric comparisons to systematic and practical methodological descriptions." (American Reference Books Annual)*

*International Aspects of Reference and Information Services*, edited by Bill Katz and Ruth A. Fraley, MLS, MBA (No. 17, 1987). *"An informative collection of essays written by eminent librarians, library school staff, and others concerned with the international aspects of information work." (Library Association Record)*

*Reference Services Today: From Interview to Burnout,* edited by Bill Katz and Ruth A. Fraley, MLS, MBA (No. 16, 1987). *Authorities present important advice to all reference librarians on the improvement of service and the enhancement of the public image of reference services.*

*The Publishing and Review of Reference Sources,* edited by Bill Katz and Robin Kinder, MLS (No. 15, 1987). *"A good review of current reference reviewing and publishing trends in the United States . . . will be of interest to intending reviewers, reference librarians, and students." (Australasian College Libraries)*

*Personnel Issues in Reference Services,* edited by Bill Katz and Ruth Fraley, MLS, MBA (No. 14, 1986). *"Chock-full of information that can be applied to most reference settings. Recommended for libraries with active reference departments." (RQ)*

*Reference Services in Archives,* edited by Lucille Whalen (No. 13, 1986). *"Valuable for the insights it provides on the reference process in archives and as a source of information on the different ways of carrying out that process." (Library and Information Science Annual)*

*Conflicts in Reference Services,* edited by Bill Katz and Ruth A. Fraley, MLS, MBA (No. 12, 1985). *This collection examines issues pertinent to the reference department.*

*Evaluation of Reference Services,* edited by Bill Katz and Ruth A. Fraley, MLS, MBA (No. 11, 1985). *"A much-needed overview of the present state of the art vis-à-vis reference service evaluation. . . . excellent. . . . Will appeal to reference professionals and aspiring students." (RQ)*

*Library Instruction and Reference Services*, edited by Bill Katz and Ruth A. Fraley, MLS, MBA (No. 10, 1984). *"Well written, clear, and exciting to read. This is an important work recommended for all librarians, particularly those involved in, interested in, or considering bibliographic instruction. . . . A milestone in library literature." (RQ)*

*Reference Services and Technical Services: Interactions in Library Practice,* edited by Gordon Stevenson and Sally Stevenson (No. 9, 1984). *"New ideas and longstanding problems are handled with humor and sensitivity as practical suggestions and new perspectives are suggested by the authors." (Information Retrieval & Library Automation)*

*Reference Services for Children and Young Adults,* edited by Bill Katz and Ruth A. Fraley, MLS, MBA (No. 7/8, 1983). *"Offers a well-balanced approach to reference service for children and young adults. " (RQ)*

*Video to Online: Reference Services in the New Technology,* edited by Bill Katz and Ruth A. Fraley, MLS, MBA (No. 5/6, 1983). *"A good reference manual to have on hand. . . . well-written, concise, provide[s] a wealth of information." (Online)*

*Ethics and Reference Services,* edited by Bill Katz and Ruth A. Fraley, MLS, MBA (No. 4, 1982). *Library experts discuss the major ethical and legal implications that reference librarians must take into consideration when handling sensitive inquiries about confidential material.*

*Reference Services Administration and Management,* edited by Bill Katz and Ruth A. Fraley, MLS, MBA (No. 3, 1982). *Librarianship experts discuss the management of the reference function in libraries and information centers, outlining the responsibilities and qualifications of reference heads.*

*Reference Services in the 1980s,* edited by Bill Katz (No. 1/2, 1982). *Here is a thought-provoking volume on the future of reference services in libraries, with an emphasis on the challenges and needs that have come about as a result of automation.*

# Reference Services for the Adult Learner: Challenging Issues for the Traditional and Technological Era

Kwasi Sarkodie-Mensah
Editor

*Reference Services for the Adult Learner: Challenging Issues for the Traditional and Technological Era* has been co-published simultaneously as *The Reference Librarian*, Numbers 69/70 2000.

The Haworth Information Press
An Imprint of
The Haworth Press, Inc.
New York • London • Oxford

Published by

The Haworth Press Information Press, 10 Alice Street, Binghamton, NY 13904-1580, USA

The Haworth Information Press, is an imprint of The Haworth Press, Inc., 10 Alice Street, Binghamton, NY 13904-1580 USA

*Reference Services for the Adult Learner: Challenging Issues for the Traditional and Technological Era* has been co-published simultaneously as *The Reference Librarian*, Numbers 69/70 2000.

The development, preparation, and publication of this work has been undertaken with great care. However, the publisher, employees, editors, and agents of The Haworth Press and all imprints of The Haworth Press, Inc., including The Haworth Medical Press® and Pharmaceutical Products Press®, are not responsible for any errors contained herein or for consequences that may ensue from use of materials or information contained in this work. Opinions expressed by the author(s) are not necessarily those of The Haworth Press, Inc.

Cover design by Thomas J. Mayshock Jr.

**Library of Congress Cataloging-in-Publication Data**

Reference services for the adult learner: challenging issues for the traditional and technological era/ Kwasi Sarkodie-Mensah, editor.
    p. cm.
    Published also as no. 69/70 2000 of The reference librarian.
    Includes bibliographical references and index.
    ISBN 0-7890-0972-2 (alk. paper)–ISBN 0-7890-0990-0 (pbk.: alk. paper)
    1. Academic libraries–Services to adult college students. 2. Public libraries–Services to adults. 3. Libraries and adult education. 4. Adult learning. 5. Continuing education. I. Sarkodie-Mensah, Kwasi. II. Reference librarian.
Z711.92.A32 R44 2000
025.5'2–dc21

00-038868

# INDEXING & ABSTRACTING

Contributions to this publication are selectively indexed or abstracted in print, electronic, online, or CD-ROM version(s) of the reference tools and information services listed below. This list is current as of the copyright date of this publication. See the end of this section for additional notes.

- *Academic Abstracts/CD-ROM*
- *Academic Search: data base of 2,000 selected academic serials, updated monthly*
- *BUBL Information Service: An Internet-Based Information Service for the UK Higher Education Community <URL:http://bubl.ac.uk/>*
- *CNPIEC Reference Guide: Chinese National Directory of Foreign Periodicals*
- *Current Awareness Abstracts of Library & Information Literature, ASLIB (UK)*
- *Current Index to Journals in Education*
- *Educational Administration Abstracts (EAA)*
- *FINDEX <www.publist.com>*
- *Handbook of Latin American Studies*
- *IBZ International Bibliography of Periodical Literature*
- *Index to Periodical Articles Related to Law*
- *Information Science Abstracts*
- *Informed Librarian, The <http://www.infosourcespub.com>*
- *INSPEC*
- *Journal of Academic Librarianship: Guide to Professional Literature, The*
- *Konyvtari Figyelo-Library Review*
- *Library & Information Science Abstracts (LISA)*

(continued)

- *Library and Information Science Annual (LISCA)*
  *<www.lu.com/arba>*

- *Library Literature*

- *MasterFILE: updated database from EBSCO Publishing*

- *Newsletter of Library and Information Services*

- *OT BibSys*

- *PASCAL*
  *<http.//www.inist.fr>*

- *Referativnyi Zhurnal (Abstracts Journal of the All-Russian Institute of Scientific and Technical Information)*

- *Sage Public Administration Abstracts (SPAA)*

*Special bibliographic notes related to special journal issues (separates) and indexing/abstracting:*

- indexing/abstracting services in this list will also cover material in any "separate" that is co-published simultaneously with Haworth's special thematic journal issue or DocuSerial. Indexing/abstracting usually covers material at the article/chapter level.
- monographic co-editions are intended for either non-subscribers or libraries which intend to purchase a second copy for their circulating collections.
- monographic co-editions are reported to all jobbers/wholesalers/approval plans. The source journal is listed as the "series" to assist the prevention of duplicate purchasing in the same manner utilized for books-in-series.
- to facilitate user/access services all indexing/abstracting services are encouraged to utilize the co-indexing entry note indicated at the bottom of the first page of each article/chapter/contribution.
- this is intended to assist a library user of any reference tool (whether print, electronic, online, or CD-ROM) to locate the monographic version if the library has purchased this version but not a subscription to the source journal.
- individual articles/chapters in any Haworth publication are also available through the Haworth Document Delivery Service (HDDS).

# Reference Services for the Adult Learner: Challenging Issues for the Traditional and Technological Era

## CONTENTS

## ABOUT THE EDITOR

**Kwasi Sarkodie-Mensah, PhD,** is Manager, Instructional Services at Boston College. He is also Adjunct Professor in the College of Advancing Studies, where he teaches one session of the required Research Methods and Data course to adult students. He is the author of over two dozen articles, several book chapters, and some 100 book and video reviews. He is active in ACRL's Instruction Section and ALA's Library Instruction Round Table Committees.

# Introduction

While the number of traditional college students has declined, the proportion of older people returning to school has seen a dramatic increase in growth. There are all indications that this trend will not slow down any sooner. Libraries of all types have been affected by this exciting influx of college bound adult students. In an era of increasing technology, when the daily lives of the world's citizens are shaped by the availability, accessibility, and evaluation of information in various formats, it becomes imperative for libraries to continue to be prepared to meet the needs of the population they serve.

In this special publication, librarians, information specialists, educators, and older adults from the United States, Canada, and Australia share a wealth of information regarding the adult learner in the age of technology.

The first section of this special volume looks at the problem of technostress and technophobia in an era of information explosion. The information age carries with it not only the strains created by the ever-increasing wave of technology, but also a fear, which if left untreated, will plunge adult learners into darkness and prevent them from making the best and most effective use of the exciting resources available to them. Anita Ezzo, Julia Perez, Gayle R. Christian, Caroline Blumenthal, Marjorie Patterson, Lucy Harrison, Brian Quinn, Deborah S. Grealy, and Kevin F. Bontenbal write about information explosion, technophobia and technostress.

Understanding the needs of the adult learner is a required ingredient in the recipe that spells successful and effective services to this special library user. Lisa Given, Sara Baron, Alexia Strout-Dapaz, Charlotte Diana Moslander, Robin E. Veal, and Anne Fox share their views, experiences, and insights into diverse issues such as envisioning the mature re-entry student, helping students make the best of the emerging technology, and the after-five syndrome, a situation all of us are too familiar with.

Theories of adult learning abound, and applying them to reference and

[Haworth co-indexing entry note]: "Introduction." Sarkodie-Mensah, Kwasi. Co-published simultaneously in *The Reference Librarian* (The Haworth Information Press, an imprint of The Haworth Press, Inc.) No. 69/70, 2000, pp. 1-2; and: *Reference Services for the Adult Learner: Challenging Issues for the Traditional and Technological Era* (ed: Kwasi Sarkodie-Mensah) The Haworth Information Press, an imprint of The Haworth Press, Inc., 2000, pp. 1-2. Single or multiple copies of this article are available for a fee from The Haworth Document Delivery Service [1-800-342-9678, 9:00 a.m. - 5:00 p.m. (EST). E-mail address: getinfo@haworthpressinc.com].

instructional services can only help us to improve what we do. We learn to practice these in the section on adult learning theories. Loriene Roy and Eric Novotny write about the contributions of learning theory to reference service and library instruction; Dorothy S. Ingram looks at the learning needs and characteristics of the adult library user; James Ghaphery explores how the similarities between contemporary adult education thought and reference services can provide us with some interesting possibilities in looking toward the future of reference in the digital era.

Distance learning is a natural when it comes to the adult learner. How do we best serve our adult learners from a distance? Helpful hints, proven solutions, and practical guidelines are provided by eleven of our colleagues. Elaine Anderson Jayne, Susan A. Ware, Patricia S. Howe, Rosemary G. Scalese, Melva Renshaw, Jon R. Hufford, Michael Middleton, Judith Peacock, C. Lyn Currie, Craig Gibson, and Jane Scales write about the adult learner and distance reference services and instruction in the United States, Canada, and Australia.

Teaching strategies of seeking, analyzing, and evaluating information go hand in hand with reference work. In the section "Reference, Instruction and Information Literacy" five of our colleagues, Hema Ramachandran, Patti Schifter Caravello, Marcia A. King-Blandford, Naomi Harrison, and Julian W. Green share with us courses, and theories of learning they have used successfully to serve and instruct the adult learner.

There are many adult learners among the special populations we serve and teach. Five articles, one on the disabled, and four on international students, examine issues and solutions we should be aware of when it comes to serving our diverse population. Katherine J. Miller-Gatenby, Michele Chittenden, Suhasini L. Kumar, Raghini S. Suresh, Christopher C. Brown, Calmer D. Chattoo, and Daniel Liestman provide detailed information in the section "Serving Diverse Populations: Disabled Patrons and International Students."

What can be more desirable than hearing from those we serve and teach? In the final section, views from those we are directly involved with are provided. "From the Horse's Mouth: Views from Faculty, Administrators, Librarians, and Students," Barbara Mullins, Betsy Park, Patience L. Simmonds, and Robert M. Fisher give us views about reference and instructional services from faculty, administrators, librarians and students.

I can say with positive certitude that the collection of articles in this collection will spark a series of challenging and stimulating conversations among my colleagues in libraries, the information profession, and other areas of education. I invite you to share your thoughts with me and the knowledgeable contributors of this volume by using the e-mail and snail mail addresses provided.

*Kwasi Sarkodie-Mensah*

# SECTION 1:
# INFORMATION EXPLOSION, TECHNOPHOBIA, AND TECHNOSTRESS

# The Information Explosion: Continuing Implications for Reference Services to Adult Learners in Academia

Anita Ezzo
Julia Perez

**SUMMARY.** The reference environment is being transformed by constant changes in computer technologies and communications, as collections and information in general become increasingly accessible electronically. Academic library users now have access to seemingly unlimited information. The explosion of information choices has implications for reference services to all users, particularly adult learners–those students older than the typical undergraduate–who are becoming a large presence on university and college campuses. This paper will explore these implications, stress the need for information literacy, and challenge academic reference librarians to assert themselves in the information arena. *[Article copies available for a fee from The Haworth Document Delivery Service: 1-800-342-9678. E-mail address: <getinfo@ haworthpressinc.com> Website: <http://www.haworthpressinc.com>]*

**KEYWORDS.** Information explosion, information overload, adult learners, electronic library, academic libraries, reference services, information literacy

---

Anita Ezzo is Science Reference Librarian, Main Library, Michigan State University, East Lansing, MI 48824 (E-mail: ezzoa@mail.lib.msu.edu). Julia Perez is Science Reference Coordinator, Main Library, Michigan State University, East Lansing, MI 48824 (E-mail: perezj@pilot.msu.edu).

[Haworth co-indexing entry note]: "The Information Explosion: Continuing Implications for Reference Services to Adult Learners in Academia." Ezzo, Anita, and Julia Perez. Co-published simultaneously in *The Reference Librarian* (The Haworth Information Press, an imprint of The Haworth Press, Inc.) No. 69/70, 2000, pp. 5-17; and: *Reference Services for the Adult Learner: Challenging Issues for the Traditional and Technological Era* (ed: Kwasi Sarkodie-Mensah) The Haworth Information Press, an imprint of The Haworth Press, Inc., 2000, pp. 5-17. Single or multiple copies of this article are available for a fee from The Haworth Document Delivery Service [1-800-342-9678, 9:00 a.m. - 5:00 p.m. (EST). E-mail address: getinfo@haworthpressinc.com].

We are currently living in a society being rapidly transformed by advances in communications, electronics, and technology. The proliferation of affordable computing and storage devices, low-cost Internet access and easy-to-use interfaces has resulted in an "information explosion"–an extreme increase in the supply and dissemination of information, particularly in digital format. The societal impacts of the "information explosion" and the dawn of the "information age" have become the subject of many books, articles, and media stories. Not surprisingly, the library literature has also grappled with this issue. Over the past fifteen years, several articles have examined the impact of "information overload" on the library user and the role of the librarian in helping patrons navigate the information floodwaters (Biggs, Bob, Hopkins, Rudd & Rudd). Of course, librarians have been helping users navigate the information world for quite some time and Korth and Silberschatz remind us that "information revolutions predate the computer age"– consider earlier "information ages/explosions" such as those unleashed by Guttenberg's invention of the printing press, Alexander Graham Bell's invention of the telephone, and the post-World War II boom in scientific research and publication (p. 140). Libraries have always been in the business of safeguarding the world's collected knowledge, developing extensive cataloging systems and classification schemes to organize and manage it all and, perhaps unintentionally, serving as information filters or monitors through their very selection practices. Traditional libraries have provided a gateway to information by providing a coherent mechanism for searching the catalog, by making catalogs universally uniform (authority control), by providing a collection of books and journals in a single location, and by offering reference assistance (McDonald, pp. 92, 94). All of these practices have served as a means of helping "people cope with and benefit from the proliferation of information." Although "today's exploding information volume and breadth of information dissemination are phenomena with historical precedents," it is our powerful computing infrastructure–hardware and software–that make this current information age unique (Korth & Silberschatz, pp. 139-140).

## THE ELECTRONIC LIBRARY

Libraries have been harnessing the latest computing technology to make information more and more accessible. Traditional card catalogs have been replaced by powerful computers that can search the online and web catalogs from one or more libraries, as well as the Internet and other electronic databases and journals. In academia, sophisticated campus networks allow users to connect remotely and conduct research from home or office without setting foot in the library. To those fortunate enough to possess the requisite configuration of computer hardware and software, the "electronic library" is accessible anywhere, anytime. Unfortunately, the "traditional" library cannot make the same claim. Fiscal constraints have generally resulted in a decline in library staffing, consolidation of public service points, reduction in service hours, and greater reliance on paraprofessionals and student assistants to provide reference assistance. Heckart speculates that the next trend may be the further development of expert systems and machine-help, so as "to provide little or no in-person help at all" (p. 252). Such an automated, self-service approach has clear implications, not only for reference services, but also for users who must become increasingly computer-savvy and information literate to step up to the challenge of becoming self-reliant information seekers.

How will academic library users fare in this information-rich environment, increasingly digitized, and searchable remotely, far from the watchful auspices of friendly reference librarians offering professional mediation? To answer this question, we must consider a second–who are these end-user searchers whom we have empowered with information self-sufficiency? While many are traditional college undergraduates 18-22 years of age, entering higher education straight from high school, increasingly, they belong to the growing body of "adult learners"–"nontraditional students" 23-25 years of age and older who are returning to school on a full-time or part-time basis after some absence to complete graduate or undergraduate studies or to take classes to fulfill job demands, improve skills, enhance employability, or simply to learn something new (Backes, p. 29; Rauch, p. 12; Wyman, p. 32). Frequently, their coursework is being completed as a part of "evening" or "weekend" college or through a distance learning or "virtual university" program. According to the United States Department of Education National Center for Education Statistics, in 1995 students 25 years of age and older comprised 43% of the total enrollment in institutions of higher education. Since projections continue to place this cohort of learners in the 40th percentile as far as the year 2007, it behooves academic librarians to examine service implications to develop a better understanding of this large clientele (p. 184).

## ADULT LEARNERS

Much has been written on the topic of adult learners and adult learning styles, yet attempts to define and characterize adult learners as a group have met with mixed success. No single definition suffices to describe this very "heterogeneous cohort of learners . . . widely diverse in their learning interests, educational goals, individual differences, experiential backgrounds, motives for pursuing learning projects, and patterns of participating in formal classroom programs" (Sheckley, p. 21). Nevertheless, while recognizing that there can be *no universal* statements which characterize all adult learners, Polson suggests the following *general attributes* which have implications for teaching and library service:

1. Multiple Roles: College is *not* a full-time occupation for the adult learner, but rather an added role which must be integrated into an already full schedule of work and family obligations, which take precedence and impact the time and energy devoted to study.
2. More Life Experiences: Adult students usually bring a broader knowledge and experience base to the classroom than the younger, more traditional student. Their experiences and prior knowledge can provide a rich foundation upon which to build new knowledge as well as create barriers to learning when established beliefs, attitudes, and practices are challenged.
3. Varied Developmental Tasks: Adult students, ranging in age from 23 to 65 years and over, represent a broad spectrum of developmental stages, each with their own accompanying life transitions, issues, and concerns, as well as age-related biological factors such as a decline in visual and/or auditory acuity, slowed reaction time, reduced energy levels, and a decrease in short-term memory.
4. Other Characteristics: Most adults are *off-campus* directed, relying less heavily on campus-based services and resources (pp. 2-4).

Attempts to account for the unique characteristics of adult learners have led to the development of a theory of adult learning–"andragogy," the art and science of helping adults learn, vs. "pedagogy," the art and science of teaching children (Knowles, p. 54). On the basis of the adult learner profile, Knowles suggests "that adults learn best in informal, comfortable, flexible, nonthreatening settings," when they are highly motivated and feel the "need to know," when they can be self-directing and participate actively in the learning process, and when they see relevance and practical applications for the learning content (pp. 54, 57-63). Teaching strategies should take these adult characteristics and needs into account; however, the very diverse nature of the adult learner cohort group suggests that, for this group, there can be "no one best way to teach" nor "one best way to learn" (Polson, p. 2). Furthermore, since "there is no single characteristic of 'adult learners' which is not present–to some degree–among all learners" (Sheckley, p. 21), the more "traditional" student might also learn better when his/her "needs and interests, life situations, experience, self-concepts, and individual differences are taken into account" (Knowles, p. 32). Sheckley suggests that the higher education system needs to recognize diversity among the entire college student population and become more responsive to the educational interests of all learners (p. 21).

## TECHNOLOGICAL CONSIDERATIONS

How can academic libraries provide better reference service in response to the changing demographics of the campus, amidst an explosion of information choices and an ever-changing electronic environment? Not without addressing some important issues and challenging some commonly-held assumptions concerning users' technological capabilities and information literacy skills. Academic libraries will continue to invest heavily in networked bibliographic and full-text databases, electronic journals, web interfaces, expert systems, etc., not only to satisfy campus-based faculty and students' expectations of remote access and to cater to user preferences for electronic vs. print indices, but also to provide the growing number of distance learners with adequate access to library materials and resources. However, since "it is expensive for users to purchase the equipment to navigate these emerging information nodes," we must not presuppose computer access and "be sensitive to those who are unable to afford it" (McDonald, p. 94). While network access on campus is likely to be powerful and reliable, off-campus connectivity will vary greatly according to the individual's particular configuration of computer hardware and communications software. Academic reference librarians will be increasingly called upon to provide technical assistance to remote users experiencing difficulties configuring their computers, downloading the necessary software to access library resources, connecting to the network, etc. Adult learners may present additional challenges, due to a wide range in computer skills. Some adult learners may be returning to school after an absence of ten or twenty years and may have never touched a computer before in their life. As Lantis and Sulewski note, these individuals "are not familiar with the names of the hardware elements, they don't understand the fundamental operations of the PC, and the buzzwords and jargon that are used in describing the technology are foreign to them." They may have "deep-seated misconceptions of what computers can and cannot do," and/or fear that they may destroy the machine with one false keystroke (p. 83). Such individuals may require one-on-one instruction and constant reassurance to help them overcome their computer anxiety.

At the opposite end of the spectrum are those adult learners who have developed considerable proficiency using computers as a part of their daily work routine. In fact, some may be exceptionally computer/technology literate and expect their educational providers (including librarians) to be equally so (Kent & Shaughnessy, p. 64). Special tact may be required to teach these users unfamiliar library applications and protocols, while acknowledging pre-existing experience and competency levels.

Regardless of previous computer experience, all learners face the inevitable problems and changes associated with electronic information resources. Servers go down and connections fail, leaving information temporarily inaccessible. Continuing efforts to improve user interfaces or to incorporate the latest "bells and whistles" result in frequent changes to the library's catalog, electronic databases, or home pages. Introductory screens are changed and options mysteriously disappear or migrate to new locations not immediately apparent, as databases are switched from one vendor to another in search of the most attractive deal. The at times seemingly constant rearrangement may be very confusing and frustrating to users, especially adult learners, whose multiple commitments impact the amount of time that can be devoted to study. The need to hunt for a missing file or to learn a new interface, after having already gained/attained a certain level of comfort and familiarity with the old one, is both irritating and time-consuming. The fact that many of these adult learners are also distance learners or other remote users accessing electronic resources more conveniently from home or office may intensify the frustration. Remote access means no kindly reference librarian is nearby to head off confusion, offer reassurance, provide guidance, or suggest alternatives. Although, theoretically, remote users can telephone or e-mail the reference desk for assistance, the majority are likely to muddle through on their own, turning instead to whatever digital "help" is available just a mouse-click away. While, obviously, libraries cannot discourage remote access nor stem the inevitable tide of change, they can attempt to minimize change simply for change's sake and become more proactive in alerting users to upcoming modifications in online systems.

Librarians also need to become more proactive in their efforts to influence the development of more intuitive and user-friendly searching software. Biggs laments that librarians "have been largely uncritical, remarkably accepting of producer-imposed limitations, and very little involved in identifying and demanding needed enhancements or changes" (p. 418). With the proliferation of products, librarians need to become "tenacious evaluators of database quality (content and search options) prior to purchase" and "assert their needs and requirements in the marketplace" (Hallett, p. 33). We need to be careful, however, that attempts to produce "user-friendly" products do not result in databases designed strictly for the lowest common denominator in end-user searchers–easy-to-use menu-driven interfaces, lacking the powerful searching capabilities librarians have come to rely on in order to conduct precise searches. With the abundance of electronic information, all users can benefit from sophisticated searching techniques that restrict searching output to a manageable size. The challenge to academic reference librarians is to teach users to make more efficient use of electronic databases. Greater uniformity of interfaces and improved online help would greatly facilitate this task.

## INFORMATION LITERACY

The explosion of information and increased options for retrieving it requires academic library users to become more "information literate"–to understand not just the information-seeking process and how to select and use appropriate library resources, but also to critically evaluate information and integrate it into their own research. Academic reference librarians, in library instruction classes, have traditionally focused on the first piece of the puzzle–information-finding skills. Unfortunately, many adult students–especially those who have been away from academia for many years–may have never received formal instruction in the use of library resources, may not be required now as graduate students to take a library skills course (Simon, p. 14), or, in the case of those "with strong academic backgrounds," may find "previously-learned skills minimally useful" in a radically-changed information environment (Steffen, p. 645). Full-time employment, family obligations, and/or enrollment in "evening" or "weekend" college or "virtual university" programs may limit current opportunities for participation in formal instruction sessions, "invariably scheduled during the day to accommodate full-time students" (Tomaiuolo, p. 51). The burden of instruction will, therefore, likely fall most heavily on reference librarians staffing the desk during evening and weekend hours. While the personal contact and individual attention afforded by the one-on-one instruction works best with adult learners (Tomaiuolo, p. 51), academic library staffing efficiencies may hamper attempts to provide in-depth assistance in a typical reference setting. The availability of librarians for research consultations on demand or by appointment and the scheduling of information skills workshops during late afternoon, early evening, and weekend hours are ways in which some academic libraries have attempted to address the instructional needs of adult students in nontraditional programs (Steffen, p. 641). If "nontraditional programs call for nontraditional hours" as Bowden and Merritt posit (p. 428), all academic libraries serving large populations of adult learners would do well to examine existing programs and services to ensure that they are available during times when adults are most apt to use them.

A greater challenge may be getting adult students to actually seek assistance. Adult learners tend to be "off-campus" directed, relying less heavily on campus-based services and resources. In a study of information retrieval techniques among graduate students in an urban university, Simon found that adult students turned to public, personal, and work libraries for resources, perhaps because they did not live on campus and/or wished to minimize the number of trips to campus. Furthermore, these students generally believed they were "adept in methods of literature searching," although many were unfamiliar with most of the library's resources, used only a few databases for their searches and rarely any print sources, did not understand the basic concepts of searching including the development of a search strategy and the identification of appropriate search terminology, and rarely utilized truncation or sophisticated searching techniques. Very few students acknowledged using database thesauri or tutorials and many asked for assistance from staff only after unsuccessfully exploring other options. Oddly enough, despite deficiencies in research skills, students were fairly pleased with their search results, although many were unable to locate relevant materials after identifying them. Once again, rather than asking for assistance, many students tended to use only what they could easily locate and did not avail themselves of interlibrary loan or other resources (pp. 82-85).

Other researchers have reported similar observations–that nontraditional students did not think they had serious research deficiencies, but rather felt they could pretty much find on their own whatever they needed in the library (Hammond, p. 329). Whether motivated by adult feelings of autonomy and a desire for independent self-directed learning or by a belief that asking for assistance implies dependence or ineptitude, this failure to utilize reference services is disconcerting to say the least. Biggs uses much stronger language in deploring "the fact that most information seeking transpires with little or no help from librarians, who have consistently failed to establish themselves as primary information professionals" (p. 411). She finds the traditional service approach to be "too impoverished" for today's information-rich environment.

> Our traditional sense of mission has led us to emphasize physical access to documents–to build large collections, resource sharing options, databases telling us what's available and where; to devise user education programs teaching use of indexes, abstracts, and catalogs most people never heard of before to lead them to journals they never heard of before so that they can read articles they never knew they needed–and often wouldn't have missed. And, increasingly, to provide such reference tools on user-friendly compact disks and end-user search systems in order to allow independence, to remove the librarian from the equation, thus obviating question negotiation and reformulation and professional structuring of search strategies. . . . by emphasizing *physical* access, we may actually reduce *intellectual* access . . . (p. 417)

## INFORMATION OVERLOAD

The retrieval of staggering amounts of information may be counterproductive–"we become so busy swallowing the news that there is no time to digest it" (Bob, p. 62). Dvorak reminds us that "there are only about 16 usable hours in a person's day, and having access to all the information in the world doesn't change that simple fact" (p. 87). In an information-rich environment the challenge of scholarship becomes not merely the acquisition of information, but the identification of the most essential or relevant materials (Hopkins, p. 306). Literary scholar, Northrop Frye stated it simply when he wrote, "scholarship is as much a matter of knowing what not to read as of knowing what to read" (p. 17). Adult learners, with their multiple obligations, must make efficient use of their library time–they do not have hours to waste in aimless exploration, "roaming around the Net finding 'cool' things to share with their friends" (Smith & Comstock, p. 6). Confronted with a dizzying array of information choices, adult learners need assistance separating the wheat from the chaff.

> They look to you, the teacher, to help them find their way through the thicket of facts and the morass of competing perspectives. They want you to help them decide what information fits their questions and problems. They want some help in deciding which information is accurate and which is not. Many want to learn how to examine information critically, so that they really understand it from their own perspectives. (Apps, p. 3)

In other words, academic reference librarians need to help adult learners become "information literate." They need to serve as information advisors, directing patrons to the best databases or print resources for their particular information need and teaching them how to focus or narrow their searches to find the most pertinent resources and eliminate the extraneous. While academic librarians have been performing this function to a limited degree, their service philosophy has more often led them to present users with the full spectrum of information options and to let the user bear the responsibility for selecting the most appropriate resources (Hopkins, p. 317). They have emphasized quantity, not quality, and have tended to shy away from an evaluative role (Berry; Biggs, p. 417). Berry warns that the continued practice of reference service in this fashion is "a recipe for irrelevance." Librarians must be willing to "interpret and vouch for information and its sources," to provide "value-added" services.

> . . . If we aspire to survive in this new age of easy access to all kinds of information, we have no choice but to elevate ourselves and our service

to this crucially needed but high-risk role of information advisor. If we don't offer this kind of professional service, who needs us?

Indeed, when many users believe that they are skilled online searchers and can pretty much find what they need on their own, when they prefer to access resources remotely without setting foot in the library, when they turn more frequently to Internet browsers for their information needs than to a live reference librarian, the path to professional obsolescence widens. In order to survive, academic reference librarians will need to redefine their role and assert themselves as information specialists. When so many users are disinclined to ask for assistance, librarians must step boldly out from behind the reference desk and find opportunities to demonstrate to bewildered patrons that there is a greater art to database searching than merely typing in the first keyword that comes to mind. They must avoid simply pointing novice searchers to workstations with no more instruction than, "It's on that machine over there; it's pretty self-explanatory and easy-to-use; come back if you have any questions." Such comments imply that little or no expertise is required in database searching, that users are expected to know everything they need to know in order to operate the system, that generally one ought to succeed on one's own, and that asking for human help should come as a last resort. Unless their goal is to be bypassed as much as possible for the sake of staffing efficiencies, academic reference librarians need to do a better job of promoting their services as a means of coping with information overload. Since end-user searching is only as good as end-user training, they need to teach users how to make more effective and efficient use of the computer to reduce searching output to manageable proportions through the use of online thesauri, limiting techniques, the location of review articles, relevancy ranking, and the like. They need to produce library pathfinders, bibliographies, and "guides to the literature" that are annotated and highly selective, focusing on the "best" or "key" resources on a particular subject and must make users "more aware of the existence and utility of these guides" (Hopkins, pp. 318, 321).

Of course, effective information filtering cannot be done in a vacuum–it must take into account each user's individual characteristics and particular information needs. The traditional reference interview becomes even more important as a means of ascertaining not just the subject area of inquiry and the amount and level of information needed, but also as a means of assessing the user's unique personal attributes. For optimum success, the reference interaction must apply the theories of andragogy and pedagogy as appropriate, adjusting teaching styles to accommodate "differences in style, time, place, and pace of learning" (Knowles, 1990, p. 31).

## CONCLUSION

In response to the changing demographics of the campus, amidst an explosion of information choices in an ever-changing, increasingly electronic environment, academic libraries must develop a new service paradigm. No longer can they afford to remain information-neutral; they must step up efforts to help learners cope with information overload by "reducing the amount of and raising the quality of information brought to the attention of the user" (Taylor, p. 58). They must increase users' understanding of the information-seeking process and teach them how to select and use appropriate library resources (print and electronic), how to critically evaluate information, and how to use information effectively for their particular research needs. In doing so, they must develop a heightened awareness of and sensitivity to the diverse nature of the college student population and become more responsive to all learners as individuals, particularly their adult clientele.

Taylor reminds us that information literacy is a gradual process and cautions that computer literacy is not to be equated with information literacy (pp. 225, 227). With the trend toward remote access and increased user self-sufficiency, academic reference librarians must clearly demonstrate that they have value to add in the information arena. Taylor implies that they do.

. . . When our society recovers from its present love affair with the computer, there will be a real need for the information generalist/professional. . . . These are those persons who, because they are technologically sophisticated *and* information literate, can begin to combine the technologies, the human intermediaries, the information content, and the delivery systems into systems of high quality to the users. . . . (p. 227)

Such is the challenge posed by this current information age. Academic reference librarians can no longer wait passively at the desk "just-in-case" they are approached. What is needed is a new service paradigm which moves beyond the "just-in-case" and "just-in-time" delivery modes to emphasize service "just-for-you." With librarians at the forefront, information seekers will safely navigate the information floodwaters.

## REFERENCES

Apps, Jerold W. *Mastering the Teaching of Adults.* Malabar, FL: Krieger Publishing Company, 1991.

Backes, Charles E. "The Do's and Don'ts of Working with Adult Learners." *Adult Learning* 8 (January/February 1997): 29-31.

Berry, John N. "Editorial: Risking Relevant Reference Work." *Library Journal* 123 (May 15, 1998): 6.

Biggs, Mary. "Information Overload and Information Seekers: What We Know About Them, What to Do About Them." *The Reference Librarian* 25/26 (1989): 411-429.

Bob, Murray. "The Information Age: Mis-, Dis-, and Overload; One Librarian's View." *The Bookmark* 41 (Winter 1983): 61-64.

Bowden, Randall and Merritt, Richard. "The Adult Learner Challenge: Instructionally and Administratively." *Education* 115 (Spring 1995): 426-431.

Dvorak, John C. "Avoiding Information Overload." *PC Magazine* 15 (December 17, 1996): 87.

Frye, Northrop. "The Search for Acceptable Words." *Daedalus* 102 (Spring 1973): 11-26.

Hallett, Karin. Quoted in Carol Tenopir, "Expert Views of the Future." *Library Journal* 123 (June 1, 1998): 33, 36.

Hammond, Carol Burroughs. "Nontraditional Students and the Library: Opinions, Preferences, and Behaviors." *College & Research Libraries* 55 (July 1994): 323-341.

Heckart, Ronald J. "Machine Help and Human Help in the Emerging Digital Library." *College & Research Libraries* 59 (May 1998): 250-259.

Hopkins, Richard L. "Countering Information Overload: The Role of the Librarian." *The Reference Librarian* 49/50 (1995): 305-333.

Kent, Elene and Shaughnessy, Mary Ellen. "Peering Into Cyberspace: An Examination of the Issues Facing Faculty and Adult Learners Entering the Realm of Distance Learning." In Visions and Revisions, Proceedings of the 16th Annual Alliance/ACE Conference, St. Pete Beach, FL, October 3-5, 1996, 63-72. ERIC Document Reproduction Service No. ED 402 511.

Knowles, Malcolm. *The Adult Learner: A Neglected Species.* 4th ed. Houston: Gulf Publishing Company, 1990.

Korth, Henry F. and Silberschatz, Abraham. "Database Research Faces the Information Explosion." *Communications of the ACM* 40 (February 1997): 139-142.

Lantis, Mick and Sulewski, Marilyn. "Overcoming Computer Anxiety in Adult Learners." In Proceedings of the 9th National Technology Literacy Conference, Arlington, VA, January 21-23, 1994, 82-85. ERIC Document Reproduction Service No. ED 381 429.

McDonald, Peter. "Science Libraries of the Future: Research in the Electronic Age." *Food Technology* 49 (April 1995): 92, 94-95.

Polson, Cheryl J. "Teaching Adult Students." IDEA Paper No. 29 (September 1993). ERIC Document Reproduction Service No. ED 395 136.

Rauch, David B. "Education for the Growing Majority: Adults." *Lifelong Learning: The Adult Years* 5 (September 1981): 10-13.

Rudd, Joel and Rudd, Mary Jo. "Coping with Information Load: User Strategies and Implications for Librarians." *College & Research Libraries* 47 (July 1986): 315-322.

Sheckley, B.G. "The Adult as Learner: A Case for Making Higher Education More Responsive to the Individual Learner." Reprinted in The Adult Learner in Higher Education: A Resource and Planning Guide (1989): 21-29. ERIC Document Reproduction Service No. ED 348 911.

Simon, Charlotte Ellen. "Information Retrieval Techniques: The Differences in Cognitive Strategies and Search Behaviors Among Graduate Students in an Academic Library." PhD Dissertation, Wayne State University, 1995. ERIC Document Reproduction Service No. ED 390 394.

Smith, Sharon and Comstock, Dan. "Teaching Internet Use to Adult Learners: The LANL Experience." Paper presented at the 1995 Conference of the Council for Higher Education Computing Services, Roswell, NM, November 8-10, 1995. ERIC Document Reproduction Service No. ED 398 916.

Steffen, Susan Swords. "Designing Bibliographic Instruction Programs for Adult Students: The Schaffner Library Experience." *Illinois Libraries* 70 (December 1988): 644-649.

Taylor, Robert S. *Value-Added Processes in Information Systems.* Norwood, NJ: Ablex Publishing Corporation, 1986.

Tomaiuolo, Nicholas G. "Reconsidering Bibliographic Instruction for Adult Reentry Students: Emphasizing the Practical." *Reference Services Review* 18 (Spring 1990): 49-54.

U.S. Department of Education. National Center for Education Statistics. *Digest of Education Statistics.* Washington, DC: U.S. Government Printing Office, 1997.

Wyman, Andrea. "Working with Nontraditional Students in the Academic Library." *The Journal of Academic Librarianship* 14 (March 1988): 32-33.

# The Information Explosion
# and the Adult Learner:
# Implications for Reference Librarians

Gayle R. Christian
Caroline Blumenthal
Marjorie Patterson

**SUMMARY.** In looking for answers to their learning and information needs, adult learners face an information explosion as one component of their complex world. While adult learners represent a wide variety of developmental stages, for information literacy, for a successful search for electronic information, each one must learn to cope with the burgeoning explosion of information. This paper explores the challenges of information gathering and examines the specific needs and characteristics of the

---

The authors are librarians at William Russell Pullen Library, Georgia State University, 100 Decatur Street, S.E., Atlanta, GA 30303. Gayle R. Christian is Associate Professor and Reference, Government Documents and Map Librarian and holds the MLS from Peabody College of Vanderbilt University. She is a member of the American Library Association, the Southeastern Library Association, and the Georgia Library Association. She is Chair of the Government Documents Interest Group of the Georgia Library Association (E-mail: gchristian@gsu.edu). Caroline Blumenthal is Associate Professor and Reference Librarian and Education Liaison and holds the MLS degree from Emory University. She is a member of the American Library Association and the Georgia Library Association (E-mail: libcab@gsu.edu). Marjorie Patterson is Instructor and Interlibrary Loan Librarian and holds the MSLS from Florida State University (E-mail: libmdp@gsu.edu). She is a member of the Georgia Library Association.

Acknowledgment is given to Dory Ingram, Human Resources Librarian at Georgia State University.

[Haworth co-indexing entry note]: "The Information Explosion and the Adult Learner: Implications for Reference Librarians." Christian, Gayle R., Caroline Blumenthal, and Marjorie Patterson. Co-published simultaneously in *The Reference Librarian* (The Haworth Information Press, an imprint of The Haworth Press, Inc.) No. 69/70, 2000, pp. 19-30; and: *Reference Services for the Adult Learner: Challenging Issues for the Traditional and Technological Era* (ed: Kwasi Sarkodie-Mensah) The Haworth Information Press, an imprint of The Haworth Press, Inc., 2000, pp. 19-30. Single or multiple copies of this article are available for a fee from The Haworth Document Delivery Service [1-800-342-9678, 9:00 a.m. - 5:00 p.m. (EST). E-mail address: getinfo@haworthpressinc.com].

*19*

adult learner in relation to information gathering. It presents strategies to assist the reference librarian in developing the necessary skills as well as methods to assist the adult learner. *[Article copies available for a fee from The Haworth Document Delivery Service: 1-800-342-9678. E-mail address: <getinfo@haworthpressinc.com> Website: <http://www.haworthpressinc.com>]*

**KEYWORDS.** Adult learners, information overload, reference librarians, databases

## INTRODUCTION

Adult learners, as library clientele, present a wide range of characteristics and needs to the reference librarian. As these adults increasingly engage in lifelong learning, they are faced with constantly changing technologies. To help them adapt, librarians must identify strategies which will facilitate learning in a swiftly changing information world. Older adults are a unique and fast growing segment of the adult population. While many of them are highly committed to lifelong learning, they often have different needs for training and assistance than do younger users.

In this article we will describe characteristics of the adult learner population and look at the learning styles of these learners, with attention to their unique learning needs. We will examine the rapid growth of information and the frequently changing variations in user access to that information. We will also describe the massive increase in information and complex library resources with implications for the adult learner. Finally, we will look at ways the librarian can facilitate success in adult library users in the midst of this information explosion. (As a working definition, we will describe "adults" as anyone older than the traditional graduate of four years of college; that is anyone 23 years of age and above.)

## DATA ON CHARACTERISTICS OF THE ADULT LEARNERS

Census data indicate that the adult population in the United States is growing. The median age of the population has increased from 32.8 years of age in 1990 to 34.9 years in 1997 (*Statistical Abstract of the United States, 1998*, p. 14). Within adult age groups, the elderly (sixty-five plus) segment of the population grew 100 percent between 1960 and 1994. It is anticipated that this segment will grow even more rapidly when the baby boomers reach 65 years of age (U.S. Bureau of the Census, 1995). This trend will inevitably be reflected in the number of adult learners in the library user population.

According to a 1996 U. S. Department of Education survey, "The Adult Learner is a growing part of the population in the academic setting, as well as in other settings. . . . Forty percent of adults participated in adult education activities in 1995, up from 32 percent in 1991. About half of the 1995 group took work-related courses, half took personal development courses, and 6 percent took courses related to a diploma, degree or certification." (Note that some respondents chose more than one category.) Adults aged 65 and over participated at 15.2 percent, primarily in personal development courses. The reported data on socioeconomic differences in adult participation rates indicated that the less skilled, the minority groups, and males had lower participation rates (*Education Statistics on Disk 1996*, 1997, Table C96).

Since adult learners represent many stages, ages, and socioeconomic levels, they possess a wide range of computer and library user skills, from the very sophisticated in technology and library usage to those with little or no experience. Both novice and sophisticated library users must learn to adapt to the continually changing electronic environment, and the library should be an integral part of the effort to meet the needs of all levels of learners.

## BACKGROUND ON LEARNING STYLES AND VARIETY IN ADULT LEARNERS

Ingram (in press) provides a useful summary of "andragogy," "the art and science of helping adults learn." She summarizes the major theories on adult learning, as well as characteristics of the adult learner. She explains the learning styles of adults and she describes how these learning styles can be used by the information specialist to help the user deal with this complex information environment.

According to Knowles (1996, pp. 255-258), adult learners tend to (1) "have a need to know why they should learn something"; (2) "have a deep need to be self-directing"; (3) "have a greater volume and different quality of experience than youth"; (4) "become ready to learn when they experience a need to know or to be able to do"; (5) "enter into a learning experience with a task-centered orientation to learning"; and (6) "are motivated by both extrinsic and intrinsic motivators."

It is useful to look at a few models of adult learning which may be applied to library research. One description of the "inquiry" model emphasizes that "the learner begins with a general need to know; finds resources as they become available or come to his attention; does most planning as the learning is in progress; and does not know initially how useful a given resource or piece of information may become" (Huey B. Long and Associates, 1989, p. 19).

King and Kitchener, in writing on reflective judgment and adult learners, used as their base the theories of John Dewey who "described a type of thinking that focuses on problems for which no clear-cut solution can be identified. . . . " Reflective judgment, as they describe it, "begins with an awareness of uncertainty," a state which the adult learner is quite experienced in handling. Recognizing uncertainty, the thinker then proceeds to reflective judgments which are "based on the evaluation and integration of existing data and theory into a solution about the problem at hand . . ." (p. 8). King and Kitchener's research also showed that reflective judgment develops in adulthood and tends to increase with age and educational level. They state that the goal for the adult learner is to strengthen reflective judgment.

Doing library research in today's complex information environment is an example of a problem with no clear-cut solution. Our goal in libraries is to help adult learners reach that level of critical thinking or reflective judgment so that they will make good decisions in selecting the information. The users must first make a decision about which resources to search. Next they must identify and locate appropriate sources within those resources, make judgments about their appropriateness, and finally integrate the data and information into their understanding of the topic before producing a written report. While a number of adult learners may feel overwhelmed by the technology and the complexity of searching and retrieval of the resources, they do have a history of complex problem-solving from previous life experiences upon which to draw. Therefore, with instruction and guidance, they will very likely learn how to sort out and cope with the complexity more readily than the younger library user.

Within the wide age span of adult learners, there are age-related differences in performance which must be recognized. Thayer (1997, pp. 16-17) summarized the psychological research pertaining to age and performance in the workplace and cited the works of Horn and Hofer (1992) and Birren and Fisher (1995). Younger adult learners have the advantage in "reasoning, short term memory, and processing speed," because these skills decline with age. At the same time "acculturation knowledge (depth and breadth of knowledge of one's culture), long-term memory, and quantitative knowledge appear to increase through most of adulthood." While performance levels for tasks based on speed decline markedly with age, performance levels of tasks based on knowledge decline very little with age. Younger adults will tend to learn the technology more quickly and will often have better technical skills. However, the younger adults will not have the same store of life experiences or "complex schema" as the more mature adults and therefore may not be as adept at making judgments about the use of resources.

## COMPUTER USAGE AND OWNERSHIP GROWS WHILE THE GAP WIDENS

A recent National Telecommunications & Information Administration (Falling through the Net II: New data on the Digital Divide, 1998) report showed that computer usage and ownership are growing rapidly. For the period from 1994 to 1997, ownership and access have grown in all segments of the population. However, there remains a "digital divide" based on race/ Hispanic origin, income, location (central city and rural areas), and other demographic characteristics. The lower socioeconomic and minority groups continue to fall further behind the more affluent population. With increased access to computers and the Internet, the adult library user is likely to be more sophisticated than in the past. However there will continue to be a disparity in the levels of skills. This difference in computer literacy means the library will need to focus on programs to encourage the computer have-nots. We must find ways to ease the fears of this new group of learners and teach them the necessary technical skills. At the same time the library must continue to respond to sophisticated users' needs for training and assistance.

## THE EXPLOSION IN GROWTH
## OF PUBLISHING AND INTERNET SITES

In looking for answers to their learning and information needs, adult learners face a vast amount of information as one component of their complex world. According to the *Bowker Annual* (1998, p. 521), production of published book titles "continued to soar" in 1996. As reported in *Ulrich's International Periodicals Directory* (1998, pp. vii-viii), serials saw an increase of 16,000 titles over those reported in 1993-94, with 8,762 serials available exclusively online or simultaneously in online and hard copy, and 2,903 serials available on CD-ROM. *Ulrich's* also noted "dramatically increased use of the Internet as a publishing medium."

## A PRESCRIPTION FOR INFORMATION OVERLOAD:
## SUMMARY OF MULTIPLE RESOURCES

Wurman (1989) states that "information anxiety is produced by the ever-widening gap between what we understand and what we think we should understand" (p. 34). He cites several "situations likely to induce 'information anxiety'", including "not understanding information; feeling overwhelmed by the amount of information to be understood; not knowing if certain information exists; and not knowing where to find information . . ." (p. 44).

Kreitzberg (1991) states that people fairly readily handle everyday sensory overload with the use of "selective attention." However, "Information overload occurs when too much information is presented for an individual to process meaningfully." The cognitive load increases when material is "unfamiliar and very complex." Kreitzberg continues, "If the user cannot make sense of the incoming material, it becomes meaningless."

In the library setting the multitude of databases available in various formats, held both directly and virtually, has made access to information "unfamiliar and complex." The mix of resources frequently includes the library's OPAC, networked CD-ROM's, online databases and Internet access. Stand-alone CD-ROM workstations for single use subscriptions and numerous non-networked U.S. government CD-ROM's in federal depository libraries may add to the complexity. Then too, statewide consortia, such as GALILEO (see REFERENCES for address) make for an even richer information environment. The availability of this wealth of information is exciting, and the capability to connect remotely enables use of the resources at any hour and in any place connected to the World Wide Web. However, this vast and complex information environment adds to the overload syndrome.

There are a number of additional challenges. These include the complication of multiple vendor databases, which sometimes overlap in coverage or even provide duplicate databases. Variations in user interfaces, search software, and points of access may cause user difficulties. This may be compounded by the requirement for separate passwords to provide valid users with access to licensed databases. Solutions for controlling enormous printing costs may entail complicated ways of charging for prints. Full-text articles are increasingly available; however, it can be difficult to determine which databases and articles are supplied in full-text. The adult learner, when faced with this multiplicity of resources, may experience confusion, frustration and even panic. Beyond these constraints, there remains the need to develop critical thinking skills to enable choosing the relevant databases and selecting the best articles and information.

In 1989 Mary Biggs (1989, p. 414-415) called for examining reference librarianship in entirely new ways, and the call is still quite relevant today. She stated, "so much is published so variously that we do not bring it together effectively, cannot always retrieve those items that would establish links among known things [which would] force the refutation or affirmation of some notions, suggest a new theory, etc. . . . "

Richard L. Hopkins (1995) provided a literature review on information overload and examined the role of library and information professionals in helping users cope with this overload. He summarized past, present and future solutions to helping users cope with the overload. Solutions with some usefulness have included the use of filtering for the "best" articles, librarian and trade produced research guides and annotated bibliographies. Technological solutions, such as the provision of electronic search systems which allow for narrowing by date, language, or other parameters, the use of relevance searching and retrieval and interactive media or "hypermedia," are likely to be increasingly useful. He stated that the need for information literacy training will continue to be an essential part of the solution.

## TEACHING LIBRARY RESEARCH SKILLS

What are some of the strategies we can use to facilitate library learning in the adult? Most obvious is teaching basic competencies of computer searching. Teaching users how to develop effective search strategies includes introducing effective screening tools and search limits such as subject discipline; time period; various levels of materials, whether primary, secondary, or tertiary; language; scholarly versus popular materials; population studied; fields within the bibliographic record; and other relevant characteristics. Skills such as using help screens, Boolean operators, truncation, and the use of thesauri to focus the search are also valuable. In addition Hopkins (1995, p. 328) states that the "neophyte user should be given a clear and accurate picture of how the scholar/researcher is able to identify and retrieve key documents in a particular area of research or study."

The material may be presented in a classroom setting or as computer based instruction with step-by-step learning. While individual instruction is ideal, it is extremely labor-intensive. Therefore, classes and self-paced electronic training materials, such as tutorials and other computer-based instruction are more practical tools. Using classrooms equipped with individual computers allows for hands-on learning. However, to be effective, direct hands-on classroom training requires more in-class time. This is particularly true if the user is learning keyboarding or basic software skills at the same time. To be even more effective the computer laboratory method requires one or more teaching assistants to monitor and help slower users keep up with the rest of the class.

Some of the adult learner preferences include small groups, one on one instruction, and training relevant to their needs and life experiences. For the less sophisticated user, as well as for many older adults, a slow pace of instruction with friendly, open exchange allows for reinforcement of learning. Ideal computer based instruction tools for adults are self-paced, with modules to enable the learner to select only the topics not yet mastered.

Offering walk-in training sessions is common at many universities and colleges, as well as public and other types of libraries. Offered at various times throughout the school year, these sessions can be attended when the need for research skills arises, thus appealing to the adult learners' particular need for information close to the time of need. Attendance at the training sessions at Georgia State University, primarily a commuter school where the average age of undergraduate students is 26 years, has been moderate. The heaviest attendance is on Saturday mornings, which is perhaps not too surprising with our high percentage of nontraditional students. It is interesting to note that female attendees outnumber male attendees in the sessions, which reinforces our continuing efforts to provide multiple modes and methods of instruction. Even with the low turnout, students frequently inquire about classes at our reference desk and some who attend the walk-in classes return to repeat and reinforce their learning. We believe that more and better publicity is essential to increasing attendance, while continuing to search for various ways to meet users' training needs. As Mary Biggs (1989) stated, outreach is "crucially important"; however, it remains quite a challenge, particularly at a largely commuter institution.

Course related classes are another frequently used method of library instruction. Cooperation between the teaching faculty and the library instructor helps ensure that the instruction is tailored to the assignment and appropriate to the learner's needs. Finding ways to encourage active learning by expanding beyond the lecture method might include "strategies such as discussions, simulations, and writing assignments that involve students in actively assimilating new information and ideas" (King and Kitchener, 1996, p. 248).

## REQUIREMENTS/TECHNIQUES FOR EFFECTIVE STAFFING FOR INFORMATION SERVICE

The reference librarian must be open to the unique needs of each adult learner. Hopkins (1995) points out that the novice researcher is generally searching for basic information and an overview, which requires providing assistance at a basic level. He compares this to the advanced user who may be quite self-sufficient, yet would benefit from learning how to improve search strategies and utilize additional databases. King and Kitchener (1994) stress the need to show respect for students regardless of the developmental levels they may be exhibiting during problem solving. Therefore, a sophisticated researcher may exhibit a lower developmental level when faced with newer library technology. The librarian must show patience and respect for the learner to encourage developing the new skills.

A friendly, relaxed librarian or staff member, who displays a welcoming and helpful attitude while placing full focus on the user, is essential for a successful reference interaction with any age group, and particularly so for the adult learners. Exhibiting a sense of humor and an upbeat attitude may be one technique the library staff might use to help relieve anxiety in the learner. Being readily accessible and moving around the patrons offering assistance is another way to achieve greater effectiveness. The librarian tends to be asked for help more often than when remaining seated waiting for questions to be brought to the reference desk. Smith's findings (1990, pp. 124-136) illustrate how librarians can turn "Timid Learners" into "Confident Learners." Smith states "The interaction with the librarian is the key to this transition," giving the learner "confidence for future interactions."

Reference librarians need a strong base of technical knowledge to provide competent assistance to the user. Excellent training and opportunities for frequent updates is necessary, since change in resources is continuous. While it may be impossible to know all of the less frequently used databases thoroughly, librarians should have the basic skills and tools to enable them to work through some of the more challenging resources. Efforts may also be made to assure adequate training of any staff or students who assist at the reference or information desk.

A willingness to admit to the patron the limits of one's technical knowledge can be an acceptable response. Adult users may be better equipped than younger people to accept as reasonable the limitations of a librarian. Using the patron's areas of expertise combined with that of the librarian can make the encounter even more successful. For example, the patron who wants to make a map of Census data may have experience in working with statistical packages and other electronic resources, while the librarian might provide introductory material on a geographic information system and the structure and content of the Census data.

Subject specialists and specialized training centers will become even more important as electronic resources proliferate. The well-trained generalist is unable to know all of the less frequently used databases and applications thoroughly. The effectiveness of service can be enhanced with subject and advanced database specialists, whether the staffing is from the reference unit, graduate students, or staff from other library units who have background in a subject area or knowledge of specialized software.

Librarians must make greater use of technology to develop electronic finding aids and pathfinders, as well as training materials on the World Wide Web. The first step is to provide clear and meaningful labeling of systems and databases on the online menus. An index to databases by subject, indicating where the database is located, and providing links to that database is very effective. Producing better introductory pages, online guides and electronic indexes with links to the sources increases the chances that the adult learners can locate the materials. Computer based instruction and online tutorials on the library's home page provide "just-in-time" assistance wherever the user is working. The technology can reinforce many of the adult learner's needs, including allowing for self-direction, providing the information when they experience a need to know it, and enabling them to approach the resources with a task-centered orientation to learning.

While teaching users to be self-sufficient is an appropriate goal, there are times when it is more expeditious for staff to perform the searches for the users. When they simply need one book or a brief search, it may be counterproductive to insist that the users learn how to navigate the technology. See Curran's article (1994) reflecting on the old adage of "teaching a man to fish."


## WORK AT THE INSTITUTIONAL LEVEL AND ABOVE


At the institutional level the librarian can promote cooperation with employers and community groups in planning, developing and distributing learning modules to directly impact the adult learner.

Preparation of excellent training materials is time consuming and costly in personnel time. World Wide Web resources such as the handout exchanges of LOEX Clearinghouse for Library Instruction, Government Documents Round Table (GODORT), Map and Geography Round Table (MAGERT) are excellent examples of efficient pooling of resources (see LOEX, GODORT, MAGERT in Reference List for URL's). Sharing guides and resources among institutions is cost effective and allows for sharing expertise. Efforts should be made to contribute to these resources.

Distance learning presents opportunities for library and information literacy instruction either as a separate course or integrated within other training courses. It allows for bridging geographical distances while potentially enabling independent learning. Use of video training and web-based exercises may be supplemented with e-mail capabilities. Computer distance learning, which ranges from distributed self-directed learning modules to computer video streaming and live interactive computer networking may also be used (Piskurich, G. M., 1996). Learner isolation may be alleviated with the integration of newer technologies into the distance learning (Beller, 1996, pp. 69-76).

More full-text scholarly materials should be made available at a reasonable cost. As user expectations rise and the motivation to retrieve journals in traditional formats falls, the availability of affordable full-text journals has not grown in proportion to the databases. The growth has been just enough to tantalize the user and raise expectations (Chronicle of Higher Education, 1998)! Increased online access to full-text journals would also benefit the adult learner by providing them access at any hour and any place.

Another role for the librarian is to work more closely with information providers and software developers to make the products and tools more user friendly. Although user interfaces are improving, the impediments to dealing with the explosion of information products continue. Also, the mode of access is frequently more complicated than necessary, with special vendor passwords and IP address demands that hamper valid remote access. Additional communication between local systems people and the vendors should be useful in resolving these issues.

## CONCLUSION

Although there are varying levels of development among adult learners, each person must learn to cope with the burgeoning explosion of information. Individual differences in learning styles dictate that a variety of instructional models be made available to adult learners to help cope with the information explosion. Other considerations include accessibility of assistance and instruction, affordability of access to the resources, funding for programs, and adequate publicizing of user services.

The long-term and short-term strategies of librarians to meet the adult learner's needs will be based on adult developmental learning theories and the needs and constraints of the adult learner. The challenge is to identify ways to provide the necessary support and training required to help the adult learners gain the tools to carry out self-directed learning.

## REFERENCES

Beller, M. (1996). Integrating New Technologies in Distance Education: Pedagogical, Social and Technological Aspects. In Y.J. Katz, D. Millin and B. Offir (Eds.). *The Impact of Information Technology: From Practice to Curriculum* (pp. 69-76). London: Chapman & Hall.

Biggs, Mary (1989). Information Overload and Information Seekers; What We Know about Them, What to Do About Them. *Reference Librarian, no. 25-26,* pp. 411-429.

Birren, J.E. & Fisher, L.M. (1995). Aging and Speed of Behavior: Possible Consequences for Psychological Functioning. In J.T. Spence, J.M. Darley, & D.J. Foss (Eds.). *Annual Review of Psychology,* 46, (pp. 329-353). Palo Alto, CA: Annual Reviews.

*Bowker Annual, Library and Book Trade Almanac,* 1998 (1998). New Providence, NJ: R.R. Bowker.

"[challenges to providing full-text . . .]" (1998). *Chronicle of Higher Education.*

Curran, Charles (1995). Perpetuating Information Overload. *American Libraries,* 26, p. 514).

*Education Statistics on Disk,* 1996. (1997) (NCES 97-076). Washington, D.C. National Center for Educational Statistics, U.S. Department of Education. (SuDocs. No.: ED 1.334/2:St 2/996/CD)

*Falling through the Net II: New data on the Digital Divide.* (1998). U.S. National Telecommunications & Information Administration. (http://www.ntia.doc.gov/ntiahome/net2/falling.html

GALILEO (Georgia Library Learning Online), (http://galileo.peachnet.ga.edu)

Guernsey, Lisa. Internet Librarians say They Must Prepare Now for Future Floods of Users. Chronicle of Higher Education, November 5, 1998.

Hopkins, R.L. (1995). Countering Information Overload: The Role of the Librarian. *Reference Librarian,* no. 49-50, pp. 305-333.

Huey B. Long and Associates (1989). *Self-Directed Learning; Emerging Theory and Practice.* n.p.: Oklahoma Research Center for Continuing Professional and Higher Education of the Univ. of Oklahoma.

Horn, J.L. & Hofer, S.M. (1992). Major Abilities and Development in the Adult Period. In R.J. Sternberg & C.A. Berg (Eds.), *Intellectual Development* (pp. 44-99). New York: Cambridge University Press.

Ingram, D. (In Press). The Andragogical Librarian. *Reference Librarian* (This Issue).

King, P.M. and Kitchener, K.S. (1994). *Developing Reflective Judgment: Understanding and Promoting Intellectual Growth and Critical Thinking Adolescents and Adults.* San Francisco: Jossey-Bass.

Knowles, M. (1996). Adult learning. In Robert L. Craig (Ed.) *The ASTD Training and Development Handbook: A Guide to Human Resource Development,* pp. 253-265. New York: McGraw-Hill.

Kreitzberg, C.B. (1991). Details on demand: Hypertext models for coping with information overload. In Martin Dillon (Ed.). *Interfaces for Information Retrieval and Online Systems: The State of the Art,* pp. 169-171. New York: Greenwood Press.

LOEX Clearinghouse for Library Instruction (http:www.emich.edu/public/library/loex.html); GODORT (Government Documents Round Table of the American Library Association) (http://www.lib.berkeley.edu/GODORT/index.html#GODORT); MAGERT (Map and Geography Round Table of the American Library Association (http:www.sunysb.edu/libmap/magert1.htm).

Piskurich, G.M. (1996). Self-directed learning. In Craig, R.L. *ASTD Training and Development Handbook,* 4th ed., p. 469-471. New York: McGraw-Hill.

Salthouse, T.A. (1993). Attentional Blocks Not Responsible for Age-related Slowing. *Journal of Gerontology: Psychological Science,* 48, 263-270.

Smith, J.C. (1991). *Public Librarian Perceptions of Library Users as Self-Directed Learners.* Syracuse University, ED.D. Thesis, (UMI Order no. AAI9026091). Ann Arbor, MI: UMI Dissertation Information Service.

*Statistical Abstract of the United States,* 1998 (1998). Washington, DC: U.S. Bureau of the Census.

Thayer, P.W. (1997). A Rapidly Changing World. In M.A. Quinones and A. Ehrenstein (Eds.), *Training for a Rapidly Changing Workplace: Applications of Psychological Research,* pp. 16-18. Washington, DC: American Psychological Association.

*Ulrich's International Periodicals Directory* (1998, 36th ed.). New Providence, NJ: R.R. Bowker.

U.S. Bureau of the Census (1995). *Sixty-Five Plus in the United States.* (Bureau of the Census Statistical Brief 95-8). Washington, DC: U.S. Bureau of the Census.

# Stress Relief:
# Help for the Technophobic Patron
# from the Reference Desk

## Lucy Harrison

**SUMMARY.** Although much has been written on technophobia and how it can be treated, little has been published on how the reference librarian can help. Limiting the time spent introducing new technologies, speaking without using computer jargon, offering instruction through different learning styles, and preparing patrons to deal with the problems they encounter are a few of the strategies the reference librarian can do to help patrons deal with their fear of computers. This article examines and defines technophobia, offers short-term strategies that reference staff can use to alleviate the anxiety of their technophobic patrons, and finally touches upon long-term solutions and changes that can be made within the library environment itself. *[Article copies available for a fee from The Haworth Document Delivery Service: 1-800-342-9678. E-mail address: <getinfo @haworthpressinc.com> Website: <http://www.haworthpressinc.com>]*

**KEYWORDS.** Technophobia, computer anxiety, reference librarians, learning styles, automation of library processes–psychological aspects

---

Lucy Harrison is Library Database Specialist, College Center for Library Automation, 1238 Blountstown Highway, Tallahassee, FL 32304 (E-mail: lucy@ccla. lib.fl.us). She received her MLS from Florida State University in 1995, and has degrees in Psychology and English from the University of Florida. She recently co-authored an article with Dr. Paul Kussrow, Florida Atlantic University, called "Learning Styles in the Library: All Students Are Equal, But Some Are More Equal Than Others," which was named by the Florida Library Association as the winning article in its 1998 Best of Florida Libraries Awards. Ms. Harrison also writes fiction, and has twice been named by eScene magazine as one of the world's best online fiction writers.

[Haworth co-indexing entry note]: "Stress Relief: Help for the Technophobic Patron from the Reference Desk." Harrison, Lucy. Co-published simultaneously in *The Reference Librarian* (The Haworth Information Press, an imprint of The Haworth Press, Inc.) No. 69/70, 2000, pp. 31-47; and: *Reference Services for the Adult Learner: Challenging Issues for the Traditional and Technological Era* (ed: Kwasi Sarkodie-Mensah) The Haworth Information Press, an imprint of The Haworth Press, Inc., 2000, pp. 31-47. Single or multiple copies of this article are available for a fee from The Haworth Document Delivery Service [1-800-342-9678, 9:00 a.m. - 5:00 p.m. (EST). E-mail address: getinfo@haworthpressinc.com].

Much has been written about how to deal with technophobia and techno-stress, in students, patrons and in library staff. The proposed solutions, how-ever, are mostly long-term and labor-intensive: Semester-long courses introducing students to the computer, relaxation training, and even systematic desensitization, none of which are much help to the frustrated reference librarian, trying to help a patron who is scared to death to touch the computer keyboard. This article will offer some ideas for short-term solutions and changes that can be easily made within the library itself. It will examine and define technophobia, discuss what strategies reference librarians can use to help the anxious patron, and touch upon some of the long-term solutions and changes that libraries can make to assist their clientele.

## WHAT IS TECHNOPHOBIA?

Technophobia was first identified as a serious problem back in the early 1980's. Dr. Craig Brod named the phenomenon "Technostress," which he defined as "a modern disease of adaptation caused by an inability to cope with the new computer technologies" (Weil & Rosen, 1997, p. 5). Matthew Maurer called it "Computer Anxiety," and defined it as "the fear and appre-hension felt by an individual when considering the implications of utilizing computer technology, or when actually using computer technology" (Maurer & Simonson, 1995/96, p. 206). In Maurer's definition, then, the patron does not even have to be using the computer to feel stress–just thinking about it is enough. Whether it is called technophobia, technostress, computer anxiety, computerphobia, or cyberphobia, it means the same thing. The patron is so anxious about using the computer that he or she becomes unable to use it, unable to learn the database, and therefore unable to find the information needed.

Technophobia is generally not a true, psychological phobia, although it may become so in extreme cases. More often, it is a heightened level of anxiety which makes learning difficult or impossible. When a patron is anx-ious, a barrier goes up in the brain, preventing any new information from penetrating or being permanently retained. In other words, he is so busy worrying about having to use the computer that nothing the reference librari-an is saying will really sink in. Various studies have found that a significant portion of any group is likely to be technophobic. Weil and Rosen put the number at somewhere between 25 and 50% (Weil & Rosen, 1997, p. 12), and a recent MCI study found it to be as high as 59%. The anxiety level will vary even within a technophobic group: Some will be so anxious they cannot learn a thing, whereas others will be very nervous, but able to grasp the basics. Rosen and Weil call these "resisters," "hesitants," and "eager adopters" (Weil & Rosen, 1997, p. 17-20). The "eager adopters" are a librarian's dream come true: No sooner is the information out of the librarian's mouth than the patron is racing away, ready to start a search. The "hesitants" are a little anxious, but willing to listen to what the librarian has to say and, if they believe that the database can really help them, they are willing to try a search. The "resisters" are the ones who are the most technophobic. They do not believe they can really figure out the computer, and even if they could, they would not be able to find any relevant information. These are the patrons who long for a return to the days of the paper Reader's Guide and printed card catalogs. These "resistors" and "hesitants" are the ones who need the librarian's help most of all, but trying to help them can be a frustrating experience for the reference staff.

## *WHO SUFFERS FROM TECHNOPHOBIA?*

In the early days of computer anxiety studies, it was believed that women and older people were most likely to suffer from technophobia. However, many studies performed over the past few years have refuted this idea. "Studies by Howard (1986) . . . Igbaria and Parasuraman (1989) . . . Ray and Minch (1990) . . . Cohen and Waugh (1989) . . . and Morrow et al. (1986) . . . each found that sex was not a significant factor in explaining differences in computer anxiety and attitudes towards computers" (Anderson, 1996, p. 63). A few studies have found differences between the anxiety levels of women and men, but it is not a causal phenomenon. If women do feel more hesitant to use computers, it is more likely due to a lack of exposure to new technology than to any hormonal or genetic traits. As Anderson relates: "Societal norms about the role of women have led to differential opportunities for women in education, particularly in mathematics, science, and engineering. . . . Studies have shown that girls view science and computers as being more male-appropriate than female-appropriate" (Anderson, 1996, p. 64).

In fact, Jacobson revealed that there may be an advantage to women using computers within a library setting: A study of high-school seniors showed that while girls may have higher computer anxiety, boys have higher library anxiety levels (Jacobson, 1991, p. 277). Thus, men may be more nervous about using the library than women, which would tend to level the playing field if in fact there was a slight discrepancy in computer anxiety levels. Weil perhaps summed it up best when, in a 1995 interview, she explained: "usually all the research has shown women tend to be a bit more cyberphobic or technophobic than men but the number, statistically, is pretty small, and I would see that more as just a cultural statement that women in general are not introduced to machinery or technology as early or expected to utilize it [as much] as men" (Interview, 1995).

The research on age and computer anxiety follows the same line of reasoning as that of women: Although there may be an increase in computer anxiety among older versus younger users, this is a factor of past experience (or lack thereof) of computers. In their 1990 article, Rosen and Maguire reported that in 17 different studies, none supported the hypothesis that age was a significant factor in computer anxiety (Rosen & Maguire, 1990, p. 181).

Previous experience with computers is the biggest predictor of computer anxiety: People who have been longer exposed to computers, and were introduced to them in the proper way, will feel significantly more comfortable using those computers. One study found that people who had taken a formal computer class or classes were "significantly less anxious than those who had not" (Fliotsos, 1992, p. 47). Other factors that may cause computer anxiety include locus of control and perceived knowledge (Anderson, 1996). In other words, if a person feels the control over their interaction with the computer is external–that they do not, themselves, control the outcome–then they will feel significantly more anxious. Likewise, if they do not feel themselves capable of performing the computer tasks, their anxiety will rise. Even playfulness may have a role in anxiety: People who were able to play around with the computer were significantly less anxious (Anderson, 1996, p. 63).

How can reference staff identify anxious patrons? One clue may be the voice. Anxious people are likely to have more errors in their speech, and more silent pauses (Harrigan, Harrigan, Sale & Rosenthal, 1996, p. 683). The voice itself may be under stress, becoming higher pitched or cracking. *The Diagnostic and Statistical Manual of Mental Disorders,* the Bible of the psychiatric profession, lists thirteen symptoms typical of panic and anxiety attacks: shortness of breath or smothering sensations, dizziness or faintness, palpitations or accelerated heart rate, trembling or shaking, sweating, choking, nausea or abdominal distress, depersonalization or derealization, numbness or tingling sensations, flushes (hot flashes) or chills, chest pain or discomfort, fear of dying, and fear of going crazy or doing something uncontrolled (Widiger et al., 1996). Obviously, most of these will not be directly observable by the reference staff. However, in addition to these internal states, there are recognizable outward symptoms. John Greist, M.D., states that "There may also be eyelid twitch, furrowed brow, strained face, fidgeting, restlessness, easy startle, and sighing" (Greist, Jefferson & Marks, 1986, p. 2). These outward signs of anxiety should certainly be a red flag to any reference librarian attempting to help a patron.

The patron may also self-identify, or attempt to self-identify, his condition to the librarian. The librarian should be careful to listen for verbal cues which will reveal the patron's anxiety over computers. The patron is unlikely to come right out and say "I'm technophobic." Instead, they will use such phrases as "I'm hopeless with computers," "I haven't used a computer before," "I'm really bad with this computer stuff," or "Don't you have a paper index we can use?" What the patron is really saying is that he is not comfortable using the computer, and does not believe that he can get the information he needs from it. Librarians should treat such concerns seriously, and not brush them off by saying, rather arrogantly, how easy it all really is.

## SHORT-TERM HELP

The demeanor of the reference librarian is very important in establishing a trusting relationship with the anxious patron, and calming him down. Dr. Greist relates the ideal role of a psychotherapist dealing with an anxious patient: "Those who have the ability to listen–and more importantly the ability to hear and understand what they have heard in some meaningful way, to explain that meaning, and to empathize and support the anxious person–can often provide substantial help" (Greist et al., 1986, p. 117). This also holds true for the reference librarian. The ability to listen, to understand, and to empathize is of paramount importance when dealing with anxious patrons. The librarian should be knowledgeable, calm and relaxed, should understand the patron's inquiry and should try to determine the patron's level of technological knowledge (Weil & Rosen, 1997, p. 45). Rosen and Weil list three crucial characteristics for any person who is teaching computers. First, "The person who is teaching computers . . . must be comfortable with that technology" (Rosen & Weil, 1994, p. 4). This would seem to be obvious to most of us, but in fact many librarians are under such time pressure that they are not able to learn every database available in their library. There are so many electronic sources available today: in-house CD-ROMs, networked CD-ROMs, databases mounted on the Public Access Catalog, databases available though dial-up connections or over the Internet. It is almost impossible for the reference librarian to know everything about every single database. Therefore, there will be times when the reference staff are learning "on the job"–they will be learning the database themselves at the same time they are teaching it to someone else. Not only is this extremely stressful for the librarian, it is also bad for the anxious patron, who needs a teacher who is comfortable with what he is teaching. One solution for this is to assign one "expert" to each of the lesser-used databases. Each staff member will then have the responsibility for learning a few databases inside out, and any patron inquiries for those specific databases can be directed to them. Of course, all staff members will need to be experts on the popular databases which are used every day.

The second of Rosen's characteristics for reference staff is that "The person who is teaching technology must be calm, clear, and very open to questions" (Rosen & Weil, 1994, p. 4). Anxious patrons are already feeling low self-esteem for having to come to the reference desk for help, and believe that they will never be able to find what they need on the computer. This feeling is not alleviated by reference staff who act bored, arrogant, or nervous, who talk in the foreign language of computer jargon, or who rush through their instruction and do not allow interruption for questions. Instead, reference staff must let the patrons know that "we are there to help them, and that no question is stupid" (Fliotsos, 1992, p. 49).

The third of Rosen's characteristics is that the staff should be non-judgmental and non-evaluative. "The introduction of technology should be in a non-evaluative atmosphere" (Rosen & Weil, 1994, p. 5). Not only does this mean that the reference librarian should keep his comments positive and specific to the problem at hand, it also means that the technology should be introduced in a non-rushed setting. That is, ideally, a patron should not be searching for material in a new database when he needs that material for a paper that is due the next day. The imposition of a deadline increases the panic in an already anxious patron. It would be better to simply retrieve the needed information for the patron first, then go on to explain the database. Thus, the pressure is taken off, and the patron can then continue to learn in a non-evaluative atmosphere.

There are some simple rules the reference staff should follow when introducing an anxious patron to the technological resources available to him in the library. These will not all be useful in every situation, and some are more appropriate for library instruction classes than for one-on-one encounters at the reference desk. Nevertheless, they should provide a starting point for librarians and other staff members looking to make anxious patrons more comfortable in the library. Some of these rules were adapted–from Michelle Weil and Larry Rosen's book *Technostress: Coping with Technology @Work @Home @Play*–to make them more appropriate for library staff, while others are my own suggestions and compilations of ideas from other studies.

## SET LIMITS

Most people are not able to focus on learning something new for hours at a time. Unless they are extremely personally interested in the topic, a forty-five minute to an hour-long session is all they will be able to handle. Research has shown that students asked to spend longer than that in learning something new will become restless, bored, and fidgety. This is good news for the instruction librarian, who is probably already limiting the sessions to fifty minutes or an hour. In academic institutions, class periods have historically been limited to an hour or so, due to this same reasoning. Students and patrons "need time to assimilate the material and to decide which parts were clear and which parts were fuzzy" (Rosen & Weil, 1994, p. 5). Reference librarians dealing with patrons on an individual basis should also use these time limits. While they may not be working with the patron directly for the entire hour–other patrons and work requirements will interrupt them–it is a good idea nevertheless to limit the time that a patron is exposed to new technologies. If the patron has spent an hour on the computer, both being instructed by the librarian and working on his own, that is more than enough for a first exposure. Suggest to the patron that he should work on something else for a while, to let the new information he has learned have a chance to be absorbed. The patron can then return the next day, or even later on the same day, with a fresh mind and a more relaxed attitude to learning the database.

For the same reason, the number of topics covered in one instruction session should be limited. Often, it is the first instinct of the reference librarian to show the patron all of the reference and electronic sources that might conceivably help them in their search. Thus, if a student comes in looking for criticism on Henry James, the reference staff might show him books on reserve, the Gales Literary Index, a set of volumes of criticism on American Authors, the Modern Language Association database, the Periodical Abstracts databases, and a myriad of other sources. This may be helpful to the extremely confident and motivated student, but for the anxious patron, it is information overload. It would be far better to introduce them to one resource at a time, with the caveat that if they do not find what they are looking for, there are many other places to search. In instruction classes, librarians should ideally cover only one database per hour-long session, and certainly no more than two. Unfortunately, in academic libraries, there is often pressure from the class professor to cover more material in a single session. Librarians may be asked to describe five or even six resources in a single hour-long session! This does not mean that the "all-day" or "half-day" seminar no longer has a place in technological instruction. Instead, the instructors of these seminars should plan for no longer than one hour learning each new database before moving on to something different, taking a break, relaxing and playing around with other technologies. "Most people who learn about a new technology need time to process their reactions (often this includes fears, insecurities, negative attitudes, negative thoughts about self or technology) and to assimilate strategies to overcome these negative reactions" (Rosen & Weil, 1994, p. 5).

Librarians should also limit the amount of jargon, or computerspeak, that they use. Using computer jargon automatically confers upon the speaker an "inside knowledge" of computers, and identifies him as a member of an elite group–the computer literate. To other members of this elite group, using computer jargon is exciting and expedites communication. To anyone outside this group, however (i.e., ninety-five percent of the human race!), using computer jargon is an exclusionary tactic which leaves them confused and frustrated. When non-computer-literate people hear terms like "baud,"

"RAM," and "client/server" being tossed around, a barrier goes up and they automatically assume they will never be able to learn what is being taught. For already anxious patrons, this can be the final straw. It is far better to use plain, clear, normal English terms for the computer processes. Instead of talking about the "bandwidth of a T1 line," call it "the speed and capacity of the telephone lines connecting the computers to the Internet." Computer jargon is not something that can be figured out intuitively–who would ever know that "boot" means to start up a computer?–and should be avoided as much as possible during the early days of teaching technology. Later on, when a patron becomes more comfortable using the computer, we can begin to explain what certain terms mean and expand his techno-vocabulary.

## GET THEM INTERESTED

It is always important, when introducing a student to new technology, to make that technology personally interesting to them. "If a technophobic student's first contact to a computer is linked to an interest or a purpose, second contact is likely" (Ross, 1993, p. 121). Ideally, a patron will first be introduced to a new database in a non-evaluative setting, where they are not under pressure to find needed materials immediately. In this situation, the reference librarian could find out any special hobbies or interests the patron holds, and perform a search that locates information on these topics. In an academic situation, the searches should be linked to the paper or assignment the student is working on. It is not enough to simply find out the student's topic and then enter that as a search term. As reference librarians know, many of the results will be inappropriate or irrelevant, and that will only serve to increase the student's frustration. Instead, the librarian should work through the results of the search with the student, identifying other possible search terms or strategies for narrowing the results. The reference staff should identify at least one specific article or abstract that could be used directly in the student's assignment. In the case of full-text articles, the librarian could even point out specific paragraphs and sentences which will support the student's thesis. Print this article out, or download it, for the student, so that they know they have at least one really good resource for their assignment. This will relax them and give them confidence to peruse the rest of their results.

Reference librarians should always be truthful and forthright with the student. Too often, librarians will over-simplify the database, explaining that it is really easy to use and filled with wonderful information, when in fact this may not be the case. Reference staff should not speak down to the patron, telling him something is easy to use in an effort to reduce his anxiety. This approach will always backfire when the patron finds out the truth about the database. On the other hand, librarians should not emphasize the difficulty of searching in certain sources, either. Instead, they should tell the patron exactly what they can expect to get from the resource, along with a realistic appraisal of its benefits and drawbacks. Do not say "This is really easy to use," or "This is the most difficult database we have." Either of those statements will heighten the anxiety of patrons. Instead, say, "The command language is kind of tricky in this database, but once you get the hang of it you shouldn't have a problem, and this is definitely the best place for you to go for information on this assignment." "It is important to emphasize the computer's usefulness" (Ross, 1993, p. 121) rather than dwell on the difficulty or ease of use.

Humor is also a powerful tool when dealing with anxious patrons. Anytime you can get someone to laugh, their anxiety level will start to drop. The physical symptoms associated with high anxiety can all be relieved by laughter (Roach, 1996). The reference librarian should not be afraid to crack an occasional joke, especially at the expense of himself or the computer. Typographical errors on the part of the librarian can be the source of a quick laugh, and to illustrate one of the shortfalls of the computer: "You and I both know what I mean when I type 'educaiton,' but apparently the computer isn't smart enough to figure it out!" Even if the student does not laugh out loud, it still relieves some of their tension. In library instruction sessions, cartoons or funny quotes can be used to great effect.

## *HELP THEM TO HELP THEMSELVES*

One of the best resources available to help patrons using electronic resources is often ignored by the reference staff, or at best referred to only briefly. This is the on-line help available in every database with the push of a button or the click of a mouse. It is essential to introduce patrons to this on-line help, as it may often be the only place they can turn for assistance. After all, the reference librarian will not always be there to help the student. Even within a library setting, the staff will often be busy helping other patrons when the student needs help. And with the advent of distance learning, more and more databases are becoming available to students in remote sites, and in their homes, over dial-up connections and the Internet. In these situations–especially if the student is using the databases late at night–there is no way to contact the reference librarian for help. The on-line help screens, then, can be a lifesaver.

Even when the reference librarian does point out the on-line help, it is often cursory: "You can push the F1 key if you need help." Instead, the student should be shown in detail how to access the help, how to navigate through its screens, and how to use the various search capabilities. In each case, whether an instruction class or a one-on-one encounter with a patron, the librarian should give students the chance to practice using the help tools as part of the training session. One major advantage of the patron using the help screens is the enormous sense of satisfaction they will have when they figure out the answer. They will have solved the problem themselves, without having to ask the librarian for assistance, and that will boost their ego and lower their anxiety levels. There are also selfish reasons why a reference librarian should train students on using the on-line help: It frees them up to assist other patrons and deal with other problems.

Patrons should be prepared to deal with the problems that will crop up. In most instruction classes and other situations where the librarian is showing students how to use the database, the searches that the instructor chooses to perform will be "idealized." The librarian has searched the database before, knows what terms will and will not work, and knows what limiting strategies will produce the best results. In the real world, we all know that things are going to go wrong: Searches are going to produce irrelevant results, printers are going to jam, Internet connections are suddenly going to freeze for no apparent reason. Teaching students to anticipate these problems, and showing them how to resolve them, can greatly increase the students' comfort level with technology. Even if the problem is not one that the students can solve for themselves, the simple knowledge that there is nothing they personally did wrong can ease their anxiety. All efforts should be made to "de-mystify" the computer for the patrons. Many people have no clear idea of the capability of the computer, assuming that it is inherently foreign and non-human. Explain to them that computers were designed by people, for people, and are filled with errors, glitches, and idiosyncrasies that reflect their human design. It is comforting for patrons to know that there is virtually nothing they can do to destroy the computer, and that it will not (a) explode, (b) melt, or (c) give them an electric shock, should they chance to push the wrong button. Explain that there will sometimes be technical difficulties associated with using the computer, and that the patron is not alone in encountering these problems.

Teaching critical thinking skills can also be extremely helpful to patrons anxious about using the computer. We have all encountered the situation where a student is helplessly looking through the medical database for information on Henry James. A simple assessment of the screen could have saved this student lots of time. Loomis and Fink, in their groundbreaking essay on instruction in virtual libraries, advocate a four-step program for teaching students how to think critically when using electronic databases. These are (rearranged slightly): (1) What am I trying to do? (2) Where am I? (3) How do I do it? and (4) What do I do with it? (Loomis & Fink, 1993, pp. 49-52).

The first step, teaching patrons to figure out what they are trying to do, is similar to conducting a reference interview. "The researcher must first state the problem, establish vocabulary control, and develop a search strategy"

(Loomis & Fink, 1993, p. 51). While these are all things that reference librarians are already doing, the student should be made aware of the process so that he can help himself through it when there is nobody else around. The second step, teaching patrons to recognize which source they are using, and whether it is appropriate for their search, may seem obvious. Reference librarians know what databases are available in their library, and recognize them when they are on the screen. Patrons, on the other hand, may not realize what is available to them, or may assume that every computer has one database with everything they need in it. Single station computers may have six or more databases loaded in a CD-ROM stacker, with more available by request at the reference desk. In addition, different databases that are manufactured by the same company may look almost identical. Thus a student may recognize the format for Ebsco's Academic Abstracts database, and assume he is searching there, when in fact he is using another Ebsco product, Health Source Plus. We must teach students to read the screen and identify which database they are using, to read database descriptions for content and years of coverage, and to examine other computers to see what else is available. The third step is to teach students how to do it, that is, how to get the information they need. Strategies such as identifying keywords, using Boolean logic, and narrowing results are often taught in the library instruction sessions (albeit sometimes very briefly) but are often neglected altogether when helping a patron one-on-one. These are valuable tools that will serve to help the student find relevant and useful results. The final step is teaching the student how to evaluate and use the information he has found. "Librarians have resisted and debated the appropriateness of adding this phase of the research process to bibliographic instruction, but it is integral to the functioning of the virtual library and, therefore, must be embraced as part of our domain" (Loomis & Fink, 1993, p. 54). It is no longer enough to simply provide students with a list of results: We must show them how to evaluate the appropriateness of each item, how to download or print out the results (and if downloaded, how to open them up again on a home computer), and how to cite these items in a reference list.

## SAY IT, SHOW IT, HAVE THEM DO IT

Everybody has his or her own individual learning style. Any given group, even a family, will have wildly different styles of learning. Learning styles are made up of four components: physical elements, social elements, environmental elements, and emotional elements (Weil & Rosen, 1997, p. 37). Physical elements are those that most people think of when they hear the term "learning styles": whether a student learns visually, auditorially, or tactually/kinesthetically (by touch and movement). Social elements include whether a student prefers to learn alone or in a group, from an authority figure or from peers. Environmental elements include time of day, heat, light, noise, and color. Emotional elements include student motivation and persistence in finishing a task. The reference librarian should recognize that each patron encountered will have a different learning style, and should take that into account when providing training. Obviously, there is no way for the librarian to know a particular patron's learning style preference, unless the patron himself communicates it. Indeed, the patron may not even be cognizant of his learning preferences on a conscious level. Instead, the librarian should offer instruction in a variety of styles.

The computer screen itself offers visual stimulus, but often the librarian is moving so fast the patron cannot locate the information on the screen. In order to reinforce this visual stimulus, the librarian should point to the screen, thereby showing exactly what is being discussed. In library instruction classes, other tools such as videos and overheads can be used. The librarian should also speak out loud, repeating instructions, commands and results, and describing the database as they move through it. This reinforces the auditory aspect of learning. Finally, and most importantly, the librarian must give the patron a chance for hands-on experimentation with the database. Tactual and kinesthetic reinforcement of learning is essential for most students. When in an instruction class, allow plenty of time for hands-on learning. In a one-on-one situation, the librarian should perform the search once, then walk the student through another while giving auditory instructions, and finally let the student perform a search on his own. This procedure is called "modeling," and allows the student to take cues from the instructor and to get hands-on experience. It does the patron no good at all to watch the librarian type everything for him. Once the librarian's hands are on that keyboard, all the student sees are hands moving on a keyboard. His attention is drawn down, to the movement of the fingers, and not to what is happening on the computer screen. The librarian should assist the student, but not do the search for him, and have him press all the keys himself.

Librarians should also offer library guides and exercises that reinforce learning styles and encourage hands-on experimentation. "Course materials should be self-paced, logical, and clear in their statement of objectives" (Ross, 121). They should allow students to work on their own or in groups, to follow a set of direct instructions or to experiment on their own, and should offer fun activities such as "treasure hunts" as well as the more traditional exercises. This way, the library guides will speak students with a wide range of learning styles, not just those who learn the way we expect them to.

## LONG-TERM SOLUTIONS

For some intensely computer-phobic patrons, a long-term exposure to computers may be the only solution. Studies have shown that students who took semester-long computer classes had significantly lower computer anxiety levels after completing the course than they did before it. These results have also been shown to stand up over the long term. Most computer classes offered are of one of two types: a semester-long, in-depth class, or a weekend or daylong workshop. Of these, the semester-long class has been shown to decrease computer-anxiety, while the shorter workshop may actually make things worse. "Workshops designed to teach computer skills can also cause anxiety . . . if the sessions are too fast-paced and overwhelming" (Deloughery, 1993, p. A26). Rosen and Weil state that their program to combat computerphobia can be completed in just five hours–given that those five hours are spread out over a five-week period. They held both group and one-on-one sessions, the goals of which were to use cognitive behavioral psychological principals to decrease computer anxiety. These anxious students were "taught to replace their negative feelings about technology with positive statements. Uncomfortable users were provided with information about computers to help dispel their misconceptions about the machines" (Deloughery, 1993, p. A26). In other words, there were no actual computers used in this program, merely psychological and behavioral treatments. However, these students were concurrently enrolled in a semester-long computer class, so they were being exposed to computers regularly outside of Rosen and Weil's class.

Did the program work? It seems to have been a success. After the course, 80% of the students were willing to use computers, 71% were confident about their ability to use computers, and half said that it would be "fun" and that they could get help if they needed it (Rosen, Sears, & Weil, 1993, p. 45). Indeed, Rosen and Weil claim that there were dramatic changes in the students who took their brief, 5-hour course. "Nearly all clients showed markedly decreased anxiety, improved cognitions, and enhanced attitudes," (Rosen et al., 1993, p. 47). These positive results apparently stayed with the students, too: "Anxiety reactions and negative conditions remained essentially absent at the 6-month follow-up" (Rosen et al., 1993, p. 43). Rosen and Weil thus suggest that the optimal strategy for dealing with technophobia is: "to develop a group program that incorporates aspects of systematic desensitization, thought stopping/covert assertion, and the information/support group" (Rosen et al., 1993, p. 48).

Maurer did not have such successful results when he tried relaxation exercises with a group of students taking a computer class. He taught muscle-relaxing exercises lasting 3-5 minutes each over the course of a semester. Despite the fact that the students did not report feeling any more relaxed by the exercises, they nevertheless were significantly less technophobic at the end of the courses. Maurer decided that it was the computer course itself, not the relaxation exercises, that were decreasing anxiety, and that "this study strongly supported the position that an introductory computer course can be effective in reducing computer anxiety" (Maurer & Simonson, 1995/96, p. 216). This might also lead us to question Rosen and Weil's results, since all their students were enrolled in a concurrent computer course: It might be the course itself, rather than the "cognitive-behavioral psychological principles" that is affecting the anxiety of the students. In either case, reference librarians should be aware of computer courses offered on their campuses, in neighborhood classes, or at other local colleges and universities, so that they can refer anxious students to them. It is not true that "familiarity breeds contempt," but rather that exposure and familiarity with computers will eventually help even the most anxious library patron.

There are also some long-term solutions which reference staff can implement within the library itself to help their patrons. The library, believe it or not, is often not the most user-friendly or comfortable place for students to conduct research and use computers. It can be intimidating, confusing, cold and impersonal. "In addition to coping with computer technology, many first-year college students are intimidated by the size and complexity of academic libraries" (Jacobson & Mark, 1995, p. 28). It is not just college students or academic libraries that are overwhelming: Patrons of any age, in any library setting, can be intimidated by the library. Environmental factors such as color, light, heat, and noise can all be manipulated to make the library a more relaxing place for patrons to work. Color, for example, affects the brain waves, the functions of the autonomic nervous system, and hormonal activities, and arouses definite emotional and aesthetic associations (Mahnke & Mahnke, 1993, p. 1). Color has long been used in psychological treatment, with "cool" colors calming mania and aggression, and "warm" colors cheering up depressive and suicidal patients. Studies have also been performed on which colors are best in libraries: "Pale or light green creates a passive effect that enhances concentration in the library environment" (Mahnke & Mahnke, 1993, p. 83). However, given the unlimited number of patrons that will enter a library, with their different personalities and learning styles, there is no one color that will appeal to everybody. "It must be reemphasized strongly that the environment in its entirety . . . must have a variety of color. The psychological power of one color will never satisfy all the needs of an environment." (Mahnke & Mahnke, 1993, p. 21). Other environmental factors should be considered: There should be noisy as well as quiet sections of the library, brightly- as well as dimly-lit areas, and warm and cool study zones. Patrons will automatically gravitate to the atmosphere that best suits their personal learning style, and will feel more relaxed and at ease there. For a full explanation of how libraries can take advantage of environmental factors to account for differences in learning styles, please refer to Kussrow and Harrison's article, "Learning Styles in the Library: All Students are Equal, but Some are More Equal than Others."

## CONCLUSION

Technophobia is a very real problem in today's libraries. It is not confined only to certain segments of the population, but may affect anyone from elementary-schoolers to senior citizens. Reference staff should be able to recognize technophobic patrons, to listen to their concerns and information needs, and to sympathize with their problems. In addition, the utilization of techniques such as setting limits on time and content covered, avoiding computer jargon, showing patrons how the database can help them specifically, teaching the use of on-line help and critical thinking skills, and allowing time for hands-on experimentation can all help to decrease patrons' anxiety about using computers and increase the chance that they will return to use them again. There are also long-term solutions that reference staff can employ, such as referring anxious patrons to semester-long computer classes, and changing the library environment itself.

Above all else, however, the reference staff should remember that the primary goal of the library is to provide information. The patron should never be allowed to leave the library empty-handed, without the resources he needs to complete his assignment, project, or personal research. After all, very few patrons come to the library in order to get experience using the computers: Rather, they come because they have an information need. It is far better for the reference librarian to perform a search himself, than for a patron to leave the library without that information need being filled. The computer search is a means to an end, not an end in itself, and any reference librarian who insists on a technophobic patron performing a search himself without finally making sure that the patron finds all the information he needs, is doing a disservice to the patron, to himself, and to the reputation of the library as a helpful institution of learning.

## REFERENCES

Anderson, A.A. (1996). Predictors of computer anxiety and performance in information systems. *Computers in Human Behavior, 12* (1), 61-77.

Ayersman, D.J. & Reed, W.M. (1995/96). Effects of learning styles, programmings, and gender on computer anxiety. *Journal of Research on Computing in Education, 28* (2), 148-61.

Barlow, D.H. & Cerny, J.A. (1988). *Psychological treatment of panic.* New York: The Guilford Press.

DeLoughery, T.J. (1993). 2 researchers say "technophobia" may afflict millions of students. *Chronicle of Higher Education, 39* (34), A25-26.

Fliotsos, A. (1992, Summer). Anxiety layering: The effects of library and computer anxiety on CD-ROM use. *The Southeastern Librarian, 42,* 47-9.

Greist, J.H., Jefferson, J.W. & Marks, I.M. (1986). *Anxiety and its treatment: Help is available.* Washington, DC: American Psychiatric Press, Inc.

Hall, L. (1997). Fighting phobias: The things that go bump in the mind [CD-ROM]. *FDA Consumer, 31* (2), 12-15. Full-text from: Academic Abstracts FullText: 9704075786.

Harrigan, J.A., Harrigan, K.M., Sale, B.A. & Rosenthal, R. (1996). Detecting anxiety and defensiveness from visual and auditory cues. *Journal of Personality, 64* (3), 675-709.

Hudiburg, R.A. & Necessary, J.R. (1996). *Coping with Computer-Stress.* New York, NY: American Educational Research Association. (ERIC Document Reproduction Service No. ED 394 495).

*Interview: Michelle Weil, PHD & CLINICAL PSYCHOLOGIST, Cyberphobia* [Online]. (1995, February 15). Retrieved March 2 1998 from the World Wide Web: http://www.businesslynx.com/interview.htm

*Is Technology Taking Over the World?* [Online]. (1997, December 25). Retrieved March 2 1998 from the World Wide Web: http://news.bbc.co.uk/hi/english/special_ report/for_christmas/_new_year/technophobia/newsid_41000/41853.stm

Jacobson, F.F. (1991, July-September). Gender differences in attitudes toward using computers in libraries: An exploratory study. *Library and Information Science Research, 13,* 267-279.

Jacobson, T.E. & Mark, B.E. (1995). Teaching in the information age: Active learning techniques to empower students. In Martin, L.M. (Ed.), *Library Instruction Revisited: Bibliographic Instruction Comes of Age* (pp. 105-120). Binghamton: The Haworth Press, Inc.

Kussrow, P.K. & Harrison, L. (1997). Learning styles in the library: All students are equal, but some are more equal than others. *Florida Libraries, 40* (7), 128-131.

Loomis, A. & Fink, D. (1993). Instruction: Gateway to the virtual library. In Saunders, L.M. (Ed.), *The Virtual Library: Visions and Realities* (pp. 47-70). Westport, CT: Meckler Publishing.

Mahnke, F.H. & Mahnke, R.H. (1993). *Color and light in man-made environments.* New York: Can Nostrand Reinhold.

Mark, B.L. & Jacobson, T.E. (1995). Teaching anxious students skills for the electronic library. *College Teaching, 43* (1), 28-31.

Maurer, M.M. & Simonson, M.R. (1995/96). The reduction of computer anxiety: Its relation to relaxation training, previous computer coursework, achievement, and need for cognition. *Journal of Research on Computing in Education, 26* (2), 205-19.

Ovens, C.S.H. (1991). Computer literacy and libraries. *The Electronic Library, 9* (2), 85-89.

Roach, M. (1996). Can you laugh your stress away? [CD-ROM] *Health, 10* (5), 92-96. Full-text from: EBSCO: Health Source Plus: 9608302433.

Rosen, L.D. (1988). *A Model Program for Computerphobia Reduction.* Cominguez Hills, CA: California State University. (ERIC Document Reproduction Service No. ED 318 466).

Rosen, L.D. & Maguire, P. (1990). Myths and realities of computer phobia: A meta-analysis. *Anxiety Research, 3,* 175-191.

Rosen, L.D. & Weil, M.M. (1994, March). What we have learned from a decade of research (1983-1993) on "the psychological impact of technology." *Computers and Society, 24,* 3-5.

Rosen, L.D. & Weil, M.M. (1995). Adult and teenage use of consumer, business, and entertainment technology: Potholes on the information superhighway? [Online]. *Journal of Consumer Affairs, 29* (1), 55-84. Retrieved March 2 1998 from the World Wide Web: http://www.csudh.edu/psych/jca.html

Rosen, L.D., Sears, D.C. & Weil, M.M. (1993). Treating technophobia: A longitudinal evaluation of the computerphobia reduction program. *Computers in Human Behavior, 9* (1), 27-50.

Ross, G.E. (1993). Strategies for addressing technophobia in nontraditional freshmen. *Collegiate Microcomputer, 11* (2), 120-122.

Russell, A.L. (1996). *Six Stages for Learning to Use Technology.* (In: Proceedings of Selected Research and Development Presentations at the 1996 National Convention). Indianapolis, IN: Association for Educational Communications and Technology. (ERIC Document Reproduction Service No. ED 397 832).

Smith, F.K. & Bertolone, F.J. (1986). *Bringing interiors to light: The principles and practices of lighting design.* New York: Whitney Library of Design.

Vitiello, J. (1998). Bedside manner [Online]. *Computerworld, 32* (5), 69. Full-text from: LINCCWeb: FirstSearch: Periodical Abstracts: 03578702.

Weil, M.M. & Rosen, L.D. (1997). *Technostress: Coping with Technology @Work @Home @Play.* New York: John Wiley & Sons.

Widiger, T.A., Frances, A.J., Pincus, H.A., Ross, R., First, M.B. & Davis, W.W. (Eds.). (1996). *DSM-IV Sourcebook: Volume 2.* Washington, DC: American Psychiatric Association.

Yeaman, A.R.J. (1992). Seven myths of computerism. *Tech Trends, 37* (2), 22-26.

# Overcoming Technostress
# in Reference Services to Adult Learners

## Brian Quinn

**SUMMARY.** One of the greatest challenges in delivering reference services to adult learners is technostress. This is a common syndrome among adults generally characterized by feelings of discomfort and unease around computers. Adult learners are particularly vulnerable to technostress because they grew up in a largely pre-computer era. Reference librarians can help alleviate technostress through several means. These include establishing a relaxed, psychologically supportive atmosphere, pacing one's instruction, and using active learning. In attempting to relieve technostress, it is important for librarians to remember that it is not only what is conveyed, but how it is conveyed that is critical. *[Article copies available for a fee from The Haworth Document Delivery Service: 1-800-342-9678. E-mail address: <getinfo@haworthpressinc.com> Website: <http://www.haworthpressinc.com>]*

**KEYWORDS.** Adult learners, technostress, reference services, alleviation, psychological support, pacing, active learning

One of the most challenging problems that librarians face at the reference desk is working with adult students. Not only are their numbers growing at colleges and universities around the country (Speer, 1996), but they are appearing at a time when reference services are becoming increasingly automated. It is thus becoming ever more common for a busy librarian at a high

Brian Quinn is Social Sciences Librarian, Texas Tech University Library, Lubbock, TX 79409 (E-mail: libaq@lib.ttu.edu).

[Haworth co-indexing entry note]: "Overcoming Technostress in Reference Services to Adult Learners." Quinn, Brian. Co-published simultaneously in *The Reference Librarian* (The Haworth Information Press, an imprint of The Haworth Press, Inc.) No. 69/70, 2000, pp. 49-62; and: *Reference Services for the Adult Learner: Challenging Issues for the Traditional and Technological Era* (ed: Kwasi Sarkodie-Mensah) The Haworth Information Press, an imprint of The Haworth Press, Inc., 2000, pp. 49-62. Single or multiple copies of this article are available for a fee from The Haworth Document Delivery Service [1-800-342-9678, 9:00 a.m. - 5:00 p.m. (EST). E-mail address: getinfo@haworthpressinc.com].

traffic reference desk to be confronted with an older student who may have little or no knowledge of computers yet nonetheless needs to use the library to complete an assignment. Such students are typically at a loss for where to begin, and may even ask in a furtive voice, "Where is the card catalog?"

When told by the librarian that the card catalog no longer exists, or that it is now on computer, the adult learner may become visibly uncomfortable, and appear confused, disoriented, or anxious. Symptoms such as these are part of a more general syndrome commonly known as "technostress," a term first used by Craig Brod in the early 1980's. Brod, a clinical psychologist, defined technostress as "a modern disease of adaptation caused by an inability to cope with the new computer technologies in a healthy manner" (Brod, 1984). Adult learners may have little experience with computers and may have managed to avoid using them, but now are faced with the realization that they can no longer do so. Adult learners often feel inadequate, embarrassed, and even frustrated by their lack of computer skills, especially if they compare themselves to younger classmates. Many realize they have a sizable handicap to overcome, and feel pressure not only to complete their assignment, but also to somehow learn computers in the process.

Students of all ages may experience technostress to some degree (Deloughry, 1993), but adult learners seem more prone to it than younger students. This is a result of what social scientists term a "cohort effect." Many adult learners were educated in the 1940's, 1950's, or 1960's, during a time when libraries were not yet automated and PC's were not in widespread use. They never had a chance to learn computers, and information technology thus seems unfamiliar, and uncomfortable. In contrast, younger students now entering college have been exposed to computers from their elementary years onward. Because they have been involved with computers from an early age, they are far less likely to feel threatened by them (Elder, Gardner and Ruth, 1987).

Adult women may be even more susceptible to technostress because of their past. Computers have traditionally been a male dominated activity in American culture, and women have in the past been socialized at home and at school to regard computers, programming, data processing, and automation generally as unfeminine. This situation may be changing now, but older women may still harbor feelings of uneasiness around computers that stem from stereotyping women as being incompatible with computers, or less capable of using them than men (Mruk, 1987). The effects of gender as well as age may combine to make this group among the most challenging a librarian will encounter in reference services to adults.

It is important to note that although technostress is a subjective, psychological reaction to a social situation, its consequences are nonetheless very tangible and real. Feelings of anxiety, tension, and apprehension may interfere with basic psychological processes such as sensation, perception, and cognition, and the result is that the adult student's overall functioning and responsiveness is impaired (Laguna and Babcock, 1997). This may in turn have a negative effect on the person's ability to operate a computer, thus creating a self-fulfilling prophecy.

More importantly for the librarian, this suggests that the adult learner suffering from technostress may not be fully capable of conducting library research adequately. The librarian who encounters a technostressed adult learner cannot, therefore, treat the person like any other student. The condition of the adult must be noted and addressed, or at least taken into account, early in the course of the reference transaction. If this is not done and the librarian proceeds to ignore the person's condition it may compound the problem and add to the stress of the adult user.

## SOURCES OF TECHNOSTRESS

The most common reason that adult learners experience technostress is because of their having grown up in a largely pre-computer era. But there are other reasons as well. It appears that technostress may have its origins early in a user's life, and may be traced back as far as early childhood. One study has found that those users who were first introduced as children to technology by their mothers were much more likely to be computerphobic (Weil, Rosen, and Wugalter, 1990). Subjects tended to recall their mothers as uncomfortable with technology, which served as a negative role model. In contrast, those users who were introduced to technology by their fathers were much more likely to have positive attitudes toward computers and feel comfortable with them. These individuals tended to recall their fathers as being comfortable and encouraging with computers (Weil, Rosen, and Wugalter, 1990). Parental attitudes toward technology thus had an important influence on their children's perception and comfort with computers. Subjects that had an initial negative experience with computers later recall these negative experiences when confronted with a computer and anticipate frustration and failure. Another formative experience that this study revealed has been associated with computerphobia and technostress and users is that their early encounters with computers were in an evaluative context that required them to perform. Usually these were educational settings in which the user was graded, which tended to create an uneasiness with technology. Users who are initially allowed to freely experiment and play with computers tend to develop much more positive attitudes toward computers generally. They are less apt to see using computers as a test or a threat and thus feel more comfortable with them. Removing performance pressure allows the natural curiosity of the user to take hold so that the user sees computer use as a form of recreation or entertainment.

This same study also found that technostressed users have a personality style that tends to make them give up when trying to solve a problem rather than persist in solving it. This tendency to quit easily often occurs in combination with another trait that prevents technostressed users from asking for help when they do not understand. Such individuals may be too anxious or proud or embarrassed to ask questions of a librarian and are thus less able to correct their errors.

The most common problems that adult users suffering from technostress face have to do with mastering the online catalog. Some users do not realize that OPACs do not automatically correct errors of entry and spelling. Many do not understand the basic principles of Boolean logic and will often type in a search string using natural language. The poor results that they obtain serve to frustrate them and discourage them, reinforcing their sense of inadequacy and aversion to technology (Bichteler, 1987).

Many times it seems like the most simple and obvious aspects of using computers are foreign to the adult user. Even something as simple as pressing the "Enter" key after typing in some search terms may be lost on adult users. Another very basic problem with web interfaces may be hand-eye coordination and the manual dexterity required to manipulate a mouse (Bichteler, 1987). Some do not know that highlighted text must be clicked on to go to the next document. Many difficulties also stem from the inability of adult students to understand the basic structure of bibliographic records and the difference between the title of an article and the title of a journal. There are also problems related to an inability to generate synonyms when the user discovers that his or her initial search terms are unable to produce an adequate number of hits.

Technostress may also result from the memory demands placed on adult learners. The adult user who is unfamiliar with computers must learn and remember various commands and principles that may seem basic to librarians but are nonetheless taxing to the mental capability of the naïve user. The adult learner must also learn a new vocabulary of technical terms and concepts that can seem fairly abstract to someone unaccustomed to using them regularly. Remembering proper sequences of commands and how to navigate databases and files in multiple formats may tax the adult learner's memory capacity to such an extent that they heighten the stress level (Sharit and Czaja, 1994). Even web-based interfaces that rely less on command-based searching than on point and click technology nonetheless require that the user understand hypertext to successfully navigate it.

An additional source of technostress is the pace at which information technology changes. Few librarians need to be convinced of this, as they themselves struggle to keep abreast of what sometimes seems like the almost daily changes that occur in hardware, software, databases, and formats. Yet while experienced computer users have learned to be somewhat flexible and adaptable to the myriad changes that are occurring all the time, the adult user trying to learn for the first time must find the pace of change an additional source of stress. No sooner has the adult learner begun to feel comfortable with a system than it is changed.

## RECOGNIZING TECHNOSTRESS IN ADULT LEARNERS

Symptoms of technostress can vary greatly from one adult user to another. Some users will be refreshingly open and overt about their feelings and actually say to the librarian, "I don't know the first thing about computers," or something to that effect. A few may even adopt a confessional tone and identify themselves as a returning student, commenting, "Look, I'm a returning student and my kids fool with these things, but I'm lost." Occasionally, an adult student will allude to their age or generational cohort and say, for example, "The last time I was in school, they still had the old card catalog." In cases like these, it is easy to detect signs of technostress, as these comments may often be accompanied by a general nervousness or discomfort in the user's overall tone and manner (Czaja and Sharit, 1993).

In other individuals, technostress may not be so obvious at all and may manifest itself in much more subtle ways. Some adults may be unwilling to admit or otherwise reveal their ignorance of information technology. Such an admission may arouse fears that it will date them or make them feel inferior or inadequate. Strong and deep-seated emotions like pride and a sense of independence may be at stake, making what would otherwise be a routine exchange for the librarian into an emotionally charged encounter. More than other students, adult learners may feel threatened by feelings of vulnerability, a loss of dignity and control. In the minds of some adults, an admission of ignorance may relegate them to the status of "non-adult," with accompanying feelings of helplessness and naivete (Czaja and Sharit, 1993).

Users such as these may try to hide their discomfort and inexperience and make comments about "not being able to find anything on this topic" even though the librarian may immediately recognize the topic as something very obvious and general. Some users may furtively ask, "Can you come out here (to the computer) for a minute?" not wishing to divulge anything more. The adult learner's body language and tone of voice may reveal what the person cannot reveal about him or herself. Frustration or anger may be present in a person's voice, and in some situations the user may avert their gaze, suggesting a sense of embarrassment or guilt at not being proficient with computers (Bichteler, 282). A halting or hesitant tone of voice may suggest unease. The librarian must be alert to such cues and recognize them as possible indicators of technostress.

## UNDERSTANDING ADULT LEARNER PSYCHOLOGY

The quality of reference service that the librarian offers adult learners can be greatly enhanced by understanding their psychology. Adults think and learn somewhat differently than younger students, so it is important that the librarian understand the adult mind. Each individual adult user will be somewhat different, yet it is nonetheless possible to make some generalizations.

One important difference between adult learners and their youthful counterparts is that adults attend school for reasons other than that it is what their parents expect of them. Many are in the midst of a turning point in their life, whether it be the result of job loss, divorce, children leaving home, death of a spouse, or lack of success in a previous academic setting. Some may be seeking skills and credentials, but others may be seeking self-affirmation, greater self-esteem, and similar psychological benefits (Ross, 1993).

The experience of entering or re-entering an academic environment after many years away from school is stressful in itself. Adults who have not done much reading, writing, or critical thinking in their life off campus may suddenly find themselves surrounded by demanding faculty and competitive students. They may find it a strain to adjust to this new environment. Unlike younger students, adults often have job, home, and family responsibilities that add to their stress level. Many enter the library with sketchy memories of how to conduct research, only to discover that the traditional paper library they remember has undergone a dramatic transformation.

Surrounded by banks of OPACs, CD-ROM towers, and young students spouting Internet jargon, it is understandable how the adult learner might feel threatened or frustrated by having no option but to search the computers. Realizing that they must somehow adapt, they may be anxious whether they can comply. Feeling simultaneously lost in this high-tech world, and yet afraid or embarrassed to ask the librarian because of concerns that they may sound ignorant, the adult learner cannot help but feel some degree of technostress (Nordenbo, 1990). Much of this reaction may be involuntary, so that the person may be noticeably uneasy.

Sitting down at the computer terminal, the adult learner is confronted with a screen and keyboard that are complex and detailed in appearance. Psychologically, this situation places great demands on the user's attention because there is more information than the user can focus on easily. The user may be unsure what to do with it all, which can create a kind of mental overload. This mental strain is a key factor in contributing to technostress.

The adult user that is faced with this situation is in need of reducing all the technical clutter by narrowing his or her concentration. Although the computer is capable of a wide range of tasks and offers a myriad array of options, the psyche of the adult user tends to be pragmatic. It is looking for relevance and specifics rather than possibilities and potential. The older the adult is, the easier he or she will recall practical applications and the more difficulty he or she will have in remembering generalities and theory (Owens, 1988).

The adult learner needs specific information, but only if it can be imparted and absorbed at an optimum pace. Generally, this rate tends to be somewhat slower than younger students, but not always. The key consideration is that the pace is comfortable for the user, so that they do not have a feeling of being rushed or bored. Librarians working with adult users can expect them to take longer to use the system, require more help while learning to use it, and make more errors in the process.

The adult learner typically goes through a psychological process of adjusting to information technology that occurs in several stages. The initial stage is often one characterized by an awareness of computers and an aversion and avoidance of them. This is followed by an initial learning stage in which the user tries to learn the correct keys and command sequences and processes that must be performed in order to search successfully. This is achieved mostly through a process of imitation, in which the adult user executes what the librarian tells him or her in a rote, mechanical fashion.

It is often at this point that the user discovers that although he or she may try to imitate the "recipe" of instructions exactly, mistakes nonetheless occur. Frustration and discouragement are common reactions, and the user requires considerable assistance by the librarian. This is usually the state when technostress reaches a peak, with anxiety and aggravation working in tandem. Only after struggling at this stage for a varying period of time does the user begin to enter the next stage, which is one of initial understanding.

In the early stage of understanding the user begins to grasp what the various sequences of commands mean and how to utilize them in particular situations. The peak technostress reaction begins to subside, and the first feelings of familiarity and comfort with the technology may evidence themselves. This may be accompanied by a new feeling of confidence, and even a degree of euphoria stemming from early success (Russell, 1995). The user has gradually moved from an initial stage of dependency to one of growing autonomy in which he or she no longer needs to depend on the librarian as much.

While this overall process usually occurs over a period of weeks or months, the same stages may occur in miniature in abbreviated form in the reference encounter. Technostress is initially strong and begins with anxiety and unease, then grows as the adult user struggles cognitively to master the technology and grows frustrated and discouraged by the difficulty of it. Faltering confidence and growing self-doubt may plague adult users to such an extent that it may actually inhibit their ability to learn and thus become a kind of self-fulfilling prophecy. Negative expectations feed on themselves and can tend to erode crucial motivational resources which are necessary if the adult learner is to mount a sustained effort and persevere long enough to make it past the most stressful stage to the subsequent early stage of success and confidence.

These initial encounters of the adult learner with computers are critical ones. If the adult learner is so overwhelmed or frustrated or confused by one or more formative experiences that they give up, it will be much more difficult to alleviate whatever technostress syndrome they may develop. Proper intervention by the librarian in the reference encounter is crucial, and can play an important role in the adjustment of the adult learner to information technology.

## INTERVENTIONS TO ALLEVIATE TECHNOSTRESS

Technostress is one of the most difficult problems that a reference librarian is likely to encounter in working with adult learners. It makes the reference encounter doubly difficult because not only does the librarian have to convey the proper research strategy necessary to meet the user's information need, he or she also has to teach the user how to use computers in order to successfully execute the strategy. In addition to this dual teaching responsibility, the librarian must also address the problem of how to reduce the adult learner's technostress level so that it does not interfere with the reference encounter and the adult's ability to learn and move toward self-sufficiency. Before any of this can even begin, the librarian must be adept enough to be able to "read" the student and recognize the symptoms of technostress.

This may sound like a formidable challenge, yet it is possible to offset whatever inexperience or age deficits the adult learner brings to the reference encounter through a combination of training, practice and design. Training is the first and most critical element in overcoming technostress, and begins with the personal qualities of the librarian. It is not enough for the librarian to impart content; how the content is communicated is also extremely important. The overall tone and manner of the librarian, the physical and verbal cues that he or she uses, can play a vital role in reducing the stress level of the adult learner.

The best way a librarian can defuse the stress that the adult user may exhibit is to be open and relaxed (Grupe and Connolly, 1995). This should have the effect of gradually lowering the user's stress level, because calm is contagious. As easy and obvious as it sounds, the busy reference librarian who has multiple users competing for his or her attention may find it hard to exude calm in the face of an anxious adult who needs in-depth, continual attention. However, the success of the reference encounter often hinges on the ability of the librarian to establish a psychologically supportive atmosphere. This includes giving them full undivided attention, listening to them carefully, and allowing them to vent whatever fears and frustrations they may have welled up within them. Often the adult learner will be painfully aware of their own shortcomings and inadequacies, but the librarian must allow them to feel comfortable enough to ask even the most obvious questions without feeling ignorant or embarrassed. Above all, the librarian must at all costs resist the temptation to show off by playing the role of the omniscient power user, and try to impress the user with a dazzling display of technical wizardry and impressive technospeak that leaves the adult learner bewildered and discouraged. Nothing is more essential than to treat the adult user with respect and as an equal and to assume a role of facilitator rather than expert. Perhaps the best approach is to adopt an attitude of unconditional positive regard, so that the user will feel as relaxed as possible (Boswell and Dodd, 1994).

Occasionally, it may not be clear at the outset just how much the adult user knows about computers. Some individuals do not show much emotion of any sort, technostress or otherwise, and in cases like this it may be necessary for the librarian to try to gauge the general level of the user's sophistication. Sometimes it is possible for the librarian to get an idea of where the user is by observing how they handle the computer and navigate the library's computer system. But other times it may be necessary to probe gently and say something like "Have you worked with computers much?" or "Have you used the library's system before?" to get an idea of how much assistance the user may be in need of, or what skill level to employ with the user. It is important to make sure initially that you are working at the same general skill level as the user, so that the adult user does not get lost or simply does not comprehend what you are trying to convey. In situations where it is not possible to sense the user's level of sophistication, the safest approach is to assume no prior skills or knowledge. This means avoiding technical jargon as much as possible and explaining things in the simplest possible terms (Hemby, 1997). There is always the risk that the librarian will underestimate the skill level of the user and come across as condescending or patronizing, but this is preferable to talking over the user's head and leaving them more confused than when they began.

## PACING AND CUES

It is also very important in working with adult learners that librarians pace themselves carefully. Not only is it very easy to assume that an adult learner knows things that may seem obvious to the librarian, but the librarian that assumes such knowledge will be more likely to explain options, functions, commands, and sequences, much faster and more casually than the user can absorb at a comfortable rate. In order to avoid this, it is a good idea to watch the user carefully and particularly what he or she is doing with the computer to see if they are able to keep up. In some instances, it is not the user but the computer that cannot keep pace, and a slowed response time may suddenly mean that the librarian's instructions are no longer in sync with the machine. The librarian's verbal narrative should always match the pacing and sequence of the commands, connections, and transitions that are occurring on the computer screen as the user is typing.

It helps to look for behavioral cues that the adult learner may exhibit that indicate that he or she is following along, or conversely, confused, uncertain, or lost. Any sign that the user is not understanding is a signal to the librarian to stop and check with the user to make sure they grasp what is being said. A certain amount of repetition may be helpful if it appears that the learner is very inexperienced, or is slow to catch on (Weil and Rosen, 1997). Repeated instructions should always be delivered with enthusiasm and respect, free of any traces of boredom or condescension. Empathy can be very helpful, because it helps the librarian to see the situation through the adult user's eyes, rather than selfishly. In the interest of clarity, it is a good idea not to digress or overexplain, because this may confuse or distract the user. Try to determine what the user really needs, then get to the point early and stick to it.

## EMPHASIZE ACTION AND DISCOVERY

It is a good idea to use active learning and stay with the technostressed adult learner through the initial phase of the reference transaction. Rather than merely demonstrating how to search a computer at the reference desk, accompany them out to a terminal and let them execute the search commands as you explain them. Resist the urge to demonstrate your proficiency or to conduct the search yourself just to get it over with. The adult learner will learn more and better by experiencing the search firsthand than by observing the librarian search. Adult learners tend to remember commands better when they initiate the commands themselves rather than sit by passively and watch someone else do it (Kelley and Charness, 1995). Do not let adult users try to get you to conduct their search for them by playing dumb or acting helpless. It will only make it more difficult for them when you leave and they are forced to search on their own. By encouraging active learning you are setting the stage for the adult to eventually become an independent learner who can be largely self-reliant.

A related approach that has proven successful in training adult learners to use computers is known as discovery learning. Using this method, the librarian encourages users to proceed at their own pace. Students are asked to do the bulk of the searching themselves, and the librarian is careful to give immediate feedback relevant to the student's search progress. The overall amount of verbal instruction is kept to a minimum so as to minimize the amount of irrelevant information (Charness, Schumann, and Boritz, 1992). Adult learners should be encouraged to not be afraid to make mistakes, and the librarian should never criticize or deride any errors that the student makes in the search process, no matter how obvious they may seem. The more the librarian is able to downplay mistakes and minimize errors, the more it will tend to bolster the self-confidence of the adult learner. Similarly, any successes, no matter how small, should be praised by the librarian.

It is essential for the librarian to maintain a positive, supportive approach throughout the reference encounter. Adult learners do not respond well to being challenged, so it helps to avoid this method, because it will only increase technostress. One of the key contributing factors to technostress is negative thinking. By exuding a positive attitude, the librarian is modeling a form of cognitive coping that the adult learner will hopefully adopt and retain after the transaction is finished. Occasionally the user may verbalize some of the negative thoughts that are running through his or her mind as they perform a search, and the librarian should be quick to counter these with positive statements (Bloom and Hautaluoma, 1990). Mindset is a very important aspect of technostress and should be addressed whenever possible during the reference encounter.

## HELP SCREENS, TUTORIALS, AND INTERFACES

Another way the librarian can help the adult learner overcome technostress and move toward greater self confidence and self reliance is by encouraging use of help screens and online tutorials. This is a strategy that is all too easy to forget in the course of a fleeting reference encounter. Yet many of the newer web-based interfaces offered for OPACs and online databases now come with fairly extensive and elaborate help screens that the adult can benefit from. It takes but a moment to demonstrate how to access, but it can open up worlds for the novice. For those adults who appear to be embarrassed asking for assistance, help screens can be particularly useful because they allow the user to maintain a degree of independence (Gist, Rosen, and Schwoerer, 1998).

Many help screens have the added advantage of offering print capability, so that the adult learner can make a copy of various commands. Having a printed copy that can be taken home, studied, and referred to when necessary is something the adult learner will especially appreciate. Most adult learners grew up in a primarily paper world, and having a paper copy in a high-tech world can be a source of familiarity and reassurance for an older student. It also serves as a memory aid that can be vital for a student who is struggling to comprehend a strange new world of screens, commands and technical jargon.

While it appears that graphical user interfaces are becoming increasingly common in libraries, many libraries may offer several different interface options. Adult users tend to have more difficulty using the older command-driven interfaces. Because commands have to be keyed in, they place heavy demands on user memory. Menu-based systems that use icons are much easier to use because all the possible commands appear on the screen. The drawback in using iconic menu systems with adult learners is that many require the use of a mouse. This demands a considerable amount of hand-eye coordination on the part of the user. Moving, clicking, and dragging with the mouse requires some practice before it can be utilized effectively. Yet lack of coordination may be less stressful than the strains on memory that are generated by command-driven systems. Overall, menu-based interfaces give the adult learner more control, and since adult learners tend to be more self-directed and independent, they generally tend to be preferable to other types of interfaces (Bates, 1996).

## REPETITION, SIMPLICITY, AND HUMOR

It is important to keep in mind that many adult learners may be encountering a computer for the first time. That means that in some cases, remediation may be required, even for something as basic as typing skills. It also means that the librarian may have to repeat the same command sequence or procedure more than once, and to be especially careful to proceed at the learner's pace, not the librarian's. What seems like a long time to the librarian may not be to the student. It helps to simplify, but never to the point of being patronizing. Proceed one concept at a time, explaining in jargon-free language, and take advantage of any slow online connections by viewing them as opportunities to summarize any important points mentioned previously.

Finally, it may help to defuse a technostressed adult learner or a tense reference transaction by injecting a little warmth and humor into the situation. An excellent way to accomplish this is for the librarian to make some reference to his or her own initial experiences with computers. No librarian is that old that they cannot remember how fumbling and tentative they were at first, and mentioning this to an adult learner can help to make them feel less fearful and less unusual. Knowing that even the seemingly omniscient librarian was at one time lost can be comforting and reassuring. Indeed, it may help to explain technostress, what it is, and how to cope with it. Above all it is important to remind adult users that technostress is a normal, common reaction that everyone experiences to some degree (Carter and Honeywell, 1991). This simple gesture can itself aid the adult user greatly in coping and realizing that it is just a phase on the long and challenging path to autonomy and mastery.

## CONCLUSION

With adult students growing in numbers, they are likely to appear at the reference desk with increasing frequency. Many did not grow up with computers in their developmental years, which is why they present such a challenge to reference librarians. Lack of early exposure to information technology makes adult learners particularly vulnerable to technostress, which often takes the form of a general feeling of discomfort and unease around computer technology. Yet older students are frequently more motivated to learn and more mature than their younger counterparts. Though age may limit some abilities, adult learners are generally as capable of learning and understanding computers as younger students (Garfein, Schaie, and Witlis, 1988). Technostress can interfere with this capability if it is not addressed and controlled in the reference encounter.

The reference librarian can play a pivotal role in helping the adult learner overcome technostress. By recognizing the symptoms of technostress, and responding in an appropriate manner, the librarian helps the adult learner realize that computers are not to be feared or avoided, but can serve as useful, even invaluable tools in the research process. This realization comes about not only by means of the instructional content that the librarian conveys, but also the manner in which it is conveyed by the librarian. Although technostress takes years to develop and is difficult to eliminate in the brief course of a reference encounter, it can nonetheless be minimized by the librarian so that the adult learner can better focus on research strategy and information content rather than be distracted by concerns about format and medium.

## REFERENCES

Bates, Reid A. "Principles of CBI Design and the Adult Learner: The Need for Further Research." *Performance Improvement Quarterly* 9 (1996): 3-24.

Bichteller, Julie. "Technostress in Libraries: Causes, Effects and Solutions." *The Electronic Library* 5 (1987): 282-287.

Bloom, Arvid J. and Jacob E. Hautaluoma. "Anxiety Management Training as a Strategy for Enhancing Computer User Performance." *Computers in Human Behavior* 6 (1990): 337-349.

Boswell, Donald L. and David K. Dodd. "Balance Theory: A Social Psychological Explanation of the Therapeutic Value of Unconditional Positive Regard." *Journal of Psychology* 128 (1994): 101-109.

Brod, Craig. *Technostress: The Human Cost of the Computer Revolution* (Reading, Massachusetts: Addison-Wesley Publishing Company, 1984).

Carter, Janet Hauser and Robert Honeywell. "Training Older Adults to Use Computers." *Performance and Instruction* 30 (1991): 9-15.

Charness, Neil, Cynthia E. Schumann, and Gayla M. Boritz. "Training Older Adults in Word Processing: Effects of Age, Training Technique, and Computer Anxiety." *International Journal of Technology and Aging* 5 (1992): 79-106.

Czaja, Sara and Joseph Sharit. "Stress Reactions to Computer-Interactive Tasks as a Function of Task Structure and Individual Differences." *International Journal of Human-Computer Interaction* 5 (1993): 1-22.

DeLoughry, Thomas. "Two Researchers Say 'Technophobia' May Affect Millions of Students," *Chronicle of Higher Education* 39 (April 28, 1993): A25-A26.

Elder, Victoria B., Ella P. Gardner, and Stephen R. Ruth. "Gender and Age in Technostress: Effects on White Collar Productivity," *Government Finance Review* 3 (1987): 17-21.

Garfein, Adam J., K. Warner Schaie, and Sherry L. Willis. "Microcomputer Proficiency in Later-Middle-Aged and Older Adults: Teaching Old Dogs New Tricks," *Social Behaviour* 3 (1988): 131-148.

Gist, Marilyn, Benson Rosen, and Catherine Schwoerer. "The Influence of Training Method and Trainee Age on the Acquisition of Computer Skills," *Personnel Psychology* 41 (1988): 255-265.

Grupe, Fritz H., and Frank W. Connolly. "Grownups Are Different: Computer Training for Adult Learners," *Journal of Systems Management* 46 (1995): 58-64.

K. Virginia Hemby. "Teaching Adults in the Business Education Classroom," *Business Education Forum* 52 (1997): 36-38.

Kelley, Catherine L. and Neil Charness. "Issues in Training Older Adults to Use Computers," *Behaviour and Information Technology* 14 (1995): 107-120.

Laguna, Kerrie and Renee L. Babcock, "Computer Anxiety in Young and Older Adults: Implications for Human-Computer Interactions in Older Populations," *Computers in Human Behavior* 13 (1997): 317-326.

Mruk, Christopher J. "Teaching Adult Learners Basic Computer Skills: A New Look at Age, Sex, and Motivational Factors," *Collegiate Microcomputer* 5 (1987): 294-300.

Nordenbo, Sven Erik. "How Do Computer Novices Perceive Information Technology? A Qualitative Study Based on a New Methodology," *Scandinavian Journal of Educational Research* 34 (1990): 43-76.

Owen, David. "Designing Instruction for Older Adults," *Programmed Learning and Educational Technology* 25 (1988): 23-27.

Ross, Gary Earl. "Strategies for Addressing Technophobia in Nontraditional Freshman," *Collegiate Microcomputer* 11 (1993): 120-122.

Russell, Anne L. "Stages in Learning New Technology: Naïve Adult Email Users," *Computers in Education* 25 (1995).

Sharit, Joseph and Sara J. Czaja. "Aging, Computer-Based Task Performance, and Stress: Issues and Challenges," *Ergonomics* 37 (1994): 559-577.

Speer, Tibbett L. "A Nation of Students," *American Demographics* 18 (1996): 32-45.

Weil, Michelle M. and Larry D. Rosen. *Technostress: Coping With Technology at Work, at Home, at Play* (New York: John Wiley and Sons, Inc., 1997).

Weil, Michelle M., Larry D. Rosen, and Stuart E. Wugalter. "The Etiology of Computerphobia," *Computers in Human Behavior* 6 (1990): 361-379.

# Technological Mediation:
# Reference and the Non-Traditional Student

## Deborah S. Grealy

**SUMMARY.** The growth of adult education on college campuses is significantly affecting college and university libraries which now must deal with issues surrounding adult and distance education, along with the proliferation of information resources and unprecedented technological change. Desktop provision of licensed electronic library resources, along with Web-based tutorials, Web-based pathfinders, and skillful mediation of electronic reference questions can help alleviate anxiety, saving valuable time for non-resident, non-traditional students by enabling them to access and utilize remotely accessible electronic library resources effectively. *[Article copies available for a fee from The Haworth Document Delivery Service: 1-800-342-9678. E-mail address: <getinfo@haworthpressinc.com> Website: <http://www.haworthpressinc.com>]*

**KEYWORDS.** Distance education, adult education, off campus library services

## *INTRODUCTION*

As increasing numbers of adult learners return to college classrooms, academic institutions are feeling the impact because their infrastructures are

Deborah S. Grealy is Reference Librarian and Non-Traditional Programs Librarian, Penrose Library, University of Denver, 2150 East Evans Avenue, Denver, CO 80208 (E-mail: dgrealy@du.edu). She received her BA and MA from Kent State University, Kent OH, her MLS from the University of Oklahoma, Norman, and is currently working toward a PhD in Higher Education at the University of Denver.

[Haworth co-indexing entry note]: "Technological Mediation: Reference and the Non-Traditional Student." Grealy, Deborah S. Co-published simultaneously in *The Reference Librarian* (The Haworth Information Press, an imprint of The Haworth Press, Inc.) No. 69/70, 2000, pp. 63-68; and: *Reference Services for the Adult Learner: Challenging Issues for the Traditional and Technological Era* (ed: Kwasi Sarkodie-Mensah) The Haworth Information Press, an imprint of The Haworth Press, Inc., 2000, pp. 63-68. Single or multiple copies of this article are available for a fee from The Haworth Document Delivery Service [1-800-342-9678, 9:00 a.m. - 5:00 p.m. (EST). E-mail address: getinfo@haworthpressinc.com].

largely designed to support traditional, residential students. Among the organizations most significantly affected are college and university libraries, which must now cope not only with the explosion of information and information technology, but with complex issues surrounding adult education. Adult students, especially those living at a distance or attending school part-time, often have complicated schedules and conflicting priorities. Unfortunately, traditional student support services do not tend to meet their needs (Sarkodie-Mensah, 132-133).

Resistance to change, lack of familiarity with resources and tools, fear of technology, and the proliferation of information pose very real barriers for students trying to use an academic library after several years away from academe. Given the exponential rate of technological change in libraries today, it is little wonder that adults returning to school hesitate to expose their vulnerability by leaping into a technological maelstrom. In addition to technostress, non-traditional students must also contend with family and career pressures, and significant constraints upon their time. Institutions which provide certificate and degree programs for the adult learner must begin to focus on students' access to information resources and their ability (and willingness) to use those resources effectively.

## MISSION

College and university libraries tend to reflect the larger teaching missions of their parent institutions. For this reason, academic librarians are committed to helping library users become information self-sufficient, rather than providing full-service information retrieval and document delivery. This pattern is beginning to change, however, as market-driven entities like the University of Phoenix offer competitive, value-added information services to adult students. "These trends will continue, and because more services will be fee-based, user satisfaction and flexibility of service delivery will become increasingly important. We will need to become more 'client focused,' and prepared to tailor services to various classes of users" (Cavanagh, 1997).

Many adult students returning to school have little or no technological savvy, while others view information as a commodity and are unaccustomed to retrieving information for themselves. Neither has much appreciation of how to use and evaluate library information resources. The former can be taught the protocols and conventions of information retrieval and become familiar with available paper and electronic resources. The latter can also be taught patterns of information retrieval and be encouraged to take ownership of their own quests for information. In time, libraries may choose to adopt more transactional models of information delivery by facilitating user-generated requests for subsidized or cost-recovery based document delivery.

## DIVERSE NEEDS

Adult education in an non-traditional academic setting can lead to unprecedented diversity in the classroom in terms of preparedness, skill level, and ability. The wide range of capabilities typically held by adult learners presents special challenges to instructors and information providers alike. "Users are varied and . . . services should take into account their nature, needs, and learning styles" (Sarkodie-Mensah, 132).

Studies are currently being conducted that will help us more fully understand how non-traditional students access and process information, how they use it, and what they retain (Rafferty, 298). Meanwhile, differences in preparedness and technological comfort levels are frequently offset by the highly motivated nature of the students. Librarians who take time to work individually with adult learners generally enjoy a gratifying return on their investment. Adult students tend to be serious in their studies. They are appreciative of individualized assistance, and eager to apply the new skills they have been taught.

## WEB-BASED RESOURCES

What are common to most adult learners are real-life constraints on time and energy. Tools that simplify the research and information retrieval process include remotely accessible Web-based library catalogs, and electronic indexes and abstracting tools that have a semblance of uniformity. Subscriptions to full-text and full-content periodicals can be delivered to desktops on demand. While these cannot (and should not) replace the library's traditional periodical holdings, easily available digital formats can be of inestimable value to the student who has limited time available to spend in the library. Use and cost studies currently underway will afford a better picture of attendant costs and paybacks involved in such Web-based distance learning support service (Schiller, 1).

"Rather than application-specific, knowledge and skills" (Anderson, 1), training in generic information technology literacy allows students to use the apparently "seamless" interface of Web-based library search engines quite effectively. By eliminating the need to learn specific command structures, students can concentrate on information content. Search strategies and information retrieval are executed electronically in an environment, which, if not transparent, is at least largely intuitive. Familiar Web-based search conventions include the use of dialog boxes and pull down menus, along with options for basic and advanced searching capabilities. Site licensing, scripted access, proxy servers, and IP limiting allow libraries to provide access to licensed commercial products without students having to worry about passwords, firewalls or other restrictions.

## WEB-BASED LIBRARY INSTRUCTION

A second strategy for assisting the adult user who accesses the library remotely is to mount a series of tutorials and pathfinders on the library's home page. Simple "point and click" tutorials provide basic information on library and information retrieval protocols like controlled vocabulary, keyword searching, Boolean logic, truncation, and word proximity searching. Instructions on basic database navigation protocols can be mounted in a similar way. An additional level of support and guidance can be supplied by linking to discipline-specific pathfinders containing annotations, locations, and hypertext links where appropriate (Grealy, 1998). More sophisticated, interactive tutorials may also be made available by using CGI-bin and Java scripts, along with multimedia and other Web enhancements. Care should be taken, however, to ensure that lower level access to the same information is available to students with less technological capability. Interfaces that permit text-based browsers such as Lynx, and other non-graphical options, facilitate access to information without contributing to technological chauvinism.

## ELECTRONIC REFERENCE

A further level of support can be provided through direct contact with reference librarians and other library faculty members. E-mail reference, telephone reference, and scheduled appointments provide personal contact and specific problem mediation. Ironically, once seen as a replacement for live reference providers, technological innovation has made human intervention more necessary than ever. The proliferation of resources in a variety of formats has led to higher volumes of reference and information interactions, and has resulted in longer transaction times at the reference desk. A wider range of choices for users gives rise to more "questions about database content, database selection, and system use" along with questions about equipment and connectivity (Summey, 108-109).

If the infrastructure of the institution allows for it, user-generated document delivery and interlibrary loan services may also be made available through walk-in, phone, fax, mail, or e-mail. Such services supplement library resources already available in paper and electronic formats, and may be provided to students free of charge, may be subsidized, or may be provided on a cost-recovery basis.

## CONCLUSION

Technology is the key to providing library services and resources to the non-traditional, adult student. Although technology may initially contribute to student technostress, the availability of electronic resources, coupled with appropriate training and support, contributes significantly to student success and satisfaction. Relevant materials are readily accessible without time and travel constraints. Technological mediation enables personal mediation of information queries, allows the student to evaluate potential materials, and provides instant gratification in terms of full-text and full-content electronic document delivery.

Electronic resource provision also addresses the important issue of equity in non-traditional service provision, since universities are obligated to provide the same level of service to off-campus students as to residential students. Electronic access to licensed information products, full-text delivery of electronic materials, Web-based training in research and retrieval methods, and electronic reference and referral services are all viable attempts at providing equal access to information to all members of the university community. Developing programs to ensure that all students benefit by services of similar quality and cost is at the heart of non-traditional and off-campus library service provision (Clark, 1).

Other issues, however, remain unresolved. "At the heart of the struggle to find a balance between a market-driven approach and a commitment to the development of students who can operate as independent thinkers and researchers, lies a debate about the role of libraries" (Stephens, 1). Availability of full-service options to non-traditional and adult students, although attractive and appropriate to their needs, raise the philosophical question of whether mediated searching and full-service delivery in an academic setting is consistent with a university's teaching mission. This question will need to be resolved at higher institutional levels where decisions regarding the rights and privileges of non-traditional students are made.

## REFERENCES

Anderson, Robert H. and Bikson, Tora K. *Focus on Generic Skills for Information Technology Literacy.* Santa Monica CA: Rand Corporation, 1998. RAND/P-8018. 6 pp.

Cavanagh, Tony. "Library Services for off Campus Students: At the Crossroads?" *The Journal of Library Services for Distance Education [JLSDE].* Vol. 1, No. 1. August 1997. 3 pp. *http://www.westga.edu/library/jlsde/vol1/1/*

Chepesiuk, Ron. "Internet College: The Virtual Classroom Challenge." *American Libraries.* Vol. 29, No. 3, March 1998, pp. 52-55.

Clark, Judith and Store, Ron. "Flexible Learning and The Library: The Challenge."

*The Journal of Library Services for Distance Education [JLSDE]*. Vol. 1, No. 2. June 1998. 5 pp. *http://www.westga.edu/library/jlsde/vol1/2/*

Faulhaber, Charles B. "Distance Learning and Digital Libraries: Two Sides of a Single Coin." *Journal of the American Society for Information Science,* Vol. 47, No. 11, November 1996, pp. 854-856.

Grealy, Deborah S. "Leveraging the Wave: The Role of Today's Academic Reference Librarian." In: *Philosophies of Reference Service* (ed: Celia Hales Mabry). New York: The Haworth Press, Inc., 1997, pp. 93-102.

Grealy, Deborah S. "Web-Based Learning: Electronic Library Resources and Instruction." In: *Distance Learning '98.* 14th Annual Conference on Distance Teaching & Learning, Proceedings. Madison WI: University of Wisconsin, 1998, pp. 133-137.

Moss, Molly M. "Reference Services for Remote Users." *Katharine Sharp Review,* No. 5, Summer 1997. 9 pp. *http://edfu.lis.uiuc.edu/review/5/moss.html*

Rafferty, Sue and Bell, Dan. "Online Learning: Does Bloom's Taxonomy Have Relevance?" In: *Distance Learning '98.* 14th Annual Conference on Distance Teaching & Learning, Proceedings. Madison WI: University of Wisconsin, 1998, pp. 297-299.

Sarkodie-Mensah, Kwasi. "The Human Side of Reference in an Era of Technology." In: *Philosophies of Reference Service* (ed: Celia Hales Mabry). New York: The Haworth Press, Inc., 1997, pp. 131-138.

Schiller, Nancy and Cunningham, Nancy. "Delivering Course Materials to Distance Learners Over the World Wide Web: Statistical Data Summary." *The Journal of Library Services for Distance Education [JLSDE]*. Vol. 1, No.2. June 1998. 8 pp. *http://www.westga.edu/library/jlsde/vol1/2/*

Stephens, Kate and Unwin, Lorna. "The Heart of the Matter: Libraries, Distance Education and Independent Thinking." *The Journal of Library Services for Distance Education [JLSDE]*. Vol. 1, No. 1. June 1998. 3 pp. *http://www.westga.edu/library/jlsde/vol1/1/*

Summey, Terri Pedersen. "Techno Reference: Impact of Electronic Reference Resources on Traditional Reference Services." In: *Philosophies of Reference Service* (ed: Celia Hales Mabry). New York: The Haworth Press, Inc., 1997, pp. 103-111.

# Challenges Faced by Reference Librarians in Familiarizing Adult Students with the Computerized Library of Today: The Cuesta College Experience

Kevin F. Bontenbal

**SUMMARY.** Adult students face several challenges in their encounters with the new computerized library of today. Having been out of school for several years many adult students are unfamiliar with the computerized revolution that has taken place within the library. Reference librarians on the other hand, face several challenges in helping adult students become familiarized with the new technologies. This article discusses some of the challenges both adult students and reference librarians face at Cuesta College, a mid-size community college in San Luis Obispo, California. Successful techniques for addressing some of these challenges are also exemplified. *[Article copies available for a fee from The Haworth Document Delivery Service: 1-800-342-9678. E-mail address: <getinfo @haworthpressinc.com> Website: <http://www.haworthpressinc.com>]*

**KEYWORDS.** Adult students, computerized library, reference services, community college

---

Kevin F. Bontenbal received his MLS from Syracuse University and is Instructional Technology Librarian, Cuesta College, San Luis Obispo Community College District, San Luis Obispo, CA 93403 (E-mail: kbontenb@bass.cuesta.cc.ca.us).

[Haworth co-indexing entry note]: "Challenges Faced by Reference Librarians in Familiarizing Adult Students with the Computerized Library of Today: The Cuesta College Experience." Bontenbal, Kevin F. Co-published simultaneously in *The Reference Librarian* (The Haworth Information Press, an imprint of The Haworth Press, Inc.) No. 69/70, 2000, pp. 69-76; and: *Reference Services for the Adult Learner: Challenging Issues for the Traditional and Technological Era* (ed: Kwasi Sarkodie-Mensah) The Haworth Information Press, an imprint of The Haworth Press, Inc., 2000, pp. 69-76. Single or multiple copies of this article are available for a fee from The Haworth Document Delivery Service [1-800-342-9678, 9:00 a.m. - 5:00 p.m. (EST). E-mail address: getinfo@haworthpressinc.com].

## INTRODUCTION

Across the country, the number of adult students returning to colleges continues to increase at an accelerating rate. According to the *Los Angeles Times*, in California; "Cal State campuses up and down the state have seen the proportion of students age 25 and over increase from 39% of the student body in 1984 to 44% last year."[1] The increase in the number of older students seems to grow proportionately with their confusion with the proliferation of technology that continues to take place within the educational environment. Many of these students are re-entering an environment that has been over run by computerization. This is especially true in the library.

As adult students venture into the library to work on class assignments and/or conduct research they often feel as though they are entering a different library altogether from the one they were used to only a few years ago. This new library, furnished with on-line public access terminals, electronic databases, CD-ROMs and Internet computers instead of a card catalog can often be intimidating to the adult student who outside of the educational environment has not been required to use computers that often, and in some cases not at all. This new computerization presents an entirely new way of accessing information in the library than most adult students are used to.

Adult students, however, are not alone in their confusion and frustration; reference librarians as well are faced with new challenges in acquainting these adult learners with the new technology. Introducing adult students to the new computerized library, and familiarizing them with the functions of these computer access points to information often proves to be a difficult and time consuming task for reference librarians. Many of these students' inexperience with technology, unfamiliarity with navigating in the Windows environment, and a basic intimidation of technology, present a new set of challenges for reference librarians. Extra time is required by reference librarians in easing adult students' fear of technology, explaining the basics of a Windows environment, and why this computerization has taken place at all–nuisances that many of us take for granted having lived through the transition.

This article will discuss the challenges and issues adult students face with the computerized library of today. It will also explore the challenges reference librarians are experiencing in familiarizing these adult students with the new computerized library. Many of the challenges and issues presented in this article have been taken directly from those experienced by adult students and reference librarians at Cuesta College. Cuesta College is a community college located in San Luis Obispo, California. Cuesta's student enrollment for Spring, 1998 reached 8,484 students, an increase of 7.6% from the previous semester. Of these 8,484 students approximately 38% are over the age of 25.[2]

## THE TYPICAL CUESTA COLLEGE ADULT STUDENT

To begin, let us first take a look at the typical Cuesta College adult student. For the purpose of clarification, an adult student is any student over the age of 25. At Cuesta approximately 38% of the student population is over 25 years old. The average age of the Cuesta College student is 26 years old. Table I shows the number of students 25 years old and older. Having such a large percentage of the student body over the age of 25 poses several challenges for reference librarians. These older students' interaction with the new technologies in the library are often vastly different then that of their younger counterparts, requiring different skills on the part of reference librarians in serving them.

One particularly observable characteristic that separates adult students from younger students is they tend to be more serious and goal oriented in their education, and do not blindly accept authority. They will spend more time searching for information and are more inquisitive about the information they find. Like many younger students do, adult students will not settle for the first article that they find. They are more critical in their research and genuinely want to learn something from the experience. However, as Mary Bludnicki points out; "while adult students have maturity and experience and are more focused on their goals, they [often] lack skills in research."[4] This lack of research skills is particularly prevalent in their dealings with the new computerized library.

## ADDRESSING BASIC COMPUTER SKILLS
## AND ELIMINATING COMPUTER PHOBIA OF ADULT STUDENTS

When it comes to computerization, one basic difference between adult students and younger students is that adult students are typically more technophobic. Many adult students have been out of school for several years and

TABLE I. Number of students 25 years old and older from Fall 1992 to Spring 1998.[3]

| Age | Fall 92 | Fall 93 | Fall 94 | Fall 95 | Fall 96 | Fall 97 | Spring 98 |
|---|---|---|---|---|---|---|---|
| 25-29 | 3260 | 1719 | 1759 | 1358 | 1138 | 984 | 1017 |
| 30-34 | 971 | 590 | 725 | 625 | 585 | 517 | 571 |
| 35 & over | 2290 | 1492 | 1738 | 1642 | 1562 | 1666 | 1674 |
| Total | 6521 | 3801 | 4222 | 3225 | 3285 | 3167 | 3262 |

carry high expectations of failure in their dealings with technology. During their absence from the educational environment many have not been exposed to computers or used them on a regular basis. This poses a challenge for reference librarians given the technological proliferation that has occurred in the library.

One beneficial approach to easing adult students' fear of computers is by making computers as friendly and non-threatening as possible. The use of non-computer analogies when explaining the functions of computers can be extremely helpful in accomplishing this goal. It is good to have a sense of humor and joke about things when they go wrong. A statement such as; "Did you try kicking it?" can often relax the tense adult student. It can also be helpful to give the computer anthropomorphic characteristics. Statements such as; "The computer does not like it when someone hits that button," or "It must be tired today," can make the students feel like the computer is not above them. Making the student feel as though it was their fault when something goes wrong will only increase their anxiety.

Being available is another good practice when dealing with adult students. Going an extra step or two with adult students lets them know they are not alone in this unfamiliar environment and will help instill the idea that the library is a friendly and helpful place. Going an extra step can be as simple as following up after the initial encounter. Do not just quickly show an adult student how to use the new on-line catalog or an electronic database. Return after a while and see how they are doing. More than likely they have encountered a problem and your return lets them know that you are there to help.

## ADULT STUDENTS
## AND THE ON-LINE PUBLIC ACCESS CATALOG (OPAC)

"Where is the card catalog?" is one of the most frequent questions adult students ask, even in this era of technology. Last year Cuesta College removed its card catalog to make room for more computer terminals. Part of the decision to remove the card catalog was also based on the fact that since the library implemented their OPAC system the card catalog was no longer updated. For the adult student equating the card catalog to the cornerstone of the library, explaining the OPAC as a better access to library materials can be a challenge for reference librarians.

It is easy for reference librarians to infer that the card catalog is a replica of the on-line catalog and how the latter is similar to the former. Mastering the on-line catalog goes beyond the simple comparison with the traditional catalog. The totally new approach to searching on-line catalogs, including the vast array of menu choices can be confusing and illogical to the student accustomed to using the card catalog to access information. One students remembers her experience; "I was terrified . . . it made me physically sick . . . I could not get the hang of the new computerized system."[5]

No matter how much time the reference librarian spends with adult students explaining the nuances of the on-line catalog, at least half, if not more, will not completely comprehend which buttons they must press to perform another search, how to tell if the item is checked out, or where the call number is displayed. Again, follow-up is a valuable practice in easing the adult student's confusion with the on-line catalog. The more reference librarians can make an adult student's initial experience a positive one the more success that student will have in their future use of the library.

## FROM OPAC TO ELECTRONIC DATABASES– A BUMPY TRANSITION

Assuming that the adult student has mastered the OPAC he or she is now faced with a new challenge: electronic databases. At Cuesta College, as is likely to be the case in other libraries, electronic databases are on stand-alone workstations. Thus, just when a student has become familiar with searching the OPAC, the proliferation of other electronic databases that have nothing in common when it comes to searching them poses another major problem for the adult student. Not to mention the difference in how each of these databases displays information. All of these inconsistencies can be confusing and overwhelming to the adult student. Often the student must spend more time figuring out how to navigate around an electronic database than evaluating the information they find. Concomitantly, the job of the reference librarian often becomes one of explaining how to use the technology rather than helping the student determine which information is most appropriate given their research question.

At Cuesta, help lists have been placed next to database computers highlighting the basic commands of each. Information packets, explaining how to search and navigate the different databases are also made available near the computer terminals and at the reference desk. Cuesta has also taken the initiative of implementing a library workbook as part of the English 1A curriculum. English 1A is a class that all Cuesta College students must take within their first year at the college.

The library workbook or Expanding Horizons, as it is called, introduces the student to the various electronic and print resources that the library contains. In completing the workbook students are required to use the OPAC, electronic databases, Internet and several traditional print indexes and references resources. Furthermore, Cuesta librarians work with the faculty in conducting bibliographic orientations. These orientations give the students a jump-start to library and research assignments and allow them to see what resources they will be using before they use them.

## THE WORLD WIDE WEB, A NEW FRONTIER

Interestingly, when it comes to the Web there is no clear delineation between misconceptions among different students. Other than basic computer phobia and inexperience with a Windows environment, the Web is as new to adult students as it is to others.

This unfamiliarity becomes prevalent when observing students using the Web. Some students will use a search engine to find a website when they already have the URL address for that website. Others do not realize that there is more information to a website than what appears in the browser window. They do not realize that they have to scroll down the page to get to this information. Some students want to know why they cannot get more information about a particular subject or topic when there is no link offered from the website they are viewing to that information. In traditional print resources the understanding that information in a particular source has limits is far more obvious than on the Web, where information is tied together through an endless labyrinths of links. Many students are also unclear as to why they are unable to send someone an e-mail when there is an e-mail link offered on a website.

These misconceptions are becoming more of an issue as instructors are increasingly incorporating the World Wide Web into their instruction and requiring students to utilize the Web for research as well as to complete assignments. As is the case with teaching electronic databases, the reference librarian often spends more time explaining the technology of the Web than that of the content of a particular website. It becomes the reference librarians' responsibility to explain to students why they are unable to connect to a particular website, why they cannot send e-mail without an e-mail account themselves, why a website that uses white fonts does not print, and how to navigate around the Web in general.

Part of the frustrations reference librarians face in helping students use the Web comes from the instructors own lack of understanding of the Web. For instance, an instructor may find some interesting websites they want their students to explore and include the URL addresses on a handout. However, when the student comes into the library to locate a particular website they may find that the website no longer exists. A common occurrence in the ever changing environment of the Web. Instructors may also ask students to search for full text journal articles or other information that is not readily available on the Web.

To address these issues librarians at Cuesta have prepared handouts on how to effectively search the Web, how to cite Web resources in a bibliography, and regularly give orientations on the Internet. This approach has helped students' understanding of the Web, but has not successfully addressed instructors' misconceptions.

## *SUCCESSFULLY FAMILIARIZING ADULT STUDENTS WITH THE NEW COMPUTERIZED LIBRARY*

There is no perfect formula for successfully eliminating adult students' fears with the computerized library of today. Each library will face different challenges and deal with those challenges based on the culture of their institution. At Cuesta College, the library has done several things to ease the fear all students, adult or younger have with the library, by making resources available that can help students with their confusion.

Some of the resources/techniques that Cuesta has implemented to help students overcome their fears with the library and help them become more familiar with the new technologies include:

- Providing handouts on basic commands, functions, and search strategies
- Labeling what resources are available on each workstation
- Conducting library orientations
- Implementing library workbook into English 1A curriculum
- Practicing patience
- Following up after initial encounters
- Being readily available

There is not one of these techniques that has worked better than another. Each challenge and each adult student is different and the best possible solution depends entirely on the situation at hand. Some adult students may learn better from a handout while others require more of a personal, hands-on interaction. Therefore, a combination of several resources/techniques can prove successful to a variety of challenges and students.

## *CONCLUSION*

The computerized library of today poses many challenges for both adult students and reference librarians. Adult students are confronted with an environment overrun by computers, each requiring different skills to operate. Furthermore, many adult students are returning to school after having been away from the educational environment for several years. During this absence many have not had the opportunities to improve upon their computer skills. Reference librarians, therefore, become responsible for familiarizing these adult students with the new technology and are challenged by trying to ease these students' fears, dispel their technophobia, and make their experience of the library a rewarding one. This is often a difficult task given the technological differences between the OPAC, electronic databases and the Internet. Ultimately, reference librarians need to be aware of the challenges, fears and unfamiliarities adult students have with the library. With such understanding, reference librarians can then begin to develop tools and practices that can help them address these challenges and fears and reacquaint adult students' with the computerized library of today.

## REFERENCES

1. Pyle, Amy. "Second Time Around." *Los Angeles Times.* 15 Feb. 1998, Campus & Career: 3.

2. The number of students age 25 and older for the past seven years were obtained from running query request against student enrollment data contained in the campus mainframe computer.

3. Ibid.

4. Bludnicki, Mary. "Supporting Virtual Learning for Adult Students." *THE Journal.* 25.11 (June 1998): 74.

5. Pyle, Amy. "Second Time Around." *Los Angeles Times.* 15 Feb. 1998, Campus & Career: 5.

# SECTION 2:
# UNDERSTANDING THE CHARACTERISTICS, NEEDS AND EXPECTATIONS OF ADULT LEARNERS TO BETTER SERVE THEM

# Envisioning the Mature Re-Entry Student: Constructing New Identities in the Traditional University Setting

## Lisa Given

**SUMMARY.** As most students attend university following high school graduation, it is not surprising that the institutional 'traditional student' discourse is one of fraternity parties and breaking free of parental control. This discourse infuses university life, and excludes mature students from the vision of those who influence students' academic careers. While educational research provides an 'adult learner' discourse, many mature students find that they are not appropriately served by their professors or reference librarians. What may help is an environment which does not presume a need and its solution based on these discourses, but one which treats all students as individuals. *[Article copies available for a fee from The Haworth Document Delivery Service: 1-800-342-9678. E-mail address: <getinfo@haworthpressinc.com> Website: <http://www.haworthpressinc.com>]*

**KEYWORDS.** Mature students, discourse, social constructionism, higher education, reference services

The promotion of 'lifelong learning,' or the idea that one's education should span one's entire life, has become a central tenet in contemporary society.

Lisa Given is a PhD Candidate in Library and Information Science, Faculty of Information and Media Studies, University of Western Ontario, London, ON, Canada N6A 5B7 (E-mail: lgiven@julian.uwo.ca).

[Haworth co-indexing entry note]: "Envisioning the Mature Re-Entry Student: Constructing New Identities in the Traditional University Setting." Given, Lisa. Co-published simultaneously in *The Reference Librarian* (The Haworth Information Press, an imprint of The Haworth Press, Inc.) No. 69/70, 2000, pp. 79-93; and: *Reference Services for the Adult Learner: Challenging Issues for the Traditional and Technological Era* (ed: Kwasi Sarkodie-Mensah) The Haworth Information Press, an imprint of The Haworth Press, Inc., 2000, pp. 79-93. Single or multiple copies of this article are available for a fee from The Haworth Document Delivery Service [1-800-342-9678, 9:00 a.m. - 5:00 p.m. (EST). E-mail address: getinfo@haworthpressinc.com].

Governments fund initiatives which promote this ideal, and universities strive to increase their offerings of continuing education programs and open their doors to adults seeking to upgrade their skills. The UNESCO report *Learning to Be* (Faure et al. 1972) first explored the concept of the 'learning society' and both the formal and informal educational activities that contribute to 'lifelong learning.' It promoted learning across the lifespan for self-fulfillment and social betterment, and served as the basis for more than two decades of research and publication by UNESCO and other internationally-recognized educational bodies on lifelong learning and lifelong education. The 'information revolution' of the last few decades has also had an impact on the rise of the importance of lifelong learning, particularly as this relates to economic change. Governments and the corporate sector encourage citizens and employees to upgrade their skills and broaden their education level to compete for jobs, promotions and success in a global economy (Hasan 1996).

This new focus on 'lifelong learning,' as both a societal and an economic good, has direct implications for the development of adult education in the next century. There are four central themes which shape society's rationale for pursuing 'lifelong learning' and which, in turn, shape the future of adult education pursuits. First, the argument is often made that regions that do not foster a 'learning society,' and individuals who do not participate, are destined to be left behind both nationally and on an international scale. Secondly, learning is crucial to all as insurance against being excluded or marginalized from social participation. Thirdly, there is a need to for constant renewal of knowledge and skills in order to keep pace with the rapidity of change that has come to typify many societies. And finally, it is important to combine productive work and learning throughout the lifespan, in order to extend the economically productive years of one's life (Hasan 1996). As more and more countries set the concept of 'lifelong learning' as a social goal with strong economic ramifications, the implications will be directly felt at all levels of education and for all students participating in educational initiatives.

## IMPLICATIONS FOR ADULT STUDENTS

Many of these four points of rationalization for lifelong learning have already had an influence on adult education pursuits. In Canada, national statistics point to a participation rate of 33% of all adult Canadians (or 1 in 3) in some form of adult learning activity (Selman et al. 1998). Within this broad group of adult learners, and across a wide range of educational activities, mature, re-entry students (or those who have been absent from formal schooling for three years or more) are increasingly participating in university degree programs. Indeed, many students now recognize that their learning will not follow a traditional, linear pattern, but will continue throughout their lives. Increasingly, educational research continues to draw attention to the problems faced by non-traditional students (including adult learners), and how their educational barriers may be overcome. In the education and library and information science literature, the focus (even implicitly) has been on the students' drive for academic success, and the role of teachers and librarians in perpetuating such success. Indeed, 'academic success' as a motivator for students' actions in the classroom, in completing assignments, and in other academic endeavours, is endemic to most of the research exploring students' academic and information-related activities.

Gloria Leckie (1996) explores many of the assumptions behind the development of undergraduate research papers which are all elements of academic success, and which continue to influence library research and practice. These include the ability to narrow a research topic, to select an appropriate database to search for information on that topic, to retrieve relevant documents from that search, and to read and analyze these documents in order to write a paper which meets the professor's concept of a 'good' paper. While Leckie's paper focuses on these assumptions in order to explore the reasons for student failure in completing such assignments, the practical components of academic success as they are defined by faculty and librarians is writ large in these pages.

The retrieval of relevant documents, particularly using electronic databases, is one of the many elements of academic success that is explored in countless studies in library and information science (see Jacobson and Fusani 1992 or Nash and Wilson 1991). The creation of complete and appropriate bibliographies is another element of academic success which has been a research focus within this discipline (see Engeldinger 1988 or McInnis and Symes 1991). Yet for many students, particularly those with competing family and/or work demands, academic success may be defined simply as completion of an assignment or taking only a small penalty on the late submission of a paper. While Jane Keefer (1993) points to the "time limitations" (336) that can affect a student's level of success, this factor (and other, similar factors) rarely sits as the marker of success itself. Instead, such elements are pushed to the periphery of the student's broader experiences of academic success, as challenges to be overcome. The concept of academic failure then, is often marked in the literature by the creation of incomplete bibliographies, the inability to find relevant citations, and the inability to properly narrow a research topic. Yet both success and failure are frequently examined with traditional undergraduates or, at least, with the presumption that a group of students have common skill levels and perspectives (see Fister 1992). Mature re-entry students, if they are included within these studies, are not usually identified.

If a learner-centered ideal is to become a reality within educational circles, it is imperative that adult learners be at the heart of this initiative. While 'lifelong learning' presumes a form of education (formal or otherwise) that stretches across the lifespan, it is the adults themselves who must alter their view of education and find a place for themselves within this new social structure. Historically, formal education has proceeded in a linear fashion and with a clear end-point: from kindergarten and elementary school, through high school, and (for some) to postsecondary programs, and (finally) the world of work. Thus, the argument was made to many generations of elementary, high, and postsecondary school students that if they stayed in school, they would be rewarded with permanent employment and security for their retirement years. While many adults have been forced to alter this view of the world in light of job cuts through corporate downsizing, or reorientation due to a change in their family lives, there are many adults who are only now waking to the harsh realities of having job skills that are obsolete or who are in need of additional programs of study.

Yet, while many adults are now beginning to reevaluate their educational pursuits in the face of new economic and social realities, the typical student at university remains the traditional student who has followed a linear educational path. Indeed there is a discourse which surrounds the persona of the 'traditional student' at universities, and informs institutional policies and practices. Prior to an examination of that discourse, its implications for adult learners, and its influence on reference service in academic libraries, a brief discussion of the nature of discourses and their influence on the social construction of identity is warranted.

## DISCOURSE AND IDENTITY

In their discussion of the social construction of self, and the relation of social discourse to this process, Davies and Harré (1990) note that

> a discourse is to be understood as an institutionalised use of language and language-like sign systems. Institutionalisation can occur at the disciplinary, the political, the cultural and the small group level. There can also be discourses that develop around a specific topic, such as gender or class. Discourses can compete with each other or they can create distinct and incompatible versions of reality. To know anything is to know in terms of one or more discourses. (45)

Discourses work to create portraits of people or groups of people, and to define these people in particular ways. Discourses manifest themselves in texts, in books, conversations, visual images, and other media. Indeed, as virtually no aspect of human life is exempt from meaning, almost anything can be read as text. Discourses, then, serve to construct the phenomena of our world through texts. As Vivien Burr (1995) notes,

> People's identities are constructed out of a variety of components or 'threads,' including those of age, class, ethnicity, gender, and so on; these 'threads' are woven together to produce the fabric of a one's identity, and they have implications for what we can (and should) do in society . . . Discourses address us as particular kinds of persons (as an old person, as a worker, as a criminal, and so on), and we cannot avoid these descriptions; they provide us with our sense of self, the ideas and metaphors with which we think, and the self-narratives we use to talk and think about ourselves. (51-54; 153)

Being a student is simply another of the 'threads' or roles in one's life and thus being a student is a component of an individual's identity, which "is constructed out of the discourses culturally available to us, and which we draw upon in our communications with other people" (Burr 1995, 51).

## THE INSTITUTION
## AND THE 'TRADITIONAL STUDENT' DISCOURSE

Burr, and Davies and Harré note that for each 'thread' of our identity, there are a limited number of discourses on offer from which we might fashion our identities. In addition, there are prevailing discourses within this limited number which seem to 'ring true' (and prevail) in our society. The 'student' thread is no exception to these rules. At postsecondary institutions, despite the growing influx of vast numbers of adult learners, a 'traditional student' discourse shapes and defines the student's identity. Further, this discourse is offered as the prevailing norm, and forms the basis for many of the institution's documents and policies. One text which offers examples of this normalized, 'traditional student' discourse, is a report on undergraduate life commissioned by my own university (Kuh 1995). In the report, no mention is made of the ages of undergraduate students, let alone how many are mature, re-entry students. The authors point to the stereotypes that surround the university as "a party school" (1995, 15), and they note that there is evidence to support such a notion. The students are described for their propensity for binge drinking, for their experiences in the residences, their exploits during orientation week, and for their involvement in student clubs and student government (1995, 15-17). There is no mention of spouses, day-care needs, or other traditionally 'adult' pursuits. Here, the 'traditional student' discourse is privileged to such a degree that there is only a cursory mention of minority groups of students–and then, only visible minorities; there is no mention of mature, international or other nontraditional groups. While one could argue that this report's apparent 'tunnel vision' is due to the fact that mature students were not included in the study's mandate, this exclusion itself is only another example of the way that the 'traditional student' discourse is normalized and perpetuated.

Another document which provides a glimpse into student life across Canada is the *1997 Graduating Student Survey at Nine Canadian Universities,* compiled by the Canadian Undergraduate Survey Consortium. In the summary of the report's major findings, the authors note that "Some prospective graduates started undergraduate studies as early as 1957 [while the] modal year at which respondents first started their present programs was 1993" (1997, 4). Apart from this admission that clearly some of the respondents were mature (and possibly re-entry) students, this group of learners is conspicuously absent from the remainder of the report. Indeed, the most striking finding of the report, as far as issues of identity are concerned, is that 46.8% of all students were dissatisfied with the measure of "concern shown by the university to you as an individual" (1997, 15). If universities continue to foster the idea of a homogenous undergraduate student body, particularly by perpetuating the 'traditional student' discourse, such findings may never be altered.

The discourse of the 'traditional student' infuses virtually every aspect of a student's life, and forms part of the hierarchical hegemony of the university, which encourages the 'normal' status quo and discourages any questioning of prevailing 'norms.' Usher et al. shed some light on this notion, by stating that

> A norm works by excluding; by defining a standard and criteria of judgement it identifies all those who do not meet the standard . . . Normalisation is not a neutral process but its significance and impact lies precisely in the fact that it appears to be neutral. The seeming 'objectivity' of a norm makes normalisation appear to be simply a neutral procedure for scientifically ascertaining people's inherent 'natural' capacities. (1997, 80)

As universities present, and reinforce, the 'norm' of the traditional student, mature, re-entry students find themselves existing outside of the norm. University orientation programs frequently include time and/or financial management workshops for those students who are away from their parents for the first time, or seminars which encourage responsible drinking practices. While these are valuable sessions, and ones which arguably meet the needs of the majority of university undergraduates, there are few equivalent sessions on offer which discuss daycare or family time management strategies, or other concerns which decades of research show to be of vital importance to mature students. For mature, re-entry students who do not fit the typical profile, they must not only fight the academic, financial and other struggles that all students face, they must also find a place for themselves within the normative practices of the institution.

## MATURE, RE-ENTRY STUDENTS–
## WHERE DO THEY FIT?

Yet such an enterprise is not necessarily that easy to fulfill. As Usher et al. note, "Even though diversity and difference may be valued, education in the modernist mode converges on the same, endeavouring to make everyone alike. Notions of progress, rationality, privileged knowledge and values, and normalisation is in-built into the educational event" (1997, 23). Activities in which adults engage, particularly as part of a formal, university degree program, fit with this process of normalisation. While universities may speak of the importance of 'lifelong learning' and have special admissions procedures for mature students, the discourse of the 'traditional (normal) student' reigns supreme. This normalization process occurs in the form of common assignments, policies, and practices, which expect (and dictate) a level of sameness, and which were created with the 'normal' student in mind. As long as institutions continue to privilege existing, 'normal' discourses, despite any claims to embrace diversity, mature students will continue to have difficulty in forging their own 'student' identities.

Indeed, the education literature shows that for many adults, returning to life as a student is not as easy as the purveyors of 'lifelong learning' would have us believe. Research conducted by Ernest L. Boyer shows "that non-traditional students–those who are older and part time–do, in fact, have an especially bumpy introduction to campus life. [They] have complicated schedules–they work and have family obligations–and yet, orientation activities and even college office hours often are not arranged conveniently for them" (1987, 49). As much of the education literature makes clear, adult learners face a number of institutional, dispositional, and situational barriers within postsecondary environments that traditional students need not overcome (Knowles 1990 and Boyer 1987). Indeed, research which explores the particular needs and problems of adult learners dates back to the early twentieth century. In 1926 the founding of the American Association for Adult Education marked the beginning of what has been a continually evolving field of academic and professional study in North America, and worldwide. In the early years, the works of Edward L. Thorndike and Eduard Lindeman spoke to the two major streams in the literature: the former, that of the 'scientific' stream, which demonstrated scientifically that adults could learn; the latter, that of the 'artistic' stream, which concerned itself with the processes governing how adults learn (Knowles

1990). The early research examined a variety of adult education pursuits, including correspondence courses for adults, continuing education and training, and citizenship study for new immigrants.

## ANDRAGOGY–
## THE THEORY OF ADULT LEARNING

While many elements for a theory of adult learning were emerging world-wide by the 1940s, these remained scattered and isolated until the 1960s. At that time, and after incorporating research from psychology, philosophy, and other disciplines, a unified theory for adult learning developed in Europe. This theory, known as 'andragogy' (or, the art and science of teaching adults), arose as an alternative to 'pedagogy,' or the theory of youth learning (Knowles 1990). The pedagogical model of learning assigns full responsibility to the teacher for making all decisions about what will be learned, how it will be learned, when it will be learned, and if it has been learned. It is teacher-directed education which leaves the learner in the submissive role of following a teacher's instructions. Andragogy, on the other hand, explores the learner's ability for self-directed learning. It elevates the role of experience in the adult learner's schooling, documents the high level of responsibility and motivation that adult learners bring to the learning environment, and explores the potent internal and external pressures that set these students apart from their younger student peers (Knowles 1968, 1990).

Based on a 'scientific' psychology of adult learning, andragogy professionalised and scientised adult education, and turned the adult learner into a site for study and professional intervention (Usher et al. 1997). Over the last three decades, andragogical principles have become entrenched in the educational literature and in practical approaches to teaching adult learners. Studies in education which explore andragogical principles offer highly descriptive accounts of the learner's experiences within the educational context. Helen Astin (1976) presents a number of papers which explore the barriers that women face in education, the role of family in women's educational pursuits, and the goals of women engaged in educational activities. Lewis C. Solmon and Joanne J. Gordon's (1981) study of adults in postsecondary education is also typical of much of the andragogical literature; here, the authors present demographic breakdowns of the adults in their study, explore the life goals and educational plans of these students, and document the implications that these elements will have on the educational experience. As with many similar studies, these texts document the various (and often, conflicting) life-roles of adult students, list the barriers to effective learning which these students face, and recommend changes based on their findings.

## THE 'ADULT LEARNER' DISCOURSE

Indeed, there are numerous elements which have been extensively documented in the literature over the past three decades, and which have become entrenched as markers of the 'adult learner.' These markers include the following, where an adult learner is known to be a person

    a. who has a wealth of 'real-life' experience which can enhance the learning process

    b. who is self-directed, knows his/her own learning needs, and has a self-concept of being responsible for his/her own life

    c. who strives for a high level of autonomy in learning

    d. who needs to know why something is necessary prior to learning it, and how it will fit with his/her life experience

    e. who is an active learner who comes to the educational experience ready to learn

    f. and, who is highly self-motivated in the learning process and is particularly driven to succeed by internal pressures (Knowles 1990, Boud 1989 and Usher et al. 1997).

In addition to these learner characteristics, the experiences of adult learners are frequently defined in terms of the negative elements of their academic lives. Usher et al. note, for example, that the adult learning process

> is characterised as one full of blockages and barriers, things which impede or hold back the self-as-learner from attaining various ends, such as efficacy, autonomy, self-realisation or emancipation which [the adult learning] tradition posits as the goal of learning. For the self-as-learner the learning process is one beset by distractions, restrictions, barriers and oppressions–all varieties of negative and feared 'otherness' which have to be overcome. (1997, 94)

The discourse of the 'adult learner' which arises from these descriptions, as reflected in years of adult education research, sits in opposition to that of the 'traditional student.' Here, adult learners, unlike their traditional counterparts, are highly motivated students who bring their 'real-world' experience to the classroom. Their separation from the institution has shown them the value of higher education, so they tend to work harder and participate at a higher level (Vakili 1993). While these findings may solve some of the institutional and situational barriers that adult learners face, this new discourse obscures our understanding of what it means to live as an individual adult learner. While the existing research is valuable for its insight into the challenges that traditional students face, many of these findings have led us to merely exchange one discourse (and social 'type') for another. Such studies do little to reveal the daily experiences of adult learners within an academic environment which does not envision them as individuals with a separate identity from that of the typical undergraduate.

In jumping from one 'student' discourse to another, the problems that adult learners face with regards to identity construction within the institution remain the same. Indeed, the mature, re-entry student must not only construct an identity for him or herself within an institution that caters to the 'traditional student' and assumes him or her to be the typical 'adult learner,' but the mature student must also battle the other identity constructs at work in his or her life. Indeed, our social group identifications (based on race, gender, age, and the like), do not presume a singular perspective based on that group identity; rather, each individual within the group "will hold a myriad of perspectives due to their different histories" (Schick 1994, 24). Thus, the mature, re-entry student, who is returning to academia after a period of separation from formal schooling, comes with his or her own, pre-formed notions of their identity. These notions have been formed through the discourses of 'parent,' 'spouse,' 'employee,' and other traditionally adult pursuits. These pre-formed 'threads' of identity have been shaped by the adult learner's interactions with his or her spouse, children, friends and colleagues, based on those persons' views of that adult's role in their lives. Thus, the addition of the 'student' thread must not only be negotiated with the institution and other students (both 'traditional' and otherwise), but also with the purveyors of all of the adult's pre-formed identities.

As well, once in the academic setting, and upon facing evidence of the 'traditional student' discourse, the adult student must grapple with feelings of conflict and discontinuity in his or her attempts to fashion an identity out of a discourse with which he/she may not identify. The adult student may, for example, feel excluded from certain clubs or social functions due to his/her age or conflicting family commitments. In the library, instruction programs which presume that undergraduates have used OPACs or CD-ROMs in high school, for example, may also exclude the adult student's experiences. At the same time, the adult learner may have to combat others' pre-formed notions of the 'adult learner,' in order to come to an identity with which he or she can abide, and to reconcile this new 'student' identity to his/her other identity threads of spouse, parent and employee. Much of the andragogical literature speaks, for example, of the adult student's high level of motivation in the undergraduate learning environment. Yet, for every student who fits such a description, there may be one who is prone to procrastination, and who will not benefit from programs and services which assume him/her to be motivated. At the same time, institutions that create programs to overcome procrastination in the 'traditional' student body (and which often presume that this problem is the result of separation from parents who kept that student motivated through high school), may not appear welcoming to the procrastinating adult.

## THE 'TRADITIONAL STUDENT' DISCOURSE AND THE ACADEMIC LIBRARY

In the academic library too, it is the 'traditional student' discourse which prevails. Instruction sessions are commonly geared to those coming directly from high school, and tend to presume that most students have used computers, and even the Internet, in their prior studies. At the reference desk, librarians may presume (often without realizing that they are doing so) that a particular student fits (or does not fit) with their vision of a 'typical' student based purely on appearances or the type of question being asked. Indeed, the library and information science literature reinforces these approaches to service by frequently referring to the generic 'undergraduate student' (see Nash and Wilson 1991 or Fister 1992). Explicit mention of mature students, or other nontraditional groups, are not made, but are instead relegated to those few articles which examine these users in isolation from their traditional peers (see Coughlan 1989 or Keenan 1989). While these latter articles do expand the field's knowledge of the special needs of nontraditional undergraduate students, they also form a larger part of the normalisation process at work in universities by placing these students as 'other' to the 'traditional norm.'

When librarians take on these approaches, by creating special programs for these students or by creating a different personal level of service to these students in answering daily reference requests, they also run the risk of perpetuating normalizing stereotypes. This is further complicated by the fact that many librarians and library and information science researchers have privileged the educational (specifically, the andragogical) literature in their approaches to serving these students. By replacing the 'traditional student' discourse with that of the 'adult learner,' librarians risk ignoring the needs of individuals at the expense of accepted types. As Sara Fine (1995) points out, once "librarians make assumptions about their own or their users' behavior and act on those assumptions as though they are true, the reference process and the flow of useful information are impeded" (17).

## WHERE DO WE GO FROM HERE IN REFERENCE SERVICES?

Whether either of the 'traditional' or 'adult' learner profiles is a true characterization of undergraduate students is a moot point; as theorists and practitioners accept them as true, they reinforce such descriptions in their research, teaching and academic policies. Indeed, if the disciplines of education and library and information science continue to accept these learner profiles, and place the adult learner in opposition to their traditional counterparts, the competing 'adult' and 'traditional' student discourses will themselves continue to be a barrier to adult learning. This leaves mature students in a position where they must grapple with their student identities in the face of a prevailing discourse with which they do not fit, in addition to struggling with matters of academic success.

Carol Schick points out that universities dismiss liberatory education and feminist philosophical points of view which encourage difference (and discourage normalisation), as these approaches run counter to the institution's inherent elitism (1994). The result then, in the context of adult learners in the university, is that the "learner-centred characteristic of adult education practice is replaced by a compliance with the structurally imposed requirements faced by both teachers and learners. The capacity of the university to dictate practice and norms is a power which it does not even pretend to share with those involved in the institution" (1994, 23), but a power with which all university participants must comply. The education and library and information science literature of the past two decades, points to evidence of disruption in the acceptance of the 'traditional student' discourse where adult learners are concerned. The lifestyle and everyday existence of the typical undergraduate has been shown to be problematic given the adult learner's 'real-life' experiences within the institution. In the research literature, the response to this clash between the adult student's world and that of the typical undergraduate has been evidenced by particular characteristics: studies which produce vast lists of barriers that mature students face, and even longer lists of how libraries (and other student services) may best serve these students. We know, for example, that the Registrar's office closes too early, that daycare is a problem, and that writing long essays after a 40 hour work week is a challenge (see Keenan 1989). And, we think that we know how to solve these problems by reacting to these findings: by extending service hours, by offering library help via e-mail, and by creating after-hour classes and tutorials for the adult learner. But is this really addressing the problem, or merely reinforcing the stereotypical beliefs that education and library and information science have clung to for decades in their search to serve these students?

## WHAT STEPS DO WE TAKE IN DESIGNING EFFECTIVE REFERENCE SERVICES FOR MATURE STUDENTS?

In order to combat the perpetuation of discursive 'types' with which few (if any) students may actually identify, library researchers and reference librarians must strive to privilege and serve the interests of individual students. The following points may serve as guiding principles to best serve the needs of mature undergraduate students:

1. We must embrace not only the existing andragogical literature, but also the newer educational literature, which questions some long-held beliefs in order to understand the experiences of individual adult students. Briton (1996), Collins (1998), and Duke (1992) provide the basis for new explorations in the theory of adult learning which library and information science cannot ignore.
2. We must question our individual assumptions related to mature students, and move away from perpetuating the 'adult learner' and 'traditional student' discourses. If we treat all users as individuals, with individual needs and problems which cannot be easily pigeon-holed for 'appropriate' reference services, we will serve all users in the best and most effective manner.
3. We must continue to implement open and neutral questioning in reference interactions. Asking questions about the information need, and not jumping to conclusions about the 'type' of user or the 'type' of question, is the best way to avoid the perpetuation of misplaced discursive practices.
4. We must strive to treat all users as individuals. While the educational literature may outline common problems and be very instructive for setting reference policies which best serve the special needs of mature, re-entry students, we must recognize that not all users will fit one profile.

## REFERENCES

Astin, Helen, ed. 1976. *Some action of her own: The adult woman and higher education.* Lexington, MA: Lexington Books.

Boud, David. 1989. Some competing traditions in experiential learning. In *Making sense of experiential learning: Diversity in theory and practice,* ed. Susan Warner Weil and Ian McGill, 38-49. Milton Keynes: The Society for Research into Higher Education & Open University Press.

Boyer, Ernest L. 1987. *College: The undergraduate experience in America.* New York: Harper & Row.

Briton, Derek. 1996. *The modern practice of adult education: A postmodern critique.* New York: State University of New York Press.

Burr, Vivien. 1995. *An introduction to social constructionism.* London: Routledge.

Canadian Undergraduate Survey Consortium. 1997. *1997 Graduating student survey at nine Canadian universities: A summary of major findings.* Winnipeg: University of Manitoba, Housing and Student Life. Photocopied.

Collins, Michael. 1998. Critical returns: From andragogy to lifelong education. In *Learning for life: Canadian readings in adult education,* ed. Sue M. Scott, Bruce Spencer, and Alan M. Thomas, 46-58. Toronto: Thompson Educational Publishing, Inc.

Coughlan, Jacquelyn. 1989. The BI librarian's new constituency: Adult independent learners. *The Reference Librarian* 24: 159-173.

Davies, Bronwyn, and Rom Harré. 1990. Positioning: The discursive production of selves. *Journal for the Theory of Social Behaviour* 20, no. 1: 43-63.

Duke, Christopher. 1992. *The learning university: Towards a new paradigm?.* Buckingham: The Society for Research into Higher Education & Open University Press.

Engeldinger, Eugene A. 1988. Bibliographic instruction and critical thinking: The contribution of the annotated bibliography. *RQ* 28, no. 2: 195-202.

Faure, Edgar, Herrera Felipe, and Abdul-Razzak Kaddoura. 1972. *Learning to be: The world of education today and tomorrow.* Paris: UNESCO.

Fine, Sara. 1995. Reference and resource: The human side. *The Journal of Academic Librarianship* 21, no. 1: 17-20.

Fister, Barbara. 1992. The research processes of undergraduate students. *The Journal of Academic Librarianship* 18, no. 3: 163-169.

Hasan, A. 1996. Lifelong learning. In *International encyclopedia of adult education and training,* 2nd ed., ed. Albert C. Tuijnman, 33-41. Oxford: Pergamon.

Jacobson, Thomas and David Fusani. 1992. Computer, system, and subject knowledge in novice searching of a full-text, multifile database. *Library and Information Science Research* 14: 97-106.

Keefer, Jane. 1993. The hungry rats syndrome: Library anxiety, information literacy, and the academic reference process. *RQ* 32, no. 3: 333-339.

Keenan, Lori M. 1989. Andragogy off-campus: The library's role. *The Reference Librarian* 24: 147-158.

Knowles, Malcolm. 1968. Andrgogy [sic] not pedagogy. *Adult Leadership* 16: 350-352.

Knowles, Malcolm. 1990. *The adult learner: A neglected species.* 4th ed. Houston: Gulf Publishing.

Kuh, George D., J. Herman Blake, Katie Branch Douglas, and Jackie Ramin-Gyurnek. 1995. *Undergraduate student life at the University of Western Ontario: Perceptions and paradoxes, final report.* Bloomington, IN: Center for Postsecondary Research and Planning, Indiana University.

Leckie, Gloria. 1996. Desperately seeking citations: Uncovering faculty assumptions about the undergraduate research process. *The Journal of Academic Librarianship* 22, no. 3: 201-208.

McInnis, Raymond G. and Dal S. Symes. 1991. Running backwards from the finish line: A new concept for bibliographic instruction. *Library Trends* 39, no. 3: 223-237.

Nash, Stan and Myoung Chung Wilson. 1991. Value-added bibliographic instruction: Teaching students to find the right citations. *Reference Services Review* 19, no. 1: 87-92.

Schick, Carol. 1994. *The university as text: Women and the university context.* Halifax: Fernwood Publishing.

Selman, Gordon, Michael Cooke, Mark Selman, and Paul Dampier. 1998. *The foundations of adult education in Canada.* 2nd ed. Toronto: Thompson Educational Publishing, Inc.

Solmon, Lewis C. and Joanne J. Gordon. 1981. *The characteristics and needs of adults in postsecondary education.* Lexington, MA: D.C. Heath and Company.

Usher, Robin, Ian Bryant, and Rennie Johnston. 1997. *Adult education and the postmodern challenge: Learning beyond the limits.* London: Routledge.

Vakili, Mary Jane. 1993. Revamping a required BI course for adult students. *Research Strategies* 11, no. 1: 24-32.

# A Close Encounter Model for Reference Services to Adult Learners: The Value of Flexibility and Variance

Sara Baron

Alexia Strout-Dapaz

**SUMMARY.** Every reference encounter is an instructional encounter. Reference services to adult learners must be as flexible as the learners' technological savvy and learning styles. Furthermore, a variety of instructional methods must be used. This study presents survey results of a sample graduate student population which is outside the mainstream of traditional college students. We present a Close Encounter Model of reference services to meet this population. *[Article copies available for a fee from The Haworth Document Delivery Service: 1-800-342-9678. E-mail address: <getinfo@haworthpressinc.com> Website: <http://www.haworthpressinc.com>]*

**KEYWORDS.** Instruction, library instruction, reference, adult learners

Sara Baron is Instruction Librarian, Texas Christian University. She is a member of the Library & Instruction Roundtables of Texas Library Association and American Library Association (E-mail: S.Baron@tcu.edu). Alexia Strout-Dapaz is Business/Reference Librarian, Texas Christian University. She is a member of Special Libraries Association (E-mail: A.StroutDapaz@tcu.edu).

The authors wish to thank the Library Administration at TCU for their financial support, our student assistants for data entry, and our colleagues who provided valuable support and feedback.

[Haworth co-indexing entry note]: "A Close Encounter Model for Reference Services to Adult Learners: The Value of Flexibility and Variance." Baron, Sara, and Alexia Strout-Dapaz. Co-published simultaneously in *The Reference Librarian* (The Haworth Information Press, an imprint of The Haworth Press, Inc.) No. 69/70, 2000, pp. 95-102; and: *Reference Services for the Adult Learner: Challenging Issues for the Traditional and Technological Era* (ed: Kwasi Sarkodie-Mensah) The Haworth Information Press, an imprint of The Haworth Press, Inc., 2000, pp. 95-102. Single or multiple copies of this article are available for a fee from The Haworth Document Delivery Service [1-800-342-9678, 9:00 a.m. - 5:00 p.m. (EST). E-mail address: getinfo@haworthpressinc.com].

*95*

## INTRODUCTION

Some reference encounters with adult learners may seem like close encounters of the third kind. Every reference encounter is an instructional one. In order to serve adult learners better, we must assess three dimensions: technological savvy, learning styles with print and electronic resources, and instructional methods provided during the encounter. Flexibility and variance in reference services is essential for meeting the information requirements of adult learners. Flexibility refers to methods used in meeting the three dimensions whereas variance refers to the scope of those methods. Our purpose with this study was to examine a sample graduate population of students seeking their Masters of Divinity degrees at the Brite Divinity School, located at Texas Christian University. Because this is a frequent user group of reference services, we tested comfort levels with computer technology, preferred methods of information access, and past technology training experiences.

One of the biggest differences between the adult, reentry learner and the 'mainstream user' is that the former may have a large gap in education. We define "gap in education" as years out of school, not a reflection of quality of education. As a result of this gap, reentry students' technological skills and learning styles must be assessed before instructional encounters. Because many people who have been out of college more than 15 years have not necessarily been exposed to technology, some may fear 'what' technology is or 'how' it can be manipulated. In contrast, 'mainstream' students tend to jump into technology and figure it out, albeit successfully or not.

## LIBRARY LITERATURE

In reviewing the literature, it became obvious that many of the assumptions regarding adult learners–and bibliographic instruction for reentry students–which were respectively elucidated in the 1960's and 1980's, still hold true. For example, Malcolm Knowles, considered that not only are "adults autonomous and independent . . . their most profound need is to be treated as a self-directing person, to be treated with respect." [1] Furthermore, librarians need "to make this learning available, to facilitate it, and in many respects, to stimulate it, to motivate it, and to sustain people's interest in a continuous learning effort."[2]

While the older literature focuses more heavily on the interaction of bibliographic instruction with the personality characteristics of reentry, adult learners, more recent library literature focuses heavily on the marketing and public relations aspect of bibliographic instruction programs for this population group. To illustrate these new marketing tactics, Patricia Weaver[3] recommends sending personalized letters to each reentry student, inviting them to schedule a personalized instruction session. This innovative tactic resulted in fuller classes and helped convince the administration of requiring library instruction sessions.

This study strives to bring the topic of reference services to adult learners up-to-date by combining historical views of reentry students and contemporary library instruction and reference standards. Our assumptions before the survey were:

1. The majority of the survey respondents have had a gap in formal education;
2. People with a large gap in education have a lower comfort level with technology; and
3. Library instruction increases a person's ability to manipulate technology.

## *METHODOLOGY*

A survey instrument was used to assess the following characteristics of a sample graduate population: gap in formal education, comfort level with technology, and the methods used to manipulate technology. We also studied library and reference use, comfort with the reference desk, and levels of technological training.

The survey consisted of 10 questions. Questions covered demographic information (age and gender); years out of school (high school and undergraduate college); level of technology use; current library and reference desk use; preferred methods for finding information (print or electronic); comfort levels with print and electronic resources; past training sessions; steps taken when confronting new resources, and definitions of information overload. Question styles included fill in the blank responses, Likert five point scale, and one open-ended. The open-ended question concerning the respondent's definition of information overload was given to a third party to code. The other questions were tabulated using SPSS 7.5 by an outside consultant.

We faced several challenges with the distribution of the survey. Due to time constraints, we were unable to do a test survey to improve the questionnaire. More importantly, the timing of the survey was not convenient for the respondents. Although our intention was to give out the survey during the last month of classes, it was delayed until the week of finals. The survey was not a priority for students taking exams. However, departmental support from the Interim Associate Dean of the Brite Divinity School greatly increased the response rate. Out of the potential pool of 170 respondents, 90 students completed the survey, thus yielding a return rate of 53%. Of those 90 surveys, 7 were invalid because only half the survey was completed.

## *RESULTS*

*Demographics.* The survey had 83 valid respondents. The average age is 37.64 with 67 being the oldest and 22 being the youngest. Of the respondents, 27 were male, 32 female and 27 did not list gender. As for gap in education, 57% of the respondents have been out of high school more than 15 years and 36% of the respondents have been out of undergraduate college more than 15 years.

*Training.* Using the Pearson Correlation, the study indicated that there is a correlation (.264) between students taking a library class and their ability to use other resources. Students attended library classes when they were scheduled by professors (.551), as opposed to attending walk-in classes. Internet training sessions moderately improve comfort level with the Internet (.284), while database training significantly increases comfort levels with both the Internet (.329) and CD-ROMs (.352). CD-ROMs and the Internet as preferred methods for finding information are also correlated (.218) (see Figure A).

*Preferences and Methods.* Younger people (years of age less than 37.64) significantly prefer electronic resources over print (.366). While older people prefer electronic resources less than their younger counterparts (.278), they also are not significantly comfortable with print resources ($-.928$). Older people (years of age over 37.64) tend to prefer the Library Catalog for finding information. Students who tend to feel comfortable "jumping right in" when facing a new online service also tend to "play with it" (.275). Age is an

FIGURE A. Past Technology/Computer Training

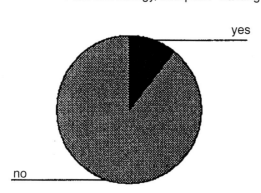

indicator of a person "playing with it," especially when correlated with the Internet. Younger people prefer playing with the Internet over training. When correlated with years out of school, respondents stated that when facing a new resource they seek training from professors (.049); get help from friends (.027); or give up (.135).

*Library Use.* People who use the library tend to use the reference desk (.183). The more comfortable people are with using the library, the more helpful they find the reference desk (.495). Older people tend to find the reference desk the most helpful. Most respondents use the library 0-5 hours a week see Figure B).

## DISCUSSION

Students outside the norm of collegiate life, namely our graduate student population with an average age of 37.64, have unique training needs. Several surprising results of the study concerned the impact of training on comfort levels with technology; comfort levels with print versus electronic sources; and the steps people take when using new technologies. Our study shows that training, even if it is over one subject database, increases students' comfort level with other resources, especially the Internet. At TCU, all CD-ROMs and databases are accessible through the library web site. This may explain the

FIGURE B. Current Library Use

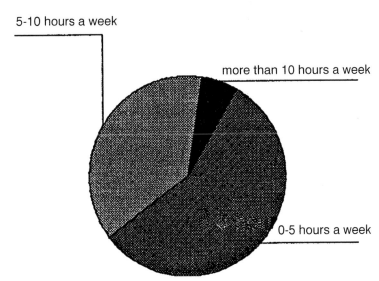

5-10 hours a week

more than 10 hours a week

0-5 hours a week

high correlation between comfort level with databases and the Internet. Even so, it is clear that with just one class, librarians have an opportunity to raise adult learners' comfort level with a variety of technologies. Considering the information needs of graduate students and the number of years out of college (36% out for more than 15 years), it is imperative that we continue to teach people about library resources and reduce their apprehensions of technology. While our assumption was that older people would prefer print resources and younger people would prefer electronic resources, we actually found that print resources tend to be a second preference for all ages. Younger people do prefer electronic resources more than older people; however, preferences for print resources are average. Comfort levels with electronic and print resources are similar in that people who are comfortable with technology are also comfortable with print. Even so, library database training is a significant predictor of print comfort levels. This can probably be attributed to the fact that we often include print resources in our instructional classes as examples of excellent resources which are alternatives to electronic resources or which are not available in electronic formats. Finally, we were interested in the steps people take when they use a new resource. Most respondents answered that they "play with it," "jump right in," "get help from friends," or "use helpsheets." They do not depend on training from professors or library classes when they face new resources. Even though respondents showed a high preference for "doing it themselves," statistics support the fact that training, either from the professor or library staff, increases comfort levels with technology.

## RECOMMENDATIONS

When dealing with adult learners who are outside the mainstream of higher education and who have had a gap in education, we argue that flexibility and variance are essential for reference services and library training. Because training in one electronic resource builds comfort levels with other electronic and print resources, we recommend a variety of training sessions on multiple resources and formats. Furthermore, helpsheets on major databases and reference works should be provided, as they are used heavily and more accessible than a library class or training from a professor. Older students tend to have some apprehension about electronic resources but are not totally comfortable with print resources either. This "limbo" may reflect an uncertainty about what resources are available and how to use them. Ideally, library training and reference services should be flexible to meet the needs of computer savvy and not-so-savvy students. In response to this survey, we propose an updated method for references services to adult learners: A Close Encounter Model.

## CLOSE ENCOUNTER MODEL

This model begins with the premise that every reference encounter is an instructional one. Every instructional encounter involves three dimensions: technological savvy (student), learning styles (student) and instructional methods (librarian). Whether at the reference desk, in a library instruction class or in personalized instruction, librarians must tailor the instructional methods to the individual's technological savvy and learning style. As a result of our survey, we know that training in *just one database* increases comfort levels with other technologies. It is imperative that the initial instructional encounter appropriately match the three dimensions of the student.

*Technological savvy.* Gauge an individual's comfort level with technology by studying her or his nonverbal and verbal communication. Did the person say she or he knows nothing about computers? Is the person confused by the mouse? Is the person having trouble seeing the screen? Is the person confused about hypertext linking? Does the person have experience with DOS and not Windows? Through simple questioning and observing, the librarian will better understand the technological savvy of the student.

*Learning styles.* In individual encounters, gauge an individual's learning style through dialogue and observation. Is the person writing down every word you say? Does the person ask you to illustrate what you are explaining? Does the person ask you to do the research for him/her? Does the person request helpsheets, online tutorials, or classes? In a group instructional setting, rather than dialogue and observations, the librarian should cover as many learning styles as possible: visual, audio, written and hands-on are some examples.

*Instructional methods.* Instructional methods must be as varied as the technological savvy and learning styles of the students. Librarians should have an array of examples, experiences, written, online help, and others. Training in library instruction needs to be provided to reference librarians through avenues such as workshops, conferences, and scholarly journal subscriptions. The instructional method used must match the student in the instructional encounter.

At TCU, we plan to adapt the Close Encounter Model and the survey results in the following ways:

1. Offer more classes which focus on one major electronic resource and print alternatives.
2. Offer classes which will accommodate beginners and novices.
3. Offer hands-on classes covering major databases.
4. Offer improved and additional helpsheets for all databases.
5. Offer more personalized, one-on-one instruction with nontraditional students.

6. Offer walk-in instruction sessions in the departmental computer lab, thus going to the students instead of their coming to us.
7. Lobby for a library methods class.

## CONCLUSIONS

There have been many articles in library literature about reference services and library instruction. This survey studies adult learners in a specific population of graduate students who are outside the mainstream of higher education. Their age coupled with the number of years they have been out of school provides some unique challenges for reference services. In addition to adapting to academe, they must also become proficient quickly in a technologically based information environment. We propose a Close Encounter Model to offer reference services and instruction that will meet a variety of information needs and create technological confidence while providing the tools necessary to manage information overload.

## REFERENCES

1. Malcolm S. Knowles, "Andragogy Not Pedagogy!" *Adult Leadership* 16 (April 1968): 351.

2. Ignacy, Waniewicz. *Demand for Part-time Learning in Ontario.* Ontario Institute for Studies in Education, Toronto, 1980: 9.

3. Patricia Weaver, "Marketing Library Instruction to Adults," *College and Research Libraries News* 58 (July/August 1997): 493-494.

# Helping Adult Undergraduates
# Make the Best Use
# of Emerging Technologies

## Charlotte Diana Moslander

**SUMMARY.** College campuses are faced with an ever-increasing number of adult undergraduates, some of whom are returning to complete degree programs, while others are coming to college for the first time. In order to teach these adult learners effectively, colleges must recognize that they have academic and social needs, as well as life experiences, that are different from those of the traditional-aged undergraduates, and adapt their educational approaches accordingly. Adult students' experiences with and beliefs about libraries and information technology also differ from those of younger students. This must be taken into account when providing library instruction to this population. *[Article copies available for a fee from The Haworth Document Delivery Service: 1-800-342-9678. E-mail address: <getinfo@haworthpressinc. com> Website: <http://www.haworthpressinc.com>]*

**KEYWORDS.** Adult students, library instruction–adults, college libraries–services to adults, public libraries–services to students, andragogy

Charlotte Diana Moslander is Assistant Director, HIV Resource Library, Bureau of HIV Prevention Services, New York City Department of Health, 225 Broadway, 23d floor, New York, NY 10007 (E-mail: cdmoslander@hotmail.com). At the time this article was prepared, she was Periodicals Librarian at Gill Library, College of New Rochelle, with the rank of Associate Professor.

She wishes to thank Carolyn Reid and Shannon Weidemann of that institution for their interlibrary loan assistance.

[Haworth co-indexing entry note]: "Helping Adult Undergraduates Make the Best Use of Emerging Technologies." Moslander, Charlotte Diana. Co-published simultaneously in *The Reference Librarian* (The Haworth Information Press, an imprint of The Haworth Press, Inc.) No. 69/70, 2000, pp. 103-112; and: *Reference Services for the Adult Learner: Challenging Issues for the Traditional and Technological Era* (ed: Kwasi Sarkodie-Mensah) The Haworth Information Press, an imprint of The Haworth Press, Inc., 2000, pp. 103-112. Single or multiple copies of this article are available for a fee from The Haworth Document Delivery Service [1-800-342-9678, 9:00 a.m. - 5:00 p.m. (EST). E-mail address: getinfo@ haworthpressinc.com].

An ever-increasing number of adults over the age of 25 are enrolling in undergraduate programs in the United States. Between 1987 and 1995, the number of students in this age group in baccalaureate programs increased by 30 per cent (from 2,923,000 in 1987 to 3,801,000 in 1995.) In 1987, 1,076,000 of these students were more than 35 years old. In 1995, this population's numbers had swelled to 1,651,000.[1]

These students come to college with life experiences and situations that are different from those of the traditional-aged (17-22) undergraduate. Adult students are less likely to be able to focus the greater part of their energy on being students, as they also tend to have obligations to spouses, children, and, sometimes, their own parents, as well as full- or part-time jobs.[2] These competing demands make the need for time management and efficient study habits critically important, but the new-to-college and the reentry students both tend to carry "baggage" from their previous experiences with schools and learning.[3] Some may not have done well in school, and, therefore, are afraid they will fail again, while others may be worried about their ability to keep up with the younger students in their classes. (This author actually had the experience of having a class of adult undergraduates ask her not to use red ink when writing comments on their work, as so many of them had negative associations with red ink and poor grades from their earlier educational experiences. The problem was solved by writing all comments in "association-neutral" green ink.)

Adult reentry students may have received instruction in the use of an academic library, but the technological advances of even the last five years will have rendered this instruction seriously out of date. Students who are just beginning their college career may have been taught how to use their high school and/or elementary school libraries, but, again, time would have made much of this instruction obsolete.[4] In addition, an academic library usually is much larger than any library previously encountered, and it often uses the Library of Congress classification system instead of the more-familiar Dewey, so students have trouble finding what they want once they actually navigate their way through the finding tools. Adults are likely to believe that everyone else in the school already knows how to use the library, and they ought to know how also, but they do not.[5]

Adult students also come to college with many different levels of experience with computer-based technologies. Some are unfamiliar with, and even intimidated by, computers; some use them in their work or at home, but are not familiar with searching databases or making efficient use of Internet search engines; others are only comfortable with one specific product or application. A small group of nurses who already held the rank of RN and were registered in a baccalaureate nursing program in order to complete the B.S.N. were interviewed informally in connection with this article. Their responses were typical of adult undergraduates the author has encountered repeatedly during her 11 years as a public service librarian in an academic library, and as a teacher of a credit-bearing course in library skills. Some used clinical programs in the course of their work, and some did not. Although they all had computers at home, some used the computer for "play" and some for word processing. Of those who used the Internet, the reported experienced ranged from "e-mail is easy, but searching the Web is not" though one who reported using the Internet for "play, weather, directions how to get places, and travel information." They all were sure they were competent in their work, but, when asked how they felt when using the library for school- or work-connected purposes, their responses ranged from "competent" to "stupid." In fact, one of the latter is so uncomfortable that she does not go into the library at the large teaching hospital where she works–she just e-mails her questions to the Nursing Librarian.

## *LIBRARY ANXIETY*

The stress these students feel when faced with using a library to find information has been reported in the library literature, studied, and identified as Library Anxiety. The condition was first described by Constance Mellon,[6] who applied her findings to the "non-traditional student" in a paper presented at the Sixteenth Library Instruction Conference in 1988.[7] In 1992, Sharon Lee Bostick developed and validated the Library Anxiety Scale as part of her Doctoral research at Wayne State University.[8] In brief, Library Anxiety arises when the student feels incompetent at using the library, but believes that no one else in the school shares this incompetence. An adult, who is accustomed to being considered competent, (perhaps even expert) at something–be it work, homemaking, or parenting–is likely to find this sudden return to youthful incompetence very stressful. Many adults are so ashamed of what they perceive as their unique incompetence that they will avoid asking for help (being "exposed") at all costs. Add the recent advances in library technology–technology with which their children may be quite comfortable–and the returning or beginning adult undergraduate is often in a very uncomfortable situation.

## *ANDRAGOGY*

"Andragogy" is derived from the Greek words meaning "adult" (actually, "man") (andros) and "leading" (agogos.) It rests upon different assumptions and uses different techniques than "pedagogy" (derived from the Greek words meaning "boy" and "leading"). Malcolm S. Knowles, perhaps the best-known advocate of this method of teaching adults, defines Andragogy as ". . . the art and science of helping adults learn, in contrast to pedagogy . . . the art and science of teaching children."[9] "The andragogical model assumes that adults enter into an educational activity with both a greater volume and a different quality of experience from youth."[10] "For the most part, adults do not learn for the sake of learning; they learn in order to be able to perform a task, solve a problem, or live in a more satisfying way."[11] Unlike their younger counterparts, adult learners tend to be motivated primarily by internal factors, not such external factors as pressure from their parents or the expectations of the social group in which they grew up.[12] Knowles also mentions that adult students often carry with them memories of prior lack of success in academic pursuits.[13] Perhaps the most important element of the andragogical model of education is the reminder that adults tend to define themselves in terms of what they have accomplished; therefore, it is important to them that their life experience be valued. When they are placed in a situation where the importance of this experience is minimized or rejected, they often feel rejected as persons.[14]

## THE ROLE OF THE LIBRARIAN

The public service and instructional services librarians are called upon to act as the andragogues who will facilitate these adult students' learning how to overcome their anxiety and become competent in the use of the academic library. Unfortunately, most academic librarians, unlike their counterparts in elementary and secondary education, were never trained as teachers, and now they find themselves faced with a group of students who may not respond well at all to the traditional pedagogical model with which the librarians are familiar from their own experience as students. Fortunately, once adult students feel confident that the librarian is there to help them, and will treat them and their life experience and areas of competence with respect, they often become enthusiastic participants in the educational process, and quite willing to tell the librarian what teaching methods work best for them. The librarian who perceives his or her role as that of expert helper, rather than authority figure, may even find that the adult students who suffer most from library anxiety will want to deal with that same librarian on a regular basis, if only because of a desire for continuity in the process of finding information for a particular course or a particular project.

## ANDRAGOGICAL TECHNIQUES

When faced with a class of adult learners or a heterogeneous age-group class that has come to the library for instruction in the use of library materials in a specific subject area, the librarian-instructor should be prepared to focus all instruction on that particular subject, so the students will be able to see an immediate application of what is being taught to the assignment at hand. In terms of teaching the use of the OPAC and other appropriate electronic resources, start out by asking the group where they are in terms of computer use. If the group turns out to be very mixed in this respect, admit that the experts will already know some of the material that will be covered, and that some of the beginners may feel lost. Apologize to both of these groups and aim for the middle, but tell them time will be left at the end to work with those who need a little extra help. (Often, by the end of the session, the "expert" students will have paired off with the neophytes, leading to spontaneous peer helping.) Exude warmth and encouragement. Support students who take the risk of admitting that they do not know something. Tell the group that the person who asks a question will not only find out the answer to the question, but will also earn the gratitude of everyone in the class who is too shy to admit ignorance on that particular point. Invite students to interrupt the presentation if the librarian uses a term they do not understand.

If all the students in the class fall into the adult learner (roughly, over 25 years of age) category, talk about library anxiety: Use the term; define it; tell them it is to be expected, especially if they have been out of school for some time. Acknowledge the fact that they are accustomed to being competent, and that they may feel uncomfortable in this new situation if they feel incompetent. Point out that children and teenagers actually are accustomed to feeling incompetent because they have known little more than learning situations for their entire lives. Tell the students that they will be given lot of information to absorb in the short time allowed, then specify what they are really going to need to know by the end of the presentation. Repeat this at the end of the presentation. If at all possible, build some practical exercises ("lab time") into the session so the students will be able to practice immediately.

Refer to the computer as a very fast, but not very intelligent, assistant with a limited vocabulary. Someone who is accustomed to having an assistant, or even to being an assistant, often responds well to this sort of personification, and becomes comfortable enough to learn how to communicate with the electronic resources in their own, very limited, vocabulary, and to understand their responses. Be prepared to answer questions about why different databases do not have standardized search languages. (Adult students, especially, understand a comparison to different brands of VCRs, or cars. Laypeople often do not realize that they are dealing with commercially-produced products when they are using library resources.) Use familiar examples: Using Boolean operators is like buying a coat: "Red or green" produces more results than "red and green."

In one-on-one encounters at the Reference Desk, adult students often need to be approached and asked whether they need any help. If the answer is "no," use the open-ended, "If you run into any problems with your search, I'll be right over at the Reference Desk–please come and get me." When working one-on-one with such students, be careful to observe any problems they may be having with the mechanical operation of the terminal or workstation. Someone who is unfamiliar with the layout of a keyboard requires a lot of patience and encouragement. Show the student where the space bar and the "Enter" key are if they are not labeled. If the librarian had difficulty learning to use a computer, that information may be shared with the student, along with how the difficulty was resolved. (This author had a lot of difficulty learning to use a mouse. First, she thought of the cable as the tail, and had it backwards, then the thing would not hold still when she tried to "click." After an expert peer got it turned around correctly, she figured out for herself that the mouse would hold still if she braced it with one hand and "clicked" with the other. After she shared this experience with a very frustrated student, he declared, "You hold the little (offspring of an extramarital liaison) down with one hand and poke it in the eye with the other!" Mechanical problem solved. On with the intellectual work.)

Be on the alert for library anxiety. If a student expresses feelings of inadequacy and incompetence, acknowledge that those feelings are real. Call them "Library Anxiety." Explain (very briefly) what library anxiety is. Tell the student that librarians have Master's degrees from schools that specialize in teaching how to handle information, and, often, considerable amounts of continuing education. Consulting a librarian when (s)he needs help becomes acceptable to the student because librarians are recognized as experts. Remind the student that computer is a stupid machine that was invented by, and is operated by, people who are smarter than it is.

The importance of readily available, well-designed, easy-to-use instruction sheets cannot be stressed too much. Use them as handouts in class. Have a rack of them clearly visible as students enter the library. Have binders (with index tabs) full of them next to every workstation. Color-code them so they can be referred to easily. (This is especially useful when the library gets very busy, as students can be referred to "the green sheet," or "the yellow sheet," to help them move through their search while the librarian is off assisting another student.)

## INSTITUTIONAL RESPONSES

Adult students are busy people. The library that provides the opportunity to make an appointment with a librarian for individual instruction and/or assistance will do much to alleviate some stress. An appointment with the librarian is something that can be planned around, just like an appointment with the dentist or the hairdresser. Being able to make an appointment with the same librarian each time one is needed provides a reassuring sense of continuity. ("This person knows what I do and don't know, so I don't have to start over every time.") Setting aside an hour or half hour from a public or instructional service librarian's schedule to provide intense, individualized instruction is a very efficient use of time, as that student is less likely to call on those at the Reference desk for help with basic searching skills or question formulation.

Allowing students to reserve a block of time at a work station is also particularly helpful to someone who may need to work around the time another adult is at home to care for the children or an infirm relative, the hours the children are in school, or a work schedule. A student who can rely upon a workstation being available when needed, even for only half an hour, will be encouraged to arrive on time with a well-formulated search strategy, and will be able to focus on the work at hand, undistracted by worries about whether (s)he will get to the next appointment on time.

Library orientations need to be scheduled with the adult students' scheduling needs in mind. If most adult students seem to be on campus during the evening or on weekends, then there need to be orientation sessions at those times. Scheduling an orientation for a time when classes are in session is not productive, as the students who are in class will be unable to attend. Treat the students like the adults they are–ask them when they would be able to attend an orientation and schedule accordingly, even if it means requiring a certain amount of flexibility on the part of the librarians conducting the sessions.

More and more colleges and universities are making the electronic resources they offer their students on campus available via the Internet. While being able to work from home at all hours can be a great convenience for the over-scheduled adult student, the same student has no one there to help when problems are encountered. The librarians in these institutions must be prepared to provide technical assistance via the telephone. At quiet times, this could be handled at the Reference desk, but the busy hours may require that someone be available at an off-the-floor workstation to take such calls. Institutions that make a commitment tó having this sort of presence on the Internet should be prepared to provide the staff and telephone lines to give their students the help they need when they are using the resources off-site.

## THE INTERNET

An increasing number of faculty members are requiring that their students find information on the Internet, and many of the students themselves are convinced that the latest information is on the World Wide Web. Because of their life experience, it is very easy to teach adult undergraduates how to evaluate web sites. Explaining what ".com," ".org," ".edu," and ".gov" mean often will lead them to think about the level of objectivity and accuracy they can expect from a given site. Asking them whether a particular piece of information has an individual's name attached to it, whether that person's credentials are listed, and what date the site was last updated all make the students aware that there are questions the information consumer should ask before accepting a piece of information as valid, complete, and up to date. The opportunity to teach students how to use a search engine efficiently often arises from their expressions of frustration that this wonderful tool that has been advertised as so easy to use is not fulfilling its promise. Adult college students often do not have time to waste surfing the 'net–a set of preset links on the library's workstations will make their lives much easier. Students who are working at home should be reminded that the library may have subscriptions to journals that will provide articles they will have to pay for if they order them from a document delivery service linked to an online database. Even cost-conscious adults often do not realize that they have already paid for access to the library's collection by paying their tuition. Again, librarians need to be prepared to provide technical support over the telephone as needed.

## PUBLIC LIBRARIES

College students often present a problem to a public library. Especially in the case of adult undergraduates, these may be people who have used the local public library for years and found that it fulfilled their information needs. They do not realize that the new needs created by their return to, or entry into, higher education cannot be met by the collection and resources of that familiar, comfortable public library. The smaller the library, the greater the burden these students' demands are likely to put on it. Also, the philosophy of public librarianship has not, as a rule, included formal instruction in the use of the library.[15] However, there are some services the public library can offer to its adult patrons who now are college students. For the student at a local college, find out whether the college has a printed list of its periodical holdings available, and, if so, ask for a copy. That way, the student who finds a citation in an index can be referred back to his or her own school, if necessary, to obtain the journal. A gentle reminder that the academic library is supposed to support the curriculum, and that the student is paying for it to do so, can be added to the referral. If the public library provides workstations through which end users can gain access to the college's electronic resources, these should be pointed out to the student. If the student is enrolled in an external degree program, recommend that he or she contact the sponsoring school and find out what arrangements have been made for library services, as it is not uncommon for such programs to have contractual arrangements for their students to have access to some large library in the area. If several students from the same program are encountered, obtain this information and keep it at the Reference desk. Adult students will also find printed information about the local public library's resources and services and how these fit in with the services and resources offered by a county or state library agency useful.

Librarians in public libraries may find that many adult information seekers who are not in college share some of the characteristics of their student colleagues. A public library that is introducing a new OPAC or computer-based index might consider offering workshops in how to use the new resource. Because some adults feel intimidated by their children's comfort with the computer, offer a few conveniently-scheduled sessions for "adults only." (Perhaps one during story hour, one during evening hours, and one on a weekend.) Workshops on making effective use of Internet resources might also be welcome. Have lots of printed instructional material available, and, if all electronic resources are not available on all workstations, label the workstations.

## CONCLUSION

Adults are going to college, for the first time or as reentry students, in ever-larger numbers. These students are likely to be justifiably concerned that their skills are out of date, and this, coupled with the daily demands put upon them by their out-of-school responsibilities, can lead to stress and anxiety. The academic librarian needs to be aware that this group may be uncomfortable with the student role, and be proactive in offering assistance. These students are most likely to be receptive to an adult-to-adult approach based upon the recognition of mutual competence and respect in which the librarian is seen as a helpful expert. The institution needs to take the adult students' particular needs into account when scheduling orientation sessions and arranging for public and instructional librarians to be available for consultation.

## REFERENCES

1. U.S. Bureau of the Census, *Statistical Abstract of the United States 1997* (Washington, DC: Government Printing Office, 1997), 190.

2. Corinne H. Mabry and Carlette J. Hardin, *From Recruitment to Matriculation: Meeting the Needs of Adult Students,* Paper presented at the meeting of the American College Personnel Association, March 1989, ERIC, ED349 831, 3.

3. Jill Mannion Brunt, "Can You Put Your Arm Around a Student on the Internet?" *Adults Learning* 7 (January 1996): 116.

4. Jeanne A. Lauber, "Adult Returning Students and Their Library Needs" (Ph.D. diss. University of North Carolina at Chapel Hill, 1995), .3.

5. Constance A. Mellon, "Library Anxiety and the Non-Traditional Student," in *Reaching and Teaching Diverse Library User Groups: Proceedings of the Sixteenth Library Instruction Conference Held at Bowling Green State University 5-6 May 1988,* ed. Teresa B. Mensching (Ann Arbor, Michigan: Pieran Press, 1989), 78.

6. Constance A. Mellon, "Library Anxiety: A Grounded Theory and Its Development," *College and Research Libraries* 47 (1986): 160-165.

7. Mellon, "Library Anxiety and the Non-Traditional Student," 77-81.

8. Sharon Lee Bostick, "The Development and Validation of the Library Anxiety Scale" (Ph.D. diss. Wayne State University, 1992.

9. Knowles, Malcolm S., *The Modern Practice of Adult Education: From Pedagogy to Andragogy,* rev. and updated ed. (New York: Cambridge, The Adult Education Company, 1980), 43.

10. Knowles, Malcolm S. and Associates, *Andragogy in Action.* (San Francisco: Jossey-Bass, 1984), 10.

11. Ibid.

12. Ibid., 44.

13. Ibid., 46.

14. Ibid., 50.

15. Margaret Hendley, "User Education: The Adult Patron in the Public Library," *RQ* 24 (Winter 1984): 191-4.

# Understanding the Characteristics, Concerns, and Priorities of Adult Learners to Enhance Library Services to Them

## Robin E. Veal

**SUMMARY.** Adult students, while often aware of library services offered by the institution they are enrolled in, often seek the familiarity and convenience of a local public library. These libraries may or may not be able to assist students with their assignment. In either case, librarians can establish an environment of good will and future support by acknowledging the unique characteristics, concerns, and priorities of the adult learner. *[Article copies available for a fee from The Haworth Document Delivery Service: 1-800-342-9678. E-mail address: <getinfo@haworthpressinc. com> Website: <http://www.haworthpressinc.com>]*

**KEYWORDS.** Adult learners, library anxiety, public libraries, reference interview

More adults then ever before are returning to school; institutions offering programs marketed to the adult learner are gaining students in increasing numbers. During the period 1988 to 1996, The National Center for Education Statistics showed an increase of 20 percent in the enrollment of students who

Robin E. Veal is Coordinator of Library and Information Services, Saint Mary's University Library Resource Center, Twin Cities Campus, 2500 Park Avenue, Minneapolis, MN 55404 (E-mail: rveal@smumn.edu).

[Haworth co-indexing entry note]: "Understanding the Characteristics, Concerns, and Priorities of Adult Learners to Enhance Library Services to Them." Veal, Robin E. Co-published simultaneously in *The Reference Librarian* (The Haworth Information Press, an imprint of The Haworth Press, Inc.) No. 69/70, 2000, pp. 113-118; and: *Reference Services for the Adult Learner: Challenging Issues for the Traditional and Technological Era* (ed: Kwasi Sarkodie-Mensah) The Haworth Information Press, an imprint of The Haworth Press, Inc., 2000, pp. 113-118. Single or multiple copies of this article are available for a fee from The Haworth Document Delivery Service [1-800-342-9678, 9:00 a.m. - 5:00 p.m. (EST). E-mail address: getinfo@haworthpressinc.com].

see are 25 years old and over (Gerald & Hussar, 1997, p. 13). However, in terms of library needs, despite being aware of library services offered to them by the institution where they are enrolled, these students tend to use a library which is familiar and convenient. This is often a public library, or perhaps a corporate or special library. While the Association of College and Research Libraries (1990) *ACRL Guidelines for Extended Campus Library Services* places the responsibility of providing library services on the institution where the student is enrolled, actual user behavior must be recognized and dealt with in the most positive way possible. Therefore, even if a library does not have the academic level of information resources to help the student, librarians can go a long way towards establishing an environment of good will and future support by understanding and acknowledging the motivations, concerns, and priorities of the adult learner.

## *PROXIMITY*

Many studies have shown that students enrolled in distance education programs patronize the most convenient library or information resource. This convenience is often defined by geography. Power and Keenan (1991) state:

> Recent studies indicate from 40 percent to 70 percent of extended campus students depend primarily upon local public libraries and second upon the more distant parent institution for their academic needs. The extended campus library resources requirements are admitted by all authors to be far beyond the capacity of most public libraries, yet public libraries are often what the user is most familiar with and are often the most accessible. (pp. 442-443)

The MINITEX Library Information Network, when drafting its "Vision Statement for Extended Campus Library Services" also concluded that students tend to use the most convenient library, whether or not it is able to provide the appropriate level of materials needed (Vision, 1995). Often in utilizing these alternative resources, adult students become frustrated because the library does not provide the academic level of information required to fulfill their assignment. Again, by recognizing and acknowledging the unique needs of adult learners, librarians may be able to establish better rapport with these students, when this happens, and students go away with positive feelings about the library, even if they were referred to a more appropriate information resource.

## *ANDRAGOGY*

How is the term *adult learner* defined? The *Encyclopedia of Educational Research* in the article "Adult Education," defines the word adult in terms of a societal role, as opposed to defining it in terms of a biological, psychological, or legal role (p. 30). It states: "An adult, therefore, is a person who has terminated continuous formal education and has assumed the roles characteristic of adult status in society" (p. 30). Key to understanding the second part of the term, *learner,* is the concept of andragogy. Knowles (1980) defined andragogy as: ". . . the art and science of helping adults learn, in contrast to pedagogy as the art and science of teaching children" (p. 43). He notes three characteristics as the most important differences between adults and children as learners. The first characteristic is the adults' *self-concept* of themselves; they see themselves as self directed (unlike a child), and expect to be treated with respect (Knowles, 1968, p. 351). Secondly, adults define themselves in terms of their *experience;* they expect their experience to be acknowledged or they feel rejected (Knowles, 1968, p. 352). Lastly, adults differ from children in their *perspective of time.* While children consider learning as something they will use in the future, adults go back to school to satisfy an immediate need, and want solutions that have immediate application (Knowles, 1968, p. 386). Therefore, adult learners want to be treated as adults, not children, and to be recognized as having a certain level of experience. They want learning to be relevant, something they can use today, as opposed to the childhood concept of "you will use it in the future."

## *LIBRARY ANXIETY*

It is important to remember when working with adult learners that they return to school with conflicting emotions. While they go back to school for a specific purpose, they often suffer from a high degree of anxiety over their new role as student. Burge (1991) describes her work with returning adult students:

> Despite my formal librarianship training and education I spent much time there just talking with students reassuring listening, legitimizing their anxieties, sharing my own anxieties about my studies, and generally trying to see the learners as adults, rather than library users. (p. 2)

In addition to fears specific to returning to school, adults are even more likely to fall victim to library anxiety; Jiao and Onwuegbuzie (1996) explain:

> Within the last ten years, library anxiety has been identified as a psychological barrier for many college students. Library anxiety is an uncomfortable feeling or emotional disposition, experienced in a library setting, which has cognitive, affective, physiological, and behavioral ramifications. It is characterized by ruminations, tension, fear, feelings of uncertainty and helplessness, negative self-defeating thoughts, and mental disorganization. (p. 152)

Mellon (1986) who first defined the term library anxiety, found that students felt that they were alone in not knowing how to use the library, and this lack of knowledge was something that they needed to keep hidden (p. 162). Mellon also concluded that feelings of being lost stemmed from four causes: (a) the size of the library, (b) a lack of knowledge about where things were located, (c) how to begin, and (d) what to do (p. 162). Kuhlthau (1991) talks about the role of feelings in the information search process. She states: "An information search is a process of construction which involves the whole experience of the person, feelings as well as thoughts and actions" (p. 326).

Both library anxiety and anxiety over the student role may prevent adult learners from asking for help. Steffen (1992) states: "Comfortable as problem solvers in their roles of parents and employees, adult students are often reluctant to display a need for assistance" (p. 200). Mellon recommends that to ease library anxiety you must first acknowledge and validate it as a legitimate concern (p. 163). When librarians do something as simple as acknowledging that libraries have undergone many changes, not just from the last time adult learners may have been students, but more recently, these students do not see their lack of knowledge as a failing on their part and may feel more comfortable asking the questions they need to ask, to utilize the library effectively.

## REFERENCE INTERVIEW

When applying the characteristics of adult learners to the reference interview, keep the following in mind:

> The first thing that adult educators typically do in a classroom situation is to take a problem census. They have their adult students identify what it is that they are curious about or worried about or concerned about. Then they build a learning program around these curiosities and concerns. Accordingly, andragogy is a student-centered, problem-oriented technology. (Knowles, 1968, p. 386)

While it may not be possible for a busy reference librarian to make as of complete an analysis as an adult educator when helping the adult learner, this method can be used in broad terms to guide the reference interview.

During the reference interview it is important for the librarian to recognize that the role of adults as students is only one part of their lives, and usually subordinate to family and job responsibilities. Therefore it is a priority for adult learners to accomplish their research goals in the most efficient way possible. For adult learners research assistance should be practical and relevant. Steffen (1992) argues:

> The library experience is also evolutionary for adult students. Although they may need to learn or relearn basic research skills, adult students

are task oriented when they come to the library. The majority use the library to complete a specific project assigned by an instructor and are interested in information and skills that will help them meet that goal, preferably as quickly and painlessly as possible. Becoming information literate is seldom a primary interest of this group. Only after several encounters with various aspects of the library are students more receptive to mastering the entire system. (p. 199)

Therefore, the reference interview needs to be brief, and quickly uncover the major concern of the adult learner. Hall (1993) states: "After the reference interview, concisely target the reference requirements and then lead the student to the most relevant sources while giving brief explanatory comments. Don't overwhelm the student!" (p. 122). When recommending resources, the following wishes of the information seeker as defined by Scepanski (1996) are especially relevant to this group of users:

. . . as wanting everything that can be gotten while sitting at a workstation. Barring that the user wants citations or pointers to information sources that are right nearby, perhaps across the room or upstairs in the library stacks. The third, and least desired of information retrieval possibilities is to identify a source available elsewhere that can be obtained, but with some delay involved; that is through use of interlibrary loan or document delivery. (p. 43)

However, in the end, the reference interview may determine that the library does not have the level of information required to complete the assignment. In this case it would be best to explain the limitations of the library in terms of successfully completing the assignment, and make a referral, so as not to waste the student's time.

Librarians who work with adult learners on a regular basis talk about the rewards of working with this group. Hall (1993) states: "The energy and motivation that this very special group of students brings to the library is real and contagious; it is exciting to work with them" (p. 123). These students often speak of their gratitude to librarians who have assisted them in overcoming the anxiety they may associate with libraries and gathering information. Rewards, from assisting adult learners, can result in greater support for the library; of course the opposite may occur if adult learners feel frustrated with the library experience. Power and Keenan (1991) argue: "Public libraries, too, are called upon to be proactive in their response to perceived needs of library users who are enrolled in academic programs yet may have limited access to appropriate library services" (p. 451). In merely recognizing and responding to the needs of adult learners, librarians can cultivate an environment of good will and future support.

## REFERENCES

Association of College and Research Libraries. (1990). *ACRL guidelines for extended campus library services* [On-line] Available: http://www.ala.org/acrl/guides/guieclss.html

Burge, E. (1991). *Relationships and responsibilities: Librarians and distance educators working together.* Albuquerque, NM: Off-Campus Library Services Conference. (ERIC Document Reproduction Service No. ED 339 383).

Darkenwald, G.G. (1992). Adult education. In *Encyclopedia of Educational Research* (Vol. 1, pp. 30-35). New York: Macmillan.

Gerald, D.E., & Hussar, W.J. (1997). *Projections of education statistics to 2008, NCES 98-016.* Washington, DC: U. S. Department of Education, National Center for Education Statistics.

Hall, R. (1993). Libraries: Improving services to non-traditional students. In G.B. McCabe, & B. Kreissman (Eds.), *Advances in library administration and organization: Vol. 11* (pp. 115-130). Greenwich, CT: JAI Press.

Jiao, Q.G., Onwuegbuzie, A.J., & Lichtenstein, A.A. (1996), "Library anxiety characteristics of 'at-risk' college students," *Library & Information Science Research* 18, 151-163.

Knowles, M.S. (1968), "Androgogy [sic] not pedagogy," *Adult Leadership,* 16, 350-352, 386.

Knowles, M.S. (1980). *The modern practice of adult education.* Englewood Cliffs, NJ: Cambridge Adult Education.

Kuhlthau, C.C. (1991), "Inside the search process: Information seeking from the user's perspective," *Journal of the American Society for Information Science,* 42 (5), 361-371.

Mellon, C.A. (1986), "Library anxiety: A grounded theory and its development," *College & Research Libraries,* 47, 160-165.

Power, C., & Keenan, L. (1991), "The new partnership: The role of the public library in extended campus services programs," *Library Trends,* 39 (4), 441-453.

Scepanski, J.M. (1996), "Public services in a telecommuting world," (Library services) (Special section: VTLS proceedings). *Information Technology and Libraries,* 15 (1), 41-44.

Steffen, S.S. & Ruther, G.S. (1992). Library services for adult students: What difference do they make? In *Exploring Our Horizons. National Conference on Alternative and External Degree Programs for Adults.* (ERIC Document Reproduction Service No. ED 351 960, pp. 196-206). Washington, DC: American Council on Education.

"Vision statement for extended library services approved," [On-line]. (1995, August 7). *The MINITEX Messenger,* 13 (1). Available: http://othello.lib.umn.edu/publ_mail/messenger/msgr-950807/index.html

# The After-Five Syndrome:
# Library Hours and Services
# for the Adult Learner

## Anne Fox

**SUMMARY.** "Communication" is the key to providing appropriate library hours and services for adult learners, students twenty-four years of age and older. This report of a survey at Western Oregon University shows that while there are some differences, the needs of both adult learners and traditional students may be similar. Both groups have a need for a variety of library hours, especially evening and weekend hours, and for remote access to both library collections and services. *[Article copies available for a fee from The Haworth Document Delivery Service: 1-800-342-9678. E-mail address: <getinfo@haworthpressinc.com> Website: <http://www.haworthpressinc.com>]*

**KEYWORDS.** Adult learners, library hours, remote access

### INTRODUCTION

Do our academic libraries meet the needs of the ever growing population of adult learners, those students twenty-four years of age and older? What are their particular needs? Just how different are their needs from those of traditional students, under twenty-four years of age? At Western Oregon Universi-

---

Anne Fox is Coordinator of Publie Services, Western Oregon University Library, Monmouth, OR 97361 (E-mail: foxa@wou.edu). She received a BS from the University of Oregon, an MLS from San Jose State University, and an MS from Oregon State University.

[Haworth co-indexing entry note]: "The After-Five Syndrome: Library Hours and Services for the Adult Learner." Fox, Anne. Co-published simultaneously in *The Reference Librarian* (The Haworth Information Press, an imprint of The Haworth Press, Inc.) No. 69/70, 2000, pp. 119-126; and: *Reference Services for the Adult Learner: Challenging Issues for the Traditional and Technological Era* (ed: Kwasi Sarkodie-Mensah) The Haworth Information Press, an imprint of The Haworth Press, Inc., 2000, pp. 119-126. Single or multiple copies of this article are available for a fee from The Haworth Document Delivery Service [1-800-342-9678, 9:00 a.m. - 5:00 p.m. (EST). E-mail address: getinfo@haworthpressinc.com].

ty I decided to conduct a survey which would attempt to answer these questions. I have surveyed our users on a regular basis over the years, but this year I added a question asking them to identify their age group, under twenty-four years or twenty-four and older.

The main focus of this survey was to review my present library hours and methods for remote access to library resources and for contacting library staff without actually coming to the library. I wanted to know if I was serving the needs of students who had little time to visit the library, especially during the day, during the regular school week. I also wanted to ask about students' preferences for contacting the library by telephone or online by computer. I am calling these various times and methods of access the "After-five Syndrome."

## SURVEY METHOD

The survey was prepared and distributed in the early summer of 1998. It was distributed in the library and also in several classrooms over a two week period. Respondents were asked how well the library hours met their needs both during the regular fall/winter/spring terms and during summer term when hours are reduced. They were also asked to suggest additional hours and to identify present hours which they found least useful (Table 1).

Presently the regular term hours are Monday-Thursday 7:30 AM to 11 PM, Friday 7:30 AM to 5 PM, Saturday 12 NOON to 5 PM, and Sunday 2 PM to 11 PM. Summer term hours are Monday through Thursday 7:30 AM to 10 PM, Friday 7:30 AM to 5 PM, closed on Saturday, Sunday 2 PM to 10 PM. Most classes are held Monday through Friday during regular terms and Monday through Thursday during summer session. There are some evening classes and weekend workshops.

Four questions were asked related to using the library remotely, including by telephone, email, or using either services or resources available from the library web page. Respondents were asked if they presently used these services, if they were aware that the services were available, and if they would use them in the future. Specific questions included how often they telephoned the library for information, research help, book renewal or other services; and if they would use email for the same type of help, and if they presently used the online catalog and various electronic databases from their home computers. These resources can be accessed from the library home page on the web from anywhere on campus and from student's home computers. They were also asked if they would use services available remotely such as a web interlibrary loan form or the "renew your own book" feature from the online catalog as they became available. Some of these services are presently in place but have not yet been widely publicized. Others are being developed (Table 1).

TABLE 1. Western Oregon University Library User Survey–Summer 1998

| **WOU Library hours: Fall–Winter–Spring Terms** |
| --- |
| Regular term hours M-Th 7:30am-11pm, F 7:30am-5pm, Sat 12-5pm, Sun 2-11pm |
| These hours meet your needs (check one):<br>Always_____Most of the time_____ Some of the time_____ Almost never _____ |
| Suggest additional hours the Library should be open:<br>M-Th_____ F_____ Sat_____ Sun_____ |
| Which (if any) of the hours the Library is presently open are least useful to you:<br>M-Th_____ F_____ Sat_____ Sun_____ |
| **B. WOU Library hours: Summer Term** |
| Summer term hours M-Th 7:30am-10pm, F 7:30am-5pm, Sat closed, Sun 2-10pm |
| These hours meet your needs (check one):<br>Always_____ Most of the time_____ Some of the time_____ Almost never_____ |
| Suggest additional hours the Library should be open:<br>M-Th_____ F_____ Sat_____ Sun_____ |
| Which (if any) of the hours the Library is presently open are least useful to you:<br>M-Th_____ F_____ Sun_____ |
| **C. Library remote services** |
| Do you telephone the WOU Library for information, for research help, for book renewal, etc.?<br>Often_____ Sometimes_____ Almost never_____ Didn't know you could_____ |
| Would you use email to contact WOU Library staff for information or research help?<br>Often_____ Sometimes_____ Almost never_____ Don't know_____ |
| Do you use the Library's online catalog and other databases from your home computer?<br>Often_____ Sometimes_____ Almost never_____ Didn't know you could_____ |
| Would you use the Library web page from your home computer for information, research help, interlibrary loan requests, and other services as they become available?<br>Often_____ Sometimes_____ Almost never_____ Don't know_____ |

At the end of the survey students were asked a few questions about themselves including their year in school, their major, and their age group.

## LITERATURE REVIEW

The literature abounds with discussions about lifelong learning, and constant retraining for a changing job or a new career, situations which will bring more and more adult learners to our campuses. Dubois calls for respecting the needs of these adult learners who will be the new majority on our campuses nationwide by 2000 (Dubois, 1996). Lintner says the complexity of higher education is changing, and that the three state universities in his state of Arizona expect over half of the students will be over 25 years of age by 2005 (Lintner, 1997).

The lives of many of these students will not be campus-centered. They will already have multiple commitments to work, to home and families, plus their education (Lightner, 1984). They want flexibility in scheduling and services, and they want an education that is relevant to their particular needs and one in which they play an active role. They want the opportunity to share their past experiences, to interact. They don't want a passive learning setting (Bowden and Merritt, 1995).

Wagschal alerts us to the need to constantly assess all sections of our user population. She defines the latest adult learners as being in two camps, the Boomers, most of whom are over 40, and the Xers, who are from 25-40. She discusses the two groups' very different past experiences and desires for the future, and the fact that the Xers and the traditional students may have more in common than the Boomers and the Xers (Wagschal, 1997).

Students of all ages may need more scheduling flexibility to meet work commitments. *Conditions in Education 1997* reports that 47.2% of full-time traditional students worked in 1995 versus 33.8% in 1970, and over 80% of the part-time traditional students have always worked, according to data from 1970 to 1995.

## *SURVEY RESULTS*

Fifty-five traditional students and seventy-two adult learners responded to the question about regular term hours. Fifty-six traditional students and 104 adult learners answered the question about summer term hours. Because the survey was conducted during the summer session some students were on campus only for summer school and gave no response to the question about regular term hours. Most of the 160 respondents answered the four questions about services by telephone, email and the web. The survey results are reported in percentages and divided into the two groups of interest, traditional students and adult learners (Table 2).

There were many similarities between the responses of these two age groups. A slightly higher percentage of adult learners answered that the present library hours met their needs "always" or "most of the time," 87.7% during the regular terms and 83.6% during summer session versus the traditional students responses of 81.8% and 80.3% respectively. When asked to suggest additional library hours most traditional students suggested later

## TABLE 2. Survey Results in Percentages

|  | Traditional students | Adult learners |
|---|---|---|
| **Regular term hours met students' needs:** |  |  |
| Always | 21.8 | 38.9 |
| Most of the time | 60.0 | 48.6 |
| Some of the time | 16.4 | 12.5 |
| Almost never | 1.8 | -- |
| **Summer term hours met students' needs:** |  |  |
| Always | 32.1 | 26.9 |
| Most of the time | 48.2 | 56.7 |
| Some of the time | 16.1 | 13.5 |
| Almost never | 3.6 | 2.9 |
| **Telephone services used:** |  |  |
| Often | 7.1 | 4.0 |
| Sometimes | 16.1 | 20.8 |
| Almost never | 39.3 | 49.5 |
| Didn't know | 37.5 | 25.7 |
| **Future email services use:** |  |  |
| Often | 7.1 | 8.0 |
| Sometimes | 26.8 | 54.0 |
| Almost never | 35.7 | 29.0 |
| Don't know | 30.4 | 9.0 |
| **Remote resources used:** |  |  |
| Often | 7.1 | 8.0 |
| Sometimes | 16.4 | 20.0 |
| Almost never | 32.7 | 30.0 |
| Didn't know | 45.4 | 31.0 |
| **Future remote services use:** |  |  |
| Often | 32.1 | 40.4 |
| Sometimes | 28.6 | 41.4 |
| Almost never | 10.7 | 9.1 |
| Don't know | 28.6 | 9.1 |

evening hours, but both groups suggested more weekend hours, both early and late.

Even though telephone contact has been our long-standing method of remote access, only 25% of all respondents indicated that they would "often" or "sometimes" use this method. Many students were unaware of the idea of telephoning the library for information or services. More traditional students, 37.5%, answered "didn't know you could" telephone versus 25.7% of the adult learners.

When asked if they would use email to contact the library more adult learners than traditional students responded positively, 62% and 34% respectively. Email has been available for students for several years, but the use of it to contact library staff for consultation or service is relatively new. The presence of the library web site with many email links will make these possibilities better known and easier to use.

The survey showed that slightly over 20% of the traditional students used the library resources remotely from their residences while about 40% of the adult learners had done so either often or sometimes. Many students, 45.4% of the traditional students and 31% of the adult learners, did not know these resources were available remotely. Our library's online catalog has been available through dial-in access for about five years and is now also available through the web. Only within the last year have many other databases become available remotely through the web.

The library is constantly developing more online remote services such as the ability to place an interlibrary loan request, renew books, or ask a reference question. When asked about the use of these library services, 60% of the traditional students said they would use them often or sometimes, and over 80% of the adult learners said they would.

## SIMILARITIES AND DIFFERENCES
## WITHIN THE TWO STUDY GROUPS

There appeared to be two major differences in responses between the two age groups. First of all, the traditional students were more likely to suggest that the library extend its evening hours than were adult learners. Secondly, the adult learners appeared to be higher users of presently available remote access to library resources and services and also appeared to be more interested in future developments of remote access.

Although there were differences in the responses between the two groups, similarities appear to outweigh differences. I would like to explore two possible reasons for the similarities in responses. First, traditional students are more likely to have both the motivations and challenges that were once attributed to adult learners. Secondly, adult learners are now more confident and computer savvy and have more job experience than the adult learners of twenty years ago.

Traditional students are taking on a variety of traits first identified as unique to the adult learners. They are now very likely to be in college primarily to prepare for a job, rather than for the general learning and social experience. Many are working at a part-time or full-time job while going to school. They may be married and even have begun a family, but with both partners continuing to pursue their degrees. It is not uncommon to see a young father doing research at the library computer stations with a baby in a stroller beside him. This would have been an unusual sight ten or twenty years ago.

Adult learners now have more experience with college and careers and with technology than in past years. Many already have one college degree and are returning to prepare for a second career. They may have worked at a well-paying job, have organizational skills and life experiences which will enhance their ability to compete academically. They may have had useful on-the-job computer experience and own a home computer. Their present employer may be subsidizing their continuing education. The days of thinking that many adult learners lack job experience and technical skills are over.

## CONCLUSIONS

The wake-up call to academic libraries is that our student population is aging and constantly changing. It is important to communicate with our students and to adapt our services to their needs and desires. Our survey appeared to show that longer library hours, more electronic access to materials and added remote and unmediated services will be very helpful to both age groups of survey respondents.

While over 80% of all respondents said the present library hours met their needs most of the time, the percentage was slightly higher for adult learners than for traditional students. This still leaves also almost 20% whose needs were not being met. It appeared from suggestions that the library should consider being open additional hours in the late evenings and on weekends.

Using the telephone or email to contact the library staff seemed to be of greater interest to adult learners than to traditional students, and almost twice as many adult learners responded that they used library resources remotely than did traditional students. This result was probably because adult learners are less likely to have a campus-centered life. They may live off-campus, generally spend fewer hours on campus, and have other demands on their time such as jobs and families. For these reasons adult learners may be more motivated to take advantage of resources and services that can be used from home or office and during times when the library building is closed.

The high percentage of both groups who were not aware of remote access to the library's resources and services showed a need for more publicity by the library and better channels of communication with users. It also appeared that the library should give a high priority to expanding the array of remote resources and services due to the high percentage of respondents in both age groups who said they would use more such resources and services as they became available.

Developing a balance between methods for unmediated services and remote access to materials with methods for personal interaction will be key to a library's success in the future. It is still important to have the physical library building, its resources, and a welcoming staff available during hours most convenient for all users. At the same time, remote access to collections and services will be increasingly important. In the future books may routinely be mailed to student's homes. Copies of journal articles may commonly be sent directly to students electronically by email. Interactive videoconferencing with reference staff may become a standard means of obtaining research assistance. The library of the future will be the library which is always communicating with its students of all ages, is clearly focused on adapting to their various needs, and which is constantly developing new and better services for both traditional students and adult learners.

## REFERENCES

Backes, Charles E. (1997), "The do's and don'ts of working with adult learners," *Adult Learning* 8 (Jan/Feb), 29-31.

Bowden, Randall and Richard Merritt, Jr. (1995), "The adult learner challenge: Instructionally and administratively," *Education* 115 (Spring), 426-33.

Dubois, Jacques R. (1996), "Going the distance: A national distance learning initiative," *Adult Learning* 8 (Sept.-Oct.), 19-21.

Lightner, Ardyce S. (1984), "The emerging adult learner: 2001," ERIC Document Reproduction Service (ED252168), 12 pp.

Lintner, Timothy. (1997), "Adults back to school: A new beginning" *Adult Learning* 8 (Jan.-Feb.), 23-24.

Mellon, Constance A. Library anxiety and the non-traditional student. In Mensching, Teresa B. (Ed.) *Reaching and Teaching Diverse Library User Groups.* 1989 p. 77-81 Ann Arbor, Michigan: Pierian Press.

National Center for Education Statistics. (1997), *The Condition of Education.* Washington, DC: U.S. Department of Education.

Wagner, Colette A. in consultation with Augusta S. Kappner. The academic library and the non-traditional student. In Breivik, Patricia Senn and Robert Wedgeworth. *Libraries and the Search for Academic Excellence.* 1983 p. 43-56. Metuchen, N.J.: The Scarecrow Press.

Wagschal, Kathleen (1997), "I became clueless teaching the GenXers: Redefining the profile of the adult learner," *Adult Learning* 8 (March-April) 21-25.

# SECTION 3:
# THEORIES
# OF ADULT LEARNING:
# IMPLICATIONS
# FOR REFERENCE
# AND INSTRUCTIONAL
# SERVICES
# FOR THE ADULT LEARNER

# How Do We Learn?
## Contributions of Learning Theory
## to Reference Service and Library Instruction

Loriene Roy
Eric Novotny

**SUMMARY.** This article focuses on some major contributions from learning theory that impact how adults learn. Following an overview of two major learning theories–behavioral and cognitive theories–the authors discuss four factors that affect learning. These are attention, perception, memory, and contiguity and practice. Other topics presented include prior knowledge effect and transfer of knowledge problems. The article closes with five recommendations for incorporating results from learning theory research into reference service and user instruction. *[Article copies available for a fee from The Haworth Document Delivery Service: 1-800-342-9678. E-mail address: <getinfo@haworthpressinc. com> Website: <http://www.haworthpressinc.com>]*

**KEYWORDS.** Learning theory, reference service, library instruction

Loriene Roy is Associate Professor, Graduate School of Library and Information Science, The University of Texas at Austin, Austin, TX 78712-1276 (E-mail: loriene@uts.cc.utexas.edu). Eric Novotny is Assistant Reference Librarian, Reference Department–Richard Daley Library, Mail Code 234, University of Illinois at Chicago, 801 South Morgan Street, Chicago, IL 60607 (E-mail: novotny@uic.edu).

The authors wish to acknowledge the influence of Dr. Duane Shell, formerly of the University of Texas at Austin, whose graduate "Psychology of Human Learning" class provided the impetus to write this article.

[Haworth co-indexing entry note]: "How Do We Learn? Contributions of Learning Theory to Reference Service and Library Instruction." Roy, Loriene, and Eric Novotny. Co-published simultaneously in *The Reference Librarian* (The Haworth Information Press, an imprint of The Haworth Press, Inc.) No. 69/70, 2000, pp. 129-139; and: *Reference Services for the Adult Learner: Challenging Issues for the Traditional and Technological Era* (ed: Kwasi Sarkodie-Mensah) The Haworth Information Press, an imprint of The Haworth Press, Inc., 2000, pp. 129-139. Single or multiple copies of this article are available for a fee from The Haworth Document Delivery Service [1-800-342-9678, 9:00 a.m. - 5:00 p.m. (EST). E-mail address: getinfo@haworthpressinc.com].

*129*

Though man a thinking being is defined,
Few use the grand prerogative of mind.
How few think justly of the thinking few!
How many never think, who think they do!

–Jane Taylor, *Essays in Rhyme*
On Morals and Manners, Prejudice
Essay I. Stanza 45

## INTRODUCTION

Isadore Gilbert Mudge, doyenne of reference service, aptly identified the secret of success for reference and, by extension, library use instruction: material, mind, and method.[1] This article is concerned with the second ingredient of this reference recipe, that of the minds of the seeker as well as his or her companion in the search for information, the librarian or information specialist. It is concerned with some of the major contributions from learning theory that impact how adults learn. The application of these theories has numerous practical implications for the provision of reference and instructional services to adults. While many of these practices are already part of every librarian's standard toolkit, they still merit reinforcement. Content is presented in three segments: (1) an overview of two major learning theories; (2) a discussion of factors that affect learning, such as attention, perception, memory, the concept of contiguity, and the role of practice; and, (3) some recommendations for reference and/or library use instruction.

## MAJOR LEARNING THEORIES

There are many definitions of learning. One simple, yet profound, definition is that "learning is an enduring change," a change that can or might be observed in someone's behavior based on some expended effort or a direct or vicarious experience.[2] Behavior is broadly interpreted and includes beliefs and skills and other expressions. Before delving into concrete examples of how adults learn, it is worthwhile to examine some of the more widely accepted theories of how learning occurs. These theories provide explanations that help build a foundation for understanding, organizing, and ultimately predicting the acquisition of knowledge. Of course no general theory will apply universally to all of the diverse circumstances encountered by library practitioners, although theories do provide guidelines for effectively planning reference service and user instruction and responding to and understanding patron needs and demands.

## Behavioral Theories

This group of theories suggests that what humans learn is based on the cues they receive from the environment. Responses that are perceived to have positive results are repeated, those that have unfavorable results are not. In this model, learning is chiefly dependent on factors outside the individual. A positive, supportive environment is needed to foster learning, where desired behaviors are encouraged and rewarded. Educators promote learning by reinforcing what they accept to be "correct" responses and discouraging the "wrong" or unproductive responses.

According to behavioral theory, instruction is most effective when (1) teachers present the materials in small steps, (2) the material is designed to elicit an observable response, (3) instructors provide immediate feedback on the learners' responses, and (4) learners move through the material at their own pace. Learning is guided by objectives, or statements of the intended outcomes. The objective determines how to measure the students' progress. An example of such an objective related to instruction-related might be: "Given 10 searches for items known to be in the collection and on the shelf, the freshman student will be able to locate call numbers for at least seven items using the electronic catalog."

## Cognitive Theories

Cognitive theorists describe learning as a process. Here, the emphasis is placed on the learner's ability to place material in context rather than the environment. Learning is described as involving rehearsal, relating new information to current information, retrieving information from memory, and organizing it into meaningful associations. Learning involves creating a set of mental representations of information and a set of processes that operate on these representations. People are perceived as being more intelligent if they represent knowledge more effectively or if they have developed a more efficient means of accessing the represented information than others. Learning occurs when the individual integrates new information into his or her own sets of mental representations. The instructor serves as a facilitator of knowledge, helping the learner organize information to optimize learning.

These theories have important implications for educational institutions. They differ primarily in the role they assign the learner. Behavioral theory assigns the active role to an authority figure. It is the instructor who determines the acceptable responses, the course content, and the overall objectives. This figure determines correct actions and apportions rewards and punishments. The learner in this model is largely a passive recipient of positive and negative stimuli. Lessons are designed to elicit a response from the learner, the response is then evaluated, and the appropriate rewards or punishments are given. An example of this type of learning in a library environment can be seen in many computer tutorials where the user is typically given a scenario and prompted for a response. Users are rewarded by being allowed to proceed only after the correct response is given.

Cognitive theories stress the role of the educator in helping learners organize new information and relate it to their prior knowledge. Prior knowledge is the totality of what an individual knows, often as a result of day-to-day experiences.[3] It is synonymous with the terms background knowledge, personal knowledge, pre-existing knowledge, and, even, world knowledge. According to a constructivist view, knowing is a cumulative effect. Roughly stated, the prior knowledge concept can be stated as the more one knows, the more additional knowledge one can acquire. Humans acquire new knowledge by building on what they already understand. Personal knowledge may help learners prepare to learn material: It provides specific examples that can be used to build theories. A reader, for example, will be better able to learn from new text if the content overlaps to some degree, but does not replicate, already known writing.[4]

Since each person's experiences are different, the learner plays a more active role in the process. The input of the learner into course content and structure is naturally much greater in this model than in a scenario using behavioral theories. According to cognitive theory, the optimum learning environment is one that utilizes active learning techniques such as group discussions.

When incorporating these theories into our professional activities, librarians need to be wary of exclusivity. It is difficult to imagine one theory that would adequately explain all learning situations. Given the complexity of human behavior it seems likely that a combination of learning theories will need to be followed and incorporated into a variety of instructional styles. The behavioral approach appears to best explain learning simpler tasks, such as memorization. This is particularly true of skills training where the task is broken down into steps and there is a correct response that can be acknowledged and rewarded. The cognitive theories appear to provide the better explanation for how people learn to perform complex tasks such as inferring meaning from context. Thus, cognitive theory might better account for how a student learns to evaluate and compare information provided by more than one reference source.

Learning is a complex task, affected by many variables. Learning is a needy, demanding, symbiotic process that requires the congruent active involvement of the learner and the instructor. If cognitive theories explain learning as an internal process, how is knowledge generated, stored, and ultimately retrieved when needed? What follows is a discussion of factors that affect learning and some examples of how to encourage or counteract their impact.

## FACTORS AFFECTING LEARNING

### Attention

Before any learning can occur, it is first necessary for the learner to attend to the task. Individuals vary in their capacity to sustain attention or focus on selected aspects of their environment for information processing rather than on all stimuli that surround them.[5] Instructors can assist students in being attentive by incorporating a variety of techniques that reduce repetition and introduce elements of novelty or unpredictability. A librarian might simply move about a seated audience while presenting materials. He or she might vary vocal tone and use natural gestures. Students might be more attentive when a variety of types of instruction is used, such as following a lecture with a demonstration which is then followed by small group exercises and hands-on presentations. Students who are allowed to summarize course content, ask questions, or otherwise contribute to the learning setting may also be more attentive.

### Perception

Perception is another process that influences how and what people learn. Perception refers to the meaning attached to inputs received through the environment.[6] How something is perceived depends both on its objective characteristics and on an individual's prior experience. For example, two people looking at a computer mouse pad will both note its physical characteristics, such as its color, shape, texture, and size. Their perceptions of its potential usefulness may vary depending on their prior exposure to computers. The variety of individual's experiences account for the differences in meaning people impart to objects. Perception is also tied to expectations. Learning is facilitated when instructors can make information more meaningful by relating it to what the learner already knows and by selecting content based on what the student expects or anticipates to learn.

### Memory

Those studying human memory are apt to describe it in terms of multiple memories or a system of memories.[7] Thus, an individual has *procedural* memory and can remember how to perform a particular task, such as how to boot-up his or her personal computer or how to use file transfer protocol. This type of knowledge can be affected by practice. Humans have *episodic* memory, the ability to recall biographical events; flashbulb memories can be easily recalled since they are associated with intense feelings. Simply attending to and perceiving information is not enough. People all receive countless streams of information every day, the vast majority of which is quickly forgotten. Stimuli or information arriving through the senses is shunted into a register where information is either erased or held briefly until it is transferred to working memory. Working memory, also referred to as short-term memory, is a location where data and processing functions must come together. Since short term memory is limited in terms of how long it call be recalled (duration) and how much can be stored (capacity), information needs to be entered into long term memory to be retained. In order to be remembered, information must be uniquely transformed and stored in long term memory where the next problem is one of retrieval.

Encoding is the process by which the information is analyzed and integrated with information already in long term memory. As anyone who has ever tried to recall an elusive phone number knows, the process of encoding information is far from perfect. Humans are biologically weak in their ability to apply knowledge to more than one context. This transfer of knowledge gap explains why patrons might not be able to consider using, for example, an index for locating articles when they are familiar with *Readers' Guide to Periodicals.*

Research indicates that educators can positively affect encoding through the use of several techniques. One way to achieve this is by *organizing* information into related categories or chunking or grouping it into larger, related units.[8] This is a way to gain additional space in working memory. Providing categories and hierarchies allows people to better relate and recall information and it aids in making a process automatic. Automaticity helps save space in working memory since it eliminates the need to concentrate on processing. The use of subject categories as aids to knowledge should hardly be a new concept for librarians and provides supportive evidence of the fact that people are more apt to remember well-organized information. Individual learners organize information when they use mnemonics, outlining, or diagraming.

*Elaboration* is another method of increasing retention. This involves linking the newly imparted information to knowledge already retained. Instructors can assist in this process by making explicit links between old and new information. For example, when discussing the online catalog with a new adult user it may help to compare it to something the user is already familiar with such as the card catalog. Similarly, an instructor in a class orienting learners to the Internet can refer to a uniform resource locator as a web site's telephone number. This allows the learner to integrate the new information into a conceptual framework already created. People can follow individualized elaboration tactics in self-study, such as visual imagery or creating mental representations of objects they are studying. Mnemonics are also a form of elaboration. Study questions that call on the reader to answer how information might be applied are also elaboration tactics as is note taking, a form of journaling rather than verbatim transcription. These activities of transforming information increase the amount of time spent processing the information, thus increasing the probability that the information will be stored in long term memory.

### Contiguity and Practice

Contiguity, or time on task, impacts learning.[9] Being in contact with information leads to more knowledge. This concept is closely tied to behaviorist experiments using stimuli and monitoring responses for cause and effect. Given a time element tied to learning, librarians may encourage contiguity. Contiguity implies that, to be remembered, information has to be in working memory and has to be frequently accessed. What is associated with the item being studied might also be recalled: If an event occurs and is followed soon after by another event, then the two events are tied together, even in memory. Thus, in teaching how to use a particular resource, an instructional librarian might reinforce, through selected verbal cues, the use of a particular search strategy. The student might, subsequently, recall the verbal cue as a step in recalling the appropriate search strategy.

Research on experts indicates that humans can acquire an expert level of performance through extensive practice over an extended period of time, though even a small amount of practice can result in learning.[10] Someone who is an expert in music performance, competition chess, or mathematics has acquired this ability through approximately four hours of structured daily practice over ten years. Practice–repetition and refinement of skills–is not inherently pleasurable, although it helps attain a level of achievement where performance becomes more enjoyable. Thus, in the nature versus nurture argument as applied to knowledge, the scale tips decidedly in the direction of nurture over any supposed innate talent. Information professionals, knowing the critical role of practice in acquiring proficiency, can reassure and model performance for beginning and intermediate skilled students, especially those who are prone to negative self-judgement.[11]

### Applying Study of Learning to Reference Service and Library Instruction: Recommendations

Arp provided five suggestions of how to apply learning theories to bibliographic instruction.[12] These guidelines are condensed as follows:

1. Conduct a needs analysis of the targeted audience and interpret results according to an ascribed learning theory.
2. Both behaviorist and cognitive learning theories advocate teaching concepts and their application. Adopt teaching techniques that do likewise.
3. Learning theories accommodate different teaching styles.
4. Measurement and evaluation of learning should be incorporated in teaching.
5. Educators should learn how to evaluate their efforts.

The final portion of this paper asks information professionals to also consider the following additional recommendations that extend Arp's guidelines.

*1. Incorporate Multiple Teaching Methods in Instruction to Reach All Learners*

Information professionals are expert learners who, like most academics, achieved academically because they excel in traditional learning settings. Information professionals may be described as convergers, deductive thinkers who prefer abstract ideas and learn best from lectures, writing papers, creating analogies or abstract models.[13] Since not all learners are alike, it is safe to state that in any group of learners there will be some who have different learning preferences from that of the instructor. While people have natural and preferred ways to learn, they can and may need to improve on their strategies. Librarians need to employ multiple teaching strategies in presenting information to assist learners in experiencing the entire cycle of learning, from study about a topic to hands-on application. Librarians working with adults have a particular responsibility to encourage and nurture a movement towards independent and self-regulated learning. For example, using interactive online tutorials as the primary mechanism for instruction and learning allows learning to occur at the desired pace and it enables the learner to avoid appearing ignorant.

*2. An Individual Learner May Enter, Exist in or Emerge from a Number of Learning Phases, Requiring Different Learning Strategies in Each Phase. The Role of the Information Specialist Must Also Adjust to the Learner's Level of Need*

Research by Shuell and Kuhlthau illustrate how learners' strategies may need to vary, depending on where the learner is in the information seeking process. Shuell discusses how learning changes in the progression from novice to expert.[14] A beginner is faced with acquiring and placing facts and disparate pieces of information into a personal knowledge base so that he or she can start to understand the subject area under investigation, what is referred to as the domain of knowledge. Simple learning strategies are helpful here, such as using mnemonics. As the beginner starts to understand relationships between facts then he or she may start to understand the content at a deeper level through refinement and restructuring. The learner needs to develop competency in this intermediate phase. The learner now must experiment with new knowledge and test it with problems, so that he or she can start to learn more abstract underlying concepts. During the third and last learning phase, the now expert learner performs tasks automatically and spends his or her time on performance.

Kuhlthau developed a model of the search process, correlating the feelings and thoughts students encountered and the actions they engaged in when moving through six stages, from selecting a topic to investigate to closing a search by beginning to write.[15] She identified "zones of intervention," or times that are ripe for mediation by the librarian.[16]

### 3. Understand that Humans Have Difficulty Transferring Knowledge

People need help in solving problems in different contexts because they may have difficulty understanding when to apply knowledge they already have. Transfer is rarely spontaneous.[17] Kuhlthau warns that when librarians focus on teaching close knowledge of sources rather than critical thinking processes, they diminish the ability of the learner to transfer skills from one learning situation to another.[18] Information specialists need to employ a variety of teaching techniques to provide learners with different opportunities to traverse the domain. Traversing the domain refers to providing multiple options for covering the same instructional territory. Each time the learner covers a topic in a new way, he or she is able to remember and recall new facets of the surroundings. The more people process information, the more likely it is that the information will be stored in long-term memory. Case-based learning is one approach that might help students learn how to transfer knowledge.[19]

A good learner is one who can develop new linkages between known facts, applying solutions that have resolved prior problems to new situations. This is the ability to think for oneself.[20] Since humans cannot prepare in advance a solution for each problem they might face, they need to develop interconnections that allow: "(a) situation-specific categorization; (b) multiple access routes to relevant case precedents in long-term memory from the details of new cases, and (c) the development of a reservoir of potential analogies when case precedents are less literally relevant."[21]

## 4. Provide Learners with an Opportunity to Share Their Knowledge

Perhaps the single defining characteristic of adult learners is their desire for input. Adults generally prefer a learning environment where they have significant input into the learning process. They feel a strong need to establish the pace and control the character of their learning experiences. Adult learners typically bring a unique set of prior experiences to an instructional setting. Students might want to share declarative knowledge, that which they can narrate. Others may want to demonstrate procedural knowledge or how they perform a task. Many learn vicariously and/or through observing. Learning is facilitated when instruction is related to these experiences.[22] In a reference context this may involve asking questions to determine how much background the patron has in this, or a similar area. This knowledge can be used to represent the new information using terms and metaphors already familiar to the patron. It is logical that the goal of a learning institution should be to encourage activities and create environments that allow adults to achieve independence and self-direction.

In an instructional setting encouraging active participation is the best way to ensure that prior experiences are acknowledged and incorporated. It is important to generate active learner involvement into the educational environment. Sessions emphasizing discussion, group exercises, and utilizing trial and error methods of discovery are best suited for the way adults learn. The librarian's role should be to provide context and background information, and to serve as a facilitator for discussion.

## 5. Learning Can Be Learned

As expert learners, information professionals have a professional obligation to assist their clients to learn how to learn. Librarians also have an obligation to become more knowledgeable about epistemology and the psychology of human learning and to formulate a formalized continuing education program that will provide him or her to synthesize new research findings. They should develop alliances with local departments of educational psychology, linguistics, and/or centers that support teaching effectiveness.

## REFERENCES

1. *Encyclopedia of Library and Information Science,* s.v. "Mudge, Isadore Gilbert.

2. Shuell, Thomas J., "Cognitive Conceptions of Learning," *Review of Educational Research* 56 (1986): pp. 411-436.

3. Alexander, Patricia A., Diane L. Schallert, and Victoria C. Hare, "Coming to Terms: How Researchers in Learning and Literacy Talk About Knowledge," *Review of Educational Research* 61 (1991): pp. 315-343.

4. Kintsch, Walter, "Text Comprehension, Memory, and Learning," *American Psychologist* 49 (1994): pp. 294-303.

5. Schunk, Dale H., *Learning Theories: An Educational Perspective* (New York: Maxwell Macmillan, 1991), p. 336.

6. Schunk, p. 148.

7. Tulving, Endel, "How Many Memory Systems are There?" *American Psychologist* 40 (1985): pp. 385-398.

8. Miller, G., "The Magical Number Seven, Plus or Minus Two: Some Limits on Our Capacity for Processing Information," *Psychological Review* 63 (1956): pp. 81-97.

9. Shuell, "Cognitive Conceptions of Learning."

10. Ericsson, K. Anders and Neil Charness, "Expert Performance: Its Structure and Acquisition," *American Psychologist* 49 (1994): pp. 725-747.

11. Zimmerman, Barry J., "A Social Cognitive View of Self-Regulated Academic Learning," *Journal of Educational Psychology* 81 (1989): pp. 329-339.

12. Arp, Lori, "An Introduction to Learning Theory," in *Sourcebook for Bibliographic Instruction* (Chicago: American Library Association, 1993), p. 12.

13. Kolb, David A., *Experiential Learning: Experience as the Source of Learning and Development.* Englewood Cliffs, NJ: Prentice-Hall, 1984; Svinicki, Marilla D. and Nancy M. Dixon, "The Kolb Model Modified for Classroom Activities," *College Teaching* 35 (1987): pp. 141-146; Bodi, Sonia, "Teaching Effectiveness and Bibliographic Instruction: The Relevance of Learning Styles," *College & Research Libraries* (1990): pp. 113-119.

14. Shuell, Thomas J., "Phases of Meaningful Learning," *Review of Educational Research* 60 (1990): pp. 531-547.

15. Kuhlthau, Carol, Betty J. Turock, Mary W. George, and Robert J. Belvin, "Validating a Model of the Search Process: A Comparison of Academic, Public and School Library Users," *Library and Information Science Research* 12 (1990): pp. 5-31.

16. Kuhlthau, Carol, "Students and the Information Search Process: Zones of Intervention for Librarians," in *Advances in Librarianship* 18: pp. 57-72.

17. Perkins, D.N. and Gavriel Salomon, "Are Cognitive Skills Context-Bound?" *Educational Researcher* (1989): pp. 16-25.

18. Kuhlthau, Carol C., "An Emerging Theory of Library Instruction," *School Library Media Quarterly* 16 (1987): pp. 94-98.

19. Spiro, Rand J., Walter P. Vispoel, John G. Schmitz, Ala Samarapungavan, and A.E. Boerger, "Knowledge Acquisition for Application: Cognitive Flexibility and Transfer in Complex Content Domains," in *Executive Control Processes in Reading* (Hillsdale, NJ: Lawrence Erlbaum Associates, 1987): pp. 177-199.

20. Ibid., p. 179.

21. Ibid., p. 181.

22. Rogers, Alan. *Teaching Adults.* 2nd ed. Buckingham, England; Philadelphia: Open University Press, 1996.

# The Andragogical Librarian

## Dorothy S. Ingram

**SUMMARY.** Andragogy is the art and science of helping adults learn. This article explores the foundations of adult learning theory, as well as current thought and practice. With special emphasis on Malcolm Knowles' Basic Assumptions of Andragogy, the article presents the learning needs and characteristics of the adult library user. These characteristics include: a psychological need to be self-directed; a preference for experiential learning; a desire and readiness to learn practical life applications; and a desire to grow and self-actualize. A discussion follows of the implications for providing more effective reference service and library instruction to adults. *[Article copies available for a fee from The Haworth Document Delivery Service: 1-800-342-9678. E-mail address: <getinfo@haworthpressinc. com> Website: <http://www.haworthpressinc. com>]*

**KEYWORDS.** Andragogy, adult education, adult learning, Knowles, self-directed learning

### INTRODUCTION

The thirtysomething mom cautiously approached the reference desk, followed at a distance by her teenage daughter. She explained that her daugh-

Dorothy S. Ingram was the former Library Human Resources Officer, William Russell Pullen Library, Georgia State University, 100 Decatur Street, S.E., Atlanta, GA 30303-3202. She holds the MLS from Peabody College of Vanderbilt University and the MS in Human Resources Development from Georgia State University. The author is a member of the American Library Association, the Association of College and Research Libraries, the Library Administration and Management Association, the Georgia Library Association, and the Southeastern Library Association. She is Vice-President, President-Elect of the Continuing Library Education Network and Exchange Round Table of ALA (E-mail: dsingram@mindspring.com).

[Haworth co-indexing entry note]: "The Andragogical Librarian." Ingram, Dorothy S. Co-published simultaneously in *The Reference Librarian* (The Haworth Information Press, an imprint of The Haworth Press, Inc.) No. 69/70, 2000, pp. 141-150; and: *Reference Services for the Adult Learner: Challenging Issues for the Traditional and Technological Era* (ed: Kwasi Sarkodie-Mensah) The Haworth Information Press, an imprint of The Haworth Press, Inc., 2000, pp. 141-150. Single or multiple copies of this article are available for a fee from The Haworth Document Delivery Service [1-800-342-9678, 9:00 a.m. - 5:00 p.m. (EST). E-mail address: getinfo@haworthpressinc.com].

*141*

ter's high school teacher had suggested a visit to the college library to find some additional materials for a report. Mom apologized in advance for her own lack of familiarity with the academic library, and for all the assistance she felt she would need in order to help her daughter. In the meantime, the high school student had already slipped confidently into an OPAC workstation and was quietly researching her topic. By the time her mother had finished sheepishly explaining her plight to the reference librarian, the student was already standing impatiently beside the elevator. "Come on, Mom!" she called softly. "I've already found what I need. It's on the third floor."

Sound familiar? If you studied FORTRAN in library school and learned about library automation while punching IBM cards and interfacing with computers the size of small buildings, then you can relate to this mother's dilemma, because you have been there. You know how it feels to have the younger generation step in and show you how it is done. And for older library patrons who have been away from the library awhile, their first trip back can be a rude awakening that requires patience and understanding from those whose job it is to provide re-training in library skills. The adult patron may be a parent escorting a son or daughter to the library for the first time; a homemaker or busy professional returning to school after a number of years; a working person on lunch hour doing research for business or pleasure; or a faculty member trying to connect with the library's resources from a remote location. No matter: As a library professional, your success in creating an older generation of library literate adults is dependent both upon your realization that adults have unique learning needs, and upon your capacity to respond to those needs. This article explores the roots of adult learning theory as well as current thought and practice; presents the needs and characteristics of the adult learner and library user; and suggests some ideas and strategies for becoming a more "andragogical" librarian.

## A BRIEF HISTORY OF ANDRAGOGY

The term "andragogy" was coined as early as mid-nineteenth century Germany to differentiate the practice of teaching adults from pedagogy, the teaching of children. Some of the scholars and theorists who have had a strong influence on the field of adult learning include:

- John Dewey, who believed that all learning is based on experience, that learning is a lifelong process, and that defining and solving problems is the central process of adult learning. For Dewey, learning was a scientific method: Faced with a real-life problem to solve, the individual forms hypotheses, collects evidence to test them, accepts or rejects the hypotheses, solves the problem, and learning has occurred. In his writings, Dewey also stressed the importance of personal reflection as a key concept in education (Cranton, 1992). Other key concepts in the work of Dewey include the importance of experience, democracy, continuity, and interaction in the educational experience (Knowles, 1990).

- Behaviorist B. F. Skinner and his colleagues, whose studies of positive and negative reinforcement inspired such current teaching practices as programmed and modular instruction, computer-assisted instruction, and ongoing feedback to provide praise for successful achievement (Cranton, 1992).

- Robert Mills Gagne, who, like Dewey, described a problem-solving cycle of learning that begins with the perception of the problem and moves through these stages: the collection of observations, the formulation and testing of hypotheses, assimilation, and ultimately the perception that the situation is no longer a problem. The field of instructional design owes much to this cycle, as well as to Gagne's description of the learning hierarchy, which he referred to as the "psychological organization of intellectual skills" (Gagne, 1977). This hierarchy includes: stimulus-response learning, motor and verbal chaining, multiple discrimination, concept learning, rule learning, problem solving, and signal learning, which is associated with stimulus-reward theory (Cranton, 1989). In his book *The Conditions of Learning,* Gagne outlined in detail the basic forms of learning and the internal (learner originated) and the external (environmental and instructor originated) conditions necessary to each.

- Humanist Carl Rogers, who believed that self-actualization of the learner, i.e., the "fully functioning" or "optimal person" (Rogers, 1969), is an educational goal in itself. Rogers wrote of the value of experiential learning, indicating that relevance of subject matter, a shift in self-perception, a non-threatening environment, active doing and participation in the learning process, and total involvement are integral to the success of the learner.

- Fellow Humanist Abraham Maslow, who thought of the adult educator as facilitator and supporter of the learner's personal growth and self-actualization. He commented, "Education in practice too often adapts the child to the convenience of adults by making him less a nuisance and a little devil. More positively oriented education concerns itself more with the growth and future self-actualization of the child" (Maslow, 1970). In his studies of human motivation, which include the motivation to learn, Maslow also described a "hierarchy of needs" that began with physiological needs and moved upwards through safety needs; belongingness and love (social) needs; esteem needs; and the need for

self-actualization. Adult educators have learned to recognize the importance of physical and psychological comfort and security, as well as
giving positive feedback, as a first step in helping adult learners to
achieve their goals.

- Critical theorists such as Paolo Freire, who described the teacher as co-
learner rather than as the traditional power figure or information provider. According to Freire's theories, the teacher and the learner have
mutual responsibility for education and growth (Cranton, 1989).
- Gestalt theorists such as Kurt Lewin, who believe that learning involves
the complete personality, rather than consisting of a series of stimulus-
response connections. Gestalt scholars believe, in fact, that the learning
process may occur in simply thinking about a problem. According to
Gestalt, learning must be well organized and structured in order to assist the learner from moving through the "disequilibrium" presented by
the tensions created in the learning situation, to a desired new state of
"equilibrium" (This & Lippitt, 1983).
- David Kolb, who developed an Experiential Learning Model to reflect
four essential types of learning abilities: concrete experience, reflective
observation, abstract conceptualization, and active experimentation. As
the learner progresses through the experiential learning process, some
abilities become more dominant, and the learner's reliance on those
evolve into an individual's preferred learning style (accommodation,
divergence, convergence, or assimilation) (Kolb, 1979).

## KNOWLES' BASIC ASSUMPTIONS OF ANDRAGOGY

The modern principles of andragogy are perhaps most closely associated
with Malcolm Knowles, who defines andragogy as "the art and science of
helping adults learn." His work clearly reflects and reiterates the concepts of
many of these earlier scholars and theorists. In his book, *The Adult Learner:
A Neglected Species* (Knowles, 1990), Knowles describes the "assumptions
of andragogy" as they differ from the more traditional, pedagogical approach. These assumptions include:

- *The need to know.* Adults must understand why they need to know
something before they become willing to invest the time to learn it.
- *A responsible self-concept.* The adult learner has a psychological need
to be both self-directed and responsible for his or her own decisions.
However, from childhood the adult has learned through conditioning to
be dependent on the educator. To assist the learner in making the transition from dependency to self-directed learning is a critical function of
the educator.

- *A wealth of life experience.* The adult learner brings life experience to the learning environment; furthermore, the adult finds more value in experiential learning than in passive learning. Each learner is a resource for the rest of the group, and, as such, he or she becomes a partner or peer to the instructor in the process. At the same time, a variety of life experiences result in an increasingly diverse population of adults with established habits and biases, creating a need for individualized teaching methodologies.
- *Readiness to learn.* The adult learner is ready to learn when there is a specific need for that learning. What is learned must be applicable to everyday life.
- *Orientation to learning.* The orientation of the learning process is problem- and performance-centered; the focus is on resolving the learner's current, real-life needs through the development of a new skill or knowledge base.
- *Motivation.* The strongest motivators to learn are increased self-esteem, greater job satisfaction, and improved quality of life.

## DESIGN ELEMENTS AND IMPLICATIONS

Based on these assumptions, Knowles also describes the necessary elements and considerations for structuring any educational experience for adult learners. They include the following, which have implications for both group library instruction and one-on-one reference desk assistance:

- *Climate of openness and respect.* Adult education should take place in an informal, comfortable environment of mutual respect and collaboration between learner and instructor.
- *Learner involvement in planning.* The learning experience should include a mechanism for planning that involves both learner and instructor.
- *Learner involvement in diagnosis of needs.* The needs assessment should involve both learner and instructor in a mutual diagnosis of the learner's desired level of achievement and performance.
- *Learner collaboration in formulation of objectives.* Learning objectives should be identified and negotiated between learner and instructor.
- *Sequenced design of instruction.* The sequence of instruction must follow the readiness of the adult to learn.
- *Experiential learning activities.* Learning activities must be experiential and relate directly to the immediate, practical needs of the learner. They must be learner-centered, and specifically problem-centered; that is, focusing on the learner's problem.

- *Mutual evaluation.* Following a period of instruction, needs should be mutually re-diagnosed, and the effectiveness of the instructional activity should be assessed by both learner and instructor.

## ADULT LEARNING AND SELF-ACTUALIZATION

At this point you may ask, "How does all of this relate to me, as a reference librarian? How can I make my adult users more comfortable? How can I become more learner-centered?" Whether your responsibilities include library instruction or one-on-one reference assistance, it helps to begin by acknowledging that the library is a classroom in the broadest sense, and that you, as a reference librarian, are frequently called upon to practice andragogy. Many adult library users, from parent to businessperson to university professor, bring with them to the library at least three critical concerns related to basic security, self-esteem, and self-actualization. These concerns are:

1. *An immediate, time-sensitive need for practical information and assistance.*
2. *A fear of looking foolish or stupid.*
3. *A desire to self-actualize through learning competencies* that will enable them to become decreasingly dependent on you and become accomplished library users in their own right.

## AN IMMEDIATE NEED

As you and your colleagues develop strategies to address your adult library users' basic needs for immediate information and assistance, here are some questions to consider:

- Is the reference area itself structured and staffed so that information needs may be addressed in a timely manner?
- Is signage adequate to lead the library user quickly to service areas?
- Could a separate information desk streamline and improve public service?
- Would a tiered service model be worth exploring?
- Are pathfinders and aids designed with the needs of the adult learner in mind?

## A FEAR OF LOOKING STUPID

To address the adult library user's fear of looking stupid is to provide a learning environment of comfort, support, acceptance, respect, and encouragement. In that environment, your efforts to educate must be collaborative and learner-centered. Here are some questions to consider:

- Do you occasionally fail to assess the user's needs correctly during the reference interview?
- Is your spoken or unspoken interaction with the adult library user free of any implication that the learner is moving too slowly or failing to understand instructions?
- Do your own time constraints pressure you to rush the library user?
- In what ways can you give positive feedback during the reference transaction?
- How can you raise the overall comfort level of your adult library users?

## A DESIRE TO SELF-ACTUALIZE

Some theorists believe that self-actualization is the ultimate goal of the adult learner. Your goal as a reference librarian is not only to assist the adult library user in addressing the immediate reference question, but also to make that user more competent and capable on each successive trip to the library. Competence is increased through practical application and guided practice. In the library instruction classroom, the most effective teaching methods are learner-centered. They may include such interactive teaching methods as class discussions, group discussions, and group projects; such individualized methods as computer-assisted instruction and multimedia; and such experiential methods as field and laboratory methods, simulations and drills. As you and your colleagues think about ways to enhance the experiential growth of adult users, here are some questions to consider:

- Are you ever tempted to solve the problem for the learner, rather than allowing him or her the opportunity to use and practice new skills?
- Do you make it a point to check back later to confirm that the user has found the correct information or has mastered the use of the database or OPAC?
- Do you use your own skills and knowledge to instill critical thinking in the user, sharing strategies for dealing with the information explosion?
- Should you consider implementing a liaison librarian model, in which reference librarians assist, involve, and collaborate with members of the teaching faculty in order to increase faculty research skills and improve the library collection?
- What other outreach activities can your library provide to assist the adult learner?

## BOB PIKE'S LAWS OF ADULT LEARNING: SOME TRAINING TIPS FOR LIBRARY INSTRUCTION

Bob Pike is known in the Human Resource Development field as the "trainer's trainer." He is famous in training circles for his creative training techniques based on these Laws of Adult Learning (Pike, 1994):

*Law 1. Adults are babies with big bodies.* As children, we learned by doing. Adults bring their own life experiences to the learning environment, and we all learn best by experience, rather than by the pure lecture method.

*Law 2. People don't argue with their own data.* Learning is more effective if the learner comes up with at least some of the ideas that are presented in class. This law is Pike's argument for incorporating group activities and projects into the classroom, in addition to the use of learner-generated "action-idea lists" of concepts or skills to be used immediately following the teaching activity.

*Law 3. Learning is directly proportional to the amount of fun you have.* Energy, involvement, and participation generated by the learners, complemented by the judicious use of humor and fun, greatly enhance the learning process.

*Law 4. Learning has not taken place until behavior has changed.* Opportunities for practice within the learning situation allow the learner to experience success in using the new techniques in a non-threatening environment.

*Law 5. Fu yu, wu yu, wzu tu yu.* Pike's translation for this phrase is roughly, "Momma's having it or Papa's having it ain't like baby having it." Learning is not complete until the learner can not only perform, but also teach other learners the new skill.

Given these "Laws," here are some questions for the Instruction librarian to consider:

- In what ways can you incorporate more experiential activities into your programs?
- How can you structure sessions to include group activities?
- What ideas do you have for increasing participation in your sessions through the creative use of fun or humor?
- How can you provide more opportunity for practice in the classroom?
- What opportunities exist for the adult learners in your sessions to teach each other?

## *CONCLUSION: WHAT MAKES A LIBRARIAN ANDRAGOGICAL?*

So what does it take to make a librarian andragogical? If we accept the theories behind the art and practice of helping adults learn, the successful "andragogical librarian" will possess these basic qualities:

*Approachability.* In her 1990 dissertation, Julie C. Smith of Syracuse University found that librarians play a unique role in creating a comfortable environment for self-directed adult learning, both in terms of physical surroundings and in face-to-face interactions with adults. According to Smith's research, this is due in large part to the ability of librarians to understand and negotiate reference inquiries; and to the basic approachability of library professionals, even by shy adults who might otherwise be hesitant to voice their needs for assistance (Brockett and Heimstra, 1991).

*Realness.* Carl Rogers states that "realness" or "genuineness" is the most basic essential attitude for the facilitator of learning. He goes on to describe this role as "a person . . . not a faceless embodiment of a curricular requirement nor a sterile tube through which knowledge is passed. . . ." (Rogers, 1969)

*Respect.* Rogers writes of "prizing, acceptance, trust . . . prizing the learner, prizing his feelings, his opinions, his person. It is a caring for the learner, but a not-possessive caring. It is an acceptance of this other individual as a separate person, having worth in his own right. It is a basic trust–a belief that this other person is somehow fundamentally trustworthy" (Rogers, 1969).

*Empathetic understanding.* Rogers describes empathetic understanding as the ability to make the learner feel that "At last someone understands how it feels and seems to be me without wanting to analyze me or judge me. Now I can blossom and grow and learn" (Rogers, 1969). In a society that often forgets to show respect for the individual, the andragogical librarian has an opportunity to stand in the adult learner's shoes and remember how it feels to be overwhelmed by technology. There are no stupid questions.

*Ability to recognize and respond to a teachable moment in the midst of crisis.* Of all the facilitators of self-directed learning, librarians are in the best position to help the adult learner solve real-life problems. As Knowles states, "Adults can best identify their own readiness-to-learn and teachable moments" (Knowles, 1990, p. 195). Even more to the point, "If you want to engage an adult in a learning program in which he'll be highly motivated, highly ready, then find out what his life crises are, and build your learning around his life crises" (Knowles, 1983).

The andragogical librarian is one who knows that whatever initiated this trip to the library was just one of those crises.

## REFERENCES

Brockett, R.G. & Heimstra, R. (1991) *Self-direction in adult learning: Perspectives on theory, research, and practice.* London: Routledge.

Cranton, P. (1989) *Planning instruction for adult learners.* Toronto: Wall & Thompson.

Cranton, P. (1992) *Working with adult learners.* Toronto: Wall & Emerson, Inc.

Gagne, R.M. (1977) *The Conditions of learning.* 3rd ed. New York: Holt, Rinehart & Winston.

Knowles, M.S. (1990) *The Adult learner: A neglected species.* 4th ed. Houston: Gulf Publishing Co.

Knowles, M.S. (1983) "How adults learn." In Baird, L., Schneier, C.E. & Laird, D. (eds.) *The Training and development source book.* Amherst, MA: Human Resource Development Press.

Kolb, D.A. et al. (1979) *Organizational psychology: An experiential approach.* 3rd ed. Englewood Cliffs, NJ: Prentice-Hall.

Maslow, A.H. (1970) *Motivation and personality.* New York: Harper & Row.

Pike, R.W. (1994) *Creative training techniques handbook.* 2nd ed. Minneapolis: Lakewood Books.

Rogers, C.R. (1969) *Freedom to learn.* Columbus, OH: Charles E. Merrill Publishing Co.

Smith, J.C. (1990) Public librarian perceptions of library users as self-directed learners. Doctoral Dissertation, Syracuse University, 1989. *Dissertation Abstracts International* 51, p. 1087A.

# Adult Learning Theory
# and Reference Services:
# Consonances and Potentials

James Ghaphery

**SUMMARY.** There is a long history of exchange between librarians and adult educators. This history not only points to previous successes but also highlights a tension of defining an appropriate focus within libraries for the provision of adult education. The similarities between contemporary adult education thought and reference services can provide some interesting possibilities in looking toward the future of reference in a digital age, both in terms of service and professional development. *[Article copies available for a fee from The Haworth Document Delivery Service: 1-800-342-9678. E-mail address: <getinfo@haworthpressinc.com> Website: <http://www.haworthpressinc.com>]*

**KEYWORDS.** Adult education, reference services, discussion groups, continuing education

## A SELECTED REVIEW

The history of adult education and libraries in America are closely intertwined. In his seminal article, "The Profession," in the first issue of the

James Ghaphery is Librarian for Instructional Technology, James Branch Cabell Library, 901 Park Avenue, Office for Information Technology, Virginia Commonwealth University, Richmond, VA 23284-2033 (E-mail: Jsghaphe@vcu.edu). He received a BA from the College of William and Mary, and an MT and MED from Virginia Commonwealth University.

[Haworth co-indexing entry note]: "Adult Learning Theory and Reference Services: Consonances and Potentials." Ghaphery, James. Co-published simultaneously in *The Reference Librarian* (The Haworth Information Press, an imprint of The Haworth Press, Inc.) No. 69/70, 2000, pp. 151-158; and: *Reference Services for the Adult Learner: Challenging Issues for the Traditional and Technological Era* (ed: Kwasi Sarkodie-Mensah) The Haworth Information Press, an imprint of The Haworth Press, Inc., 2000, pp. 151-158. Single or multiple copies of this article are available for a fee from The Haworth Document Delivery Service [1-800-342-9678, 9:00 a.m. - 5:00 p.m. (EST). E-mail address: getinfo@haworthpressinc.com].

*American Library Journal,* Melvil Dewey concluded by tying the future of the profession to the transformation of the librarian from "a mouser in musty books" to an individual who is "in the highest sense a teacher" (1876). More than a century later, American Library Association President Barbara Ford drew on the vocabulary of adult education in calling for "lifelong learning" opportunities for librarians, staff, and the general public (1998). Indeed much of the American Library Association's efforts are connected to adult education. This is clearly reflected in the charges of various divisions and round-tables such as the Public Library Association, Reference and User Services Association, Continuing Library Education Network Exchange Round Table, and the Library Instruction Round Table.

Likewise, the field of adult education has often drawn upon library resources and librarians. Early adult education efforts in colonial America, such as Benjamin Franklin's Junto, centered on access to books within collective, public and personal libraries (Stubblefield and Keane, 1994). Further, Malcolm Knowles, in his history of adult education, not only traced the relationship between adult education and libraries, but also cited successful outreach efforts from the library community to other educational professionals (1976).

Several works from the library literature have thoroughly detailed the history of adult education in the context of the library. Among these, C. Walter Stones' article "Adult Education and the Public Library" (1953), Robert Lee's *Continuing Education for Adults through the American Public Library, 1833-1964* (1966), Lynn Birge's *Serving Adult Learners: A Public Library Tradition* (1981), and Connie Van Fleet's "Lifelong Learning Theory and the Provision of Adult Services" (1990), are especially noteworthy. Despite the fact that these works were written over a period of four decades, a number of interrelated issues emerge. Foremost, the American library enjoys a long history of educational outreach and support to a wide variety of adults. Given this record, there remains the difficulty of defining what exactly constitutes adult education in libraries. This difficulty surfaces in the long running debate over the level of service and support that should be offered for library adult education.

## DEFINING A LEVEL OF SERVICE TO ADULTS

It is indeed hard to mention any library service that does not in some way contribute to the potential for adult learning. From a well cataloged book to the reference interview, the efforts of libraries create structures and avenues for learning. The level of service for adult education, on the other hand, brings the difficulties in definition to the fore. The debate has revolved around how much initiative librarians, apart from their traditional roles, should take in designing or leading adult education programs. Dilemmas of decreasing budgets and increasing demands make these choices even more contested.

Amidst historical swings of emphasis among such areas as reader's advisory services, community outreach programs, and library instruction, the library has remained central to the continuing education of adults. The educational contexts are as diverse as our library systems including university libraries in conjunction with an organized curriculum of study, public libraries for vocational or recreational research, and special libraries such as a state archives for genealogical research. Especially interesting is the degree to which the library literature and adult education theory have charted parallel courses. Van Fleet effectively argues that the 1852 Report to the Boston Public Library contains the philosophical kernel of the 1970's educational concept of lifelong learning. She states, "Obviously then, lifelong learning theory and the underlying foundations of the public library have much in common: both recognize the importance of continuing universal education for vocational and personal development" (p. 170).

## LINDEMAN AND KNOWLES

Modern adult education theory has developed among many avenues, theorists, and practitioners. Among these, the work of both Eduard Lindeman and Malcolm Knowles is fundamental. Lindeman's *The Meaning of Adult Education,* spoke passionately about the unmet needs of adults learners (1920). Always central to his conception of adult education was the importance of the individual's experience. Lindeman argued that the adult's experience was too often marginalized in the educational process. He stated, "The resource of highest value in adult education is *the learner's experience* . . . Too much of learning consists of vicarious substitution of some one else's experience and knowledge" (p. 9). Building on the ideas of Lindeman, Malcolm Knowles constructed the model of andragogy:

> For more than four decades I have been trying to formulate a theory of adult learning that takes into account what we know from experience and research about the unique characteristics of adult learners. Originally (in *Informal Adult Education,* 1950), I organized my ideas around the notion that adults learn best in informal, comfortable, flexible, nonthreatening settings. Then in the mid-1960's I was exposed to the term *andragogy. . . .* And it seemed to me to be a more adequate organizing concept . . . (1990, p. 54)

Like Lindeman, Knowles never drifted far from the individual's experience. Other essential components of andragogy include the importance of the overall context of learning for adults. This context must take into account the relationship between what is to be learned and the learner's life as well as the "why" behind any learning endeavor. For example, think of the Library of Congress classification system. Knowles would maintain that if you wanted to teach this system to adults, you must do so in the overall context of their quest for a specific book as opposed to setting up a class every Thursday night on cataloging practices.

## THE REFERENCE INTERVIEW AND ADULT LEARNING THEORY

As the preceding example demonstrates there are many specific similarities between adult learning theory and the philosophy behind reference services. We do not regularly offer classes on discrete facets of librarianship, but teach at the reference desk from the patron's need. The reference interview is especially illustrative of Knowles' life centered model of education. Where adult learning theory focuses on the needs of each adult as an individual, the reference transaction by its nature is already individualized. More important than the presence of a self motivated learner (or patron with a research question), is the transaction between the instructor and learner. The heart of the reference interview speaks to the importance of communication between librarian and patron. This communication, through the use of open ended questions serves as a goal clarification for both the librarian and the learner. In terms of adult learning theory, this interaction would be characterized as "facilitation" or helping the adult learner map or clarify his own course of study. This facilitation process is guided by the listening and questioning skills of the facilitator.

## COLLABORATIVE LEARNING

Another hallmark of adult learning theory is the concept of group interaction (Brookfield, 1986). Collaborative learning acknowledges both the social nature of learning and the richness of personal experience that each person in a group can bring to an educational setting. In the traditional reference setting it is hard to envision directing a patron toward another researcher and suggesting that they compare notes or chat about their research. While librarians, deservedly, serve as the primary experts for research consultation and each patron has the right to consider the reference interview as confidential, it is important to consider the potential of collaborative learning and how it might be employed within and outside the walls of the library.

I am often intrigued by the learning which occurs when our students give each other advice in the reference area. At their best, these interactions often result in mutual learning, where both students come to understand a wider breadth of the research possibilities at the library. At their worst, without professional guidance, misinformation can easily be distributed. This dilemma is a good illustration of the fine line an adult education facilitator must walk between too much or too little intervention in a collaborative learning environment. I should also note that our student population at Virginia Commonwealth University is very diverse and like many colleges and universities is made up of a large percentage of returning adult students. In a recent ACRL 1997 conference paper, Dolores Fidishun has recognized the intersection of this changing demographic and adult learning practices and has elaborated some interesting recommendations and challenges to the library community.

While not advocating the abolition of the reference desk as an efficient vehicle for delivering quality research advice, I believe that we can look toward supplemental services that may capitalize on collaborative learning techniques. That is, we should be able to provide a space both for group interaction and professional input. The emerging environment of digital reference offers us new opportunities to link our users up with one another. Listserv technology has been employed by a number of college and university libraries as a mechanism for students to post questions and for librarians to engage in extended conversations about research. Likewise, electronic reference is reaching a large remote population through sites such as the Internet Public Library. Our net of referral possibilities has also been greatly expanded when we consider the variety of listservs or synchronous electronic conferencing where discussions of highly specific issues are taking place beyond traditional geographical boundaries.

Collaborative learning theory has also impacted instruction throughout the educational system as more and more students and adults are called on to wrestle with problems in small groups or teams. In touring two newly constructed libraries (Virginia Theological University and Eastern Michigan University), I was struck by the architectural acknowledgement of this shift as numerous group study rooms were included, complete with wiring and white boards. It will be interesting to see if such rooms welcome librarians as well as students. That is, if the group has a research question, must they trudge over to the reference desk or can a group consultation take place in the study room or through the wiring? In terms of venturing into the areas of collaborative learning, such pre-formed task oriented groups seem like a logical starting point and could offer a compelling field of study.

It is interesting to consider epistemological questions and the librarian's role in these types of conversations. If one believes that knowledge can be created through interaction, then much is to be gained from opening up the reference interview to a larger group. That is, while the librarian has valuable research advice as a subject matter and research specialist, other participants in the group may pose valid questions and advice as well. The fundamental question does return to "role." If listservs and groups are valid research tools, then should the librarian merely refer a patron to an appropriate list or should the librarian be an active participant within the list? As an institution committed to education, does the library have a role in hosting virtual discussions on pressing local or global issues? The reference librarian is certainly well poised in terms of training and experience to become a rich resource in such an arena.

## CRITICAL REFLECTION

Contemporary adult education theorists have emphasized the overall quality of the educational experience. Stephen Brookfield has elaborated a distinction between "training" and "education" (1986). Training, for Brookfield, involves the teaching of discrete skills while education deals with deeper issues of personal reflection and the development of a critical awareness. In a similar spirit, Jack Mezirow sees the educational endeavor as a means to question, challenge and transform our previously held beliefs and values (1990).

The resources for this type of education are certainly present in a library setting where competing voices sing out next to each other on the shelves or from amongst growing digital collections. Do we step into these larger goals of adult education or simply maintain a setting where critical reflection may or may not occur? These contemporary rubrics go to the heart of the debate over the level and type of library adult education that we offer.

The emerging issues of information literacy dovetail with the ideas of critical reflection. An information literate person is "able to recognize when information is needed and have the ability to locate, evaluate, and use effectively the needed information" (American Library Association Presidential Committee on Information Literacy, 1989). These skills are intertwined with the ideas of critical reflection and adult education, especially when we move beyond simple retrieval of specific information to the more complex information tasks of analyzing competing theories and reconciling them with one's own beliefs. It is this personal struggle for meaning that educators such as Brookfield and Mezirow look to as the heart of the educational enterprise. Such a struggle offers the opportunity for significant learning and reflection. In terms of teaching information literacy skills, we may do well to search for these teachable moments when information retrieval interacts with personal value clarification and meaning making.

## CONTINUING PROFESSIONAL EDUCATION

In the area of continuing professional education, the concept of critical reflection gives us a powerful avenue for renewal and engagement. Donald Schon has offered a challenging portrait for all professions (1986). He argues that the telltale sign of a professional is not to be found in the certification process or in a scientific body of knowledge. Instead, he looks to the zone of actual practice where such preparation can only take one but so far. In practice, the professional must make difficult decisions that do not fit neatly into pre-defined categories. While Schon writes about professions in general, the following is arrestingly descriptive of the reference process: "She [the professional] responds to the unexpected or anomalous by restructuring some of her strategies of action, theories of phenomena, or ways of framing the problem; and she invents on-the-spot experiments to put her new understandings to the test" (p. 35). Schon sees this type of action as more artistic than scientific and calls for such ongoing reflection to resonate throughout our understanding of and thoughts about the profession.

We, as professionals, must take advantage of the accrued knowledge from each reference interview and interaction. The potential of such an artistic professional is greatly enhanced by reflection on past practices. Why did I recommend that particular source? What questions did I ask the patron? This ability to reflect both during and after the reference encounter is especially critical as we chart new areas of reference. Such reflection can serve as a basis for creatively moving into new realms of digital reference.

## CONCLUSION

Looking to and reflecting upon other disciplines can challenge our own preconceptions and values. In the case of adult education, I have merely scratched the surface of the potential alliances. The historical precedent is strong for collaboration across these disciplines. More importantly, the challenges of our current age reach beyond singular solutions and paradigms. The time is ripe for greater exchange between librarians and adult educators. The process would serve to enrich both parties and more importantly present dynamic and exciting educational opportunities for library patrons.

## REFERENCES

American Library Association Presidential Committee on Information Literacy (1989), *American Library Association Presidential Committee on Information Literacy: Final Report.* Online: <http://www.ala.org/acrl/nili/ilit1st.html>.
Brookfield, Stephen (1986), *Understanding and Facilitating Adult Learning,* San Francisco: Jossey-Bass.

Dewey, Melvil (1876), "The Profession." *American Library Journal 1 (1)*, 5-6.

Fidishun, Dolores (1997), "Can We Still Do Business as Usual? Adult Students and the New Paradigm of Library Service." *ACRL 1997 National Conference Papers.* Online: <http://www.ala.org/acrl/paperhtm/c25.html>.

Ford, Barbara (1998), "Lifelong Learning: Global Reach and Local Touch." *American Libraries 29 (3)*, 33.

Internet Public Library. Online: <http://ipl.si.umich.edu/>.

Knowles, Malcolm (1950), *Informal Adult Education,* New York: Association Press.

Knowles, Malcolm (1977), *A History of the Adult Education Movement in the United States,* Huntington, New York: Robert E. Krieger Publishing Company.

Knowles, Malcolm (1990), *The Adult Learner: A Neglected Species,* 4th ed. Houston: Gulf Publishing Company.

Lee, Robert (1966), *Continuing Education for Adults through the American Public Library 1833-1964,* Chicago: American Library Association.

Lindeman, Eduard (1926), *The Meaning of Adult Education,* New York: New Republic.

Mezirow, Jack (1990), *Fostering Critical Reflection in Adulthood,* San Francisco: Jossey-Bass.

Stone, C. Walter (1953), "Adult Education and the Public Library" *Library Trends 1* (April), 437-453.

Stubblefield, Harold and Patrick Keane (1994), *Adult Education in the American Experience,* San Francisco: Jossey-Bass.

Van Fleet, Connie (1990), "Lifelong Learning Theory and the Provision of Adult Services," In *Adult Services: An Enduring Focus for Public Libraries,* edited by Kathleen Heim and Danny Wallace. Chicago: American Library Association, 166-211.

# SECTION 4:
# FROM A DISTANCE:
# PROVIDING REFERENCE
# AND INSTRUCTIONAL
# SERVICES
# FOR THE ADULT LEARNER

# The Librarian as Bricoleur:
# Meeting the Needs of Distance Learners

## Elaine Anderson Jayne

**SUMMARY.** Like bricoleurs, instructional librarians, especially those who provide instruction to distant learners, use a "tool-box" of materials and means to address the needs of adult learners. They also need to be adaptable and resourceful, staying abreast of current research and technologies in order to create an instructional repertoire (bricolage), to deliver services comparable to those that on-campus students receive. This article describes adult learners' needs and the variety of tools used to reach students in one university's instructional program. *[Article copies available for a fee from The Haworth Document Delivery Service: 1-800-342-9678. E-mail address: <getinfo@haworthpressinc.com> Website: <http://www. haworthpressinc.com>]*

**KEYWORDS.** Distance learners, distance education, instruction, bibliographic instruction, bricolage, bricoleur, Western Michigan University, instructional programs

## INTRODUCTION

It's 6:45 p.m. and you've just arrived at your university's regional center after a long drive. You rush to the computer lab to ready it for your seven

Elaine Anderson Jayne is Instructional & Continuing Education Librarian, Dwight B. Waldo Library, Western Michigan University, Kalamazoo, MI 49008-5080 (E-mail: elaine.jayne@wmich.edu). She received an MA in Anthropology from the University of Michigan and an MILS from the University of Michigan.

[Haworth co-indexing entry note]: "The Librarian as Bricoleur: Meeting the Needs of Distance Learners." Jayne, Elaine Anderson. Co-published simultaneously in *The Reference Librarian* (The Haworth Information Press, an imprint of The Haworth Press, Inc.) No. 69/70, 2000, pp. 161-170; and: *Reference Services for the Adult Learner: Challenging Issues for the Traditional and Technological Era* (ed: Kwasi Sarkodie-Mensah) The Haworth Information Press, an imprint of The Haworth Press, Inc., 2000, pp. 161-170. Single or multiple copies of this article are available for a fee from The Haworth Document Delivery Service [1-800-342-9678, 9:00 a.m. - 5:00 p.m. (EST). E-mail address: getinfo@haworthpressinc.com].

o'clock class, only to discover that for one reason or another some of the computers are not in working order. So once again, it's time to relax, be flexible, and use that old standby-the blackboard–then have students double up on the working computers to practice with hands-on exercises. Looks like it's going to be an evening when you adapt to the situation and draw upon a variety of materials. It's time to be a bricoleur.

Bricoleur is a useful concept. The French term for a handyman who performs odd-jobs, bricoleur was appropriated by the anthropologist Claude Levi-Strauss to describe the resourcefulness of a tribesperson who uses the materials at hand–odds and ends–to construct something entirely new.[1] Instructional librarians, especially those who teach distant learners, are not unlike bricoleurs. They often need to adapt to new and unexpected teaching situations. They must also stay abreast of current research and technologies and apply them to create an assortment of instructional "tools" (bricolage) which can be drawn upon as needed to facilitate instruction and learning. Bricolage, then, may be considered an instructional librarian's toolbox, including both a sufficient assortment of materials and their creative application to provide services, in this case services to distant learners that are comparable to those available to on-campus students.[2]

At present, a growing number of distance education librarians in the United States deliver instruction through a wide variety of means for their universities.[3] This paper will provide a profile of distance education students and describe the instructional program, students, and "tools," at one particular university, Western Michigan University (WMU).

## WHO ARE THE ADULT LEARNERS?

The 1990s have seen a significant increase in the number of adult students engaged in distance education.[4] Fostering this growth are numerous interrelated economic and demographic factors, most of which relate to employment: an aging work force, postponed retirement, and a competitive marketplace characterized by constantly changing technologies. Many adults are turning to lifelong learning in order to maintain job skills throughout their careers. Statistics compiled by the National University Continuing Education Association add detail to these generalizations about the workplace:

- The labor force is now growing more slowly; those already in it will be forced to adapt to technological change.
- There has been a concomitant rise in the enrollment of adults in post-secondary education, and approximately half the courses they take are job-related.[5]

Most of these adults are college graduates employed full-time and completing higher degrees or specialized programs to advance in their profession. In addition to their jobs, these students may have family responsibilities, and part-time enrollment provides them with a flexible alternative to traditional attendance. Unlike the enrollment of traditional full-time students, the enrollment of part-time students has soared, and the majority of them are women over the age of 35 who are pursuing higher degrees.[6] In response to this growing demand, an increasing number of public institutions of higher education are offering distance education classes. There is also a flowering of consortiums and new institutions that were never dreamt of previously. These include Western Governors University, the University of Phoenix, and various collaborative ventures between colleges and businesses.[7]

## *WESTERN MICHIGAN UNIVERSITY'S OFF-CAMPUS PROGRAM*

Western Michigan University (WMU) has a student body of over 26,500, and the University's off-campus program is the state's second largest, offering courses for two doctoral, twenty masters, and seven undergraduate degree programs.[8] The profile of the approximately 3,200 students in these programs in many ways mirrors national trends:

- Most of the students are in their 30s and 40s
- Ninety-four percent of the students are employed
- Women represent 70.6% of this group[9]

As elsewhere, these students have become an increasingly important component of WMU's graduate student population, and now represent 43% of the university's total graduate head count enrollment.

At WMU, off-campus learning is offered by the University's Division of Continuing Education in a variety of modes: (1) satellite-delivered television courses, (2) compressed video interactive television (CVIT), (3) e-mail, especially in educational technology classes, (4) the World Wide Web, and (5) self-instructional courses using videotape and print materials. However, the majority of students attend classes taught by professors at five regional centers in southwest Michigan and at two additional sites in other parts of the state. Nearly all of the classes are offered in the evening or on Saturdays, since most students work full-time.

None of the regional centers has a library. However, Western Michigan University Libraries are able to provide off-campus students with comparable access to research materials. The online catalog is available to all students with computer/modem access, whether at home or at one of the center's computer labs. Also offered are over 60 bibliographic databases through

OCLC's FirstSearch system and Lexis-Nexis access. A document delivery service uses the U.S. mail and U.P.S. to deliver materials directly to these students at their home addresses. Students first submit requests for books or articles at the regional centers they attend, and then the requests are faxed to the University Libraries' Resource Sharing office, which sends the materials to the student within two working days.[10] The same office processes materials for class reserves and sends them to the appropriate center. Interlibrary loan of articles not owned by WMU Libraries may be requested through an electronic form.

## HOW DO THE NEEDS OF DISTANCE LEARNERS DIFFER?

Distance alone puts these students at a disadvantage. Unlike their on-campus counterparts, they do not have easy access to reference librarians who can help them with a variety of research needs–everything from focusing a topic to choosing terms and a database for an online search. Even though the online catalog may provide call numbers in their shelf list sequence, off-campus learners lack the opportunity to browse and explore what a library provides. Additionally, student peer support may be lacking, especially if classes are not delivered in person at an instructional site.

Adults may also differ from traditional students in the way that they learn. As suggested by a large body of literature, mature students are more likely to integrate the new material that they are learning with accumulated life experiences, and they often feel they have little time to waste because they may be juggling several roles, including full-time employment.[11] Not surprisingly, adults are motivated learners who are more problem-centered than subject-centered in their approach to learning. On the other hand, returning after a long absence from the classroom, their learning skills may be weak, and the competitive academic environment may be intimidating. Finally, computers can be expected to add yet another layer of anxiety. Returning students may be inexperienced in using everything from word processing programs to the World Wide Web, and frequently experience technical problems with their home computers. The problem then, is how to take into account these many variables affecting distance learners, as well as other factors such as their individual learning preferences (auditory, visual, etc.) in order to help them become effective researchers.

## INSTRUCTIONAL BRICOLAGE AT WMU

A broad blueprint for our instructional program is the University Libraries' *Statement on Information Literacy,* which defines the skills and competencies an information literate person should possess.[12] This ideal, however, bumps up against the reality of staffing limitations. For off-campus courses, one full-time librarian plus a half-time librarian are assigned to provide instruction and reference assistance to 3,300 continuing education students.[13] We have found that no one approach is in itself *the* answer, partly because of the variety of student needs, learning styles, and technological skill levels, but also because the impediment of distance limits the number of in-person sessions we are able to deliver. As a result, we must use a "tool-box" of approaches, both high and low-tech in order to reach as many students as possible and in multiple ways. I will briefly describe five general approaches that we have developed.

## CLASS-RELATED INSTRUCTION

WMU's continuing education librarians work as "circuit riders" delivering class-related instruction in computer labs at the university's five regional centers, all but one of them over an hour's drive from the main campus. Included in these instructional sessions are an explanation of the services available to distance learners (e.g., the university's excellent document delivery service), a demonstration of the use of the online catalog and bibliographic databases, and hands-on practice time for the students. The sessions, which last at least an hour and take place at the request of professors, have been well received by both professors and students.

One-hour sessions, however, are not long enough to cover adequately library services, to demonstrate the catalog and available databases, to provide hands-on time for students to practice, and to answer many of the students' questions. Rarely is there time to address such important topics as research strategy or the evaluation of sources. Because continuing education students are much more isolated from personal contact, we attempt to compensate by urging students to contact us by phone or e-mail if they have subsequent problems.

Another difficulty is that professors are reluctant to request class-related instruction. Because classes normally meet twelve times or less during a regular semester, many feel formal library instruction deprives them of precious time needed for subject instruction. Moreover, adjunct professors may not be fully aware of this library service, even though fliers are sent to all teaching faculty at the beginning of each semester. One way to promote library services and class-related instruction despite these impediments, is to follow up the fliers with telephone calls to offer short twenty-minute presentations in the classroom. These truncated class visits provide the opportunity to promote two other services, Open Labs and the distribution of a *Library Guide for Continuing Education Students.* Professors have responded positively to these "cold call" offers, and the presentations turn out to be an effective use of time, since several can be scheduled in one evening.

## *THE* LIBRARY GUIDE

A detailed *Library Guide for Continuing Education Students* is distributed at library instructional sessions, in-class presentations, and at Open Labs. Students may also request a copy at any of the regional centers. Formerly, students were given nineteen separate handouts compiled from those used in the main library. While these were helpful, their lack of organization and overlapping information was sometimes confusing. Created two years ago to provide a single integrated source of information about the Libraries' services and databases, this more inclusive guide serves as both an introduction to new students and a handy reference for more experienced users.

In creating the guide we took into account examples from a literature search and several library guides from other institutions received on loan from LOEX. We also tried to minimize library jargon and to explain all specialized terms.[14] Although it means a thicker document, we used 12 point font for an older audience that might find small type more difficult to read. Highlighted boxes throughout the *Guide* emphasize important points or examples.

The contents of the *Guide* include a detailed index, contact and help referral information, a schema of the research process, an explanation and examples–both simple and advanced–of how to search available databases. All of WMU's electronic resources are listed with a brief description, as well as instructions for accessing them. Also included is a subject guide to all the databases. A section on searching the World Wide Web suggests starting points, such as the Libraries' home page. In addition, the *Guide* includes sample forms for requesting services and provides maps to and of the campus.

These contents are photocopied and then stapled between colored heavyweight covers, so the *Library Guide* is only slightly more expensive to produce than the packets it replaces. Each semester it is updated to reflect changes, especially in database offerings.

The *Guide* has proven to be very successful and is now being used as a primary resource in training student reference assistants in the main library. The results of a 1997 survey of ninety continuing education students who had received a *Library Guide* at the beginning of the semester showed that two weeks later, almost half were using it as a reference for services or for searching databases. Eighty-nine of the students said that they would recommend it to a friend.

## OPEN LAB PROGRAM

Another instrument in our bricoleur's toolbox is Open Lab sessions. At the beginning of each semester, several 2-3 hour time slots are reserved at each regional center's computer lab for "open labs," which are drop-in help sessions for students. A schedule for these is posted to indicate when a librarian is available to offer individualized help, and students are encouraged (though not required) to sign up in advance.

## REFERENCE SEARCH ASSISTANCE

Students may complete a form for search assistance, listing their topic, search terms used, and databases tried. Regional centers then fax these forms to the continuing education librarians who, if material on a student's topic cannot be found on available databases, use fee-based databases to search the topic. This service has fallen into disuse, as it began before the university acquired its more than 60 electronic databases. Now, students are encouraged to phone or e-mail continuing education librarians whenever they encounter difficulties with searching or with computer connectivity.

## LIBRARY SKILLS CLASS

Comments by students on class evaluations brought to our attention the need for additional instruction, perhaps in a more formal venue. In fall 1997, the possibility of offering a one-credit class was discussed with Continuing Education administrators, who moved quickly to have the class approved. Initially a series of four of these classes was scheduled and the first taught at the main campus in the 1998 spring semester, with subsequent classes to be taught at various regional centers on a rotational schedule. Before the initial class began, students were sent questionnaires on their majors, degree programs, and computer and Web skill levels, so class content and examples could be tailored to their individual needs. As it turned out, the first class attracted a heterogeneous group; there were students enrolled in continuing education classes, traditional on-campus students, and one entering international student. Represented were eleven different majors from chemistry to communications.

Because so many students hold full-time jobs, the class was scheduled for two successive Saturdays, and since each session lasted from 9:00 am. to 4:00 p.m., it was team taught by a continuing education librarian and a librarian from the main campus. Class time needed to be structured carefully, both because it would be difficult for students to sustain attention in an all-day class and because our agenda was necessarily ambitious. We planned to give students an overview of the structure of databases, to introduce the search process, and to teach search protocols for the OPAC and two electronic bibliographic database systems. We also wanted to introduce three other Web-based bibliographic databases and to include a unit on searching the World Wide Web.

As much as possible, we taught this material in an evaluative context using active learning techniques such as hands-on practice, group exercises, and class discussion, in addition to our lectures and short demonstrations. Our teaching methods also required students to move back and forth between computer terminals and a nearby seating area throughout the day. Short walking tours of a particular area or service point in the library were likewise combined with breaks to provide additional variety in a long instructional day. The group reconvened for question and answer sessions, and at the end of each day's session students had free time to conduct their own searches.

Exercises enabled students to practice online catalog and bibliographic database searching and to compare databases by searching the same topic in four databases. Students learned how to convert a topic from conversational language into a search statement using ERIC descriptors and Boolean operators. A lively discussion on authority and authenticity emerged after students completed an evaluation activity in which they were asked to judge preselected Web sites.[15]

Students were appreciative of what they had learned in the class, and this was confirmed by their positive written course evaluations. Nevertheless, they had useful suggestions in response to which we planned to "fine tune" the syllabus and materials for the course for the fall 1998 classes.

## ADDING BRICOLAGE

With our on-campus colleagues we share the challenge of limited staffing as well as the goal of reaching a large number of students–whether it be over 20,000 students on campus or 3,000 off-campus. Increasingly, we also share the problems of remote users. Widespread access to electronic resources has had the effect of making all students 'distant learners,' whether they are in their dorm rooms or at remote locations hundreds of miles from campus. The convergence of these two otherwise disparate student groups offers new opportunities for collaborating with our on-campus colleagues in creating instructional materials. By employing new technologies judiciously we can create cross-over tools, such as Web-based tutorials, that can be modified to do 'double duty' and to reach audiences with different skill levels. With no foreseeable increase in staffing, we plan to retain and improve the tools in our instructional program that are the most effective, for example class-related instruction, the library guide, and the credit class in library skills. And we will continue to add new elements selectively as the need for them arises. Having a variety of tools and instructional strategies in our bricoleur's repertoire allows us to more effectively meet the needs of our students.

## REFERENCES

1. Levi-Strauss, Claude. *The Savage Mind,* trans. George Weidenfeld and Nicholson Ltd. Chicago: University of Chicago Press, 1967, pp. 16-20.

2. The *ACRL Guidelines for Extended Academic Library Services,* originally drafted in 1982 and revised in 1990, has once more been revised and submitted to the ALA Standards Committee for approval at the 1998 ALA Annual Convention. This most recent version states: "Students and faculty involved in extended academic programs are entitled to library services equivalent to those provided for students and faculty in traditional campus settings."

3. The Extended Campus Library Services Section (ECLSS), which has recently voted to change its name to Distance Learning Section, is one of the fastest growing sections of ACRL. In January 1998, ECLSS had a total of 1,043 members, an increase of 13.25% from the 921 members reported in January 1997. American Library Association, Association of College and Research Libraries, Extended Campus Library Services Section, *ECLSS Newsletter.* 7 1998: 1.

4. Maryhelen Jones has pointed out that the term, 'distance education' is "as porous as the boundaries" between the many variables of time, place, and technology employed, as well as the type of institution offering instruction (Jones, Maryhelen and Moore, Thomas J. "Providing Library Support for Extended Learning Programs: A Partnership Model." In *Libraries and Other Academic Support Services for Distance Learning,* Greenwich, CT: JAI Press, 1997, p. 1). The profusion of meanings for distance learning reflects technology's impact on the variety of programs and delivery systems. In this article 'distance learning' will be used to describe instruction that takes place at sites removed from the traditional campus environment.

5. National University Continuing Education Association. *Lifelong Learning Trends: A Profile of Continuing Higher Education,* 5th ed., Washington, DC: University Continuing Education Association, 1998, pp. 13, 17.

6. Ibid, 29.

7. As of February 1998, twenty-one colleges and private corporations from sixteen states and Guam are participating in Western Governors University, a "virtual university" with no campus. Enrollment is projected at 95,000 by the year 2006. The University of Phoenix, operated for profit by the Apollo Group, has more than 100 campuses and learning centers in thirty-two states, as well as in Puerto Rico and England. As an example of a cooperative venture, San Jose State University is offering an animation course, co-sponsored by Warner Brothers Feature Animation. See Blumenstyk, Goldie. "Western Governors U. Takes Shape as a New Model for Higher Education," *Chronicle of Higher Education,* 6 February 1998, A21; Strosnider, Kim, "An Aggressive, For-Profit University Challenges Traditional Colleges Nation-

wide," *Chronicle of Higher Education,* 6 June 1997, A32; Strosnider, Kim, "Operator of University of Phoenix Opens Five New Sites in Four States," *Chronicle of Higher Education,* 6 March 1998, A42; and Winkler, Ellen V., "Teaching the Magic of Animation, At a Distance," *Chronicle of Higher Education,* 8 May 1998, B9.

8. From Western Michigan University's *Fall 1998 Off-Campus Class Schedule.*

9. Visser, James A., Dean, "Presentation to the Faculty Senate Executive Board," delivered February 25, 1997.

10. In 1996-1997, this office received a total of 5,888 document delivery requests: 282 for books, 4,913 for articles, and 693 for ERIC documents.

11. Knowles, Malcolm S. *The Modern Practice of Adult Education: From Pedagogy to Andragogy,* 2nd ed., New York: Cambridge Books, 1980, pp. 44-45; Knowles, Malcolm S. *The Adult Learner: A Neglected Species,* 3rd ed., Houston: Gulf, 1984, p. 12.; and Merriam, Sharan B. and Rosemary S. Caffarella. *Learning in Adulthood,* San Francisco: Jossey-Bass 1991.

12. University Libraries, Western Michigan University, *Statement on Information Literacy,* January 29, 1997.

13. In the 1997-1998 academic year, 89 students attended Open Labs and 409 received class-related instruction, leaving 2,802 students without instruction.

14. Especially useful in creating our *Library Guide* were ideas and suggestions from: Federal Library Committee Task Force on Public Relations, "Guidelines for Library Handbooks" (ERIC Document ED 067-137,1972); Heller, Paul and Betsey Brenneman (1988), "A Checklist for Evaluating Your Library's Handbook," *C&RL News 49,* (February), 78-79 and Metter, Ellen and Elizabeth Willis (1993), "Creating a Handbook for an Academic Library: Rationale and Process," *Research Strategies 11,* 220-232. LOEX loaned library guides produced by Central Michigan University; The University of Calgary; and the Auraria Library Handbook from University of Colorado at Denver, Metropolitan State College of Denver, and Community College of Denver. The article by Peterson, Lorna and Jamie W. Coniglio. "Readability of Selected Academic Library Guides" *RQ* Winter 1987 was a useful reminder to keep terms as transparent as possible to general readers.

15. Our exercise was modeled upon one created at U.C.L.A. in which students judged preselected web sites. See Grassian, Esther and Zwemer, Diane, "Hoax? Scholarly Research? Personal Opinion? You Decide!" (Los Angeles: University of California, Los Angeles, 1998), <http://www.library.ucla.edu/libraries/college/instruct/hoax/evlinfo.htm>.

# Interactive Reference at a Distance:
# A Corporate Model for Academic Libraries

Susan A. Ware
Patricia S. Howe
Rosemary G. Scalese

**SUMMARY.** Distance education's steady evolution from correspondence courses to virtual classrooms poses a significant challenge to the delivery of library services. Success in achieving widespread electronic access to library catalogs and online databases serves only as the foundation for meeting this challenge. Full evolution to virtual library services demands the addition of dynamic and interactive electronic reference services. The Telebase Help Desk service is one model of an Internet-based interactive reference service. *[Article copies available for a fee from The Haworth Document Delivery Service: 1-800-342-9678. E-mail address: <getinfo@haworthpressinc.com> Website: <http://www.haworthpressinc.com>]*

**KEYWORDS.** Interactive online reference service, virtual reference service, distance education, adult students, telebase

## INTRODUCTION

Distance education's steady evolution from correspondence courses to virtual classrooms poses a significant challenge to the delivery of library

Susan A. Ware is Assistant Librarian, Penn State University, Delaware County, 25 Yearsley Mill Road, Media, PA 19063 (E-mail: saw4@psu.edu). Patricia S. Howe is Senior Information Specialist, Winstar Telebase, Inc., 435 Devon Park Drive, Suite 600, Wayne, PA 19087 (E-mail: phowe@telebase.com). Rosemary G. Scalese is Manager of User Services, Winstar Telebase, Inc. (E-mail: rscalese@telebase.com).

[Haworth co-indexing entry note]: "Interactive Reference at a Distance: A Corporate Model for Academic Libraries." Ware, Susan A., Patricia S. Howe, and Rosemary G. Scalese. Co-published simultaneously in *The Reference Librarian* (The Haworth Information Press, an imprint of The Haworth Press, Inc.) No. 69/70, 2000, pp. 171-179; and: *Reference Services for the Adult Learner: Challenging Issues for the Traditional and Technological Era* (ed: Kwasi Sarkodie-Mensah) The Haworth Information Press, an imprint of The Haworth Press, Inc., 2000, pp. 171-179. Single or multiple copies of this article are available for a fee from The Haworth Document Delivery Service [1-800-342-9678, 9:00 a.m. - 5:00 p.m. (EST). E-mail address: getinfo@haworthpressinc.com].

services. Success in achieving widespread electronic access to library catalogs and online databases serves only as the foundation for meeting this challenge. Full evolution to virtual library services demands the addition of dynamic and interactive electronic reference services. Pioneering experiments in virtual reference services have employed text-based communication in MOO (Multi-User Object Oriented) environments and video-conferencing within local area networks.[1] Though promising, their success has been limited. While interactive, the MOO's object oriented environment requires special navigational commands that may confound novice or infrequent users. More personalized, visual communication and application sharing are possible with videoconferencing, but at present, the limited bandwidth and the traffic congestion of local area networks hamper communication quality and stability. As a result, most video reference services must restrict service to selected computer sites that have ISDN or T-1 telecommunications lines that support high quality audio and video transmission. In contrast, Winstar Telebase, a commercial information service, has developed an interactive reference service based on widely used and distributed Windows or Internet chat technology. Since 1984, Telebase librarians have used an integrated system of chat communication, real-time transaction log analysis, online reference tools, and multi-tasking to provide interactive database search assistance to their subscribers. As the virtual university gravitates to the Internet, the Telebase Help Desk may serve as a model for academic libraries.

## THE VIRTUAL UNIVERSITY

As higher education moves rapidly and aggressively to develop technology-based distance education programs, the Internet appears to offer the greatest potential for widespread course distribution. Technologies ranging from satellite and television broadcasting to video and Internet conferencing are delivering distance education courses and services. According to the National Center for Education Statistics,[2]

- 62% of public 4-year and 58% of public 2-year institutions of higher education offered distance education courses via audio, video, or computer technologies in fall 1995,
- Another 25% planned to offer technology-based distance courses in the next three years,
- 75% of the institutions surveyed planned to increase or start to use two-way interactive video or computer-based technologies in the next three years.

More than 700,000 students were enrolled in 25,730 different distance education courses offered by public and private institutions in academic year

1994-1995.[3] The majority of distance education students are mid-career professionals seeking higher education for career change or advancement. These working adults are emerging as the fastest growing segment of higher education and are expected to be the majority in the next century.[4]

Unlike traditional campus-based programs, distance programs permit the students to control the time, place and pace of their education. Ironically, while departure from tradition is a major factor in distance program enrollment, virtual re-creation of the campus tradition of dynamic discourse and interpersonal relationships is a major factor in distance student persistence. Drop-out studies have discovered that the frequency and nature of student-institutional contacts and the speed of feedback to student-initiated contacts are significant variables in both persistence and degree completion.[5] By offering high quality channels of communication, distance education programs can facilitate the personal involvement between students and the institution that is needed to foster both social integration and collective affiliation. Key institutional affiliations include relationships with faculty, administrators and academic support services. In response to the need for more and better opportunities for communication, distance education programs are constantly working to provide student access to the full range of support services including advising, career planning, financial aid, tutoring and library services.

## DISTANCE EDUCATION AND LIBRARY SERVICES

Academic libraries have made great strides in providing remote access to and delivery of information resources. A survey of 44 leading distance education programs in the United States found that 59.5% offered remote access to the library catalog, 43% provided access to library online databases, and 67.6% offered library reference service.[6] Another 1994-1995 survey of 1,225 nationally representative two-year and four-year, public and private higher education institutions found that 56% offered distance education courses with an electronic link to the institution's library.[7]

At the 1998 American Library Association annual conference, the Distance Learning Section of the Association of College and Research Libraries approved a revision of its guidelines for off-campus library services. The 1998 *Guidelines for Distance Learning Library Services* acknowledges the growing technological innovations in the transmission of information and reaffirms a commitment to equitable library support for all students, in both campus-based and virtual university communities. Moreover, the revised guidelines emphasize adherence to the highest quality standards for distance learning library services.[8] This strong national commitment to full and effective library services for distance learners demands that academic libraries meet the challenge of providing timely, interactive reference service.

## THE TELEBASE MODEL

Telebase, a division of the Winstar Corporation, is an information gateway service that offers web-based or windows-based access to a host of popular bibliographic and full text databases. Most Telebase subscribers are members of online services such as CompuServe, Prodigy and America Online. However, a growing number are subscribing independently through a web-based registration module. The Telebase gateway offers subscribers access to the same databases that are standard fare in academic libraries (DIALOG, Wilsonline, OVID, Dun and Bradstreet et al.). Reference questions come from working adults, college students, and occasionally, children. The heaviest users are small business entrepreneurs looking for information to support management and investment decisions. In all cases, users come to the Telebase Help Desk (also known as SOS) seeking immediate assistance in conducting a productive and cost-effective database search. The cost of a search varies greatly depending on the type and depth of information retrieved. Prices range from $.50 for 5-10 bibliographic citations or abstracts to $2.00 for the full text of a newspaper or magazine article. Company financials and credit reports range in price from $12.00 to $85.00. Users are not charged for reference service.

Using online chat, real-time transaction log analysis, online reference tools, and multitasking, Telebase librarians help online searchers analyze their needs, select the most appropriate databases, and design or revise their search strategies. If a search question requires a special subject mastery or language proficiency, the transaction can be transferred seamlessly to the terminal of a subject or language specialist in the reference room or to one who is telecommuting. The Telebase Help Desk service is a model for negotiating reference queries and providing timely, relevant search assistance online.

## QUERY NEGOTIATION

Timely feedback is critical to effective online query negotiation. Computer systems research affirms that most computer users become annoyed and will disconnect if delays in feedback exceed 8-12 seconds.[9] At the same time, librarians require more than 12 seconds to examine a question and compose a thoughtful reply. The Telebase solution to this dilemma is the "tab." Tabs are brief, pre-recorded messages that can be retrieved and transmitted in 3-5 keystrokes or mouse clicks. They are used, primarily, to assure users that they are still connected and have not been forgotten. Tab messages include routine greetings and salutations, probing questions, progress reports and replies to frequently asked questions (Figure 1). Since instructions that are too complicated or detailed are often misinterpreted or ignored, tab responses are kept short and succinct.

## FIGURE 1. Selected Tabs

**Greetings and Salutations**

> Hello. This is Jean. May I help you?
> **992:** My pleasure, please SOS anytime we can be of service.
> **994:** Have a happy holiday!
> **997:** You're welcome. Good luck with your search.

**Probing Questions**

> **80:** Can you tell me more specifically what you want to find about this?
> **81:** Do you need the full text of the articles on line, or will references or abstracts be sufficient?
> **85:** What kind of information about that company are you hoping to find?

**Hold/Delays**

> **2:** Can you hold for a minute while I check that for you?
> **3:** Still checking, please hold.
> **7:** I am going to test a search now, please hold.
> **22:** Your question is rather complex. Please allow me some time to type in an answer or search instructions.

**Basic Search Instructions**

> **121:** You can use **AND**, **OR**, **NOT** and ( ) to combine search terms.
> Use **AND** to find articles with ALL the terms.
> TELEPHONE **AND** REGULATIONS **AND** ONLINE SERVICES will find articles that include all of these words.
> Use **OR** to find articles containing ANY one of the terms;
> AGREEMENT **OR** TREATY **OR** PACT will find articles that include any of these terms.
> Use **NOT** to find articles that DO NOT contain selected words:
> JAZZ **NOT** UTAH will find articles about jazz, but not about the Utah Jazz basketball team.
> Use **Parentheses** ( ) when combining **AND** and **OR** in a search statement.
> (QUARTERLY **OR** ANNUAL) **AND** REPORT will find articles about either Quarterly Reports or Annual Reports.
> **122:** The **slash mark** (/) is used to retrieve variant word endings. For example, ECONOM/ will retrieve ECONOMY or ECONOMICS or ECONOMICAL. When you use a slash mark, leave a space immediately after the slash.
> **123:** Do not use punctuation like quotation marks, exclamation marks, commas, and hyphens.

**Responses to Frequently Asked Questions**

> **601:** Financial information from Annual Reports for public companies can be found in the following databases: S&P CORPORATE DESCRIPTIONS PLUS NEWS, DISCLOSURE ONLINE or MEDIA GENERAL PLUS. Information on private companies is limited. However, you may try D&B BUSINESS REPORTS which has D&B credit ratings/payment analysis reports. You may also find consolidated financial statements for most companies, both public and private, from the Business Information Reports of this database. However, reports may not be available on all companies. In that case, an alternative would be to search DUN'S MARKET IDENTIFIIERS or AMERICAN BUSINESS DIRECTORY for some general background information.
> **615:** BOOK REVIEW DIGEST covers adult and juvenile fiction and nonfiction from 1983 to the present. To be included in this file, a book must have been published or distributed in the US or Canada. Nonfiction books must have received at least two reviews published in a selected list of periodicals. (This list does NOT include Publishers' Weekly.) Works of fiction must have received at least three reviews. Reviews must have appeared within 18 months of a book's publication. Textbooks, government publications, and technical books in law and the sciences are excluded.

Although the non-verbal cues that play such an important role in establishing rapport in face-to-face reference are absent, effective textual communication can be equally reassuring. In fact, a recent study of computer-mediated communication concluded that the absence of misleading, distracting, or prejudicial physical appearance cues online can reduce the influence of looks, gender, and race and raise the importance of information and expression in interpersonal interactions.[10]

Throughout the online reference transaction, Telebase librarians empathize with the user, describe what is being done, explain why it is being done, and suggest how much time the task will take. In addition, users are reassured by the written transcript of the transaction that is displayed on their screens as the discussion proceeds. This scrolling transcript is always available for review during the reference negotiation and for printing at its conclusion.

## TRANSACTION LOG ANALYSIS

A historical analysis of Telebase reference transaction logs revealed that over half of its users were infrequent searchers who were unfamiliar with the format, coverage, and search features of specific databases. Their common search problems involved the improper use of Boolean and truncation operators, ineffective keyword search phrases, and spelling errors. Although online help text appeared in strategic points throughout the system, many users still needed or preferred personal assistance.[11] A similar profile of user experience, search problems, and help preferences is reported in a number of transaction log studies of academic library searching.[12]

While academic library systems have limited transaction log analysis to historical studies, the Telebase system makes possible real-time transaction log analysis to support reference service. If searchers consult the Help Desk or SOS before leaving a database, their transaction logs are captured and are available for the librarian's review. Key transaction data captured include:

- the name of the service and the specific database
- the user's search history (database fields with commands and terms entered in each field)
- the number of prior successful searches (retrieved hits) and failed searches (retrieved 0 hits)

With real-time transaction data, Telebase librarians can begin to diagnose the user's search problem immediately. Common search errors such as misspellings, command errors, and inappropriate databases are quickly detected, and replies can be composed for immediate response. Transaction data not only assist in a quick response, but also speak for users who are unable to articulate their needs clearly during the negotiation. Examples of captured transaction logs appear in Figure 2 and Figure 3. In Figure 2, the user's search problem is clearly displayed. This patent search failed for two reasons. A space must be entered between the country code and the patent numbers (US 462887), and the Boolean command OR is required to search for multiple patent numbers in a single command statement (US 4628877 OR US 4168593). In Figure 3, Chrone's Disease is misspelled.

## *MULTITASKING*

The issue of response time becomes even more critical after the query has been negotiated. At this point, the librarian needs time to consult ready reference sources and test search strategies in different databases. While the librari-

FIGURE 2. Windows Transaction Log

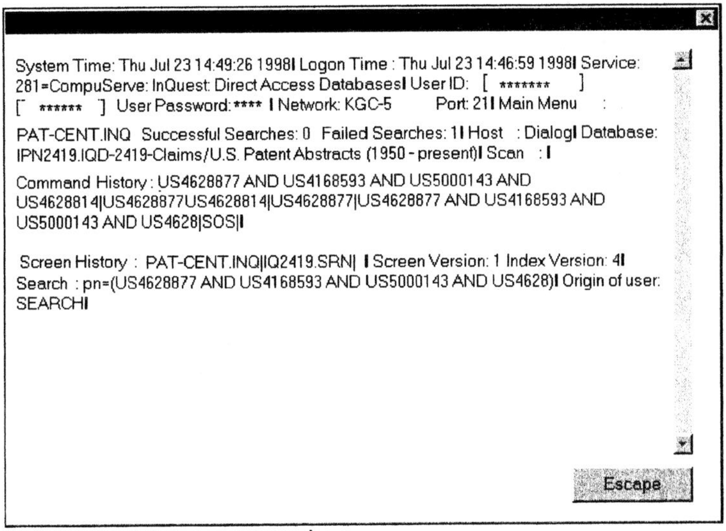

FIGURE 3. HTML Transaction Log

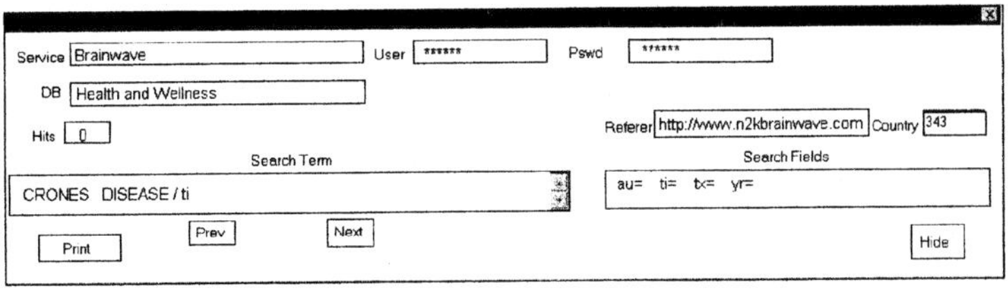

an searches, intermittent communication must be maintained with users so that they understand what is being done, how much time each task will take, and what progress has been made. Telebase librarians coordinate all of these online activities by conducting multiple tasks simultaneously in separate windows.

For ready reference searching, a host of online reference tools have been bookmarked for quick access. They range from dictionaries and subject glossaries to DIALOG Bluesheets and a variety of individual database search codes. In addition, online reference tools are created locally based on frequently asked questions. Alternate windows are used to test search strategies in different databases. Multiple windows allow selections from test search results to be copied and pasted into the reference chat window and transmitted to the users for their review.

## THE FUTURE OF DISTANCE LIBRARY SERVICES

In a comprehensive and analytical review of present and future issues in remote reference services, Bernie Sloan stresses the importance of librarian/ user collaboration in an age of digital libraries.[13] He concludes with a challenge to libraries to provide the human touch of reference service to widely dispersed clients whenever and wherever they want it or need it. How to serve distant users was also a topic of stimulating discussion at a 1998 American Library Association Midwinter meeting. The interest expressed there gave rise to a summer Library of Congress Institute, "Reference in a Digital Age," where participants grappled with some of the major issues of delivery and quality of reference in a digital environment.[14] In addition, daily discussions of current practices and problems take place on DIG_REF, a listserv devoted to issues in digital reference service.[15] While listserv reports of email reference services are common, real-time interactive reference remains elusive.

To participate fully as reference providers in technology-based distance education, libraries must forge on to develop and implement real-time interactive reference services that function much like the Telebase Help Desk. One such effort is underway at Temple University where librarians Sam Stormont (formerly a librarian at Telebase Systems) and Marc Meola are developing an interactive reference service using several web-based chat and conferencing programs. Ultimately, they hope to incorporate chat, a whiteboard, application sharing, and audio-visual features.[16]

The role of the university library in the virtual age of higher education will be determined in large part by the level of interactivity achieved. Electronic access to collections has secured the library a role as an information repository in a virtual environment, but only when interactive reference service is mastered will the library play an active and integral role in distance higher education.

# REFERENCES

1. *Reference Services in the ILP MOO.* Internet Public Library. [http://www.ipl. org/moo]; Tona Henderson, "Moving Towards a Virtual Reference Service," *Reference Librarian* 41/42 (1994): 173-84; Kathleen M. Folger, "The Virtual Librarian: Using Desktop Videoconferencing to Provide Interactive Reference Assistance," *ACRL 8th National Conference* (1997): [http://www.ala.org/acrl/paperhtm/a09.html]; Susan Lessick and others, "Interactive Reference Service (IRS) at UC Irvine: Expanding Reference Service Beyond the Reference Desk," *ACRL 8th National Conference* (1997): [http://www.ala.org/acrl/paperhtm/a10.html].

2. *Distance Education in Higher Education.* Washington, DC: National Center for Education Statistics, 1997.

3. Ibid.

4. Jill M. Galusha, "Barriers to Learning in Distance Education," *The Infrastruction Network* (1997): [http://www.infrastruction.com/articles.htm].

5. David Kember, "A Longitudinal-Process Model of Drop-Out in Distance Education," *Journal of Higher Education* 60 (May/June 1989): 278-301.

6. *Survey of Distance Learning Programs in Higher Education.* New York: Primary Research Group, 1997.

7. *Distance Education in Higher Education.*

8. Email correspondence with Harvey Gover, Chairman, 1998 ACRL Guidelines Committee, August 23, 1998.

9. Ben Shneiderman. *Designing the User Interface: Strategies for Effective Human-Computer Interaction.* 3rd ed. Reading, MA: Addison-Wesley, 1998, 367.

10. Joseph B. Walther, "Computer-mediated Communication: Impersonal, Interpersonal, and Hyperpersonal Interaction," *Communication Research* 23 (February 1996), 3-43.

11. Lise M. Dyckman and Brian T. O'Connor, "Profiling the End-User: A Study of the Reference Needs of End-Users on Telebase System, Inc.'s EASYNET," *Proceedings of the National Online Meeting* (1989): 143-202.

12. Deborah D. Belcic and others, "Using Transaction Log Analysis to Improve OPAC Retrieval Results," *College and Research Libraries* 59 (January 1998): 39-50; Christine L. Borgman, "Why are Online Catalogs Still Hard to Use," *Journal of the American Society for Information Science* 47 (1996): 493-503; Larry Millsap and Terry Ellen Ferl, "Search Patterns of Remote Users: An Analysis of OPAC Transaction Logs," *Information Technology & Libraries* 12 (September 1993): 321-343; Patricia M. Wallace, "How Do Patrons Search the Online Catalog When No One's Looking?" *RQ 33* (Winter 1993): 239-252.

13. Bernie Sloan. *Service Perspectives for the Digital Library: Remote Reference Services.* (December 1997). [http://alexia.lis.uiuc.edu/~sloan/e-ref.html].

14. *Reference Service in a Digital Age.* (June 29-30, 1998). Library of Congress: Washington, D.C. [http://lcweb.loc.gov/rr/digiref].

15. Access DIG_REF discussion archives: [http://www.vrd.org/Dig_Ref/dig_ref. html].

16. Email correspondence with Sam Stormont at Temple University, Philadelphia, PA, July 24, 1998.

# Reference Provision
# in Adult Basic and Community Education:
# An Unusual Model

## Melva Renshaw

**SUMMARY.** Reference services at ARIS are provided by a team of five staff–four educational professionals and one information services professional. This unusual structure was developed in response to the needs of teachers and practitioners in the adult literacy and basic education (ALBE) field in Australia. This paper describes ARIS and its activities, explains how reference services are provided and identifies factors that may influence the effectiveness of this model of service. It finds that although a full evaluation is required, this model is effective in providing services that meet the particular needs of teachers in this particular field. *[Article copies available for a fee from The Haworth Document Delivery Service: 1-800-342-9678. E-mail address: <getinfo@haworthpressinc.com> Website: <http://www.haworthpressinc.com>]*

**KEYWORDS.** Adult literacy and basic education, reference service, reference staff

---

Melva Renshaw is Information Services Officer, ARIS, the Adult Education Resource and Information Service, Language Australia. (ARIS is pronounced as in Paris). She has a Bachelor of Arts from the University of Melbourne (1996) and graduated from Charles Sturt University in 1997 with the Graduate Diploma of Applied Science (Library and Information Management). Renshaw is a member of the Australian Library and Information Association and has worked in public, corporate and special libraries for more than 12 years.

She would welcome comments on this paper which can be sent to ARIS, GPO Box 372F, Melbourne 3000, Australia (E-mail: melva@nllia.gov.au).

[Haworth co-indexing entry note]: "Reference Provision in Adult Basic and Community Education: An Unusual Model." Renshaw, Melva. Co-published simultaneously in *The Reference Librarian* (The Haworth Information Press, an imprint of The Haworth Press, Inc.) No. 69/70, 2000, pp. 181-192; and: *Reference Services for the Adult Learner: Challenging Issues for the Traditional and Technological Era* (ed: Kwasi Sarkodie-Mensah) The Haworth Information Press, an imprint of The Haworth Press, Inc., 2000, pp. 181-192. Single or multiple copies of this article are available for a fee from The Haworth Document Delivery Service [1-800-342-9678, 9:00 a.m. - 5:00 p.m. (EST). E-mail address: getinfo@haworthpressinc.com].

## INTRODUCTION

### Aims

The Adult Education Resource and Information Service, ARIS,[1] proactively supports the adult education development needs of Victorian community based providers through professional development activities, dissemination of information, advice provision, and special projects that arise. The ARIS reference services are only part of these activities, and their unusual structure reflects this. To examine them without describing the broader activities of ARIS, is to take them out of context however. This paper will attempt to describe ARIS and its activities, explain how reference services are provided and identify factors that may influence the effectiveness of this model of service. Since descriptions of similar models have not yet been located, this paper will perhaps provide a starting point for more comprehensive examination of this kind of model.

### Clients

Most ARIS clients are teaching English language literacy and numeracy to adults of English-speaking background. Most are working in community houses or Technical and Further Education (TAFE) colleges, and are sessional or part-time workers with limited training in adult education.[2] Many have taught in primary or secondary schools before moving into the adult field where they have completed some professional development activities and may have started one of the tertiary qualifications in adult education that are now available.

Community houses are usually small local organisations who are often very busy, with limited resources to cope with the demands made on them. Funding cuts to literacy programs have been significant in recent years, so limited finances are available for development activities or the purchase of resources. Frequent and significant changes in government policy and funding arrangements have ensured an unsettled and demanding workplace for many teachers.

A number of clients are university staff and researchers who seek the most recent publications and journals in a given topic area and are usually quite proficient information seekers. ARIS also assists increasing numbers of people involved in workplace or vocational training, many of whom have little qualification or experience in adult education, and have received funding of some kind to conduct training or develop resources for use in the workplace. Most clients are from Victoria but ARIS also assists people from all over Australia and overseas.

In general, the adult literacy and basic education (ALBE) field is something of a 'poor relation' to the broader education sector in Australia. It has a comparatively low profile and funding level, and its diverse activities mean that a single label is difficult to find and thus, market. Many people are unaware that there is a significant need for assistance for English-speaking background people and mention of 'adult literacy and basic education' usually prompts a response about the large number of immigrants Australia accepts.

The ALBE field could be described as relatively young as it has really only begun to produce its own literature in the past 30 years or so. Generally, journals devoted to the topic have only appeared in the last 20 years and there are few indexes of relevant articles and papers.

Overall, our clients generally require advice on program administration and reporting, funding procurement, ways to use and where to find good resources for use with their students, and recommended professional development reading materials.

## Activities

With these clients and needs in mind, ARIS provides a diverse range of services. Each year, a number of workshops and seminars are conducted on a range of topics. "Introduction to the CGEA" (Certificates in General Education for Adults),[3] "Using the NRS" (National Reporting System),[4] "What Makes a Good ALBE Resource?" and "Adult Numeracy Teaching: Making Meaning in Mathematics"[5] have been popular over the years.

These activities are only one part of the initial aim of the service which was to provide educational advice 'from one professional to another' on theoretical and practical issues to do with adult education. This service has continued and expanded, and the small body of resources which initially supported this function has grown into a collection which now supports 'standard' reference services.

ARIS also disseminates information on ALBE resources and professional development activities by publishing periodicals, information sheets and mini-bibliographies. The *ARIS Resources Bulletin* contains reviews and abstracts of recent materials and the *ARIS Monthly Memo* lists forthcoming conferences, seminars and workshops. *Multiple Choice* and *Australian Language Matters* provide information to community providers and the wider language field respectively. ARIS also publishes and distributes resources in the adult basic education field and sells over 50 titles.

Project work involves ARIS staff in a range of activities. In 1996, they redeveloped the CGEA and so are well-placed to provide advice and assistance to teachers on this curriculum. Current projects include the development of distance learning materials, and "ANAMOL," Adult Numeracy Assessment and Materials On-Line, which involves isolated numeracy teachers in an action research project. One of the ARIS Co-ordinators, Dave Tout, is a member of the steering committee of the International Life Skills Survey, and Jan Kindler, the other ARIS Co-ordinator, manages Language Australia's Adult Literacy Research Network which funds and disseminates adult literacy research across Australia.

In all these areas, the service and its activities are largely directed by clients and their needs. Workshops are prepared to address the latest professional development issues, resources are acquired in areas in which teachers are currently working, and periodicals attempt to address 'hot topics' as they arise. One of ARIS' key aims is to assist clients who work outside metropolitan Melbourne, so as many activities as possible are conducted in rural Victoria.

### ARIS Staff and Their Responsibilities

ARIS requires a number of staff who have professional qualifications, current or recent experience in adult literacy and basic education and numerous other skills. Staff need a good understanding of the sorts of students the clients may have, and the kinds of situations in which they work. They must be able to conduct workshops, provide advice on a wide range of topics, evaluate appropriate resources and journals, and edit and prepare newsletters and journals. Other tasks include handling queries, referring students to ALBE providers, indexing and abstracting, and writing submissions. ARIS is fortunate to have four staff (2.1 effective full-time, who will be referred to here as 'professional staff'). They have experience in teaching all areas of literacy and numeracy and have taught learners from a range of backgrounds and in a range of situations, for instance in prisons, and in isolated rural areas. Each staff member also has a particular area of expertise such as numeracy, or oral language. ARIS also needs at least one library professional and the current Information Services Officer (IS Officer) has some limited experience in tutoring in adult basic education. The IS Officer's tasks include reference duties, acquisitions, subject cataloguing, circulations, journals management and website management.

It must be emphasised that since all professional staff are part-time (except the IS Officer), in their 'other' lives they are practising in the ABLE field in a variety of ways, which brings current and invaluable experience to the service. As mentioned earlier, this is typical of workers in this field, many of whom hold a number of positions in various workplaces.

## THE REFERENCE SERVICES

### Resource Collection

Clearly, many ARIS activities rely or draw on the resources collection, in particular, the *ARIS Resources Bulletin.* Professional development activities and project work rely heavily on the collection. It now contains approximately 3000 items (including audio, video and software programs), and subscribes to some 100 journals. On average, 35-40 people come in and use the collection each month with approximately this number contacting the service via phone, fax or email. Each month, 75-80 items are borrowed with approximately one third of these being mailed to clients.

ARIS actively seeks to acquire up-to-date practical and theoretical works from around the world, in the fields of adult community education and adult English language literacy and numeracy. Searches on educational databases, including ERIC, VOCED[6] and AEI[7] and a range of other Australian databases are also conducted.

The collection is subject catalogued using a thesaurus based on the *Australian Thesaurus of Education Descriptors*,[8] and arranged on the shelves using only the major descriptor. All four professional staff and the IS Officer are involved in selecting and abstracting resources and indexing journal articles.

The collection has also expanded recently to act as a clearinghouse of materials developed under certain government funding programmes. This service is known as the LANRC (Language Australia National Resource Center) and is accessible via the Web.

### Reference Services

Before giving examples of information requests, it is perhaps useful to consider just what constitutes reference work. Katz states that the reference process "is the process of answering questions"[9] and (without in the least, suggesting that this is all there is to it) he provides a "good pragmatic start" to finding a useful definition.[10] As mentioned above, many people come to ARIS for educational advice and this perhaps fits under Bopp and Smith's "Guidance" category of reference services[11] which includes "Readers' advice" and "Research advice and consulting." A sample of the information requests ARIS receives may clarify this:

- from researchers and university students, statistics on the number of people with literacy problems in Australia or the world. Since this is very difficult to reduce to a numerical response, considerable background and explanation is usually given to the client. ARIS has also prepared an information sheet on the topic.
- from adult learners, the best way they can improve their literacy and numeracy skills. Depending on their situation, they are often referred to a local community or other provider.
- from teachers wanting to integrate reading, writing, numeracy and oral tasks, resources on a given topic at a given literacy or numeracy level.

- from program administrators, the requirements they must fulfil to run a particular course.
- from volunteer tutors, advice on assisting a student with a particular learning disability, or learning style.
- from researchers, guidance on literature reviews.
- from people accessing the ARIS website, how to search the web version of the database of resources.
- from people returning to or entering the field, suggestions for catching up on the latest issues, or how to access appropriate networks of practitioners.
- from editors and researchers, citation details for a given article or for materials by a particular author.

To try and split requests according to definitions is problematic because distinctions are rarely clear, and in practice, many requests are handled by any one of the four professional staff or the IS Officer. There are some requests that can only be handled by a staff member with particular expertise. Then for example, the Manager of the Adult Literacy Research Network provides advice on funding sources for possible projects, and it is the IS Officer who conducts on-line searches. In practice, many queries are handled in tandem by a professional staff member and the IS Officer. All staff would agree with Katz's dictum that "often the simple questions can develop into complex ones,"[12] and so are ready to seek assistance from others when necessary.

Other associated tasks highlight this model of reference service. All four professional staff and the IS Officer are responsible for selecting new resources and abstracting them once they have been catalogued. Similarly, all five are involved in indexing journal articles, especially in the subject areas in which they have expertise. Development and maintenance of the thesaurus of subject terms is a team task. Circulations tasks too are handled by all staff. The shared responsibility of these tasks highlights the extent to which reference service provision is an integrated part of the overall ARIS service and an integral part of the work of all the professional staff.

## FACTORS INFLUENCING THE EFFECTIVENESS OF THIS MODEL

What are the aspects of this kind of operation that are particularly helpful or difficult for users? To begin with, the literature on reference services has given considerable attention to the kinds of staff that libraries should employ. A lengthy study of relevant journals and indexes[13] reveals the following pertinent discussions.

### What the Literature Has to Say

There has been much discussion on the relative merits of library assistants, officers or technicians providing reference services. This includes the kinds of queries that they should handle, whether they should work alone and types of training that are beneficial. For example, Smith and Bopp believe that with proper training and support "nonprofessionals supplement and complement professional reference service, but are not expected to replace it."[14]

To a lesser extent, the employment of other kinds of professionals in libraries has been addressed. Writers generally concentrate on professionals such as computer, management or marketing specialists. For example, Herbert S. White is quite categorical in stating that "only librarians can be allowed to do that which librarians are educated uniquely to do" and other professionals must understand "what they are qualified to do and what they are not. . . . "[15] Interestingly, a 1995 *SPEC Flyer*[16] found a willingness on the part of a significant number of research libraries to employ non-M.L.S. qualified staff in reference positions (13%) but that there was a wide gap between this willingness and the actual making of appointments. Unfortunately reasons for this gap were not investigated.

The value of librarians specialising in a particular area or becoming 'subject specialists' is quite widely discussed and seems often well regarded. It is perhaps surprising then that so little has been written on the possible value of subject professionals that are not library professionals.

Alone, none of these discussions address the kind of model in operation at ARIS. In particular, description of a similarly structured reference service is yet to be located and the author would welcome direction to any of which readers are aware. (The Adult Literacy Information Service (ALIO) in Sydney works in the same field but the information service there has a number of library professionals who provide reference services.)

In an attempt to flag the outcomes, both positive and negative, for users of this model, the following list of key tasks and skills was developed from a number of reference materials.[17] The list in part follows the steps in a reference interview and points to possible areas of improvement for ARIS.

### Skills and Tasks Involved in Reference Service Provision at ARIS

#### Initial Welcoming and Contact

All visitors to ARIS are offered assistance and information soon after they arrive. It is hoped that this will begin to establish some sort of rapport with ARIS staff so that they will feel free to seek further help. It often seems that professional staff have some advantage in this process, as their experience and empathy with practitioners in the field seems to help visitors feel at ease. This also helps them in communicating their request and in expressing uncertainties about their line of inquiry.[18]

*Clarifications and Negotiation of What the Person Needs*

During the process of determining just what information or advice is needed, professional staff are able to 'speak the same language' as users and can ascertain their needs very effectively. That they know the jargon and acronyms in the field, as well as the broader 'ALBE-speak' is a distinct advantage for users.

Further, professional staff are well versed in the wider theoretical concepts and constructs of the field and have a working knowledge of current and historical developments. Their awareness from personal experience of the challenges practitioners face on a day-to-day basis is also invaluable in helping them determine the subject, scope and purpose of the user's needs.

Smith and Bopp[19] very usefully discuss the way in which patrons come to reference services with preconceived sets of expectations about their needs and how they will be assisted, and how reference staff may need to recognize and perhaps question these expectations. It could be argued that when initially assisting an ALBE student, teachers face an almost identical situation. Many teachers realise that it is quite usual for a student's first request or comment to be quite different from their actual needs or concerns. This is often the case in the reference interview. The first statement of what the patron needs, is often an approximation in some way of what they require. Staff need to be able to listen carefully and patiently, and be prepared to clarify exactly what is needed during the current discussion, and during subsequent discussions. In this area, ALBE teachers could be said to have received invaluable experience in preparation for reference work. Just as for ALBE teachers, staff need to confirm that the user is satisfied with the service provided and for ongoing requests, continue to check that the assistance provided is appropriate.

*Locating and Providing Appropriate Information*

In the ARIS situation, this may range from locating the telephone number of an educational provider to searching for bibliographic information, so a number of skills are required. It is necessary to have a good grasp of how the literature of the field is structured, how it has developed and has been produced, and how it can be accessed using indexes and other tools.

It is also necessary to have a reasonable familiarity with the items held in the collection, how they are organised and how the tools available make these items accessible. Staff must also be able to translate the borrower's description of their needs into the language of the tools that access the collection.[20]

If the user must be referred elsewhere, knowledge of sources and services, such as other special libraries and union catalogues, and how they can be accessed is also necessary. Networking with other information services is invaluable here also.

Clearly in this area, professional staff may not be as proficient as possible, although from personal, and on-the-job experience their knowledge would not be insignificant. All ARIS staff are responsible for abstracting new materials and indexing journal articles, which certainly helps them to locate current materials when requested.

It is in this area, that the literature located on the training needs of library assistants and technicians could be most useful. In practice, since professional staff are all part-time, it is often difficult to make time to provide training, and for that training to be reinforced with later exercises. The list of baseline subject competencies prepared by Benefiel, Miller and Ramirez[21] could also be useful although it was developed for larger academic libraries, so may need some variation for special libraries.

In terms of referrals to useful contacts in the field and the provision of educational advice, professional staff should be able to locate and provide this information very effectively.

## Providing Critical and Evaluative Advice on Information Located

Again, the working knowledge that professional staff have of the needs and situations of users is invaluable here. "The ability to determine what is good, bad, or indifferent for a given individual with a given question is the heart of the matter."[22] Clients need staff to select, analyze and evaluate information[23] so that their needs are met. This extends to providing ideas on ways to use or develop materials for a particular person in a particular situation and so professional experience is vital. Similarly, clients quite often ask for information that has been superseded, or about administrative requirements that authorities have amended and so they can be advised appropriately.

## Other Outcomes for Clients

A brief note must be made of other advantages and disadvantages for clients. The current assignment of tasks such as abstracting and indexing has a dual advantage for clients as it ensures that reference staff are aware of current issues in the literature. It also contributes to staff members' own professional development. Since all ARIS professional staff are part-time, when clients seek the expertise of a particular person, it is not always easy to catch them. However, this does enable (or requires) staff to participate in other ALBE workplaces which thereby keeps them fully up-to-date on what is happening in the 'real world' of ALBE. Funding too must be mentioned. Increased resources would enable various improvements, for example, training for professional staff and purchase of a public access terminal. As mentioned above, limited funding is not unusual for providers and services in the ALBE field.

## How Well Does ARIS Provide Reference Services?

This is difficult to ascertain as until October 1997, only anecdotal evaluative information in a number of forms was available. Unsolicited comments and letters of thanks were almost always positive and visitors coming for the first time often commented that a friend or colleague had found ARIS very helpful.

In October 1997, an evaluation[24] of the service was conducted using phone and in-person interviews, and a mailed questionnaire. Feedback on the whole service was very positive but unfortunately, analysis of the reference service was limited to four questions. However, over 96% of respondents found that the staff were helpful and informative and that the resources in the collection were useful. Difficulties associated with using the service, included distance (from user) and the loan period. No comments were made regarding the effectiveness or otherwise of the reference staff.

A more thorough evaluation of reference service provision would be most useful, perhaps against performance measures identified by an Australian working party for reference services.[25]

## CONCLUSIONS

The unusual structure of ARIS reference services was developed in response to the needs of teachers and practitioners in the ALBE field in Australia. Other models of service in which a combination of information service professionals and educational professionals provide reference services have not yet been located.

The are a number of areas in which this model may bring distinct advantages to clients. For example, in terms of subject knowledge and ease of communication in the reference interview, professional staff can bring invaluable skills and experience.

In terms of bibliographic knowledge and searching skills, professional staff may not be as proficient as information services professionals. At ARIS, this is often balanced by the professional staff and the IS Officer working in tandem to assist clients.

Although a full evaluation is required, there has certainly been sufficient informal feedback from clients to indicate that this model of service meets their needs. How it can be developed and improved to keep up with their needs is the challenge at hand.

## REFERENCES

1. Language Australia receives Victorian government funding to run ARIS. ARIS supports adult educators, particularly those involved in adult literacy, English language and numeracy in community based providers and TAFE (Technical and Further Education) colleges.

2. Ian Kendall, Community Education Tutors: Their Needs and Aspirations, Melbourne: Adult, Community and Further Education Board, Victoria (ACFE), 1993. pp. 12-26.

3. Jan Kindler et al., Certificates in General Education for Adults, Melbourne: Adult, Community and Further Education Board, Victoria (ACFE), 1996. This is the most widely used adult basic education curriculum in Australia.

4. Sharon Coates et al., National Reporting System, Canberra: Department of Employment, Education and Training and Australian National Training Authority, 1995.

5. Dave Tout and Betty Johnston, Adult Numeracy Teaching: Making Meaning in Mathematics, Melbourne: National Staff Development Committee for Vocational Education and Training, 1995.

6. Vocational Education and Training Database, Leabrook, S. Aust.; National Centre for Vocational Education and Research, 1990- <http://www.ncver.edu.au/voced. htm>.

7. Elspeth Miller (ed.), Australian Education Index, Melbourne: Australian Council of Educational Research, 1958- .

8. Elspeth Miller and Margaret Findlay, Australian Thesaurus of Education Descriptors, 2nd ed., Melbourne: Australian Council of Educational Research, 1996.

9. William A. Katz, Introduction to Reference Work Volume I: Basic Information Sources, 6th ed., New York: McGraw Hill, 1992. p. 3.

10. Katz, p. 3.

11. Richard E. Bopp and Linda C. Smith, Reference and information services: An introduction, Englewood, Colo: Libraries Unlimited, 1991. pp. 12-14.

12. Katz, p. 16.

13. Library and Information Science Abstracts: LISA, [CD-ROM], Bowker-Saur, 1969-June 1998. ; Australian Library and Information Science Abstracts: ALISA, [CD-ROM], Melbourne: Informit, 1982-March 1998. ; Elspeth Miller (ed.), Australian Education Index, Melbourne: Australian Council of Educational Research, 1958-June 1998. ; ERIC, Washington: ERIC Clearinghouse on Assessment and Evaluation, 1976-1998. <http://www.ericae.net/scripts/ewiz/amain2.asp>.

14. Bopp and Smith, p. 21.

15. Herbert S. White, "Professional Librarians and Professionals in Libraries," Library Journal 116, (January 1991): 75.

16. John G. Zenelis and Jean M. Dorrian, SPEC Flyer 212: Non-Librarian Professionals, Washington: Association of Research Libraries, 1995. pp. i-ii.

17. For example: Candace R. Benefiel, Jeannie P. Miller and Diana Ramirez, "Baseline Subject Competencies for the Academic Reference Desk," Reference Services Review 25 (Spring 1997): 83-93; Bopp and Smith, p. 42-55; Guidelines for Behavioral Performance of Reference and Information Services Professionals, Washington: RASD Ad Hoc Committee on Behavioral Guidelines for Reference and Information Services, 1996. <http://www.ala.org/rusa/behavior.html>; Miriam Tees, "The Reference Librarian in the Small Information Center: Selection and Training." The Reference Librarian 14 (Spring/Summer 1986): 61-65.

18. As recommended in Bopp and Smith, p. 44.

19. Bopp and Smith, p. 47-48.

20. Katz, p. 17.

21. Benefiel, Miller and Ramirez, especially pp. 91-93.

22. Katz, p. 34.

23. Tees, p. 62.

24. Vivian Faraj, ARIS: An Evaluation of Services, Melbourne: V. Faraj, 1997.

25. Rosemary Cotter et al., CAVAL Reference Interest Group Working Party on Performance Measures for Reference Services: First Report, Melbourne: CAVAL, 1995, especially pp. 25-28.

# The University Library's Role in Planning a Successful Distance Learning Program

## Jon R. Hufford

**SUMMARY.** This article examines the role a university library plays in planning the student support services that are so crucial to a successful distance learning program. The content of the paper is based on the experience the author acquired as a member of Texas Tech University's Distance Learning Council. The Council's efforts to plan, prioritize, and develop a distance learning program that will include strong support from the Library are emphasized. The work of the Distance Learning Council and its committees is discussed when it relates to the TTU Library's contribution to the program. *[Article copies available for a fee from The Haworth Document Delivery Service: 1-800-342-9678. E-mail address: <getinfo@ haworthpressinc.com> Website: <http://www.haworthpressinc.com>]*

**KEYWORDS.** Distance learning, student support services, collaboralism

A transformation is occurring in how universities teach students. New technology, changes in the makeup of student bodies, with adults, minorities, women, and foreign students participating in ever increasing numbers, and distance learning are major components in this transformation. The University Continuing Education Association recently published a report titled *Lifelong*

Jon R. Hufford is affiliated with Texas Tech University Library, 18th and Boston, Lubbock, TX 79409.

[Haworth co-indexing entry note]: "The University Library's Role in Planning a Successful Distance Learning Program." Hufford, Jon R. Co-published simultaneously in *The Reference Librarian* (The Haworth Information Press, an imprint of The Haworth Press, Inc.) No. 69/70, 2000, pp. 193-203; and: *Reference Services for the Adult Learner: Challenging Issues for the Traditional and Technological Era* (ed: Kwasi Sarkodie-Mensah) The Haworth Information Press, an imprint of The Haworth Press, Inc., 2000, pp. 193-203. Single or multiple copies of this article are available for a fee from The Haworth Document Delivery Service [1-800-342-9678, 9:00 a.m. - 5:00 p.m. (EST). E-mail address: getinfo@haworthpressinc.com].

*Learning Trends: A Profile of Continuing Education* (1998). This report describes several of the trends bringing about this transformation. One trend is the great potential of the adult population in the United States for participation in distance learning. According to the Association's report, distance learning has become an appealing alternative for working adults with career and family responsibilities who want to enhance their education. Other trends include the fast and consistent growth of jobs in occupations requiring more education, and the increased number of American households that have access to technology-based instruction (*Lifelong Learning Trends*, 1998, p. 23, 79, 85).

## THE UNIVERSITY'S ROLE

Universities are facing challenges and are offered opportunities in this new learning environment. Careful planning and determined action are needed to successfully meet the challenges and take advantage of the opportunities. Experiments in distance learning that have no clear goals will very likely fail.

One of the challenges is that, although greater demands are being placed on universities, resources have not grown proportionally. Given this situation, a plan of action can go a long way towards narrowing the gap between new demands and available resources. The planning requires a long-term strategic approach. This approach should include an analysis of the environment, making strategic choices, and setting and prioritizing goals. A liberal dose of imagination and action are also necessary. Throughout the entire planning process, it is vitally important that the university faculty and staff responsible for the program focus on the key elements of the new learning environment. These key elements include recognizing the need for new educational systems, correctly identifying constituents that the distance learning program will serve, developing support services for the constituents, developing a good technical infrastructure and a cooperative network for sharing information and experiences, and acquiring skilled staff (Pohjonen, 1997, p. 369-371).

Another challenge is that views on education, learning, and information technology change quickly in today's environment. In fact, the life span of particular electronic learning environments that are dependent on particular technologies is becoming shorter all the time. Some of these environments are already out of date when they are introduced to the public. The rapid growth of knowledge and technology is responsible for this short life span. Because of this rapid development, universities must learn to respond faster and plan better. Also, they must spend sufficient amounts of money, time, and staff talent during the developmental phase of a distance learning program (Pohjonen, 1997, p. 371-2).

## THE LIBRARY'S ROLE

More than anything else, the success of a distance learning program depends on the distance learning courses offered. A significant factor contributing to the success of these courses is the ease with which students can accomplish the library research needed to complete the assignments their professors give them (Edge, 1995, p. 10). Library personnel are expected to assist distance students in several ways. In general, the goals of a comprehensive university library support program for distance education should include reference services, information literacy instruction, and document delivery services. The successful implementation of these goals depends on library staff projecting its traditional ethos of service to the patrons to also include distance learning students.

## LITERATURE REVIEW

Institutional planning for distance learning is reasonably well documented, especially in unpublished form. Several of the materials available include information about library contributions to distance learning. Whereas unpublished documents are available that treat planning in some depth, published materials tend to cover the topic in a cursory manner. Several of the unpublished documents are available in the Educational Resources Information Center (ERIC) Microfiche Collection. Also, several online documents are available on Web sites that define an institution's vision or plan of action for distance learning. Like the published materials, these online documents tend not to be developed plans. Rather, they are advertising instruments for distance learning programs. The ERIC Collection includes materials on the more traditional kind of distance learning that state universities and community colleges have been delivering for years through television, radio, and video and audio cassettes. Information on planning the kind of distance learning that is associated with the computer tends to be more readily available on the Internet, though it can also be found in unpublished documents in the ERIC Collection.

*Role of Libraries in Distance Education, SPEC Kit 216,* an ERIC document that is dated July 1996, reports on the results of a survey of 119 Association of Research Libraries members that gathered information about distance learning initiatives in ARL libraries. The specific objectives of the survey were to identify libraries involved in distance learning activities and their level of involvement, to determine the kinds of library services delivered to remote patrons, and to ascertain the management and support levels provided by libraries for distance learning programs (Snyder et al., 1996). Additional statistics on distance learning are available in the National Center for Education Statistics' issue brief: *Distance Education in Higher Education Institutions: Incidence, Audience, and Plans to Expand* and in its statistical analysis report: *Distance Education in Higher Education Institutions* (National Center for Education Statistics, 1998 and 1997).

A subject guide to Web-accessible resources concerned with library support of distance learning is available at a site titled *Library Support for Distance Learning* (http://www.lis.uiuc.edu/~sloan/libdist.htm) (Sloan). In addition to links to general sites on distance learning, it includes links to several Web-accessible papers and articles that provide a critical perspective to distance learning. There are also links to over 50 Web-accessible papers, articles, and reports dealing specifically with library support for distance learning and more than 60 individual library sites that include descriptions of how these libraries offer services to distance learners.

Information on distance learning policy at all levels of higher education is available on the Western Cooperative for Educational Telecommunications' Web site (http://www.wiche.edu/telecom/telecom.htm). The Cooperative is a membership organization established in 1989 by the Western Interstate Commission for Higher Education (*Western Cooperative for Educational Telecommunications,* 9 October 1998). Also, the State University of New York's University Distance Learning Panel recommendations are available on the World Wide Web *(The SUNY Learning Network)* at http://sln1.esc.edu/admin/sln/original.nsf, and a review of the policies guiding the Western Governors University is available online. The WGU, consisting of seventeen higher education institutions, began its initial pilot program phase in February 1998 (Edwards, 17 February 1998).

Documents are available in the ERIC Collection that report on the planning efforts of state educational agencies in the area of distance learning. *Toward a State of Learning (Achieving the Vision III); Strategic Planning for the University of Maryland System* (1995) provides an overview of the challenges facing the institutions belonging to the University of Maryland System in the coming years and the strategic planning efforts that the institutions' administrators and faculty will have to take to meet these challenges. *Coming of Information Age in California Higher Education* (1997), authored by the California State Post-secondary Education Commission, documents the vision this agency has for distance learning in California's future. This report presents an overview of some of the major issues facing California higher education as it moves into the Information Age. "Administration, Management and Policy," chapter nine of *Distance Education: A Systems View* (Moore and Kearsley, 1996), discusses distance learning issues related to planning, staffing, resources, budgeting, scheduling, quality assessment, and policy making.

Two ERIC documents discuss distance learning activities in foreign countries. *China's Radio and TV Universities and the British Open University: A Comparative Perspective* (Runfang, 1997) examines the origins, objectives, structures, costs, funding, programs, and teaching and learning of the radio and television universities in China and the British Open University. The author discusses the growth and development of higher education and the philosophies underpinning practice at these institutions. *Determining the Scope of Online Delivery at a Traditional Research-based University* (Mason, 1996) includes a brief summary of the key factors that have facilitated the implementation of the online delivery of teaching programs at the University of Melbourne (Australia), including the importance of strategic planning.

## TEXAS TECH UNIVERSITY'S PLAN OF ACTION

With the intention of meeting the challenges and benefiting from the opportunities associated with the transformation that is taking place in higher education, the Texas Tech University administration formed the Telecommunications Infrastructure Fund/Distance Education Vision Committee in the fall of 1996. In an effort to encourage a sense of involvement and commitment at all levels across campus, faculty from various departments, departmental chairpersons, associate deans, directors, and a vice-provost were asked to participate as members of the Committee. The Committee's assigned task was to develop a vision statement for the future of distance learning at the University. The main theme of the Committee's final report (May 27, 1997) was that, by early in the next century, the University should become a national leader in changing the paradigm of higher education through distance learning (Texas Tech University, 1997, part 2).

The "Vision" Committee recommended in its report that a permanent administrative unit be created that would be responsible for insuring the university's ability to achieve this position of leadership. More specifically, the unit would be responsible for facilitating the development and delivery of distance learning and for fostering collaborative distance learning relationships with educational institutions throughout West Texas. The report recommended that the unit concentrate on four areas: distance learning infrastructure and operations, distance learning program development, coordination and support, and information services and technologies. The unit would insure that the academic components of the institution become equipped and supported at the level necessary to provide their constituencies access to and the benefit of developing distance learning and information technologies. Further, the unit would interface with other academic units on campus, respond to the inter-institutional distance learning challenges within Texas, and take advantage of new developments in distance learning and information technology which impact the University's mission.

The University President accepted the Committee's recommendations and, late in 1997, appointed the Vice-Provost for Outreach and Extended Studies to be the administrative officer responsible for the unit. The Vice-Provost for Outreach and Extended studies serves permanently as the Distance Learning Council's chair. At the same time, the President accepted the recommendation that a Distance Learning Council be created to advise the Vice-Provost and to assist in providing strategic direction for the distance learning program. The Council is a standing body with representation from each of the major academic and service units of the University. It is presently responsible for developing policies that will define distance learning priorities and activities. When completed, these policies will guide the overall development and implementation of distance learning at Texas Tech University (Texas Tech University, 1997, p. 2-3).

In addition, the Distance Learning Technology Committee was created as a standing subcommittee of the Council. This Committee will be responsible for the ongoing development of recommendations for campus computing and network standards and design, system computing and network standards and design, distance learning classroom design, interactive video systems design, and satellite and other alternative delivery systems. The Committee also will coordinate the review, evaluation, and demonstration of new technologies for potential adoption and application in the distance learning programs of the University. The Council will be able to appoint additional standing and/or ad hoc committees when the need arises.

## THE DISTANCE LEARNING COUNCIL AND ITS COMMITTEES

Early in 1998, the chair of the Distance Learning Council set up working committees to address the Council's responsibilities. Each council member is assigned to one of these Distance Learning Council committees. Each committee has undertaken to study its assigned area and then write a report that will include recommendations for its area of responsibilities. Working committees are in place to address student services and course management, faculty issues and programs, and institutional relations and issues. Although it is likely that these committees will sit for several months, it is unclear at this time whether they will continue to exist once all the reports are completed.

## THE STUDENT SERVICES
## AND COURSE MANAGEMENT WORKING COMMITTEE

An area frequently neglected in the development of distance learning programs is student support services. Support for students at a distance in-

cludes registration, enrollment, and transcript services; access to student
advisors; academic counseling; and financial aid services. Also included are
such services as access to library and research materials, bookstore services,
timely receipt of instructor materials for courses, technical support, and communication with other students.

The Distance Learning Council decided early on to make student support
services an important part of Texas Tech University's distance learning program. Several members of the Council identified library services as being
especially important. The fact that the Associate Dean of the University
Libraries and the Libraries' Coordinator of User Instruction are members of
the Council has helped to reinforce this belief.

With this in mind, the chair of the Distance Learning Council established
the Student Services and Course Management Working Committee. The
Committee's members include the University's Director of Extended Learning, who is serving as chair, the Libraries' Dean and Coordinator of User
Instruction, the Director of the University Transition Advisement Center, and
the Associate to the Vice President for Student Affairs. Some of the Committee's more important responsibilities are developing an inventory of potential
constituents to be served, defining their characteristics, identifying the elements of the learning context for constituents, identifying market forces
driving educational requirements, developing approaches for providing service, and developing uniform guidelines for support services for distance
students. These responsibilities will serve as a framework for writing the
Committee's report.

The Student Services and Course Management Committee began its work
in February of 1998 and has met several times since. However, the original
goal of completing its report by the end of the summer turned out to be
unrealistic. Efforts to write the report have continued into the fall, with no
prospect for completion in the foreseeable future.

Nevertheless, much discussion and research on policy issues such as those
discussed below have and will continue to take place. The Committee recognizes that thorough and careful policy development is a key component of a
successful distance learning initiative. Its rationale is that all too frequently
the toughest distance learning policy questions remain unasked. Also, some
issues may seem minor at first and thus receive minimal consideration. Yet
later on these issues often become major stumbling blocks to a successful
distance learning program. Asking the really tough questions early in the
policy development process can go a long way towards avoiding potential
policy pitfalls and contribute to the quality, rigor, and strength of a distance
learning program. With this in mind, the Student Services and Course Management Working Committee has approached its responsibilities in a deliberate manner.

The Committee has discussed on several occasions the issue of what should be the appropriate level of service for distance learning students. It decided that Texas Tech University's distance learning student must be offered the same level of service quality that on-campus students receive. The Committee is acting on the assumption that it is critical for a program's student service policies to be developed with quality service to the distance students always in mind. Committee members have found it helpful when discussing policies to work through the steps that students must take to learn about courses and programs, enroll in them, participate in the classes, and successfully complete a distance learning course or program. The Committee is firmly convinced that strong student service policies can greatly increase a distance learning program's chances for success.

Another issue that the Committee is discussing is whether a single department or office should handle all questions from distance learning students who may have difficulties in any number of critical areas, including computer-related connection problems, registration glitches, undelivered textbooks, or advisement options. Would a single office serve the students best? If so, which office should be responsible? Or should there be a central office or clearinghouse that refers students to other offices or departments for specialized assistance?

## TEXAS TECH UNIVERSITY LIBRARIES' SERVICES CURRENTLY IN PLACE FOR DISTANCE LEARNERS

The Libraries are well positioned to support distance learning at Texas Tech University. The primary means of providing library services to Texas Tech University's distance students is through Internet access to the Libraries' Web site. The University's Academic Computing Service provides Point-to-point Protocol (PPP) accounts for access to Web-based electronic resources requiring user validation/IP addresses. The cost of these accounts to distance learning students is $45.00 per semester plus long distance phone charges. Telnet access to the Texas Tech University Libraries' online catalog and several other databases are also available.

Several resources that provide valuable services to distance students are available on the Libraries' Web site. A link on the site introduces distance students to all the services available to them. This same electronic document is also available as a printed handout. The Web site also provides access to reference assistance. Distance students can submit questions on the site and expect to receive answers either on the same day the questions were submitted or the morning of the next workday. Additional links provide current news about the Libraries, a staff directory, and links to Internet resources compiled by the Libraries' subject librarians. The staff directory includes e-mail links to subject librarians and other staff personnel. There is also a tutorial available on how to conduct library research and online forms for requesting delivery of University-owned material and interlibrary loans. Both the library-owned and interlibrary loan materials that are requested using the forms can be mailed or faxed to a distance student's home or office. Finally, distance students have access to scanned materials placed on reserve by instructors at the Electronic Reserve link on the Libraries' Web site, and there are countless full-text resources available on the site and throughout the Internet.

Upon request, distance students who want to avoid purchasing a bar-coded Texas Tech University ID card are mailed a library card with a bar-code. The bar-code number is necessary for access to all databases requiring user validation. Also upon request, a TexShare library card will be mailed to distance students. This card permits the holder to borrow books from other Texas academic libraries.

The Texas Tech University Libraries will have additional services made available to distance students in the near future. The Libraries will soon have a proxy server that will provide direct access to Web-based databases restricted by Internet Protocol (IP) addresses, thus bypassing the need for a Texas Tech University Point-to-point Protocol (PPP) account. Students will then be able to use America Online (AOL) or other Internet providers to access all Web-based resources supplied by the Texas Tech University Libraries.

Another service that will be implemented soon is desktop (computer to computer) delivery of articles to patrons from Texas Tech University Libraries and interlibrary loan sources. Renewal of books, requests for "recalls" of books and other material checked out to someone else, and accessing personal borrowing information, such as information on books currently checked out or overdue items, are other services that will be made available in the next few months.

## *TEXAS TECH UNIVERSITY LIBRARIES' SERVICES IN THE PLANNING STAGES*

There are several services for distance students that Texas Tech University Libraries may adopt soon. Some of these services are a distance learners' Web page, an 800 phone number, a library card that is electronically transmitted to students, customized library instruction, express delivery of Library materials, and the establishment of a Library team that would coordinate distance learning services and respond to future needs.

## *CONCLUSION*

As was pointed out earlier in this article, careful planning and determined action are prerequisites to successfully meet the challenges and take advantage of the opportunities in the new learning environment. The strategic approach required should include an analysis of the environment, making strategic choices, setting and prioritizing goals, imagination, and action. The university faculty and staff responsible for the distance learning program must recognize the need for new educational systems, correctly identify constituents, develop adequate support services, develop a good technical infrastructure and a cooperative network for sharing information and experiences, and acquire skilled staff. Also, universities must respond to new developments quickly and be ready to spend sufficient funds for development.

A university library's role in this strategic planning is to provide the best possible support for distance learning courses. A significant factor contributing to the success of the courses is the ease with which students can accomplish the library research needed to complete the assignments their professors give them. Generally, the library support that makes success possible includes reference service, information literacy instruction, and document delivery services. Ultimately, the successful implementation of these services depends on library staff projecting their traditional ethos of service to the patrons to also include distance learning students.

Texas Tech University, with strong support from the Library, has taken a strategic approach in planning its distance learning program. The formation of the "Vision" Committee that authored a vision statement, the establishment of a distance learning administrative unit with a council to assist and advise it and council committees that are developing recommendations for defined areas in distance learning are developments that reflect careful planning and determined action. When completed, the committee reports will include the results of such activities as environmental analyses, making strategic choices, and setting and prioritizing goals.

## REFERENCES

California State Post-secondary Education Commission. (1997, February). *Coming of Information Age in California Higher Education.* Sacramento: California State Post-secondary Education Commission. ERIC Document Reproduction Service No. ED 405 768, microfiche.

Edwards, J. (1998, February 17). Western Governors University Begins Pilot Phase. [online]. Available: HTTP: http://www.westgov.org/smart/vu/pilotrelease.html

*Lifelong Learning Trends: A Profile of Continuing Higher Education* (5th ed.). (1998). Washington, DC: University Continuing Education Association.

Mason, Jon. (1996, July 7-10). *Determining the Scope of online Delivery at a Traditional Research-based University.* In *Learning Technologies: Prospects and Pathways. Selected papers from EdTech '96 Biennial Conference of the Australian Society for Educational Technology* (pp. 77-81). Melbourne, Australia: Society for Educational Technology, University of Melbourne. ERIC Document Reproduction Service No. ED 396 731, microfiche.

Moore, Michael G. and Greg Kearsley. (1996). "Administration, Management and Policy." In *Distance Education: A Systems View* (pp. 172-196). Belmont: Wadsworth Publishing.

National Center for Education Statistics. (1997). *Distance Education in Higher Education* (NCES 98-062). Washington, DC: U.S. Government Printing Office.

National Center for Education Statistics. (1998). *Distance Education in Higher Education Institutions: Incidence, Audiences, and Plans to Expand* (NCES 98-132). Washington, DC: U.S. Government Printing Office.

Pohjonen, Juha. (1997, December). "New Learning Environments as a Strategic Choice." *European Journal of Education, 32*, 369-377.

Runfang, Wei. (1997, May). *China's Radio and TV Universities and the British Open University: A Comparative Perspective. ZIPP Papiere 104.* Hagen, Germany: Fern University, Institute for Research into Distance Education. ERIC Document Reproduction Service ED 407 601, microfiche.

Sloan, Bernie. (n.d.). Library Support for Distance Learning. Graduate School of Library and Information Science. University of Illinois at Urbana-Champaign. [online]. Available HTTP: http://www.lis.uiuc.edu/~sloan/libdist.htm

Snyder, Carolyn A. and others, comps. (1996, July). *Role of Libraries in Distance Education. SPEC Kit 216.* Washington, DC: Association of Research Libraries. ERIC Document Reproduction Service No. ED 398 930, microfiche.

The SUNY Learning Network. (n.d.). [online]. Available HTTP: http://sln1.esc.edu/admin/sln/original.nsf

Texas Tech University. Telecommunications Infrastructure Fund/Distance Learning Vision Committee. (1997, May). "A Vision for Distance Learning at Texas Tech University." Lubbock, TX: Texas Tech University.

University of Maryland. System Administration, Adelphi. (1995, October). *Toward a State of Learning (Achieving the Vision III). Strategic Planning for the University of Maryland System.* ERIC Document Reproduction Service No. ED 405 765, microfiche.

Western Cooperative for Educational Telecommunications. (1998 October 9). [online]. Available HTTP: http://www.wiche.edu/telecom/telecom.htm

# Library Services to External Students from Australian Universities: The Influence of Flexible Delivery upon Traditional Service Provision

Michael Middleton
Judith Peacock

**SUMMARY.** Distance education services provided by a number of Australian university libraries are considered. Attention is paid to agreements between libraries, library staff involvement in program and information skills development, evaluation of services, and the evolution of online delivery. This paper establishes that little provision is made for the specific support of the adult learner in distance education and argues that flexible delivery initiatives are diminishing the distinction between on- and off-campus services, irrespective of client-base. *[Article copies available for a fee from The Haworth Document Delivery Service: 1-800-342-9678. E-mail address: <getinfo@haworthpressinc.com> Website: <http://www.haworthpressinc.com>]*

**KEYWORDS.** Distance education, higher education, academic libraries, World Wide Web, educational change, adult education, library role, open universities, Australia, user needs information

Michael Middleton and Judith Peacock are respectively Senior Lecturer, School of Information Systems, and Reference Librarian, Gardens Point Library, Queensland University of Technology, 2 George Street, Brisbane, Queensland, Australia (E-mail: m.middleton@qut.edu.au and j.peacock@qut.edu.au).

The authors would like to thank Tony Cavanagh, Christine Cother, Jo Kellett, Olga Lipsky, Susan Lutley, Jenny McCarthy, Jennifer Redding and Mary Anne Secker for discussions and input into this paper.

[Haworth co-indexing entry note]: "Library Services to External Students from Australian Universities: The Influence of Flexible Delivery upon Traditional Service Provision." Middleton, Michael, and Judith Peacock. Co-published simultaneously in *The Reference Librarian* (The Haworth Information Press, an imprint of The Haworth Press, Inc.) No. 69/70, 2000, pp. 205-217; and: *Reference Services for the Adult Learner: Challenging Issues for the Traditional and Technological Era* (ed: Kwasi Sarkodie-Mensah) The Haworth Information Press, an imprint of The Haworth Press, Inc., 2000, pp. 205-217. Single or multiple copies of this article are available for a fee from The Haworth Document Delivery Service [1-800-342-9678, 9:00 a.m. - 5:00 p.m. (EST). E-mail address: getinfo@haworthpressinc.com].

## INTRODUCTION

Within the last decade we have seen rapid expansion of facilities for remote provision of education. In the higher education sector, the accompanying procedures have been variously called external studies, open learning, distance education, off-campus instruction and flexible delivery. Much endeavour has been devoted to making definitional distinctions, and to determining the effectiveness with which they may be undertaken.

These educational approaches all assume a greater reliance upon resource-based independent learning with an expectation that libraries or resource centres will complement educational materials. Libraries themselves must reconcile limited funding for acquisition with a greater diversity of information sources, notably those that may be delivered digitally.

Life long learning is a common contemporary social and political aspiration. It brings with it attendant pressures on the more mature members of society to re-enter what, for many, are educational structured and administered quite differently to those of previous experience. Learning characteristics of adults have been identified to the extent that educational processes may be tailored to their needs. As most participants in distance education are adults, such refinements must also incorporate appropriate and timely methods of information resource provision and service delivery.

Distance education is long established in the Australian university environment–hardly surprising, considering the size and population distribution within the country. For example in 1910 the University of Queensland followed the lead of the University of London and provided distance education opportunities for teachers (Australia, National Board of Employment, Education and Training, 1992).

Here we investigate, within the Australian university sector, the way in which distance education has been advanced within a framework of resource and service provision that is integrated with learning management with reference to the learner as adult.

## ADULT LEARNING

Educators have been at some pains to distinguish the special characteristics and needs of adult learners. If a tertiary level student enrolled in conventional mode may be reckoned as relatively young, studying full time, having good access to academic staff, and attending tutorials and lectures in the customary manner, then adult learners will be upwards of their mid-twenties, studying part time, and often making use of educational materials that give them greater flexibility of learning styles.

The features that distinguish adults as learners have been widely discussed in the educational literature. They may be described in summary as: (a) self-direction that provides a degree of autonomy of pursuit of knowledge within a critical framework; (b) collaborative approaches using the experience of peers as a resource; (c) motivational factors such as progress towards well-defined goals; (d) incorporation of new material within an existing framework of comprehension; (e) using their own experience as a resource, and (f) competing study time, workplace and domestic priorities.

As adults have multiple roles, responsibilities and opportunities, they exhibit an orientation to education and learning singularly different to that of the adolescent learner. Since they often involve themselves in learning of their own volition, their motivation may be in accord with long range goals, and be applied to specific problems. However, it is doubtful that the reaction against perpetuation of upper middle class values by the higher education system that precipitated adult learning in England (Trump, interviewed by Scott, 1988) continues to be a specific force. In Australia at least, labour force reform, in conjunction with initiatives of earlier governments to create a multi-skilled workforce, has had a significant bearing.

The accumulated and consolidated life experience of adults may itself be a threat to self-concept if the learning experience promotes a transformation away from the foundation of past experience on which self-concept is based. This reserve of experience makes adult learners themselves important learning resources. However, they may not have the level of self-understanding to embark upon an unsettling process of learning that can take them away from the comfort of the known and understandable, to the insecurities that may be associated with assimilation of new knowledge.

Adult physical, psychological and social developmental changes will influence their receptiveness to learning. This may be associated with realigned personal goals associated with different family circumstances or a different energy level (Brookfield, 1986, p. 30).

In a learning context, adults are therefore more likely to: (a) plan effective use of appropriate learning resources; (b) establish and carry out self-directed learning plans; (c) validate their learning objectives with personal performance measures; (d) make use of experience for accomplishing learning objectives; (e) pursue curiosities for their own enlightenment; (f) anticipate their own learning needs with respect to identifiable competencies; and (g) accept and act upon constructive feedback on performance.

These principles lend themselves to flexible delivery for which we use the definition given by Chalmers (as cited in Clark & Store, 1998): "the provision of learning and assessment opportunities in modes which serve to increase the degree of student control over when, where, how and at what pace they learn." Such flexible delivery may of course include that to remote students.

## DISTANCE EDUCATION AND LIBRARY ROLE

The 'distance' in education has been widely interpreted. For example, it may be psychological, economic or cultural and not distinguishable purely by geography (Burge, Snow & Howard, 1989); the geographic distance may be quite small or, to some extent, irrelevant. In fact, over half of Australia's 'distance education' students live within metropolitan areas (Australia, National Board of Employment, Education and Training, 1992).

Irrespective, the participants in distance education have an expectation that the resource basis for their learning is equivalent to that of on-campus students. This places a burden on libraries to provide the resources and services that on-campus students seek for themselves.

The part to be played by libraries has been considered in some detail in a variety of environments (Burge, Snow & Howard, 1989; Heery, 1996; Jagannathan, 1996; Shklanka, 1990). These writers and others emphasise: (a) the importance of reliable and equitable access to the resources of host institution libraries; (b) the need for development of course materials with reference to incorporation of resource materials; (c) the need for joint development by academics and librarians of course materials; (d) the need for promotion of library services; (e) the need for dialogue between learners and instructors to be supported by organised mechanisms for information access; (f) the need to carry out evaluation of library resource provision as part of course evaluation; and (g) the need for evaluation of library system utilisation.

An example of library system evaluation is described by Wilson (1995) who measured increases in confidence among isolated undergraduate students in 12 study areas. Only two groups, health science and library studies, increased in confidence in use of remote online sources during the course of their study. This was attributed to course context in the case of library studies students, but was not explained in the case of health science students. Although work such as this give some insight to conduct of users, Burge, Snow and Howard (1986) contend that there has been little evidence of development of an adult-learner centered model of library use behaviour.

## LIBRARY PRACTICE

Many practical examples of library participation contribute to fulfilling their role. Among these are: (a) assigning specific library positions and duties for supporting distance learners; (b) providing a service for supply of materials that are complementary to course materials through post or courier; (c) making arrangements with local libraries such as public libraries or educational libraries, that may include joint purchasing of materials, reciprocal borrowing and interlending rights; (d) provision of catalogue access through networked arrangements or by access to local institutions that provide such access; (e) user assistance via call center or similar help service, allowing students to make requests and enquiries by post, fax or telephone; (f) searching electronic databases on behalf of students who then receive the results by post or email; (g) facilitation of teleconferencing or videoconferencing; (h) provision of photocopy vouchers; (i) provision of training in study skills and information skills through off-campus centres, short residential courses, videocassette, networked material, or CD-based material for home PCs; (j) promotion by means of introductory material in print and digital form with contact information so that beginning students are given an idea of what to expect in relation to lending and access policies.

An Australian survey of higher educational library support, for what were then termed external students, was conducted a decade ago (Croker & Grimison, 1989). The resulting document itemised services offered by 49 higher educational institutions that offered some form of external studies.

The data collection form that was used illuminates what might be expected from such institutions. Respondents were asked to indicate whether facilities provided included: (a) an answering service; (b) requests received by mail or telephone; (c) loans of audiovisual material, books, periodicals or prescribed texts; (d) free or paid photocopying services; (e) utilisation of postal service; (f) return postage paid for students; (g) information/referral services; (h) interlibrary loan for undergraduates and/or postgraduates; (i) online searches free or for a fee; and (j) service availability hours. Figure 1 is a consolidated summary of responses to some of these data that we have prepared.

With the restructuring of the higher education system in Australia, many of the institutions that responded to this survey have now been amalgamated into larger entities. In the next section we elaborate on how a number of them have modified services since that time.

## RECENT AUSTRALIAN DEVELOPMENTS

We collected information from a number of prominent institutions involved in the area of distance education, and confined the survey to tertiary institutions that provide formalised distance support through their libraries. Although the Vocational Education and Training sector in Australia also provides significant distance education support through the Technical and

FIGURE 1. External services–Australian academic libraries derived from Croker and Grimison (1989).

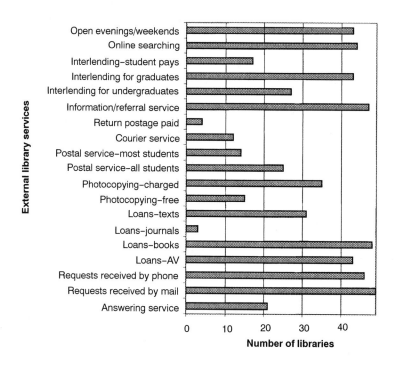

Further Education [TAFE] institutions, we have confined our analysis to the universities.

Information was gathered by structured telephone interview of specialist librarians involved in distance education. We sought information on: (a) agreements with other libraries for local support of students; (b) library staff involvement with program development through acquisition of supporting resources, instructional design or integration of information methods into course design; (c) promotion of library use either by faculty, by librarians directly through courseware, or in orientation packages; (d) evaluation of resource provision, or of information methods within courses; (e) development of online support through networks for access to resources; (f) development of information skills packages; and (g) special provision for adults that takes account of motivational, vocational, information technology exposure or other factors thought to be distinctive.

## AGREEMENTS WITH OTHER LIBRARIES

Australian universities provide usage and borrowing privileges to a range of external students, however their policies vary widely. A comparative list of such policies is available on the Internet (Deakin University, 1998). The universities work within this policy framework, often modulated by regional arrangements such as that of QULOC (Queensland University Libraries Office of Cooperation), and CAVAL (Cooperative Action by Victorian Academic Libraries).

Arrangements with public libraries did not extend beyond interlibrary loans. Although several of the universities have formerly attempted specific collection maintenance within remote public libraries, most of these arrangements are moribund or terminal. The exigencies of supporting remote students whose locations vary from year to year, and of monitoring materials in collections, has meant such arrangements have not been viable. Collections established at other libraries have been dismissed as a consequence.

While common practice relies heavily upon reciprocal arrangements for borrowing privileges, little provision has been allowed for on-site training in distant locations. Some use has been made of the TAFE Open Learning Centres for such training, but there are no formal arrangements in place.

The increasing availability of public Internet resources in public libraries through government funding at both state and federal levels (initiatives such as the regional telecommunications infrastructure fund 'Networking the Nation'), has assisted access for remote students. For example, Biloela Public Library in central Queensland has multiple Internet workstations.

## STAFF INVOLVEMENT WITH PROGRAM DEVELOPMENT

Librarians can make the following types of contributions in course teams: assisting the course writer(s) in identifying appropriate literature and network resources to support preparation .of the course; providing advice about networked electronic resources and Internet materials to which students can have access; providing information literacy components of the course; providing advice about the variety of learning resources that may be employed in relation to the place, mode and pace of delivery; and ensuring that staff in the Library know about new products and modes of delivery before student support issues arise (Clark & Store, 1998).

Most of the libraries surveyed have a structure of liaison or subject librarians within the main library structure. It is these librarians rather than off-campus librarians who have direct involvement in course development. However, their association has been mainly to ensure that appropriate library materials are acquired, rather than to assist the academic teaching staff to develop course-specific packages. An exception to this is in the health studies area at Edith Cowan University. Although other aspirations were expressed to participate in package development, we did not identify any other examples, except for collaborative efforts with library or information studies courses.

There is, however, a developing trend to devolve the instructional development, design and delivery of courses in distance mode to specialised work units external to faculties or libraries. These units may include specialist graphic designers and curriculum designers and assist in the development and delivery of print-based materials. At QUT, this includes complete instructional and editorial assistance, desktop publishing and printing of course resources. As a recent phenomenon, no formal links between such services and existing library services have been established, and collaborative efforts appear to be on an ad hoc basis.

## PROMOTION OF SERVICES

Most libraries produce packages of print material for enrolling students. These are either integrated into single volume introductory material, or are provided as modular fliers. This material is usually replicated on World Wide Web [WWW] sites with the list of contents forming links to informative material. Some libraries provide additional information via newsletters, either available in print or accessible online.

## EVALUATION OF SERVICES

Evaluation pertaining to support resources and services provided by libraries is predominantly incorporated as resource provision questions under the umbrella of course evaluation. This is in addition to in-house library evaluation of service support and information provision. We did not learn of any evaluations of organised interface provision to resources.

## DEVELOPMENT OF ONLINE SUPPORT

Australian universities in general make extensive use of the Internet for delivery of material. Universities with distance education services invariably maintain WWW pages that promote the off-campus service, provide information specific to distance students, provide avenues through forms, email or hyper-links to assistance catalogues and reference services. Table 1 lists example sites for such services in Australia.

TABLE 1. Australia university distance education sites.

| Institution Library | Service | URL |
|---|---|---|
| Central Queensland University | Off Campus services | http://www.library.cqu.edu.au/offcampus/ocs.htrn |
| Charles Sturt University | Distance Education Library Services | http://www.csu.edu.au/division/library/decont.htm |
| Deakin University | Off Campus Library Service | http://www.deakin.edu.au/library/ocserv.html |
| Edith Cowan University | External Library Services | http://www.cowan.edu.au/library/live/ext00001.htrn |
| Griffith University | Off Campus Library Services | http://rnedea.itc.gu.edu.au/lils/mg/distance.htrn |
| James Cook University | Off Campus Library Service | http://www.jcu.edu.au/gen/Library/offcamp.html |
| Monash University | Remote Library Services Unit | http://www-mugc.cc.monash.edu.au/glib/esu/flsuguide.htm |
| QUT | External Library Services | http://wwwlib.qut.edu.au/services/external/ |
| RMIT | External Services | http://www.lib.mit.edu.au/external/overview.html |
| University of New England | Off Campus Services | http://www.une.edu.au/library/ocshome.htm |
| University of South Australia | Distance Education Library Service | http://www.unisa.edu.au/library/fds/dels/dels.htm |
| University of Southern Queensland | Off Campus Library Services | http://www.usq.edu.au/library/offcamp/offcamp1.htm |
| UNSW. St George Campus | External Services | http://www.library.unsw.edu.au/~stg/extbroch.html |

This is done regardless of formal distance education procedures. Typical of such an approach is the Integrated Learning Environment in QUT's Faculty of Information Technology (Peacock & Middleton, 1997) makes use of an Internet interface integrated with CDROM material for delivery of course and learning materials. As do many similar universities that support distance education services, QUT Library makes no distinction between the online services for on- and off-campus users.

Many of the services traditionally provided exclusively by External Library Services (ELS) units are now provided, or supported, by those other sections within the library that have extended their services via electronic means. External students, for example, now have comprehensive access to bibliographic databases, allowing for a degree of autonomy in satisfying information needs. In light of recent technological innovations, current services provided by such units have been adapted accordingly, with emphasis on alterations to administrative procedures and information provision.

Extensive use is made of email as a communication tool, and distance users can also retrieve detailed information from the WWW pages of ELS units and lodge requests for information electronically via email or web-based forms. At QUT Library, discussion lists (implementing listserv technology) have also been implemented to provide support for distance students. Plans for further WWW-based developments include utilisation of QUT Library's E-Reserve and an electronic document delivery service. At this stage it is envisaged that the latter will operate independently of the Regional Document Delivery Project in which the library also participates with neighbouring universities. However, similar user authentication procedures and an automated registration procedure to ensure strict adherence to copyright ordinances are envisaged.

The number of external students currently make use of the electronic services is growing, and the impact of technology upon the role of ELS and their incorporated procedures has been significant. This is typical of many off-campus units, which estimate the proportion of distance students making regular Internet access at 25-40%. With continued emphasis in the wider educational arena on electronic delivery of information, the Internet-based services, in tandem with traditional service provision, will continue to dictate a focus.

Widespread use has been made of existing networks to mount a comprehensive selection of electronic databases at QUT, on CDROM or via the Internet, and all effort has been made to provide external access to these databases. The Library holds current subscriptions to approximately 135 databases, appropriate in content to support undergraduate usage through to research needs and spanning all subject disciplines.

There is also use of the network to provide reference services. For example Deakin University library staff make use of concurrent session facilities on workstations to combine address and bibliographic search information for forwarding search results for reference queries (Cavanagh, 1997).

## INFORMATION SKILLS PACKAGES

Online provision of library instructional material for downloading and was developed in Australia by Open Learning Australia (1998). However the former Open Learning Library Information Service is now provided by the University of South Australia which is supplanting such packages with more up-to-date material. Most libraries provide general instructional material directly from library home pages with variations on help facilities. Some extend the use of instructional facilities with downloadable PDF files. Central Queensland University provides catalogue self-instruction software for downloading as executable files. In some cases, computer disks that include such material as catalogue instruction are provided in orientation kits.

Orientation sessions for distant users are provided personally by some universities. For example the University of Southern Queensland employs regional liaison officers who among other things provide introductory library presentations. There is little evidence of extensive use of video or teleconferencing technologies to enhance or promote library services, although some have commenced trialing weekend and evening orientation sessions to provide face-to-face contact with beginning students. There is also evidence of specifically designed user education classes for those students located within a geographically acceptable distance from the home institution.


## SPECIAL PROVISION FOR ADULTS

It was widely acknowledged that the conventional distance learner is adult. However, there is little accommodation for the variable learning styles, motivational agendas and diverse experiential backgrounds of these students in the design, delivery and support of courses.

Some universities provided specialised library facilitation for remote students. For example the University of South Australia has a team dedicated to external information requests. They make use of a closed collection dedicated to distance students. Central Queensland has a team of assistants who continually staff enquiry lines to handle requests or redirect them to appropriate Faculty librarians.

Nevertheless, adults are not singled out for special treatment as distance learners. The likelihood of this happening would seem to be diminishing as flexible delivery lessens the distinction between on- and off-campus delivery.


## CONCLUSION

Burge (1991) has argued that intelligent use of technology should guide librarians toward a more sophisticated approach to the existing strengths, learning goals, and living and learning style preferences of distance learners as they cope with the stresses of their societal roles. She feels that this approach should be learner-centreed and collaborative in nature.

Academics have increasingly turned to information technology to support self-directed learning. Information skills are an essential component of the life-long learning process (Wilson, 1994). The wide utilisation of the Internet has meant that the information skills must be both about it and on it, presenting challenges to librarians in delivery of these information skills. These are being addressed in a variety of stimulating ways in Australia.

The flexible delivery that the Internet enhances means that distance is less a factor in delivery of these skills. Increasingly the on-campus roles of reference librarians are being mirrored in support for the entire student population, as external services become less differentiated.

Educational shifts in higher education impact substantially upon the teaching and learning experiences provided to students. The recent convergence of distance education and flexible delivery presents a major challenge to tertiary education, particularly in the current climate of economic rationalism. Although technological innovations are providing an avenue by which many of previous impediments to the efficient provision of distance education may be overcome, these innovations may themselves be impediments to adult learners whose prior educational experience has not included computer-based delivery of materials. Libraries must remain responsive to the needs of their clients by demonstrating a willingness and flexibility to adopt and adapt technology into the development of flexible and accessible reference and instructional programs to support institutional initiatives in course delivery.

## REFERENCES

Australia. National Board of Employment, Education and Training. (1992). *Changing patterns of teaching and learning: The use and potential of distance education materials and methods in higher education.* Canberra: NBEET.

Brookfield, S.D. (1986). *Understanding and Facilitating Adult Learning.* San Francisco: Jossey-Bass.

Burge, E.J., Snow, J.E. & Howard, J.L. (1989). Distance education: Concept and practice. *Canadian Library Journal,* vol. 46, no. 5, pp. 329-35.

Burge, E.J. (1991). *Relationships and responsibilities: Libraries and distance educators working together.* Opening Keynote Address for the Off-Campus Library Services Conference (Albuquerque, NM, 1991).

Cavanagh, A.K. (1997). Library services for off campus students: At the crossroads? *Journal of Library Services for Distance Education,* vol. 1, no. 1. [Online] HTTP: *http://www.westga.edu/library/jlsde/jlsde1.1.html*

Clark, J. & Store, R. (1998). Flexible learning and the library: The challenge? *Journal of Library Services for Distance Education,* vol. 1, no. 2. [Online] HTTP: *http://www.westga.edu/library/jlsde/jlsde1.2.html*

Croker, C. & Grimison, C. (1989). *Library services for external students: A guide.* Canberra: LAA Special Interest Group on Distance Education.

Deakin University Library. Document Supply Section (1998). *Borrowing privileges for external students at tertiary libraries in Australia 1998.* [Online]. Available HTTP: *http://www.deakin.edu.au/library/borrpriv.html*

Heery, M. (1996). Academic library services to non-traditional students. *Library Management,* vol. 17, no. 5, pp. 3-13.

Jagannathan, N. (1996). Library and Information Services for Distance Learners. *Resource Sharing & Information Networks;* vol. 11, nos. 1-2, pp. 159-70.

Open Learning Australia (1998). *Open Learning Library Information Service: OLLIS* [Online] HTTP: *http://www.ola.edu.au/providers/ollis.htm*

Peacock, J. & Middleton, M.R. (1997). Mixed mode education by default: Implications for library user services. *ALIA DESIG Conference 'Shifting Sands: Distance education in times of change,'* Wagga Wagga. [Online] HTTP: *http://www.fit.qut.edu.au/InfoSys/middle/contrib/DESIG97.html*

Scott, R.N. (1988). The University of Oxford's approach to adult and continuing education. *Journal of Academic Librarianship,* vol. 14, no. 1, pp. 15-23.

Shklanka, O. (1990). Off-campus library services–A literature review. *Research in Distance Education* vol. 2, no. 4, pp. 2-11.

Wilson, V. (1994). Developing the adult independent learner: Information literacy and the remote external student. *Distance Education.* vol. 15, no. 2, pp. 254-278.

Wilson, V. (1995). Learning to learn: The acquisition of information literacy by isolated students of Edith Cowan University. *Education for Library and Information Services: Australia,* vol. 12, no. 1, pp. 19-31.

# Facilitating Adult Learning:
# The Role of the Academic Librarian

## C. Lyn Currie

**SUMMARY.** This paper considers the instructional role of the academic librarian and examines the contribution adult learning theory makes to the practice of teaching information literacy skills. It explores those principles of effective practice in facilitating adult learning which apply to the teaching–learning transactions in the library. It describes the aim of facilitation as one of encouraging self directed, empowered adults and confirms the role of the academic librarian in facilitating the development of critical thinking, creative problem–solving and informed decision making in adult learners. It also examines the concept of information literacy and how this contributes to adult lifelong learning. *[Article copies available for a fee from The Haworth Document Delivery Service: 1-800-342-9678. E-mail address: <getinfo@haworthpressinc.com> Website: <http://www.haworthpressinc.com>]*

**KEYWORDS.** Adult learning, facilitation, self directed learning, information literacy, lifelong learning

## *INTRODUCTION*

Adult learning theory with its emphasis on developing the skills of the learner rather than transmitting the content of the discipline provides a useful

---

C. Lyn Currie is Head, Education Library, University of Saskatchewan, 28 Campus Drive, Saskatoon, Saskatchewan, S7N 0X1, Canada (E–mail: currie@sklib.usask.ca).

[Haworth co-indexing entry note]: "Facilitating Adult Learning: The Role of the Academic Librarian." Currie, C. Lyn. Co-published simultaneously in *The Reference Librarian* (The Haworth Information Press, an imprint of The Haworth Press, Inc.) No. 69/70, 2000, pp. 219-231; and: *Reference Services for the Adult Learner: Challenging Issues for the Traditional and Technological Era* (ed: Kwasi Sarkodie-Mensah) The Haworth Information Press, an imprint of The Haworth Press, Inc., 2000, pp. 219-231. Single or multiple copies of this article are available for a fee from The Haworth Document Delivery Service [1-800-342-9678, 9:00 a.m. - 5:00 p.m. (EST). E-mail address: getinfo@haworthpressinc.com].

framework for academic librarians involved in teaching information skills. Information skills education based on conceptual and critical thinking models and using the teaching methodologies of adult learning theory is an achievable if challenging objective for academics and librarians in higher education institutions (Wilson, 1994).

Academic librarians have turned in recent times to an examination of the learning process, learning styles of adults and teaching strategies appropriate for adult learners in their efforts to realize the mandate of higher education to "create people who can make informed decisions, creatively problem solve, and think critically and responsively" (Burge, 1989). There is increasing evidence in the literature (Sheridan, 1986; Keenan, 1989; Oberman, 1991) of the application of adult learning theory to the development of user education in libraries. The concept of user education has expanded to encompass training in the skills implicit in Knowles' (1990) definition of the adult independent learner. The notion of information literacy is implied in the critical thinking skills that characterize the independent, self-motivated lifelong learner. Oberman (1991) observed that by 1987 the importance of critical thinking processes in information literacy was well recognized in the bibliographic instruction movement. Conceptual learning, analysis and evaluation of information and the transferability of skills across disciplines have become familiar themes long espoused in the theory and practice of library user education (MacAdam, 1989).

To adopt an adult learner-centered approach implies a move away from totally controlling the teaching and learning situation in the direction of collaboration in an effort to assist learners to become critically reflective and independent individuals (Galbraith, 1991). Since adult learners enter the library with intentions, memories and styles of learning the librarian must work to develop helping or trust relationships with them, playing the role of "more capable peer" (Carr, 1986). The librarian assumes the role of a collaborator or facilitator rather than an expert.

## ADULT LEARNING THEORY

Knowles' (1980) concept of andragogy has done much to shape the practice of adult education. His andragogical model, the process by which adults learn, is characterized by a mutually respectful, informal, collaborative style of teacher/student relationship which uses experiential techniques and is based on several key assumptions about adult learners:

- they are motivated to learn
- their orientation to learning is life-centred
- experience is the richest resource for their learning

- they have a deep need to be self-directing
- their individual differences increase with age.

The two distinguishing characteristics of adult learning most frequently advanced by theorists are the adult's autonomy of direction when learning and the use of personal experience as a learning resource (Simpson, 1980).

Brookfield (1986) provides a succinct summary of the principles of adult learning specified by adult learning theorists (Gibb, 1960; Miller, 1964; Kidd, 1973; Knox, 1977; Brundage and Mackeracher, 1980; Smith, 1982; and Darkenwald and Merriam, 1982): Adults learn throughout their lives, with the negotiations of the transitional stages in the life-span being the immediate causes and motives for much of this learning. They exhibit diverse learning styles–strategies for coding information, cognitive procedures, mental sets and they learn in different ways, at different times for different purposes. As a rule however they like their learning activities to be problem-centered and to be meaningful to their life situation and they want the learning outcomes to have some immediacy of application. The past experiences of adults affect their current learning, sometimes serving as an enhancement, sometimes as a hindrance. Effective learning is also linked to the adult's subscription to a self-concept of himself or herself as a learner. Finally adults exhibit a tendency towards self-directedness in their learning.

The development of self-directed learning skills is central to Knowles' model of lifelong learning. He defined these skills as the ability to:

- develop and be in touch with curiosities
- perceive oneself objectively and accept feedback about one's performance non-defensively
- diagnose one's own learning needs in the light of models of competencies required for performing life's roles
- formulate learning objectives in terms that describe performance outcomes
- identify human, material and experiential resources for accomplishing various kinds of learning objectives
- design a plan of strategies for making use of appropriate learning resources effectively
- carry out a learning plan systematically and sequentially
- collect evidence of the accomplishment of learning objectives and have it validated through performance (Knowles, 1990:174).

As self-directed individuals with a certain amount of life experience, adult learners are desirous of learning those things they perceive necessary to help them cope effectively with their real-life situations. The demands of the adult learner are those of self-direction, relevance, usefulness and the opportunity to integrate life-experiences with learning experiences (Keenan, 1989). According to Burge (1998) adult learning is all about construction (how adults create their own framework of knowledge) and confusion (when learners attempt to organize a mass of incoming information); achievement, affiliation and acknowledgement (feeling competent and being connected to others); relevance, responsibility and relationships (relating life experiences and personal knowledge to learning, accepting learner responsibility for learning and establishing collaborative relationships which create a climate that allows for talking in order to think, making mistakes, letting go of old ideas and attitudes and being open to anything new) and expression through which the learner is able to see himself perform, hear himself think, compare thoughts and skills to those of his peers and open his mind to feedback.

## FACILITATING ADULT LEARNING

Brookfield (1986) identified six principles of effective practice in facilitating adult learning:

- Participation in learning is voluntary
- Effective practice is characterized by respect among participants for each other's self worth
- Facilitation is collaborative with facilitator and learners engaged in a cooperative enterprise
- Praxis is at the heart of effective facilitation–a continual process of activity, reflection, collaborative analysis, further reflection
- Critical reflection is fostered
- Self-directed empowered adults are nurtured.

Adult learning is best facilitated when learners are engaged as participants in the design of the learning, when they are encouraged to be self-directed, when the educator functions as a facilitator rather than a didactic instructor, when the individual learner's needs and learning styles are taken into account, when a climate conducive to learning is established, when the learner's past experiences are utilized in the classroom and when learning activities are deemed to have some direct relevance or utility to the learner's circumstances.

An effective teaching and learning encounter as described by Galbraith (1991) is one which involves a transaction between facilitator and learner that is active, challenging, collaborative, critically reflective and transforming. The essence of the transactional process is to move adult learners toward independence and responsibility for their own learning. The most common elements of the transactional process are collaboration, support, respect, freedom, equality, critical reflection, critical analysis, challenge, risk taking and praxis. Adult learning methods most appropriate to the transactional process include discussion, simulation, learning contracts, inquiry teams, case method, critical incident, and mentoring. Facilitating adult learning requires an understanding that facilitators and learners bring into an educational encounter varying personalities, personal and professional experiences, levels of sophistication and various cultural and ethical backgrounds. Different approaches are necessary within the teaching and learning process because of the diversity, variability and varying levels of expectations of the learners, the subject matter presented and the varying intellectual domains of the learners.

## THE FACILITATOR-CHARACTERISTICS, ROLES AND SKILLS

The personality characteristics and interpersonal and human relations skills of the facilitator are central to the success of Knowles' andragogical approach. The attributes of caring, trust and respect are essential characteristics for the facilitator of adult learners. Brookfield (1986) suggests a facilitator should recognize and understand the diversity of adult learners, provide a climate conducive to learning, provide a contextual setting for the exploration of new ideas, skills and resolutions, provide a forum for critical reflection and have the ability to assist adults in the process of learning how to change their perspectives, shift their paradigms and replace their way of interpreting the world. Implementation of these requires the facilitator to be technically proficient in content and instructional planning areas as well as highly competent in interpersonal and human relation skills.

The best thing the facilitator can do is act as a collaborative colleague in the learning endeavour. By using a collaborative approach to agree on the learning objectives, adult learners can increase their understanding of and commitment to achieving the objectives, understand the relationship between current and desired proficiencies, reflect on questions that need addressing, and acquire a framework for learning how to learn beyond the present program (Knowles, 1980).

The transition from teacher to facilitator of learning requires a shift in role from content transmitter to process manager and involves performing a different set of functions requiring a different set of skills that include relationship building, needs assessment, involvement of learners in planning, linking learners to learning resources and encouraging learner initiative. Adult educators need to be more concerned with learning processes rather than learning products, with the learner first. In adult learning the life experience of learners and their needs for discussion demand that facilitators pay careful attention to dialogue and process. As learning involves moving from one developmental stage to the next, it becomes the role of the facilitator to perceive correctly where the individual exists on the developmental scale and to assist, not only in allowing the learner to master each new stage, but also in challenging the learner to confront the next one (Keenan, 1989).

The facilitator's roles are diverse given the multifaceted nature of adult learning and the settings in which it occurs. The facilitator may be the challenger, role model, mentor, coach, demonstrator, content resource person and learning guide. According to Mackeracher (1996) the facilitator is a very influential component of the learning environment through the provision of guidance, structure, information, feedback, reinforcement and support. The facilitator's role is often regarded as assisting adults to complete learning efforts that they as learners have defined. This view emphasizes the primacy of the learner, grants a substantial measure of control to learners and places learning directly in the context of the learners' own experiences. The difficulty in accepting this is that it assumes a high degree of self-knowledge and critical awareness on the part of adult learners. For the educator it is not always easy to accept adults' definitions of needs as the operational criterion for the development of curriculum, design of programs or evaluation of success.

Facilitators of adult learning need to be proficient in the instructional planning components of needs assessment, context analysis, objective setting, organizing learning activities and evaluation if they are to be effective in helping adults learn. Through needs assessment facilitators can review their assumptions about the educational needs of adult learners and be responsive to those needs. Context analysis considers the societal trends and issues. Adult learners have perceptions of standards, expectations and opportunities that are directly related to their purpose for being engaged in the learning exercise. Understanding these allows the facilitator to contribute to decisions on using learning activities to strengthen problem solving, specify mastery levels, and helping learners use educational strategies that enable them to use or deflect influences that encourage or discourage them to learn and apply (Knox, 1986). The way that learning activities are selected and organized must be rational and based on the educational objectives, the adult learner's characteristics, current proficiency levels and preferred learning styles as well as the facilitator's own perspective and experience.

## THE LIBRARIAN AS FACILITATOR

The preference in adult education for a facilitative and collaborative role as opposed to an authoritative role of teachers applies well to the teaching learning transactions that occur in libraries and was supported in the findings of a study conducted by Carr (1986) of adult learners in public libraries. He concluded that a relationship based on collaboration, reciprocity, empathy and trust was critical between the learner and the librarian. Success was determined by the learner's desire and commitment to learn and the librarian's effectiveness in nurturing self discovery in the learner.

In recognizing and becoming sensitized to the adult learner's need for self-direction and independence the librarian functions much more as a facilitator than an information manager with a shift in emphasis from providing information to offering the learner the ability to see a number of approaches to achieving the predetermined goal. The goal of academic library user education should be to assist users in their efforts to integrate and exploit the power of library resources in their preferred information-seeking styles. By empowering students to master their own research strategies the librarian is reinforcing the individual's need for self-accomplishment and self-direction (Keenan, 1989).

Burge (1991) points out the academic librarian also needs to mediate creatively between the pragmatic world of adult learners and the high technology world of information. The technological shifts towards macro, global-sized networks for information organization and storage may in turn promote a shift toward micro-sized, communal psychological arenas for meeting the achievement and affiliation drives of adult learners. Intelligent use of technology ought to drive librarians towards a more sophisticated approach to the existing strengths, learning goals, living and learning style preferences of adult learners.

## LIFELONG LEARNING AND INFORMATION LITERACY

The publishing of *A Nation at Risk* in 1983 by the U.S. National Commission on Excellence in Education called for active learning that prepares students for lifelong learning, active citizenship and risk taking. It claimed that through resource based learning students could master information retrieval and evaluation skills that will be useful for learning throughout their lives. They could become information literate (Breivik, 1989). An information literate person was later defined as one who:

- recognizes the need for information
- recognizes that accurate and complete information is the basis for intelligent decision making
- formulates questions based on information needs
- identifies potential sources of information
- develops successful search strategies
- accesses sources of information including computer-based and other technologies
- evaluates information

- organizes information for practical application
- integrates new information into an existing body of knowledge
- uses information in critical thinking and problem solving (Doyle, 1992).

These information literacy skills of finding, reading, analyzing, interpreting, applying and communicating information are the foundation for living effectively and being employed productively. They require the use of critical thinking skills to focus on an issue or question, analyze arguments, ask clarifying questions, evaluate reliability of sources and examine assumptions (Ennis, 1987).

To acquire the information literacy skills that are essential to lifelong learning and active citizenship learners need to begin by developing more sophisticated information management skills. Breivik (1989) believes that the six elements of a good learning experience will come together only when librarians and faculty cooperate in shifting the focus toward library-based learning. For Breivik a good learning experience is one which imitates reality, is active, individualized, responsive to a variety of learning styles, accommodates constantly changing information and where the environment is least threatening,

## LIBRARY INSTRUCTION FOR INFORMATION LITERACY

The potential value of library instruction in facilitating integrated learning and the development of lifelong learning skills is receiving more attention in curriculum planning. Library instruction programs have evolved from descriptions of reference sources, to the use of conceptual frameworks and a thorough going application of cognitive theory to library instruction. The importance of providing users with a conceptual foundation for library information seeking has been extolled within library instruction for years. Lancaster (1972) concluded that users encountered the greatest difficulty in conceptualization and formalization of information needs, selection of appropriate terminology and development of search strategies that could exploit the interactive power of online systems. More recent research tends to confirm his early findings. Tuckett and Stoffle (1984) emphasized the central goal of library instruction as self-reliance on the part of library users, to develop those who have the ability to conceptualize the type and scope of information needed to address a problem, envision the steps required to obtain that information, determine the type of sources which would be appropriate, ascertain if such sources exist, rethink either the type or scope of information needed and make judgements about the quality, pertinence and reliability of the information generated through this process.

Oberman (1991) has commented on the shift in focus in library instruction from an initial concern with lower level cognitive objectives on the Bloom (1984) taxonomy of knowledge and comprehension to the highest cognitive objectives of analysis, synthesis and evaluation. Since problem solving is a critical component of successful library research there is now an emphasis on the role that analytical reasoning abilities and problem solving skills play in the process of library research. The use of learning cycles and guided design by Oberman (1982) is one example of library instruction which engaged the learner in a series of activities that demanded the use of abstract reasoning abilities to work through a problem related to information research. In this problem-solving approach to user education there is a direct transfer of responsibility from the instructor to the student which clearly incorporates andragogical/collaborative principles (Sheridan, 1986). More recently Shapiro and Hughes (1996) have argued that information literacy should be conceived broadly as a new liberal art that extends from knowing how to use computers and access information to critical reflection on the nature of information itself, its technical infrastructure and its social, cultural and philosophical context. They identify seven dimensions of literacy which enable individuals not only to use information and information technology effectively and adapt to their constant changes but also to think critically about the entire information enterprise and information society. Those dimensions include:

- tool literacy–the ability to understand and use the practical and conceptual tools of current information technology;
- resource literacy–the ability to understand the form, format, location and access methods of information resources;
- social structural literacy–knowing how information is socially situated and produced;
- research literacy–the ability to understand and use the IT-based tools relevant to the work of today's researcher and scholar;
- publishing literacy–the ability to format and publish research and ideas electronically in textual and multimedia forms;
- emerging technology literacy–the ability to adapt to, understand and make use of the continually emerging innovations in information technology; and
- critical literacy–the ability to evaluate critically the intellectual, human and social strengths, weaknesses, potentials and limits, benefits and costs of information technology (Shapiro and Hughes, 1996).

Library users need sound conceptual models in order to successfully negotiate complex interactive library systems. With the constant evolution of data access and communication technologies in libraries there is great need for rapid dialogue between library staff and learners. Such dialogue is part of the mediator and educator roles of librarians and may determine, to a large degree, the extent to which the learner develops the necessary critical and analytical skills for independently using information resources and learning effectively.

## LIBRARY INSTRUCTION AND THE ADULT LEARNER

Libraries have confronted the question of how to accommodate the varying knowledge, skills, experience and attitudes of adult learners. The pervasiveness and importance of these diverse factors suggest that new approaches to instruction allowing flexibility and alternate learning experiences for individuals according to their learning styles and a mix of approaches to content presentation will be necessary to educate users (King and Baker, 1987). Academic librarians have been limited in their experience shaping instruction to account for adult learning needs since they are often placed in situations with limited time and no control over class composition. As a result their instructional aims are often cognitive rather than affective and behavioural. As Burge (1991) observed, in working with adult learners one is continually confronted with the problem of how to move learners sensitively and consistently out of their "teach me" passive, receptive attitudes and develop in them the skills and desire to take responsibility for their learning. By way of example she asks: How willing are your learners to spend the time needed to learn the skills for independent navigation around the data networks?

Huston and Oberman (1989) advocated the use of collaborative techniques in library instruction claiming adults are best taught by educating them in a manner that engages their personal conceptual frameworks and building on their experiential frameworks and reminding them of what they do know. This in recognition that an effective teacher encourages mutual confrontation and collaboration and allows adults to choose what they need to know. Keenan (1989) called for an emphasis to be placed on individualization of teaching and learning strategies since adults bring to any learning environment a greater quantity and a different quality of experience. She suggested such approaches as meeting with small groups, encouraging group discussion allowing students to question and come to an understanding of how and why user education can be beneficial to them and setting up situations which foster peer-helping activities.

Hensley (1991) has effectively argued that learning style and learning transfer theories can enhance the ability of reference staff to provide quality instruction at the reference desk and contribute to the development of a library user's information-seeking skills. A major desired outcome of the reference desk interaction is the ability of the user to transfer what is learned from one interaction to a new situation. Initial learning and retention of that learning is key to the learning transfer process. He advocates matching the reference librarian's interaction with the user's learning style thereby enhancing clear communication, retention of information imparted and ultimate transfer of learning to new situations. Some strategies he proposes include focussing on understanding the information/instructional need from the user's perspective, sequencing responses into segments that create opportunity for further learning and time for the user to engage in the instructional process, awareness of possible shifts in learning style because of stressful or unfavourable conditions for learning, and providing alternative information sources.

Academic librarians have discovered the imperative to actively pursue a balance involving interaction and cooperation among faculty as course planners, librarians as facilitators of research objectives and students as learners (Baker,1989). Many possibilities exist for such cooperation between librarians and faculty for improving student learning particularly if librarians assume an active role as facilitators of critical thinking. If the academic librarian suggests alternative sources to a student, encourages a student to consider an author's reputation and expertise, engage students in active dialogue concerning their assumptions and prejudices about a topic, authorities or varying perspectives on an issue offered by different disciplines they are facilitating critical thinking (Gibson, 1989).

## CONCLUSION

Wilson (1994) has argued that a paradigm shift needs to occur if academic libraries are to make assistance to the adult learner the central objective of library service. Through their continuing advocacy of the library as "a vehicle for self transformation through the life span of the individual" (Carr, 1986), and promotion of information literacy for lifelong learning librarians are beginning to manage that paradigm shift thus claiming a niche for the academic library in the development of the adult learner.

The role for the academic librarian involves being a proactive mediator between information and the learner, sensitive and skilled in interviews and consultation, able to provide appropriate learning resources and teach the learner to be independently skilled in using data sources and libraries.

Since the process of adult learning involves the learner in critical analysis of information and confident explorations and analyses of their own and other people's knowledge the ultimate question for the academic librarian becomes one of personal agency according to Burge (1991). If the academic librarian wants to be able to select the most appropriate models of teaching (given the characteristics of adult learners), talk the right language with educators, cater for the style differences in cognition and learning and respond empathetically to learners' affective and cognitive problems without feeling out of depth, future education and training in adult education is advocated. In terms of those societal trends affecting the learning and lifestyle preferences of adults the librarian has an unprecedented opportunity for significant innovative practice.

## REFERENCES

Baker, Betsy (1989). Bibliographic instruction: Building the Librarian/Faculty partnership. *Reference Librarian* 24, 311-328.

Bloom, B.S. (Ed.) (1984). Taxonomy of educational objectives: The classification of educational goals. New York: Longman.

Breivik, Patricia Senn (1989). Politics for closing the gap. *Reference Librarian* 24, 5-16.

Brookfield, S. (1987). *Developing critical thinkers*. San Francisco: Jossey-Bass.

Brundage, D.H. and Mackeracher, D. (1980). Adult learning principles and their application to program planning. Toronto: Ministry of Education.

Burge, Elizabeth J. and others. (1989). Developing partnerships: An investigation of library-based relationships with students and educators participating in distance education in Northern Ontario. Toronto: Ontario Institute for Studies in Education. ED 311 902.

Burge, Elizabeth J. (1991). Relationships and responsibilities: Librarians and distance educators working together. Off Campus Library Services Conference, Albuquerque, New Mexico. ED 339 383.

Burge, Elizabeth J. and Roberts, Judith M. (1998). Classrooms with a difference: Facilitating learning on the information highway. 2nd ed. Montreal: McGraw Hill.

Carr, David (1986). The meaning of the adult independent library learning project. *Library Trends* 35, 327-345.

Darkenwald, G.G. and Merriam, S.B. (1982). Adult education: Foundations of practice. New York: Harper and Row.

Doyle, Christina S. (1992). Final report to National Forum on Information Literacy. ED 351 033.

Ennis, Robert (1987). A taxonomy of critical thinking dispositions and abilities. In Joan B. Baron and Robert J. Sternberg (Eds.) *Teaching thinking skills: Theory and practice.* New York: W. H.Freeman and Co., 1987.

Galbraith, M.W. (1989). Essential skills for the facilitator of adult learning. *Lifelong learning: An omnibus of practice and research* 12, 6, 10-13.

Galbraith, M.W. (1991). Facilitating adult learning: A transactional process. Malabar: Robert E. Kreiger.

Gibb, J.R. (1960). Learning theory in adult education. In M.S. Knowles (ed.) Handbook of adult education in the United States. Washington, DC: Adult Education Association of the U.S.A.

Gibson, Craig (1989). Alternatives to the term paper: An aid to critical thinking. *Reference Librarian* 24, 297-309.

Hensley, Randall (1991). Learning style theory and learning transfer principles during reference interview instruction. *Library Trends* 39, 3, Winter, 203-209.

Huston, Mary and Oberman, Cerise (1989). Making communication: A theoretical framework for educating end users of online bibliographic information retrieval systems. *Reference Librarian* 24, 199-211.

Keenan, Lori (1989). Andragogy off-campus: The library's role. *Reference Librarian* 24, 147-158.

Kidd, J.R. (1973). How adults learn. New York: Cambridge Books.

King, David and Baker, Betsy (1987). Human aspects of library technology: Implications for academic library user education. In Mellon, Constance A. (Ed). *Bibliographic instruction: The second generation*. Littleton: Libraries Unlimited.

Knowles, M. (1980). *The modern practice of adult education: From pedagogy to andragogy*. New York: Cambridge.

Knowles, M. (1990). *The adult learner: A neglected species*. 4th ed. Houston: Gulf Publishing.

Knox, A.B. (1977). *Adult development and learning: A handbook of individual growth and competence in the adult years*. San Francisco: Jossey-Bass.

Knox, A.B. (1986). *Helping adults learn*. San Francisco: Jossey-Bass.

Lancaster, F.W. (1972). Evaluation of online searching in MEDLARS (AIM-TWX) by biomedical practitioners. University of Illinois Graduate School of Library Science *Occasional papers* 101.

MacAdam, Barbara and Kemp, Barbara (1989). Bibliographic instruction and critical inquiry in the undergraduate curriculum. *Reference Librarian* 24, 233-244.

Mackeracher, D. (1996). *Making sense of adult learning*. Toronto: Culture Concepts.

Miller, H.L. (1964). *Teaching and learning in adult education*. New York: Macmillan.

Oberman, Cerise and Linton, Rebecca A. (1982). Guided design: teaching library research as problem-solving. In Oberman, Cerise and Strauch, Katina (Eds.) *Theories of bibliographic education: Designs for teaching*. New York: Bowker.

Oberman, Cerise (1991). Avoiding the cereal syndrome, or critical thinking in the electronic environment. *Library Trends* 39, 3, Winter, 189-202.

Shapiro, Jeremy J. and Hughes, Shelley K. (1996). Information technology as a liberal art: Enlightenment proposals for a new curriculum. *Educom Review* 31, 2, March/April, 31-35.

Sheridan, Jean (1986). Andragogy: A new concept for academic librarians. *Research Strategies* 4, 4, 156-167.

Simpson, E.L. (1980). Adult learning theory: A state of the art. In H. Lasker, J. Moore, and E. L. Simpson (eds.) *Adult development and approaches to learning*. Washington, DC: National Institute of Education.

Smith, R.M. (1982). Learning how to learn: Applied learning theory for adults. New York: Cambridge Books.

Tuckett, Harold W. and Stoffle, Carla J. (1984). Learning theory and the self-reliant library user. *RQ* 24, Fall, 58-65.

Wilson, Vicky (1994). Developing the adult independent learner: Information literacy and the remote external student. *Distance Education* 15, 254-279.

# Going the Distance
# (and Back Again):
# A Distance Education Course Comes Home

Craig Gibson
Jane Scales

**SUMMARY.** University 300, a course on research and Internet skills, was originally developed at Washington State University for the distance education program. Using a critical thinking approach to the contemporary information environment, the course has grown, evolved, and been transformed into a general education course for the main campus at the university. The course's history shows how strong administrative support and beneficial collaborations across the university trans-

Craig Gibson is Associate Director, Information Services, George Mason University, Fairfax, VA. He was previously Head of Library User Education at Washington State University. He holds an MLS from the University of Denver, an MA in English from the University of Mississippi, and a BA in English from West Texas State University. He is active in the American Library Association, the ACRL Instruction Section, and the Virginia Library Association. Jane Scales is Extended Degree Librarian, Washington State University, where she coordinates library services and user education for distance education students. She holds a BA in Russian from Indiana University, an MA in German from Ohio State University, and an MLIS from the University of Kentucky. She specializes in humanities, social sciences, and government documents reference, and collection development in Slavic literatures and languages, and library science. She is very active in the WSU Libraries' User Education program, teaching Internet skills classes, and currently coordinates the campus version of the credit research skills course GenEd 300, "Accessing Information for Research."

[Haworth co-indexing entry note]: "Going the Distance (and Back Again): A Distance Education Course Comes Home." Gibson, Craig, and Jane Scales. Co-published simultaneously in *The Reference Librarian* (The Haworth Information Press, an imprint of The Haworth Press, Inc.) No. 69/70, 2000, pp. 233-244; and: *Reference Services for the Adult Learner: Challenging Issues for the Traditional and Technological Era* (ed: Kwasi Sarkodie-Mensah) The Haworth Information Press, an imprint of The Haworth Press, Inc., 2000, pp. 233-244. Single or multiple copies of this article are available for a fee from The Haworth Document Delivery Service [1-800-342-9678, 9:00 a.m. - 5:00 p.m. (EST). E-mail address: getinfo@haworthpressinc.com].

formed the course into an emerging key component of the university curriculum. *[Article copies available for a fee from The Haworth Document Delivery Service: 1-800-342-9678. E-mail address: <getinfo@haworthpressinc. com> Website: <http://www.haworthpressinc.com>]*

**KEYWORDS.** Distance education, research skills, Internet skills, critical thinking, general education, curriculum reform

## INTRODUCTION

One of the most rapidly developing issues in the late 1990s for librarians, faculty, administrators, and all involved in higher education, is the need to reach beyond the confines of the traditional campus and the walls of the traditional library to place-bound students. "Distance education," variously defined, is hardly new, of course, having been offered through correspondence courses, guided exercises, television courses, and other means for decades. The great demographic changes of the 1990s, however, are pushing higher education to accommodate the greater numbers of an older working student population–through sophisticated instructional delivery wherever students happen to live and work. At the same time, business and industry seek employees with greater ability with critical thinking and problem-solving, and also technological skills–employees who continue to learn on the job. These abilities and skills, of course, are also needed in students regardless of their age, location, or demographic profile. Critical thinking and problem-solving in a highly fluid, information- and technology-intense environment are therefore the "common denominators" in distance education and traditional campus-based education. This article shows how a distance education course, originally conceived and designed to develop these skills, was redesigned to fit the requirements of a traditional campus student population–a very different "reverse direction" of course development in a university curriculum.

## ONE UNIVERSITY'S RESPONSE

The emergence of distance education as an opportunity for universities has led some of them to develop major programs to reach out to the nontraditional, place-bound student. Washington State University (WSU), with its original campus located in Pullman in rural eastern Washington, is one such university. A land-grant university, it has a strong mission for outreach to the entire state, and has developed other campuses–in Spokane, Tri-Cities, and

Vancouver–as well as a strong Extended Degree Program for place-bound students in rural areas and smaller communities throughout the state. This Extended Degree Program has employed videotaped courses and printed course guides, developed by faculty in cooperation with instructional designers, video producers, and administrators, for a number of years. Students throughout Washington and other states elect to take courses through this program because of its quality and service level.

Administrators in WSU's Extended Degree Program early realized that library resources and services are crucial components of a successful distance education program. They worked with librarians to develop special document delivery services and reference assistance for students regardless of their location. This cooperative working relationship between Washington State's Extended Degree administrators and librarians has been especially fruitful in insuring equity of access to electronic resources subscribed to for all university students, even though the complexities of licensing database subscriptions for a multi-campus university and its widely scattered student population remain a challenge.

## ANOTHER ROLE FOR THE LIBRARY:
## A CREDIT COURSE

In 1995, administrators in Washington State's Extended Degree Program approached the library about another opportunity: that of developing a special, for-credit distance education course to teach students research and Internet skills. From contacts with and surveys of current and prospective students, the administrators knew that there was rapidly increasing interest in learning how to use the Internet as well as more traditional information resources. The need for a special course, linked conceptually with the social science curriculum then in place for extended degree students, loomed large in 1995. We were part of these early discussions, along with the Director of Libraries and Extended Degree administrators. Because of collegial working relationships among librarians and Extended Degree administrators, this planning phase went smoothly and quickly. One-half FTE staff member, it was decided, would assist with developing the course in the library, in addition to document delivery responsibilities; the Head of the Library User Education also would be assisted with course development by a video producer and a course guide designer. Another important early decision was to involve a reference librarian with extensive Internet experience in writing those sections in the course guide on Internet skills.

An administrative decision about curricular level and placement of the course was made at this point. It would be called University 300 because it would fit within the university's set of general, non-department-based "service" courses for all students. It would be designated a junior (300-level) course because the content would be developed for students with a designated major–in this case, the social science major common to all students enrolled at that time in the Extended Degree Program.

## CONTENT ISSUES

Several pedagogical issues quickly came to the forefront. We considered instructional design issues early on–content, instructional delivery, and assessment–but content was most important at this stage, as instructional delivery was largely predetermined by the Extended Degree Program's standard delivery methods. Content issues, however, had to be decided upon quickly for the prototype of the course. Working with the Extended Degree Program Coordinator, we developed an outline of topics and sample assignments. At the same time, we began working with the video producer on experimental taping sessions to become comfortable with "camera presence" and to understand more about adapting instruction from traditional classroom settings to videotape for distant students.

One basic point about the content of the new course was the need to link it conceptually with the social science curriculum then in place in the Extended Degree program. Students could choose courses in anthropology, business, criminal justice, history, political science, psychology, and sociology, all adapted to the video- and course-guide format from traditional courses taught by faculty on either the WSU-Pullman campus or the other WSU campuses. The course was therefore especially developed with the needs and interests of social science majors in mind. One whole chapter in the course guide focused on the scholarly communication system in the social sciences and on the differing vocabularies of the social science disciplines, so that students could understand the necessity of selecting the appropriate search terms later in database searching.

The content of the new course was also greatly influenced by our belief that any approach to information access and use in the 1990s must be based on a firm conceptual grasp of the entire "information landscape": that the basic concepts of the information environment should be taught, not just the rapidly changing specific features of database interfaces and software tools. Specific features of tools and resources would be taught when appropriate and necessary, but they would not be the " foundation" or the primary focus. In addition, we insisted that students have ample opportunity to apply their conceptual knowledge, that they put their newly gained concepts to work through critical thinking and actual experience. These two foundations–conceptual frameworks, critical thinking applications–determined all instructional design decisions for the course.

Although hardly new in library instruction circles, the "conceptual frame-works" approach would be tested in the distance education environment because students would not have access to traditional academic libraries and would have to develop greater metacognitive and critical thinking abilities to monitor and extend their own understanding of information resources in the absence of palpable and visible library collections and librarians. This pedagogical challenge suggested that students receive a special type of "scaffolding" in this course: They would read and hear about the concepts of the course through videotapes and course guide, but test their understanding through repeated scenarios and case studies as well as practice exercises. The scenarios and case studies would develop the students' ability to "self monitor" and grasp ill-structured information and research problems before beginning practice exercises in search strategy or evaluating sources. Other opportunities for "self-monitoring" would be included as self-study exercises, a standard feature in distance education courses, where students must have opportunities to try out their own understandings of new content, often in the absence of peers or instructors.

## INSTRUCTIONAL DELIVERY/COURSE TOPICS

The initial distance education version of University 300, developed in 1995, followed the standard instructional delivery methods of the Extended Degree Program: videotaped lessons, and printed course guide with accompanying exercises. The course guide itself served as the textbook. After developing the course outline, we clustered the course topics into fourteen lessons, a close match to the University's fifteen-week semester. Because of the complexity of some topics and the need for sustained student practice, several of those topics were carried from one lesson to another. For example, the course as first developed had three lessons on database searching and four lessons on the Internet. The initial course outline is shown in Table 1.

A videotape, each 30 minutes in length, was developed for each lesson. We worked with a video producer and his assistants in selecting locations with appropriate lighting, developing scenarios for role playing, and including techniques to encourage prospective students to become actively engaged with the ideas discussed in the videotapes. Several experts on course topics were interviewed to provide variety: The Assistant Director for Library Systems, for example, spoke about electronic information issues in one video, while the Assistant Dean of Liberal Arts reflected on discourse communities and vocabulary issues in the social sciences in another. The planning and set-up time required for producing each video was, of course, much more than the actual taping time: Each 30-minute video required approximately eight to twelve hours of advance preparation.

TABLE 1. Outline of Original Course

| Lesson | Topic | Lesson | Topic |
|--------|-------|--------|-------|
| 1 | Course Introduction/ Information Landscape | 8 | The Online Catalog |
| 2 | Scholarly Communication and Information System in the Social Sciences | 9 | Evaluation of Information |
| 3 | Question Analysis Applied to Social Science Research Topics | 10 | The Internet: Basic Concepts |
| 4 | The Electronic Toolkit | 11 | The Internet and its Information World |
| 5 | The Art of Database Searching: Basic Concepts | 12 | The Internet: Resource Discovery Tools |
| 6 | The Art of Database Searching: Advanced Strategies | 13 | The Internet and Research in the Social Sciences |
| 7 | Online Services: First Search™ and UnCover™ | 14 | Course Review and Summary |

The other vehicle for instructional delivery, the course guide, was written in the summer of 1995. It included relatively stable information about scholarly communication, search strategies, and database concepts–but also information reflecting the current state of the Internet at that time. Detailed explanations of Gopher, FTP, and WAIS were included, along with explanations of the World Wide Web, at that point in 1995 just beginning its phenomenal growth. The chapter on the online catalog was relatively sparse because the Libraries were in the process of implementing a new integrated library system, replacing a locally developed one.

The course guide attempted to facilitate critical thinking in students through scenarios and case studies. The scenarios written for the first course guide showed the "ill-structured" nature of much research, particularly that in the social sciences. The scenarios figured prominently in the course guide chapter on question analysis, a transferable method for analyzing a research topic in any discipline. Here is one example of a research scenario given as an assignment:

> *You are intrigued by the way politicians always seem to have perfect answers for dealing with the crime problem. Every election sees candidates for offices at all levels promising to "get tough on crime" through*

*stiffer sentences, more prison-building, and other remedies. You discover the rates for various types of crimes vary drastically from locale to locale in the United States, and your instructor suggests that you investigate community policing and model neighborhood crime prevention programs. You decide to focus especially on the latter. How will you find information on these programs?*

The scenario approach offered students an opportunity to understand something of the "big picture" about the information environment before plunging into the specifics of database searching and Internet filtering. The scenarios also approximated real assignments that students might receive in criminal justice courses or other social science courses.

## EARLY EXPERIENCES WITH THE COURSE

Though the course was offered in Fall 1995 for the first time, and received student enrollment, most of these first enrollees had to complete the course in the Spring semester of 1996. There were several reasons for this–most notably, lack of computer access by some who enrolled. Other students who secured Internet access experienced glitches with various access modes. For example, America Online[TM] subscribers could not telnet to the WSU library catalog and were limited, for the most part, to email and the nascent World Wide Web. The various email applications used by students presented problems at times as well, particularly when they wanted to send in their assignments as attachments. It was too difficult to provide instructions for these kinds of routine activities that were so dependent on the quirks and configurations of various online companies. We discovered as well that many students enrolled in University 300 as they first began to experiment with computers, online vendors, and research itself. Consequently, one of our first lessons was to make clear to students the difference between the services and assistance they should expect from their Internet service providers, and what we could offer. In subsequent semesters, it became mandatory that students have computer and Internet (specifically telnet) access.

Beginning in Spring Semester 1996, University 300 began to use a private listserv to facilitate student-instructor discussion and communication. The listserv provided students with a means to develop a community with their distant classmates, and helped them understand that research is a community effort. Even with recent changes in the course, the listserv continues to be used, despite other methods of communication now available on the Web (bulletin boards and other web-based guestbook-like programs)–because listservs remain a standard means of professional communication in the "real world."

## TRANSFORMATION OF THE COURSE

Almost immediately after the course was developed, it needed revision. From the Fall of 1995 to the present, changes in technology, the Internet, and the WSU campus environment compelled further refinements in University 300. A chronological overview highlighting these developments is shown in Appendix 1.

In the Fall of 1997, the Director of the General Education Program secured a grant from the William and Flora Hewlett Foundation Education Program entitled "Building a Research Track in General Education at Washington State University." A section of the grant provided for the expanded development of University 300 for a support mechanism for social science majors to a more general and stable platform which could serve students in the humanities, sciences, or social sciences. A series of meetings was held among the Libraries, the WSU Writing Center, the Student Advising and Learning Center, and interested teaching faculty to plan for a larger-scale implementation of University 300, to facilitate its adoption into the General Education Program. This collaborative effort, and support from these individuals and programs, assisted the Libraries in understanding the pedagogical, administrative, and political issues related to establishing a new course on campus.

While these discussions progressed, the University 300 course material–a revision of the original fourteen lessons–was reformatted for eight Web-based modules, with subsections accessible via hyperlinks on the University 300 course materials page. A team of librarians wrote text, provided research assistance, and created digital photographs and images for the modules. In the subsequent semester, video streaming was introduced into several of the modules, as clips from the original course videos were chosen and formatted for the Web. The Student Advising and Learning Center provided support for the coding of the modules into HTML. The current version of the course material is outlined in Table 2.

## *OTHER CHANGES*

The discussion of academic discourse and discipline-specific research was expanded to include a short history and background of the humanities and the sciences. Research examples throughout the text of the course material were edited to include scenarios from other academic disciplines. The most significant component of this expanded research focus, however, could not be contained in text, but had to come alive in the classroom when University 300 was "linked" to targeted three-credit research-oriented courses. In Spring semester 1998, for example, three librarians, representing the sciences, social

## TABLE 2. Outline of Current GenEd 300 Course

| Lesson/Module | Topic | Lesson/Module | Topic |
|---|---|---|---|
| 1 | Course Introduction: Libraries, Modern Research, Library History, Research Models | 5 | Database Structure: Concepts, Structure, Language |
| 2 | Information Landscape: Growth, Formats, Types, and Producers of Information | 6 | Database Searching: Introduction, Database Choice, Search Vocabulary, Planning a Search |
| 3 | Academic Disciplines: the Sciences, Humanities, and Social Sciences | 7 | The Internet: Cultural Aspects, Technical Issues, Searching the Internet |
| 4 | Question Analysis: Introduction, Research Scenarios, Formal and Informal Sources, Summary | 8 | Evaluation of Information: Bias, Relative Objectivity, Criteria |

sciences, and humanities, taught sections of University 300 to students enrolled in a cluster of courses focused on the Umatilla tribes of Washington and Oregon. This "course cluster" included two 400-level history courses, a 400-level science course, and a 200-level English course.

Offering University 300 in Spring semester 1998 on campus presented a number of logistical issues not evident or pressing the course's distance education format, where students tend to be more self-motivated, and in which there is more of a fluid, less time-dependent exchange between student and instructor. New grading policies, syllabi, attendance policies, student recruitment strategies, classroom dynamics and other issues, which had largely been non-existent or certainly more straightforward with distance education students, needed to be explored and worked out. These same challenges of implementing a process-oriented course on campus continues to be worked out, with added administrative concerns as the program grows. The results of linking the one-credit research course to a three-credit offering were successful in the view of students who had enrolled. Typical student responses to end-of-semester evaluations reflected a sense of achievement in fulfilling the research goals of their linked course, and the realization that formal research is a rich and challenging endeavor that warrants critical thought and skills not previously understood.

The fall of 1998 saw the official adaptation of University 300 into the General Education program, when the course's prefix changed to GenEd 300, and the full implementation of the course on the Pullman campus. A combination of librarians, academic instructors, and graduate students currently teach GenEd300. The collaborative partnership between the Libraries and the General Education program, especially, has resulted in significant programmatic and administrative developments to the course. Pedagogically, the constructivist model of learning, present in the course since its inception, has been encouraged and strengthened through a series of workshops. This theory of learning, allied with some crucial elements of the critical thinking movement, holds that students build upon prior knowledge–in this case, prior research experience and information evaluation abilities gained in other courses and outside of the university. Instructors create opportunities for students to interact, discuss, try out, explain, evaluate, and reflect on the research process as they learn to incorporate more conceptual knowledge into their experience.

The administrative duties related to the maintenance of GenEd 300 evolved and increased greatly. However, the Libraries received significant support and assistance from the university. The Student Advising and Learning Center, for example, has provided a half-time coordinator to work with the Libraries on the training of instructors, and to support the logistics of creating course sections, scheduling instructional lab time, and working with faculty to develop "links" between content and research skills.

## LOOKING AHEAD–AND WHAT WE'VE LEARNED

The future of GenEd 300, both in its distance education and on-campus versions, looks very promising at this point. WSU teaching faculty are very supportive in recommending it to students. Of course, success brings new challenges. For the GenEd 300 program to expand, it must develop a comprehensive training plan and support mechanisms for graduate students to teach methods of question analysis, information access, and evaluation within the context and philosophy of the course. More effort must be focused on increasing the interactivity of the current web-based modules. Finally, more formal and reliable assessment of the course needs to be implemented.

We believe that the course's history shows the commonalities of learning issues among distance education students and traditional campus students, despite their many differences; that sound learning theory is useful in any context; that research skills make the most sense when linked with students' growing understanding of disciplines, their vocabularies, and their habits of mind and techniques of investigation; that administrative support is crucial not only in initiating new courses but in sustaining and "scaling" them to wider purposes; and that fruitful collaborations produce unexpected and happy benefits.

## ACKNOWLEDGMENTS

This history and development of Univ300/GenEd 300, a complex and rewarding experience, show the support of many individuals, programs, and departments at Washington State University. We would like to thank the following for their contributions:

Janet Kendall and Muriel Oakes of Extended University Services; Rick Gay, video producer for the Extended Degree Program; Margie Rose, graphics specialist for the Extended Degree Program; Richard Law, Director of General Education; Susan McLeod, Associate Dean of Liberal Arts; Nancy Baker, Director of Libraries; James Elmborg, former Head of Library User Education; Alice Spitzer, Sharon Walbridge, Janet Chisman, and Sarah Symans, WSU librarians of various specialties; Amy Beasley, current administrative assistant for the GenEd 300 program; Kristine McBride, Extended Degree Library Services; Bill Condon and Joel Norris of the Writing Center and GenEd 302 program; Jean Henscheid of the Student Advising and Learning Center; Darin Saul, Center for Environmental Education; students enrolled in the course itself; and many faculty at WSU who have shown an interest in, and supported the development of, Univ300/GenEd300.

## APPENDIX 1

Semester Timeline of Course Development in University/GenEd 300

| Semester | Course Development |
| --- | --- |
| Summer 1995 | University 300 first developed for Extended Degree students |
| Fall 1995 | University 300 (distance education version) first offered |
| Spring 1996 | Course taught for second time, with implementation of listserv to facilitate instructor-student discussion |
| Fall 1996 | First major course guide revision precipitated by changing Internet environment and newly added library databases |
| Fall 1997 | Course content further modified and adapted for the Web; course received support from Hewlett Grant through the WSU General Education Program |
| Spring 1998 | University 300 taught for the first time on the Pullman campus in pilot form |
| Fall 1998 | Course prefix changes from UNIV to GenEd 300. GenEd 300 taught concurrently on campus and through Extended Degree Program |

# SECTION 5:
# REFERENCE, INSTRUCTION AND INFORMATION LITERACY

# Reference Services
# to Police Officer Students
# at the School of Police Staff and Command,
# Traffic Institute, Northwestern University

### Hema Ramachandran

**SUMMARY.** This paper focuses on the reference services provided by librarians at the Transportation Library for the police officer students enrolled in the School of Police Staff and Command, Traffic Institute, Northwestern University (Evanston, Illinois). Although this program is unique, the wealth of experience gained over several years can be useful for others who are planning and implementing services for adult learners within an academic environment. The Transportation Library's unusual organizational culture–a corporate library within an academic setting– and a variety of clients necessitates "changing gears" and services to meet the needs of each group. *[Article copies available for a fee from The Haworth Document Delivery Service: 1-800-342-9678. E-mail address: <getinfo@haworthpressinc. com> Website: <http://www.haworthpressinc.com>]*

Hema Ramachandran is Technical Reference Librarian, California Institute of Technology, Pasadena, CA 91125. She worked at Northwestern University from November 1993 to September 1997 (Hema@library.caltech.edu).

The author wishes to acknowledge her former colleagues at the Transportation Library: Dorothy Ramm, Mary McCreadie and the Head of the Transportation Library, Roberto Sarmiento. All of them made great suggestions, offered encouragement and found errors in the final stages of the writing of this paper. Last but not least, the author wants to thank her husband, Dr. R. Sethuraman, for being the first to read this article and offering his expert advice and encouragement when it was needed the most!

[Haworth co-indexing entry note]: "Reference Services to Police Officer Students at the School of Police Staff and Command, Traffic Institute, Northwestern University." Ramachandran, Hema. Co-published simultaneously in *The Reference Librarian* (The Haworth Information Press, an imprint of The Haworth Press, Inc.) No. 69/70, 2000, pp. 247-258; and: *Reference Services for the Adult Learner: Challenging Issues for the Traditional and Technological Era* (ed: Kwasi Sarkodie-Mensah) The Haworth Information Press, an imprint of The Haworth Press, Inc., 2000, pp. 247-258. Single or multiple copies of this article are available for a fee from The Haworth Document Delivery Service [1-800-342-9678, 9:00 a.m. - 5:00 p.m. (EST). E-mail address: getinfo@haworthpressinc.com].

**KEYWORDS.** Police officers, law enforcement officers, reference services, adult learners, library services to professionals, library instruction, bibliographic instruction, Northwestern University, Traffic Institute, School of Police and Command

## INTRODUCTION

In a recent article entitled "Library Instruction for the Professions: Information Needs and Libraries," Carol Hammond and Eleanor Mitchell, address an engaging issue that has hitherto gained little scholarly attention (Hammond and Mitchell, 1997). The authors underscore the importance of instruction and reference services for professionals such as architects, psychologists, accountants and practitioners in recreation/tourism. Traditionally, those employed in "research-oriented fields," including the medical profession, have ready access to information within their discipline. But what about those engaged in the "less research-oriented professions?" Since the information needs of the latter are just as valid and important, how are librarians meeting their needs? It is precisely this less explored question and topic that my paper investigates, using as a case-study the School of Police Staff and Command (SPSC) which is part of the Traffic Institute (TI) at Northwestern University. This article thus extends the dialogue initiated by Hammond and Mitchell, and hopefully provides a framework for further research and studies in other contexts and situations.

Hammond and Mitchell ask some pointed questions that set the tone for this article. For example they write:

> In the current information environment of rapid change and technological innovation, planning library instruction programs the university and enter the profession, is increasingly challenging. Can we really develop lifelong skills, or just skills that help students get through college? Are we teaching concepts that are flexible enough to serve students as the information world around them changes dramatically? How do those who enter the professions look for the information they need? Do our programs prepare them for finding information on the job? (p. 79)

An analysis of their survey results of professionals in Arizona draws many useful conclusions. I summarize below some of the main points, which I found illuminating:

- Library instruction programs are relevant and needed for those who enter professions.
- Librarians should adjust the content of instruction from library instruction to information instruction.

- Librarians should also provide opportunities for practitioners to upgrade information-finding skills especially in the use of electronic resources.
- Administrators and library service providers should explore improved access to academic libraries and special services that might be developed for users from the professions.

Before turning to a full description of what, how, where, and when the SPSC program is run at the Traffic Institute, Northwestern University, I want to briefly explain its relevance to Hammond and Mitchell's article. The program at Northwestern University's (NU) Transportation Library (TL) has been addressing the very same issues, that Hammond and Mitchell identified, and the librarians have shifted the "content of instruction from library instruction to information instruction." This pedagogical strategy empowers the SPSC students (police officers in mid-level positions) to use the information-seeking skills beyond the scope of the class assignments to using the techniques gained to hone their decision-making processes in their day-to-day work situations. As one of the top private research institutions, Northwestern University has extended its educational and research privileges not only to the police officers from all over the United States but also to the four corners of the world. Given the fact that regular admission to the undergraduate and graduate programs at Northwestern University is highly competitive, the SPSC program provides a unique opportunity for the police officers to have access to the library and other resources as any other regular student on campus. More importantly, the gaining of TI certification after the successful completion of the courses provides an enormous leverage and high premium in terms of further advancement in their career, especially in taking on responsible management positions. This unique community service thus provides a model of ways other private institutions with rich endowments can bring the diverse community to the university, and the university to the community. In fact a survey of the graduates of the TI program, such as the one conducted by Hammond and Mitchell, may prove useful and illuminating.

## *TRANSPORTATION LIBRARY, TRAFFIC INSTITUTE AND THE SCHOOL OF POLICE STAFF AND COMMAND*

The Transportation Library (TL) at Northwestern University (NU) provides support for the Transportation Center and the Traffic Institute (TI). In addition to one of the largest transportation collections in the world, TL also has a major collection of law enforcement and criminal justice material to support the information needs of the Traffic Institute. The Traffic Institute was established in 1936 to provide training for police officers in traffic law enforcement and accident investigation and it has later broadened its scope to include other areas of police operations, in particular management and administration. One of the main educational arms of TI is the School of Police Staff and Command (SPSC), which since 1983 has been providing a dynamic 10-week police management program designed for police managers and their agencies. The main objective of the program is to provide officers, drawn from mid and upper-level supervisory ranks, with the knowledge and skills necessary for assuming increased responsibilities in administrative staff or line command positions. Officer-students must be prepared to complete upper-division (i.e., junior and senior-level) university course work. Accreditation of the program has been approved through the University College of Northwestern University, and all students who successfully complete the program can transfer 18 upper division, undergraduate semester credit hours from the University College to other academic programs. The curriculum includes a class in Information Resources for Law Enforcement Managers taught by librarians at the Transportation Library.

On-campus SPSC courses are held twice a year; about 40 officer-students converge in Evanston from around the country (and in fact the world) and live on campus for the durations of the consecutive 10-week program. In addition to the on-campus program, several SPSC classes are presented off-campus each year at sites across the country. During my time at Northwestern University (1993-1997) there were about 8-12 offsite classes a year. TI contracts with a law enforcement agency (e.g., Detroit Police Department, Ohio State Highway Patrol) and provides instructors and materials; the agency provides a venue and local support.

## REFERENCE AND INSTRUCTION SERVICES

This paper will focus on reference services provided by the librarians at the Transportation Library to support the on-campus program. This special volume of *The Reference Librarian* is devoted to the topic of reference services to adult learners, but since reference service and information instruction are inevitably dovetailed together, it is important that I begin with a brief description of the library instruction program.

TL has always provided on-campus support to SPSC but it was Jo Cates, Head of the Transportation Library (1991-1993), who proposed, developed and implemented the offsite instructional program with Renee McHenry (Head of Public Services) and expanded and formalized the on-campus support. Upon my appointment as Reference and Instruction Librarian, in November 1993, I continued the basic program following the original model developed by Jo and Renee. As is the case with any instructional program, it is constantly under review and many changes were made from 1993 to 1997 (the time of my departure). For instance, any classes that are held within a 50 mile radius of Evanston receive the ½ day library instruction class on campus rather than having the instruction librarian travel to the offsite location. My paper is based on my experience with program and services as they existed during my time there. The unique offsite program was the focus of a paper presented at the *Special Libraries Association Annual Conference* (Rama-chandran, 1996).

Prior to his or her arrival on campus, each student in the program is sent a comprehensive packet of information about the Transportation Library–its policies, hours, location, contact information and the like. The packet in-cludes materials on how to access the online catalog and how to search for criminal justice material; a listing of resources in TL and other NU libraries compiled by Dorothy Ramm entitled *Finding Criminal Justice in the Trans-portation Library,* and other relevant information. In addition to these vital resources, TL has also developed a web page especially for the SPSC stu-dents entitled *Selected Internet Resources in Criminal Justice Resources* (http://www.library.nwu.edu/transportation/cj.html).

The class session *Information Resources for Law Enforcement Managers* taken during the first week of the 10-week program equips and orients the students to effectively use library and information resources to conduct their research. In fact, instead of a crammed one-hour session of library instruc-tion, the library instructor (in recognition of the importance and complexity of information research) is allotted a half-day slot to cover the gamut of the whole research process. The following topics are covered: effective research skills; library and information resources in criminal justice and law enforce-ment; use of the various library and information tools (online catalog, period-ical indexes, online databases, and the Internet) and critical evaluation skills. The on-campus presentation is interwoven with online demonstrations of these resources, an orientation tour of TL, and a chance to begin the literature search. It is a major challenge to cover all this material in a way that the students can grasp the essentials without being overwhelmed by the vast amount of information. It is also a challenge for the instruction librarian since the information has to be staggered and presented methodically to the stu-dents.

From the onset of the orientation session, which is usually scheduled on the first Friday afternoon of the ten-week course, to the students' graduation, it often feels like one is in a "Quicktime" movie! Within a few days, the students have to select and submit a research topic to their instructor. In exploring their potential research topic, the students work closely with the librarians in order to determine whether there is enough published material on the topic. The students are in class all day (8:00-4:30 pm, Monday-Friday) and can only visit the library at the end of the day, during their lunch hour or on Saturday. This presents a logistical headache as students often arrive en masse at the end of the day!

## IMPLEMENTATION OF A NEW SERVICE

To alleviate the pressure of attending to many students at once, and serve the SPSC students better, the library established a new procedure with the Fall 1996 class. Special help sessions were scheduled the week following the class. The addition of a "sign-up sheet," eliciting student's name, research topic and the date of the planned visit to the library, have helped to refine the process. The instruction librarian can then do some preliminary work, especially vital with the less directly police related topics. The pre-scheduled visit forces the students to focus immediately on their proposed topic, and come to the library planning to work. Extra librarians are on duty the following week from 4:30-7:00 pm weekdays, lunch times and on the two subsequent Saturdays.

The additional service has worked extremely well and has become an integral part of the program. For one week the whole library focuses on the needs of the police students. Instead of the traditional policy of having one librarian on duty, the new strategy calls for two persons on duty (two librarians or one librarian and one support staff member), and a student assistant (if possible), available at the most critical time–4-5 PM weekdays. At that time the Transportation Library had 4.5 librarians (this includes the instruction librarian and head of the library), three support staff members and a team of student assistants. All of the librarians at the Transportation Library elect to do an evening and/or Saturday shift. One of the librarians is assigned to assisting the police students, while the other one takes care of telephone and other onsite requests. Naturally, beyond the "special help week" the students continue to receive quality reference assistance as and when it is needed.

The librarian on duty conducts a 'reference interview' with each student and instructs him or her in the use of the online catalog. This includes the unique in-house TRAN database of periodicals articles held by the library. From that point on the student is encouraged to examine the various databases and continue to critically review citations, select relevant items, and ultimately retrieve items from the shelves. Other relevant online databases (*National Criminal Justice Reference Service* database, *Sociofile, PsychInfo, PAIS, ABI Inform, Nexis/Lexis,* etc.) and print sources (*Criminal Justice Abstracts, Criminal Justice Periodicals Index*) as well as other relevant reference sources are utilized as warranted by the topic. Student assistants complete the teamwork by providing assistance in locating items on the shelf, directions in using equipment and other routine tasks.

There are many tangible benefits in approaching reference work from a customer-oriented perspective. In addition to the obvious advantages to the police students, the new approach to reference benefits the librarians as well:

- Less stress all around–for the police students, student assistants, the instruction librarian and the department.
- In each onsite class there are always some police students who commute to Evanston and this service is of special benefit to them in scheduling study time and family life accordingly.
- Librarians can consult on difficult topics at shift changes. Naturally each librarian has his or her own unique strengths and can lend a different perspective to the topic on hand.
- I found that helping several students at the same time (without other interruptions), is liberating and very rewarding and actually helps to develop, observe and refine one's own reference and instructional techniques. It is a rejuvenating experience as one observes inexperienced library users literally grow in confidence in front of one's eyes. It was also interesting to observe group dynamics amongst a special group of users.
- Unlike in the past, when student assistants were deluged with more requests than they could handle, the new strategy takes the burden off the student assistants.
- It is also an opportunity for the student assistants to watch us and learn reference and public service techniques and for their supervisor to provide some on the spot student training. The "student team" became experts themselves and many of them offered to the officers helpful suggestions of potential research topics.
- When the police students have learned how to use the information tools, there is less stress in later weeks for the library staff as most of the police students progress to the next step in the research process–gathering material, requesting inter-library loan requests, and so on.

## SHIFTING GEARS, SENSITIVITY AND GROUP DYNAMICS

One of the major challenges for the Reference/Instruction librarian and all who work in the Transportation Library is the necessity and ability to "shift gears" swiftly to match the broad spectrum of onsite, telephone and virtual (email) patrons. Without missing a heartbeat and often simultaneously, one has to serve the needs of undergraduates, graduates, faculty, researchers, external patrons, such as transit officials and consultants, and police students. The police student is a very special type of patron–they may be on the one hand at the freshmen level in terms of library experience, but on the other hand be at the mid-point of their professional careers. Conversely, they may also be concurrently enrolled in a Bachelor's or even Master's degree program and have substantial experience in using library and information tools. In fact we have noticed that in the past three to four years the use of Internet and other research tools has dramatically increased in this user population. However, the gap between the info-sophisticate and the info-novice has widened over the past few years, as the law enforcement profession is becoming a degreed profession. So, it can be seen from this scenario that the librarians have to tread very cautiously in ascertaining the level of library experience of each student. On the surface this may appear to be an onerous task but I believe that this is one of the skills that experienced reference librarians have learnt on the job and can instinctually tune into the patron's level of knowledge. In some cases patrons will self-identify that they are novices to library research; in many cases they will not. Failure to ascertain the level of library experience in the reference interview process can result in either not adequately serving the needs of the student–resulting from not providing appropriate instruction in the use of various tools–or adopting a patronizing tone that can be very off-putting to the student. As more and more adults return to universities to further their education, librarians are finding that their clientele no longer consists of the three traditional groups–undergraduates, graduates and faculty–but that the "adult learner" adds yet another layer of complexity. The Transportation Library represents a very good example and case study of an organization, which has traditionally served all these groups in an exemplary fashion.

Group dynamics and behavior are also at play in this particular situation and the librarians must be aware of issues of rank and peer politics. Often an older police student of a higher rank and less experience with computerized databases may be working beside a younger/junior officer who knows much more. This is not an unusual situation since the younger officers are often more computer literate. However, one has to be highly sensitive to issues involving group dynamics since these officers may belong to the same jurisdiction and must resume their position in the hierarchy when they return to work. In view of this fact it is wise and appropriate of the librarian to remember at all times that we–students and librarians–are all professionals and not embarrass the novice library user in any way. In order to be sensitive and bring the inexperienced police student(s) to the level of other competent library users, the librarians try to provide assistance and instruction on a confidential one-on-one basis. Since students, frequently arrive en masse it is often a challenge for the librarians to achieve this goal. It is interesting to note at this juncture that confidentiality is assured by the one-on-one nature of the contact method, phone or email, for the offsite classes.

## ADULT LEARNERS

It would be easy, and maybe in some ways less time-consuming, to do the research and present the students with all the relevant books and journal articles but it would not give the students first-hand experience about the research process or foster a sense of accomplishment. Therefore all the staff at TL aim at showing, instructing, and guiding the students to conduct their own database searching and retrieving materials. But the staff remains attentive and offers assistance as needed throughout the process. After a few years of in-depth experience in working with this user population, it is very easy for the librarians to fall into the pattern of magically zeroing in on the required material. However, we must remember that this is a new venture for the student and we must let them learn for themselves the mystical ways of the catalog and online databases. Part of this process is to allow them to make mistakes and treat it as part of the learning process. Marirose Coulson's recent article in Information Outlook makes an excellent argument for allowing mistakes to happen:

> Adults fear making mistakes, but mistakes are crucial to learning. When one makes a mistake, awareness is heightened. . . . A mistake also adds value because it forces the trainee to try again, which increases retention. Repetition reinforces skill development. The key is to create an environment that allows discovery and one where making a mistake is okay. Adults want to be self-directed. . . . Adults are motivated to learn and prefer a task-centered approach rather than memorization. (Coulson, 1998)

With adult learners, I find it inappropriate to adopt the role of the all-knowing librarian and insist they do it my way. Rather I allow the student to make their own decisions but I am always there to offer solutions. I like to think of myself as the "Information Guide" or a facilitator pointing the way to the ultimate goal. In the same vein, several writers have articulated similar sentiments in a cogent and eloquent manner. For example, Jacquelyn Coughlan reviews some of the articles on "teaching styles" as they relate to adult learners which bears repeating in the context of this paper:

> Sheridan recommends the "power of persuasion, sharing and example over those of dominance and manipulation." She further observes that an effective teacher encourages mutual confrontation and collaboration; and discourages destructive comparisons and patronising attitudes; and perhaps most importantly, allows adults to choose what they need to know. Knox's idea of the necessary qualities for teachers are concern and respect for adults with varied backgrounds, and a sense of humor,

responsiveness, and flexibility. Gartner says that the teacher "must be-come a co-learner who adopts a learner role, so that he/she can provide the student with a model of desirable learner behavior." (Coughlan, 1989. See also Sheridan, 1986; Knox, 1980; and Gartner, 1977)

## PROFESSIONAL INFORMATION NEEDS

One of the major underlying philosophies in the SPSC program is to foster in the participants the idea that the skills that they acquire are not only useful for writing their research paper but of paramount importance when they return to work. The Transportation Library has a very special relationship with the law enforcement community and encourages the students to contin-ue using the library and its services even after they graduate. By the same token, the library continues to provide reference and document delivery services, by phone, email and onsite, on request. Students are told to recom-mend TL and its services to their colleagues–even to those who did not attend the program. So the librarians have two complementary goals in serving the students in the program–the immediate goal of assisting them in gathering materials for their research paper and the long-term goal of exposing the law enforcement officers to the wealth of library and information tools for future research projects.

It is interesting to note at this juncture an article by Marc Levin, which reports on a research project of the information-seeking practices of local government officials. He makes a very compelling argument on the impor-tance of accessing relevant and timely information for effective decision-making:

> Moreover, local officials have to speed up their decision-making to make the public's demand for shorter lead times between identifying problems and announcing appropriate remedies. Declines in public sup-port and financing and the soaring costs of poorly planned policies have put additional pressures on the local government decision-making. To respond effectively to the increased complexity and urgency of policy-making, local government officials must rely on their ability to access relevant, accurate and timely information. (Levin, 1991, p. 272)

His study found that the officials recognize that they require different types of information–directories, legal information, developments in the field, information on local agencies and internally produced information–to make informed decisions. However, they are frustrated or display a lack of awareness of the process of obtaining external library-based resources. From this it can be seen that the support provided by Northwestern University's

Transportation Library to the law enforcement community plays a major role in providing a much needed service to a segment of local government officials who otherwise may not have access to such information.

## CHARACTERISTICS OF THE POLICE STUDENT USER GROUP

What is it like to provide reference services and teach law enforcement officers? Of all the patron groups that I have had the privilege of serving in my career thus far, serving this group has brought me the most job satisfaction. Each officer on the program knows that their agency has invested a great deal of money and time in sponsoring them to attend this program. Each of them has been selected by their Chief of Police as the one who will benefit most from this program and that they in turn will be better managers. They are highly motivated, disciplined, organized, focused, professional, and ultimately grateful for any and all help that we give them to achieve their goals. They understand the importance of education for themselves, their families and their agencies. They appreciate that the skills they acquire in this program will make them better police managers, facilitate better decision-making and ultimately equip them to serve their communities well. I have a better appreciation of the law enforcement profession and have also benefited from learning about their life and professional experiences. It is also very rewarding and satisfying to receive telephone calls, email messages and visits from graduates of the program who turn to the Transportation Library for their on-the-job research needs.

## CONCLUSIONS

Although this is a case study, there are many conclusions that we can draw and apply to other situations in academic libraries. It is safe to conclude that reference librarians have more and more demands made on them today and have to provide more services often with fewer staff resources. Add to this mix the complex world of electronic databases, shrinking collections, and the changing nature of pedagogy and it is easy to conclude that our usual way of doing business may have to change. Many academic reference departments are rethinking the traditional models of reference services spurred on by the increase in the numbers of adult learners, distance education users and remote access of electronic resources. It would be prudent to take a hard look at the user population and the level of traffic at the reference desk and reallocate staffing. For instance on a campus where the majority of students are commuters and combine work and study, alternative means of providing reference services may not only be helpful to the students but also improve the quality of service for all. The problem is particularly acute when each student who approaches the desk needs in-depth research assistance. The department could offer, for instance, drop-in reference help sessions, reference by appointment, and extensive email reference. These are all ideas that can probably be implemented with existing resources and ensure that all students get assistance in a timely fashion, while at the same reducing the traffic and congestion at the reference desk for the more routine enquiries. However, these changes to the traditional reference model require the cooperation of the entire reference team to ensure its success.

## REFERENCES

Coughlan, Jacqueline. "The BI librarian's new constituency: Adult independent learners." *Reference Librarian,* Vol. 24, 1989, pp. 159-173.

Coulson, Marirose. "Great expectations: Reach to teach." *Information Outlook,* September 1998, pp. 13-15.

Gartner, A. and Riessman, F. *How to individualize learning.* Bloomington, IL: Phi Beta Kappa Educational Foundation, 1977.

Hammond, Carol and Mitchell, Eleanor. "Library instruction for the professions: Information needs and libraries." *References Services Review,* Vol. 25, No. 2, Summer 1997, pp. 79-87.

Knox, A.B. *Teaching adults effectively.* San Francisco: Jossey-Bass, 1980.

Levin, Marc A. *"The information-seeking behavior of local government officials."* American *Review of Public Administration,* Vol. 21, No. 4, December 1991, pp. 271-286.

Ramachandran, Hema. "Offsite instruction for police officers," *87th Special Libraries Association Annual Conference,* Boston, MA, June 10, 1996. (A transcript of the paper and others in the session "Teaching Research Skills: Innovative Strategies for Library Use Instruction" is at http://www.library.nwu.edu/transportation/slatran).

Sheridan, J. "Andragogy: A new concept for academic librarians." *Research Strategies,* Vol. 4, Fall 1986, pp. 156-167.

# Library Instruction and Information Literacy for the Adult Learner: A Course and Its Lessons for Reference Work

Patti Schifter Caravello

**SUMMARY.** The creation of a course, offered through UCLA University Extension, called "Research Methods for Fiction, Nonfiction, and Film Writers" was motivated by the observation that many adult learners lack information skills and the opportunity for formal library instruction. The content and format of this librarian-taught course have changed through the years both to incorporate more electronic resources and to employ more active learning methods. This article describes the need for the course, the course content and its evolution, and the active learning exercises employed. What an academic reference librarian derives from teaching such a course informs reference work with adult learners, whether or not they are part of the university community. *[Article copies available for a fee from The Haworth Document Delivery Service: 1-800-342-9678. E-mail address: <getinfo@haworthpressinc.com> Website: <http://www.haworthpressinc.com>]*

**KEYWORDS.** Library instruction, adult learners, adults, adult programming, active learning, information literacy, continuing education

Patti Schifter Caravello is Reference Librarian and Instructional Services Coordinator, UCLA Charles E. Young Research Library, Box 951575, Los Angeles, CA 90095-1575 (E-mail: patti@library.ucla.edu).

[Haworth co-indexing entry note]: "Library Instruction and Information Literacy for the Adult Learner: A Course and Its Lessons for Reference Work." Caravello, Patti Schifter. Co-published simultaneously in *The Reference Librarian* (The Haworth Information Press, an imprint of The Haworth Press, Inc.) No. 69/70, 2000, pp. 259-269; and: *Reference Services for the Adult Learner: Challenging Issues for the Traditional and Technological Era* (ed: Kwasi Sarkodie-Mensah) The Haworth Information Press, an imprint of The Haworth Press, Inc., 2000, pp. 259-269. Single or multiple copies of this article are available for a fee from The Haworth Document Delivery Service [1-800-342-9678, 9:00 a.m. - 5:00 p.m. (EST). E-mail address: getinfo@haworthpressinc.com].

## ADULT LEARNERS AND LIBRARY INSTRUCTION

Writers, independent researchers and other adults whose occupation or interests require information skills are at a distinct disadvantage when they walk into a modern research library. This is particularly so at the nearest university library which may, or may seem to, offer the greatest breadth of resources. The array of electronic resources alone is enough to mystify; the absence of a card catalog enough to disorient; and the feeling one is an outsider is enough to intimidate even the most earnest adult learner. The pace of information technology has been so fast in recent years, it is a challenge even for librarians to keep up with it. Adult learners now encounter libraries which are very different places than when they were in school. The library can even seem to change between visits, as databases relocate and new tools appear. In reference desk encounters, what adult learners often receive is bits and pieces of information (how to find this journal, where to find that fact), not a cohesive strategy or set of concepts to guide them through unfamiliar systems and topics.

Those who are not college students have few opportunities for formal library instruction, especially that which addresses a variety of information competencies. Descriptions of library and Internet instruction sessions in public libraries can be found in the literature and on the Web,[1] but the literature is sparse when compared to that on academic library instruction. Programs at college and university libraries, including resource-based, conceptual, discipline-specific, and course-integrated instruction, are typically available only to the university population.

Library instruction for adult learners should take into account precepts of adult learning theory, in which emphasis is placed on developing independent learning skills rather than on transmission of knowledge alone, the teacher is more a facilitator of the learning process, and a central goal is the creation of independent learners who think critically.[2] These principles, which are also used to varying degrees in academic library instruction, provide "an ideal framework for the teaching of information literacy"[3] to which they are so naturally allied.

Library instruction was not likely an integral part of adult learners' prior education, hence many have little if any past research skills training to recall during the reference interview. Lacking the time, personnel, and in some cases the mission to spend a lot of time with "non-students" or "off-campus users," academic reference librarians often gear their approach to getting such users through this library visit, whether or not that includes teaching them skills, concepts, or strategies they can use again. This approach works for some, particularly one-time library users, but it is ineffective for the adult learner who has recurring or ongoing information and research needs. It is an open question whether adults can become information literate on their own or with only reference desk assistance.

## A COURSE APPROACH

When University of California Los Angeles (UCLA) reference librarian and writer Mona McCormick had the idea for a course on library and information skills for the adult learner in the early 1980s, technological changes had already hit most academic libraries. At that time, the adult learner seeking a fruitful and efficient session in the research library faced all the obstacles described above when he simply encountered an online catalog. McCormick proposed the "Research Methods for Writers" course to the Writers' Program of University Extension, the large and well-established continuing education arm of UCLA whose programs are adult-focused and "committed to meeting the lifelong educational needs and interests of adults and working professionals."[4] With its open admissions policy, the Writers' Program attracted, then as now, fiction, nonfiction, poetry, play, and screen writers. The course, with its focus on the writer/researcher, was a natural fit.

The goals of the course have not changed substantially since its inception. Phrased in the terminology of the late 1990s, they are:

- to foster information literacy in the adult learner
- to provide practical as well as conceptual assistance for the information and research needs of the independent writer or researcher
- to introduce tools of the modern research library and virtual library
- to create a more substantive librarian–adult learner connection and shared vocabulary which can be valuable at any reference desk

## INSTITUTIONAL SUPPORT

UCLA University Extension produces a course catalog every quarter. This publication is the main source of publicity for the course. Extension also takes care of enrollment, fees, photocopying, and other administrative matters. Because the course is given on Saturdays, when the library's instruction classroom is not being used, I have been able to use it for this class. The classroom has facilities for live demonstrations of the online catalog, electronic indexes, and the Web. By agreement with Extension, there is a cap of 25 students for the course. I have found this necessary due to the types of hands-on activities employed and the desire to get to know the students and have them find me accessible. There is usually a waiting-list for the course, indicating a need for it in the community.

For librarians who might like to introduce a course like this, finding the opportunity or institutional support might be a challenge. But avenues like university extension and continuing education at colleges or community colleges may be receptive to a proposal for this type of course, and they provide many advantages. They are accessible to most people in the community, non-threatening to adult learners with varying educational backgrounds, and they usually do not require matriculation in a particular school or program. Academic locales have classrooms, library materials, and computer workstations and resources, all of which are utilized during the course. Adult programming in large public libraries would be another avenue to pursue.

### COURSE FORMAT

McCormick experimented with course formats (six weeks, one evening a week; two whole days on one or two weekends). The two consecutive Saturday format worked best, as it allowed large chunks of time in which to cover a lot of ground and perform in-class exercises, and it gave the students a week between classes to experiment, do an assignment, or come up with questions. I have taught the course almost every year since 1987 using the two-Saturday format (9:30 a.m. to 4:30 p.m. both days).

Although most students and the instructor–adults with jobs and families– appreciate that the course spans only a week, some students see this as a disadvantage; they need more time to absorb all the material and to practice what they have learned while still enrolled in the course. It cannot be emphasized enough how much it means to these adult learners to have access to, and interaction with, a librarian in the context of this course. They finally have the full attention of someone who knows the library and research strategy, who can demystify online systems, relate search concepts to their research topics, and provide systematic clues to the information world's complexities. Although it is all, technically, over in a week, follow-up through email, in-person consultation, and instructor feedback to final projects extends the course for some students. And, naturally, student and instructor alike hope that the librarian-adult learner connection continues well past the end of the course, in all the libraries they visit.

With respect to pacing and moving through the intensive two-day format, I have found the following to be most important with adult learners:

- to vary the format and pace during each of the two days (with lecture, group activity, independent exercises, tour, online demonstrations, and hands-on activities with books and computers)
- to reinforce the units of instruction with hands-on practice
- to use the library's classroom as home base, and also use other areas of the library
- to provide time for students to speak and ask questions

## LECTURE AND ONLINE DEMONSTRATIONS

The first objective is to convey the concept of the systematic search strategy. This is often the first time these adult learners have heard a discussion of the possible steps and sequences a particular query might entail and the significance of search strategy to independent learning and research. As student research interests vary, I do not address the structure of particular disciplines, but the idea of the systematic and critical approach to information. Until now they have found articles serendipitously, bounced from one source to another as a ball in a pinball machine, maybe getting lucky, maybe not. This has been solitary work; some have thought they alone were confounded by the process, although many somehow became familiar with, even proficient in particular tools or strategies. The search strategy discussion undergirds the whole course, is outlined in a three-page handout, and is usually an eye-opener to the students.

Other lecture topics spread over the two days reflect various information competencies and include:

- mechanics of research (systems for keeping track of citations, notes, and search strategies)
- controlled vocabulary
- key aspects of online catalogs (attributes most systems have in common)
- evaluating reference tools and information they provide
- periodical indexes and abstracts
- biographical research methods
- critical thinking in the research process

Imparting these concepts and strategies in short lectures immediately followed by online demonstrations and/or active learning exercises helps keep a balance between "transmission of knowledge" (to which at least some time must be devoted) and emphasis on "learning processes" (the key to the development of independent learners).

Online demonstrations provide a context for some of the lectures and an opportunity to turn the students' research topics into actual online searches. The topic of controlled vocabulary only begins to make sense during the online catalog demonstration. Likewise, with the entire morning of day two devoted to strategies and tools in the search for periodical and newspaper articles, online demonstrations of various indexes are critical. Many adults are not yet, or not effectively, using the World Wide Web, and even those who are benefit from a demonstration which covers search techniques and ways to evaluate materials found on the Web. All the demonstrations contain a conceptual element and a practical lesson, both of which are important to adult learners who appreciate the why and the how.

## *ACTIVE LEARNING EXERCISES*

1. *Topic Sharing and Defining:* As an ice-breaker on the first morning I ask each student to describe to the class the research topics they are, or expect to be, working on and what they hope to learn in the course. I use this information throughout the two days to emphasize certain tools or strategies and to illustrate searches in databases. The students use their topics in the subsequent active learning exercises to make the sources come alive and the lessons more meaningful to them. This exercise helps the students see that others are in similar predicaments about research. My part in the exercise is to be the reference librarian, openly asking questions of some of the students to clarify the topic's parameters, the type of information sought, or to see if a certain source was checked. This provides insight into how a topic should be defined and an information need expressed. These mini-reference interviews are kept brief for best effect, to give everyone a turn in the time allotted.

2. *Fact-Finding Exercise #1:* On the first day, I engage the students in the first of two one-hour fact-finding exercises. These are small group, hands-on activities with reference books I bring to the classroom. After introducing the idea and methods of evaluating reference tools, I read examples of biased encyclopedia articles, disagreement in facts between reputable reference tools, and cases where only the tool's preface describes what is really covered. The students in groups of two or three look critically at two reference works, handed out randomly. In their packets is a list of all the reference tools used in the exercise which they or their classmates will examine (almanacs, fact books, chronologies, specialized encyclopedias, word books, directories, geographical tools, and quotations books).

After examining each of the two tools' preface, organization, indexing, and content, the students come up with two questions each source can answer. This makes the exercise a little like the TV game show *Jeopardy!* where the answer is a question. When the time is up, one person from each group reports to the whole class the title of the reference book used and two questions it answers.

In the course of this activity, adult learners gain a new perspective on the sources of information available. They invariably ask me or their partner such questions as, "why would you use this one," or "how *is* this one organized," "where does this data come from," or "don't you think this is too limited/too ambitious?" Before they settle on what questions they will read to the class (which are as much to amuse as to share information), they have usually already asked the right questions about the tools themselves and had their awareness raised. For the sake of keeping to the schedule, I ask them not to share all of what they learned about the tool, but just to read the two questions. This activity is more about critical thinking in the search for information than where to go for specific information, but students often get ideas for reference works to try later, and make notes on their book lists.

3. *Fact-Finding Exercise #2:* On day two, in the classroom with other reference books brought in from the library's Reference room, students in groups of about five or six rotate every fifteen minutes to each of four stations. At each station is a group of reference books with a common purpose: (1) sources for finding pictures and photographs, (2) sources that take you beyond the UCLA Library, (3) statistical sources, and (4) sources for tracking the 20th Century. In their packets the students have a list of all the books. There is a set of questions for each station, and students, working together or independently, use the books to try to answer as many questions as they can in the time allotted.

People derive different benefits from this exercise, as learning styles vary. Some will spend most of the time looking carefully at one or two sources at each station and miss the other sources. Others, eager to see as many books as possible, focus on finding answers to the questions and make discoveries about the books that way. A few are interested in taking notes on their list of sources to remind themselves to use the book in the future, and they do not concentrate on the questions. All of these are valid outcomes, reflecting different learning processes and styles. While a few students are frustrated when they cannot get to all the books and all the questions, this exercise is always rewarding in some way. Its goals, similar to those of the first fact-finding activity, are to develop a critical approach to reference tools and facts, to recognize various categories or types of reference tools, most of which are not yet online, and to learn by doing and have some fun.

4. *Bibliography Exercise:* In the final exercise of the first day, students learn about the value of bibliographies in research, and how to find and interpret them. In their packets is a bibliography in which each citation is written in a different style. I start out by asking for the active participation of the students in trying to decipher the references. This leads them to look carefully at citations, often for the first time, and to ask the right questions to interpret them. As this is a very dry topic, turning it into a lively guessing game somewhat redeems it. Once we have covered "In" references, book and journal citations, abbreviations, and other details, the students go to the library's Reference Room for the main part of this exercise.

The students use any volume of *Bibliographic Index* to find a bibliography related to their topics. After copying down the reference, they use the online catalog to find the item. Alternatively, they may start with the online catalog under a Library of Congress subject heading plus "bibliography." The exercise requires that they apply what they learned, or get clarification on what they missed, in the online demonstration. I facilitate the activity by remaining available for questions as they search. When the students are able to locate the bibliography in the stacks, they feel a certain sense of satisfaction. This activity reinforces several of the day's topics: search strategy, understanding citations, and the use of the online catalogs.

5. *Periodical Indexes:* On day two, each student selects an index and then uses it to find at least one article on his or her topic. Most opt for an electronic index. As the students spread out to use the workstations, I again rove and look over their shoulders to be available to answer their questions. They have to find the periodical's location in the library using the online catalog if the index does not provide the location. This exercise is a practical application of what was just covered in the lecture and demonstration, and is the type of structured exploration and immediate reinforcement I have found to be invaluable in teaching adult learners.

6. *Biographical Search:* Under revision is another active learning exercise in which the *Biography and Genealogy Master Index* and *Biography Index* were used and the biographical information evaluated. I am altering it to include the Web in the search for and evaluation of information about people, a change facilitated by the increased number of workstations in the library which access the Web. The goal of the revision is to incorporate the electronic and further emphasize evaluation over mechanics.

## FINAL PROJECT

Students are encouraged, though not required, to do a project which asks them to utilize the search strategies and some of the tools covered in the course. Its end product is a set of eight index cards on which are noted: the scope of the topic, a citation to a bibliography on the topic, two periodical article citations, a list of relevant Library of Congress subject headings, two books found with those headings, and a book found using the bibliography or the lists of references in the articles or books. All citations are annotated. On the back of each card containing a citation, the source of the reference is noted. In this way students are encouraged to be aware and critical of the process by which they find information. I return the projects by mail, with notes and reactions to the work done and suggestions of additional strategies to try for their topics.

## EVALUATION

At the conclusion of the second day, the students fill out University Extension's course evaluation forms. The forms ask about satisfaction with the course content, the instructor, and the course materials, and they provide ample space for narrative comments. These and students' informal comments and questions have been very helpful in developing the course year to year. I provide no pre-test of knowledge nor a post-test to check what was learned. The goal is for the course to be a key step in the process of becoming information literate, not for it to bring the students all the way there or to certify that particular skills have been acquired. Adults with their different interests and backgrounds do not all expect or derive the same thing from the course. The final project places the student at the beginning of a research endeavor; it affords the opportunity to use the concepts, apply what was learned, and receive individualized assistance. As tempting as it is to try to obtain the quantitative feedback a post-test might provide, I consider the final project the next logical step in the process and a better way for adults to conclude the course experience.

## EVOLUTION OF THE COURSE

The two days are jam-packed with lessons, information, and activity. It is fair to say that the course flirts dangerously with information overload. Adult learners' educational and research experiences vary widely, and one cannot predict the varieties in a given group of adults. Covering too much content can turn some people off, yet this process energizes others. It is a hard balance to strike, but instructor openness to questions and follow-up emails can make the difference to the few who feel 'overloaded.'

I revise the course content to keep it current with advances in information retrieval. This has meant including more electronic resources, especially those which students can access on home computers. Web skills and evaluation techniques, for example, are now crucial to independent researchers who, without any training, can waste time on the Web and run the risk of seeing it as their primary or only research tool. Other changes have been pedagogic: The inclusion of more active learning exercises keeps it lively, helps to reinforce the lessons, and reaches adults with different learning styles. "Nothing beats a walk-through," as one student put it.

Sometimes the changes necessitate trade-offs, which can be beneficial. Where I used to cover particular dictionaries and encyclopedias in depth, I now use encyclopedias just to illustrate the lecture on evaluating reference works. Students then apply the evaluative concepts during the fact finding activities. Instead of spending time with the mechanics of printed periodical indexes and the card catalog, I now teach online tools and the importance of being in the right database for the query. When I added a demonstration of the Web to the course, I had to shorten the online catalog demonstration to make time for it. This meant paring down that demonstration to its most essential points, particularly those which enhance other types of online searching–controlled vocabulary, Boolean techniques.

## LESSONS FOR REFERENCE WORK

Teaching the course provides the librarian-instructor with a greater understanding of the anxieties about modern libraries shared by many adult learners. It helps clarify what and how adult learners need to be taught, their desire to be more self-sufficient and competent, and their feelings about the library: computer phobia, embarrassment, and feeling overwhelmed, just to mention a few. Teaching the course lets the librarian see up close what kinds of things confuse adults when they attempt to apply what the librarian has told them. Such understanding can alter approaches at the reference desk with adult learners.

Many of these users, particularly those with ongoing information needs, want to achieve some measure of independence even when they seem to request more hand-holding of the librarian. This behavior results at least in part from the fact that sporadic reference desk encounters may not cover search strategy concepts and vocabulary, or provide guided practice; yet these are often needed in order for adults to understand and carry out what the librarian has advised. Perhaps only a course or other instruction program can provide this, while affording adults the time and space to integrate the new concepts and skills into their knowledge base. Keeping this in mind, the reference librarian can still increase effectiveness with the adult learner by:

- recognizing when to infuse the reference transaction with wider search strategy advice and information concepts in addition to answering the specific question
- defining all the jargon or terminology employed when providing instruction
- demonstrating how to use the database (or other tool) and when time permits, watching them use it so they can ask for clarification on the part that confused them
- recognizing that adult learners are often project-focused, and in need of time-saving tips and skills they can have success with immediately; little successes seem to increase interest in the larger process, while confusion and failure increase frustration and alienation
- offering ways, such as handouts and electronic or Web-based tutorials, to help adult learners become more self-sufficient

When veterans of the course approach me at the reference desk, they invariably convey that they feel less fear and intimidation than before in using the library. Then they will say, "Just remind me of some strategy or tool." I find we have a shared vocabulary that I can call upon during the reference interview and that I can build on as we talk. With most adult learners this is not the case, and words like database, index, or subject heading can confuse them completely. It is always easier to move my former students along faster and more successfully than I can other adults seeking reference assistance.

## CONCLUSION

The course approach offers adult learners sustained access to an information professional as they seek a level of information literacy they could probably not achieve on their own. The course employs teaching methods well-suited to people who, unlike full-time undergraduates, are not engaged daily in academia, with the concomitant opportunities for learning. A course can provide practical skills which adults seek, a critical approach to information sources and research strategies which challenges them, and a conceptual framework upon which to base further exploration in the process of learning.

## REFERENCES

1. For example, Vanessa Burford, "Public Library Instruction: A Novice's Experience," *Research Strategies* 15 (Spring 1997): 106-111; Shelly Adatto, "Helping Users Help Themselves: User Workshops at Seattle Public Library," *PNLA Quarterly* 56 (Winter 1992): 9-10; *Los Angeles Public Library-Central Library Calendar of Events* (1998). Available [Online]: <http://www.lapl.org/admin/EventsCa110.html> [27 October 1998]; *Houston Public Library Public Online Training Program* (1998). Available [Online]: <http://www.hpl.lib.tx.us/events/pubtrain.html> [27 October 1998].

2. For a summary of adult learning theory and its relationship to information literacy skills, see Vicky Wilson, "Developing The Adult Independent Learner: Information Literacy and the Remote External Student," *Distance Education* 15 (2) (1994): 254-278. For a succinct list of adult learning principles for librarians to keep in mind, see RUSA-SUPS Services to Adults Committee, *Adult Programming: A Manual for Libraries,* RUSA Occasional Papers, no. 21 (Chicago: Reference and Adult Services Association, American Library Association, 1997), pp. 15-16. For teaching techniques with adults, see Michael W. Galbraith and Bonnie Zelenak, "Adult Learning Methods and Techniques," in *Facilitating Adult Learning: A Transactional Process,* ed. Michael W. Galbraith (Malabar, FL: Krieger Publishing Co., 1991), pp. 103-133, and Constance C. Blackwood and Barbara A. White, "Technology for Teaching and Learning Improvement," in *Facilitating Adult Learning,* p. 156.

3. Wilson, p. 261.

4. *UCLA Extension: Welcome* (1998). Available [Online]: <http://www.unex.ucla.edu/welcome.htm> [27 October 1998].

# Adult Students:
# Wandering the Web with a Purpose

Marcia A. King-Blandford

**SUMMARY.** In the spring 1997, the Adult Liberal Studies Program at the University of Toledo invited proposal to design, develop, and teach a seminar course specifically for the adult learner. Our adult learners must learn to move seamless through the Internet, web-based interfaces and stand alone CD-ROMs. The course proposal, "Wandering the web with a purpose: Using the Internet for information and research," was accepted as a four credit hour course and is specifically geared for adult learners who range in age from their early 30s to late 70s. *[Article copies available for a fee from The Haworth Document Delivery Service: 1-800-342-9678. E-mail address: <getinfo@haworthpressinc.com> Website: <http://www. haworthpressinc.com>]*

**KEYWORDS.** Adult learner, information literacy, World Wide Web

Each spring at the University of Toledo (UT), the Division of Individual and Specialized Programs (ISP), located within University College, invites the faculty to submit proposals for seminar classes for the Adult Liberal Studies (ALS) program. The Adult Liberal Studies program is specially designed for the over 25 year old adult student who wants to return to school to either finish a four year college degree or start one. This is an opportunity for UT faculty to collaborate across college and department lines, teach an

---

Marcia A. King-Blandford is Assistant Professor, Library Administration, Reference Librarian, Carlson Library, The University of Toledo, Toledo, OH 43606-3399 (E-mail: mkingbl@utoledo.edu).

[Haworth co-indexing entry note]: "Adult Students: Wandering the Web with a Purpose." King-Blandford, Marcia A. Co-published simultaneously in *The Reference Librarian* (The Haworth Information Press, an imprint of The Haworth Press, Inc.) No. 69/70, 2000, pp. 271-285; and: *Reference Services for the Adult Learner: Challenging Issues for the Traditional and Technological Era* (ed: Kwasi Sarkodie-Mensah) The Haworth Information Press, an imprint of The Haworth Press, Inc., 2000, pp. 271- 285. Single or multiple copies of this article are available for a fee from The Haworth Document Delivery Service [1-800-342-9678, 9:00 a.m. - 5:00 p.m. (EST). E-mail address: getinfo@haworthpressinc.com].

inter-disciplinary topic or teach in a pet area of interest. The specialized nature of the audience, adult students, and the nature of the course design, seminar-style, allows the faculty a great deal of academic freedom in the how, what, when, where, and why of an area. All proposals are reviewed and notification of acceptance of a proposal is made in early May in time for the upcoming fall's registration. Seminars can be taught fall, spring or summer semesters; they are offered both on campus, at university off-site locations, and through the distance learning modules. Since these seminars are taught over and above the normal workload, a stipend of $2250 is given to each faculty member chosen to teach. [1]

## GETTING STARTED

In the spring of 1997, with an absence of any for-credit information literacy courses being offered at the University of Toledo, the Adult Liberal Studies seminar program created an opportunity to design, develop, and teach an information literacy course specifically geared to the adult student. The special information and research needs of the adult students were well known to the reference staff at Carlson Library. The brief reference interview for adult students was not enough; scheduling a one-on-one individual instruction appointment with a librarian just did not fit into their packed Franklin planners. Carlson Library, as an OhioLINK member, offers its faculty, students, and staff a web-based interface for searching the OhioLINK central catalog (74 members composed of two-year and four-year public higher education institutions, private institutions, and the State Library of Ohio), the electronic journal center, full-text reference sources, and more than fifty subject specific research databases.[3] The adult student familiar with the "old card catalog" must not only ask for help to find information and conduct research but also ask how to use the computers. For the adult student who does not work on a computer or whose computer experience does not include Internet access, using a keyboard and mouse presents definite challenges. Each of us remembers that first experience with a mouse; it seemed an impossible feat to get the arrow to the right place on the screen. This is much more than the "library anxieties" of the traditional college age student. The adult student, in addition to learning how to navigate the college environment, i.e., parking, standing in lines, shuffling from office to office, meeting with advisors, touch-tone registering, closed out required courses, and bookstore expenses, must also strengthen their study, note taking, and time management skills. The adult student is different from the traditional age student because their reality is different.[4] They have responsibilities for work, family, and home that brings additional stresses to bear on their goal of getting a degree.[5] By the time the adult student reaches the academic library, their perseverance has already been tested. The adult student soon discovers that the library is as foreign to them as any of the other academic endeavors they have recently faced.

The Adult Liberal Studies seminar provided an opportunity to create a supportive environment for the adult student. The information literacy seminar entitled, "Wandering the web with a purpose: Using the Internet for information and research," would provide a hands-on learning experience for the adult student.[6] The four goals of the seminar were:

1. Students would understand the language of the Internet in relationship to information retrieval skills.
2. Students would be able to identify and select the appropriate search engine for their information needs.
3. Students would be able to evaluate and verify the information retrieved.
4. Students would be able to utilize the most appropriate Web resources for classroom assignments and research projects.

The fifteen week, semester long course, would serve as a foundation for both locating information via the Internet and conducting library research using the various OhioLINK web-based resources. The seminar would be taught in one of the University's computer classrooms since Carlson Library does not have its own computer classroom. Not teaching the seminar in the library turned out to be a real advantage. Since the computer classroom was "remote" from the library, it immediately re-enforced the idea that working with library resources did not necessitate actually being in the library. For most of the adult students in the seminar class, this notion had never been fully realized. They associated the concept of library resources with being physically in the library building. Additionally, many of the adult students had recently purchased a home computer system complete with Internet access. Since all registered UT students can use UTNET as their Internet provider free-of-charge, the announcement of this perk to the adult students was revolutionary to them. These two factors, remote library use, and free Internet access from their homes, laid the groundwork to introduce the adult student to the reality of desktop access.

## *LEARNING ALL I DID NOT KNOW*

No previous teaching experience was enough preparation when it actually became time to teach this three credit hour seminar course. A year before, the experience of team teaching a pilot English course with an English department faculty member had provided an opportunity to really get up in front of a class of undergraduates as both librarian and teacher. Yet, all the details of teaching were left to the experienced faculty person, e.g., classroom selection, day/times, bookstore orders, and signing extra students into the class. Although establishing the curriculum, alternating teaching topics and grading papers was a joint exercise, the "team approach" with an experienced faculty lessened the actual teaching responsibilities. It was like riding in a car instead of driving. Additional classroom teaching experience had come from the University's First Year Information initiatives. Teaching three semesters of a one credit hour First Year Information (FYI) class for the College of Business at the University more closely paralleled the one-shot library instruction classes that are part of every instruction librarian's comfort zone. The 37 traditional age college students, fresh out of high school, resembled all the other freshmen students who participated in the mandatory library instruction sessions for their required English composition classes. The First Year Information course was a requirement that must be endured. Since the FYI Coordinator for the College of Business once again handled the teaching details, the real details for teaching were silently taken care of. This would be the first attempt as pure teaching faculty; "perhaps it wouldn't have happened, if [I] had known just how much work it would be."[7]

The first introduction to the details and responsibilities of teaching is the "wait list" of students who want to get into the seminar course after it has "closed." It was a shock to learn the Information Literacy seminar had closed after the second day of registration. A student currently enrolled in the spring 99 course waited three semesters to finally get into the course. By request, the seminar had been restricted to 24 students. The number of computers in the classroom dictated this decision; the idea was to have one student per workstation. This was a critical component of the original design of the seminar. The original design of the seminar allowed the students a supportive environment in which to try for themselves, make mistakes, try again, and hopefully, succeed. If the desired goal of efficiency and effectiveness was to be achieved, each adult had to learn to work independently on their own. As their first phone calls and email messages were received, it was the clues from the students themselves asking to be put on a waiting list or asking if the size restrictions of the seminar could be lifted that served as the first dose of reality. This seminar course was a "go" complete with waiting list. It was in the panic of the moment, that the idea of the class also being offered as a distance learning module was born.

Thirty adult students were allowed to officially register for the information literacy seminar held during fall semester 1997. It would meet on Tuesday evenings from 5:30 until 8:30 p.m. All thirty students were required to meet in the classroom for the opening class session. A self-assessment of computer vocabulary, computer knowledge, computer experience, and searching skills was given to each student.[8] Each student was also asked on the self-assessment to rate his or her computer comfort and computer use on a scale of one to five, with five indicating strong and frequent computer use. A 5 rating was defined as sending and receiving email with attachments on a daily basis, using some type of word processing package, and searching the Internet with a graphical web browser. Each student was also required to explicitly state his or her expectations for the seminar. After reviewing the course goals and objectives and the course syllabus, the self-assessments and course expectations were collected. As each adult student introduced himself or herself, their responses were discussed. Adult students who rated themselves a 4.5 or above were invited to take the course as a distance learning module. The decision to make all lecture notes, class outlines, class exercises, projects and assignments, midterm and final examinations, available from the instructor's home page could also easily support a group of distance learners. All class members would be able to access the home page and correspond with the instructor via email, fax and telephone. For the groups of adults participating as distance learners, prompt responses to email and meeting project and examination deadlines would count for class participation. After identifying the distance learning group, the self-assessments and ratings allowed the remaining participants to be grouped together by skill levels. The students who self-rated themselves a 3 or 3.5 were asked to "help" other students in the course.

## MEETING THE STUDENTS AT THEIR SKILL LEVEL

One approach to teaching to the range of computer skills for the adults would be to encourage the new beginners to arrive 30 minutes before the start of the regular class. This "pre-class" was created by the suggestion of one of the students. During this half-hour, such basics are turning on/off the computer, booting up, passwords, selecting and opening the Web browsers and vocabulary were emphasized. Understanding the jargon of the computer was an important first step to understanding the tasks to be performed. The students who had given themselves a rating of 0 or 1, had a high level of anxiety about computers and held to the belief that they could "break something" and "make the whole system crash." The 30-minute time frame became beneficial because it allowed the new users to start ahead of the more comfortable computer users. It also allowed the necessary repetition of computer basics and vocabulary that would have slowed the momentum of the class. Additional visual aids were also brought in for the pre-class; these materials were optionally made available to everyone else.

Course preparation for the adult student is intense. To teach consistently and coherently is overwhelming. No one-shot instruction, no team-taught pilot program, and no First Year Information class provided the amount of experience needed to teach for a three hour block of time week after week. Pacing the class materials for three hours while the adult students were working on the computers and trying to take detailed notes proved to be one of the biggest challenges during the first weeks of the seminar. Expectations of the amount of materials that could be covered and grasped were unrealistic. The need for step by step instructions coupled with the need for repetition was also underestimated. Unlike teaching the traditional age college students who rarely ask a question, the adult students were quick to ask questions. "Why? "How?" and "What?" were the most frequent questions asked during the first few weeks of class. Even when the adult student could not articulate what he or she did not understand, they knew enough to stop the momentum of the class by shooting their hand into the air. Giving the adult student time to understand and thoroughly practice each new skill is a more desirable teaching moment than covering a specific amount of content. After the first semester of this course, each of the three required projects for the course were offered in various skill levels. The projects were labeled X,Y, or Z; each adult student could pick the skill level of the project that was most appropriate for them. They were encouraged to be fair and yet challenge themselves. The distance learning students had to complete each project at the X level. Class management was the second teaching detail that was learned the hard way.

The third introduction to the details of classroom teaching for the adult student is the time outside of class that must be made available to them. The adult students needed a great deal of reassurance. Adult students know their strengths and weaknesses; they are very realistic about themselves and what they expect to gain. Adult students are willing to admit they don't understand, show their frustrations, and act overwhelmed, and are quick to announce they are ready to quit.[9] Where the traditional age college students rarely approach the instructor until the last days of the course, adult students are quick to come to the instructor for input about their status in the class. To help convince the adult students that they could do the work for the seminar, it was necessary to provide opportunities for each student to demonstrate their new knowledge. This was a pivotal point. Asking a panicked individual to act like the instructor and demonstrate what they knew and what points were still confusing was the results of the adult students' own frustration about "not catching on quickly," and feeling they really could not work on the computer.

## THE ADULT AS A STUDENT

The adult student is a serious student. They are making real sacrifices to get or finish a degree.[10] Unlike the traditional age student who does the minimum, learning for the adult student is not about memorizing or reading the text or just showing up. The adult students bring an intensity and an interest to the course; they want to be able to apply what they have learned in the classroom to their lives. They are like sponges, ready and willing to absorb all there is to know. Adult students linger after class; they do not watch their watches and jump up to leave at the stroke of the clock. Now, after four semesters of teaching the information literacy seminar for adult students, being readily available outside of the scheduled class time is critical. Adult students need the instructor to answer their constant email requests, take their weekly telephone calls, meet with them individually at a computer and provide constant reassurance in order for the adult student to strengthen their skills, gain confidence in their abilities and become successful. This is the safety net outside of the classroom. Adult students need the individual support and attention of the faculty. This is a key to their success. This is also the third teaching detail that had to be experienced to be learned.

The fourth teaching detail is the importance adult students place on class attendance and the emphasis they give to grades. There was an attendance sign-in sheet each week, optional class exercises for practice, three projects, an in-class midterm examination and a take-home final. The adult students were constantly questioning what their grade was NOW. Keeping the grade book handy was a new experience. After the first semester of the course, a detailed graph of the possible points with the corresponding grades was distributed so that the individual student could continually figure out where they stood in terms of their attendance and grade. This graph also alleviated any surprises. The same questioning attitude the adult students bring to the class is brought to how tests, projects, and assignments were scored. Adult students are willing to fight for themselves. They want to earn good grades and they know that good grades are a measure of their success as a student.

## OUTCOMES AND SURPRISES

The final detail of classroom teaching was perhaps the most surprising. Knowing where the adult students had started and watching the growth of skills and knowledge over the fifteen-week seminar was mind-boggling. Towards the end of the semester a checklist was developed to help identify the skills and competencies that had been demonstrated during the seminar.[11] Each class member had to evaluate him or herself. This assessment was done in addition to the official course evaluation developed and distributed by the Division of Individual and Specialized Program.[12] If an adult student still did not feel comfortable with a particular skill, concept or vocabulary term, an individual appointment was set-up outside of class to allow further work on this area. Watching adult students move between search engines, locate and request monographs through OhioLINK's central catalog, search full-text databases for journal articles, copy/paste citations and/or text into documents made everything worthwhile. Were they fast? No. Yet, to paraphrase Isadore Mudge, these adult students could make the right choices at the right time with the right amount of information in the right format.[13]

## ADULT STUDENTS AND DISTANCE LEARNING

The distance learning students had the freedom to complete the course on their own time and in their own space. This was a testament to the best of distance learning education.[14] The adult students took a responsible attitude towards keeping in touch via email, asking questions, completing assignments and worrying about their grades. This group of distance learners would have been bored in the classroom setting where their peers were "just beginning" or "still figuring things out." Already competent in email, and searching the Internet, their information retrieval skills did not need to be developed but to be further strengthened and refined. A greater emphasis for this group of eight students was on efficiency and effectiveness. Introducing this group of students to the organization of electronic information and demonstrating search strategies moved this group of students to the next level of desktop access. The initial group of distance learners had all rated themselves as "very strong" and "daily users of the Internet." Yet, at the close of the seminar, each individually expressed how much they had learned; the most common refrain was, "I can't believe all I didn't know." Information evaluation, toggling between web browsers, searching the most appropriate subject specific research database, knowing how to begin, these were all tasks identified to strengthen the already existing skills of the distance learning group. There was as much interaction with the distance learning adult students as with the regular classroom students.

## FUTURE DEVELOPMENTS

Now after four semesters, an advanced information literacy seminar is being developed. The original information literacy course will be its pre-requisite. The adult students have requested a continuing course. The adult students share a common goal that is often voiced as their desire to "look good to their grandchildren, children, and co-workers." Melvin Dewey, the original champion of librarians, was always working to rally librarians into new areas of community involvement and education.[15] This same vision and spirit of librarians as leaders reminds us all to keep trying pressing ahead to take advantage of the tools available right here and now. Where the typewriter and mass printing were the tools of Dewey,[16] the tool of this age is the Internet. Librarians, hearing Dewey's call to action, are rallying information seekers to take full advantage of this here-to-stay technology, the Internet.

## *CONCLUSION*

Teaching this information literacy seminar course each semester has instilled a new appreciation of the other teaching faculty at the University. Like other instruction librarians in other academic setting, there was a continual push to get the faculty to use the instruction options available. It takes a lot of work and even more initiative by a faculty member to bring their students to the library and/or coordinate a library assignment with the library's resources. If faculty members are not keeping up with their own field of study and keeping up with the technology, it follows that the same faculty will not put themselves "out there" for all to see their weaknesses. No amount of cajoling by the academic library will bring this faculty member on board for library instruction.

The view of library instruction from the "other side" is different now. The role of library instruction must be more consultative and less formula. Since undergraduate education is more content driven than graduate work,[17] undergraduate library instruction needs to be focused more on identifying information retrieval skills and strengthening existing skills than the emphasis on the research process itself. Save the research process for the audience for which it is intended. Teaching information literacy to adult students and to traditional age undergraduates in a for-credit course means acknowledging and building upon existing skills. It is starting with the basics that will build towards the research process. Academic librarians need the visibility of being in the classroom. The need for information literacy classes is real; if made available, the students will come because the Internet is the bridge between undergraduate education and the world of work. Curriculum developments for information literacy start with the standard competencies to be gained. The Institute for Information Literacy at the national level and state level organizations, like Ohio's OELMA (Ohio Educational Library Media) are working to identify and name these specific competencies.[18] These efforts are the real stepping stones in teaching information literacy; parallels can be found in the reading and literacy curriculum long accepted in education circles.[19] In this Internet age, here is the role that no other professional can play. The librarian is the best person in the best position to teach the information literacy skills that will be used to learn what is best on the Internet. Working with adult students in the classroom and invitations to broaden the information literacy curriculums within specific departments and programs has re-enforced a long held belief that academic librarians have a rightful place as teaching faculty in today's university community. Classroom teaching, curriculum development, and closed-out information literacy courses will go a long way to justifying the role of academic librarians while meeting a need that will take all students from college to career.

## REFERENCES

1. Memo to submit ALS seminar proposal to University College, April, 1997.

2. Hammond, Carol Burroughs. "Nontraditional students and the library: Opinions, preferences, and behaviors." College & Research Libraries. 55, July '94, p. 323-41.

3. "OhioLINK in Brief. . . ," OhioLINK Update, 4 (2), September 1998, p. 3.

4. Kaplan, Philip L., and Iris M. Saltiel. "Adults who do it all: Balancing work, family, and school." Information Age, May/June, July/August 1997, p. 17.

5. Ibid., p. 18

6. King-Blandford, Marcia. ALS proposal, "Wandering the Web with a Purpose. . . " ALS seminar proposal, Division of Individual and Specialized Programs, University College, The University of Toledo, April 1997. See Appendix 1.

7. "Letter from the Publishers," Toledo Parents Magazine, March 1998. p.[2] The exact quote went "great things are accomplished because we didn't know hard that would be when we began."

8. ALS 3060 Self-Assessment, The University of Toledo. See Appendix 4.

9. Kaplan, Philip L., and Iris M. Saltiel. "Adults who do it all: Balancing work, family, and school." Information Age, May/June, July/August 1997, p. 18.

10. Eastmond, Daniel V. "Adult Learners and Internet-Based Distance Education," In Cahoon, Bard, editor. Adult learning and the Internet. New Direction for Adult and continuing Education. No. 78. San Francisco: Jossey Bass, Summer 1998, p. 38.

11. ALS 3060 Checklist. See Appendix 5.

12. University College Course Evaluation, The University of Toledo.

13. Mudge, Isadore, Guide to Reference Books, 6th ed., p. xiv.

14. Association of College and Research Libraries. Distance Learning Section. ACRL guidelines for distance learning library services: The final version, approved July 1998. College & Research Libraries News 59 (9) Oct. '98, p. 689-94.

15. Vann, Sarah K., editor. Melvil Dewey: His enduring presence in librarianship. Littleton, CO: Libraries Unlimited, 1978, p. 198.

16. Ibid., p. 165.

17. Blau, Peter M. The Organization of Academic Work. 2nd ed. News Brunswick: Transaction Pub., c1994, p. [1].

18. Http://www.ala.org/acrl/infolit.html and OLA/ALAO/OELMA Joint Task Force on Implementing the Recommendations of the Task Force on Library Instruction, High School of College, Nancy O'Hanlong, Chair, April 1990.

19. Ransom, Grayce A. "Teaching conceptual vocabulary skills," Chapter 8, in Preparing to teach reading. Boston: Little, Brown and Company, c1978. This particular text was chosen because of its use as a standard in training reading teachers. It was of particular interest because of the similarities with today's information literacy efforts.

## SUPPORTING WORKS

Cahoon, Bard, Adult Learning and the Internet. New Direction for Adult and Continuing Education 78. San Francisco: Jossey Bass, Summer 1998.

Drueke, Jeanetta. "Active Learning in the University Library Instruction Classroom." Research Strategies, 10 (2) Spring 1992, pp. 77-83.

Kissane, Emily C. "Critical Thinking at the Reference Desk: Teaching Students to Manage Technology," RQ 32, Summer 1993, p. 485-489.

Kraus, Marie A. "What Library Schools Teach about Library Support to Distant Students: A Survey," The American journal of distance education, 1994, pp. 20-35.

Miller, Marian I and Barry D. Bratton. "Instructional Design: Increasing the Effectiveness of Bibliographic Instruction," College and Research Library 49, Nov. 1998, pp. 545-549.

Nahl-Jakobovits, Diane. "Bibliographic instructional design for information literacy: Integrating Affective and Cognitive Objectives." Research Strategies 11, Spring 1993, p. 73-88.

Oberman, Cerise. "Unmasking Technology: A Prelude to Teaching, Research Strategies 13 (1) Winter 1995, p. 34-39.

Schmersahl, Carmen B. "Teaching Library Research: Process, Not Product." Journal of Teaching.

Weingard, Darlene E. "A Reminder about Andragogy," Journal of Education for Library and Information Science 37 (1) Winter, 1996, pp. 79-80.

# APPENDIX 1

## Syllabus

<u>Instructor:</u>      Marcia King-Blandford
Office: 1024, CL
Office Hours: By appointment
email: mkingbl@utoledo.edu

<u>Course Description:</u>

Introduction to utilizing the World Wide Web for information and research to support the needs of the undergraduate student. The goal of this course is to move towards "knowledge management." The objectives of this course are as follows: to develop and refine the information retrieval skills; to develop a critical thinking approach to the Web environment; and to develop a personal information management system. A successful student will know the language of the Web and its environment; to able to search, evaluate, and utilize the information retrieved from the Web; know how and when to choose a needs specific searching approach; distinguish information format on the Web; and download, print, email, paste information. Class will meet in Room 1250 University Computer Center. Each student will have their own workstation. At least one formatted disk is required. There is no required text.

<u>Course Grades:</u>

Extra credit is always an option with prior approval by the instructor. It is the responsibility of the student to notify the instructor of a change in their enrollment status.

The grade will be reflected by:

25%    <u>Class participation and attitude.</u>
Your presence and participation are an important part of this course.

Be here, be active, and be involved.

25%    <u>Quizzes, mid-term, and Final Examination.</u>
Short quizzes on language, a mid-term and a final examination will be given to access your knowledge. A portion of both the mid-term and final examinations will be hands-on.

50%    <u>Assignments and Class Presentations.</u>
Five assignments will be completed for the course. A written description of the assignment, the requirements, and due dates will be distributed according to the schedule outlined in the course syllabus.

Class Activities:

| | |
|---|---|
| Week of January 12 | Getting started. |
| Week of January 19 | Getting started on the Web: navigation and language. |
| Week of January 26 | Search engines: who, what, when, where, and why<br>Assignment #1: Email. |
| Week of February 2 | Email, gopher, and listservs. |

Class Activities (continued):

| | |
|---|---|
| Week of February 9 | Information and news sources on the web.<br>Assignment #2: Search engine evaluation |
| Week of February 16 | Business/Marketing/Advocacy sources on the web. |
| Week of February 23 | Library (public and academic) resources on the web. |
| Week of March 2 | Mid-term examination. |
| Week of March 9 | No class: Spring Break |
| Week of March 16 | Library (public and academic) resources on the web.<br>Assignment #3: Website evaluation. |
| Week of March 23 | Government, health and science resources on the web. |
| Week of March 30 | The web and word processing. |
| Week of April 6 | Information management.<br>Assignment #4: Web bibliography. |
| Week of April 13 | No class |
| Week of April 20 | Class presentations with written documentation. |
| Week of April 27 | Review.<br>Assignment #5: Showing what you know |
| Week of May 4 | Final examination: Check schedule for date/time/place. |

It may be necessary to make changes to the syllabus. Any changes to the syllabus will be given in writing.

January 13, 1998

## APPENDIX 2

### Adult Liberal Studies Seminar Proposal

**Name:** Marcia King-Blandford     **College/Department:** Carlson Library, 530-2842

**Seminar Title:** Wandering the web with a purpose: Using the Internet for information and research

Identify the category most appropriate for this proposed seminar:

### Social Sciences seminar

**Description of seminar** (One or two sentences)

This seminar would introduce the adult/returning student to information retrieval and research using Netscape. It would cover a range of topics from the language of the Internet to selecting search engines to identifying useable Web sites and accessing UTMOST and OhioLINK resources. In addition to efficiently and effectively retrieving usable information, focus would also be placed on evaluating information and incorporating Web-based information into assignments and research projects.

### Course objectives stated as learning outcomes:

Students would understand the language of the Internet in relationship to information retrieval skills.

Students would be able to identify and select the appropriate search engine for their information needs.

Students would be able to evaluate and verify the information retrieved.

Students would be able to utilize Web resources for classroom assignments and research projects.

### Course requirements:

None

### Instructional resources (including textbooks, reference materials, videotapes):

Web sites would be "bookmarked" and utilized as text/reading assignments.

Optional use of one of the standard workbooks like Baldwin and Poirer's *The Research Process and the Internet*, as a course resource.

### Outline of topics and activities in proposed seminar:

Compare and contrast a web search using two different search engines.

Monitor and evaluate a Web site of choice in your subject area for authority, timeliness, reliability, etc.

Midterm examination on the language of the Internet and various search strategies.

Research a specific subject based topic utilizing Web resources and identify relevant sites.

Final examination on course material covered.

Evaluation: Articulation of information retrieval skills in a Web-based information system.

Guest speaker on Internet use.

### Special instructional needs for seminar, such as technology, space, labs, etc.:

Class needs to meet in a computer lab like 1250 UCC.

# APPENDIX 3

**ALS Student Information**

Please complete the following:

Name_____

Local Address_____

Daytime Phone _____ Evening Phone _____

Fax _____ Email _____

I use a computer: ___never ___ rarely ___on occasion ___frequently ___daily

I use: ___email ___word processing packets ___computer CDs ___Yahoo or other search engines

___other: _____

My work requires the use of a computer.    ___yes    ___no

I have a computer at home.    ___yes    ___no

I have Internet access from my home.    ___yes    ___no

I have Internet access from my office.    ___yes    ___no

Why I am taking this course:

What do I expect to learn from this course?

Please circle the rate that best describes your computer use:

| Rarely use computers or just do one specific task. | Use a computer some; can type; have been out on the Internet. | Receive send email, with attachments; use word processing package; use search engines. |
|---|---|---|

| 1 | 2 | 3 | 4 | 5 |
|---|---|---|---|---|
| Low use | | | | High use |

# Breaking the Mold:
# Using Educational Pedagogy
# in Designing Library Instruction
# of Adult Learners

Naomi Harrison

**SUMMARY.** This paper delineates the special characteristics of the adult learner, emphasizing their high level of motivation and their diverse learning styles. It introduces the 4MAT® System, an instructional model developed by Bernice McCarthy, PhD which provides a systematic approach to delivering instruction that especially addresses the learning styles of adults. As a learner-focused model for adapting curriculum and instruction to the diverse needs of students, 4 MAT gives teachers/librarians a framework in which to design learning activities in a systematic cycle. The system encourages librarians to use multiple methods of instruction so as to reach students more effectively, regardless of the individual's learning style. The paper concludes with a library instruction unit designed by using the 4MAT® System. *[Article copies available for a fee from The Haworth Document Delivery Service: 1-800-342-9678. E-mail address: <getinfo@haworthpressinc.com> Website: <http://www.haworthpressinc.com>]*

Naomi Harrison (MLS, Indiana University; MA Human Resources, Webster University) is Reference Librarian/Coordinator of Library User Instruction, Olin Library, Rollins College, 1000 Holt Avenue-2744, Winter Park, FL 32789 (E-mail: nharrison@rollins.edu)

4MAT® and Excel are registered trademarks of Excel, Inc. Used by special permission.

[Haworth co-indexing entry note]: "Breaking the Mold: Using Educational Pedagogy in Designing Library Instruction of Adult Learners." Harrison, Naomi. Co-published simultaneously in *The Reference Librarian* (The Haworth Information Press, an imprint of The Haworth Press, Inc.) No. 69/70, 2000, pp. 287-298; and: *Reference Services for the Adult Learner: Challenging Issues for the Traditional and Technological Era* (ed: Kwasi Sarkodie-Mensah) The Haworth Information Press, an imprint of The Haworth Press, Inc., 2000, pp. 287-298. Single or multiple copies of this article are available for a fee from The Haworth Document Delivery Service [1-800-342-9678, 9:00 a.m. - 5:00 p.m. (EST). E-mail address: getinfo@haworthpressinc.com].

**KEYWORDS.** Adult learner, 4MAT® System, learning styles, instructional model, curriculum, library instruction

One urgent need in library instruction is to identify and use a practical, effective educational model of pedagogy for teaching adult learners in today's library environment. The ability of instruction librarians to prepare students to navigate successfully through the profusion of information, both print and non-print media, and our method of delivery of instruction must be broadened and specifically encompass strategies that appeal to the diverse approaches students have to learning.

The challenge to instruction librarians is to break out of the traditional lecture approach to lesson design by using more active learning processes and strategies, as well as the more reflective modes of teaching. This challenge requires librarians to explore the educational theories and practices of classroom instruction colleagues. We need to ask such questions as the following: What do we know about our user–the adult learner? What pedagogy do we need to embrace in designing our instruction? How can we effectively guide these students through strategies of learning that will enhance their ability to become self-directed independent learners of library resources in this technological age?

## *ADULT LEARNERS*

As reference/instruction librarians we work with reentering adults as well as traditional-age college students with varying learning styles and anxieties about the use of the library and its many resources. The Higher Education Amendments (P.L. 99-498), passed by Congress in 1985 define "adult learner" as

> An individual who by reason of personal circumstance, age, gender, disability, minority status, income, rural isolation, economic or educational disadvantage, marital status, presence of dependent children, lack of or need for new employment skills . . . or other significant barrier is not a traditional student, and engages in some form of structured post-secondary study to improve the individual's knowledge, information skills, or employment opportunities.

In establishing P.L. 99-498, Congress made the following findings that are germane to this discussion:

1. the increasing incidence of relocation and dislocation of industries and workers, the entry and reentry of adults into the labor force, and the

rapid rate of change in technology, the economy, population demographics, and social conditions, necessitate significant improvement in postsecondary educational opportunities for adults in all stages of life;
2. the majority of adults who continue their education do so for job-related and career-oriented reasons . . . ;

\*    \*    \*

3. enrollment of adult learners approaches or equals that of traditional students in postsecondary institutions and such enrollment patterns are changing the demography of postsecondary education;
4. . . . such institutions need to adapt themselves to integrate adult learners (United States Statutes at Large, 99th Congress: 2nd Session, 1986).

Finally, the adult education law authorizes program and planning grants "to help strengthen the capacity of postsecondary institutions to respond to the continuing educational needs of adults." In so doing, the federal government, among its many provisions, encourages the development and innovative use of technology and the training of personnel to improve their ability to serve adult learners.

The special needs of the adult student have been well documented in both the education and library literature. The term "andragogy," which means the teaching of adults, first appeared in the education literature in 1933. In 1986, Jean Sheridan described adult students as having unique psychological and educational needs and considered different teaching styles that accommodate those needs in the context of library instruction. Adult students are generally much more independent than traditional students; and they are likely to have to juggle jobs and family responsibilities along with their schoolwork. Thus, adult students are often highly motivated and committed to their education (Vakili, 1993). Their diversity in age, race, educational preparation, life experience, and intelligence requires a broad-spectrum approach to teaching combined with individualized instruction. Many adult students prefer a more informal approach to education, where collaborative, hands-on learning is encouraged. Vakili (1993) asserts that "being actively engaged in a course and solving practical problems are important to them." Clearly, adult higher education students benefit from different institutional services and teaching styles than those offered to traditional students.

## INSTRUCTIONAL MODES

The Council on Continuing Education, as discussed in the Sheridan (1986) article, advocates a "collaborative and personalized" approach to teaching, which promotes active participation, provides feedback, reinforces basic skills, moves from the simple to the complex, and helps the learner apply new knowledge beyond the educational environment. Further, it suggests that the curriculum should relate to the learner's experience or needs, with the instructor acting as facilitator. Several examples of successful collaborative learning techniques with adult learners are cited in library literature. Carr (1980) says that since adult learners enter the library with "intentions, memories, and styles of learning," the librarian must work to develop helping or trust relationships with them, playing the role of the "more capable peer." The librarian becomes a collaborator or facilitator rather than an expert. Oberman (1983) developed a problem-solving approach using a question analysis technique which she calls "a watershed for the bibliographic education movement." In her approach there is a direct transfer of responsibility from the instructor to the student which clearly incorporates collaborative principles. Huston (1983) uses collaborative techniques with both faculty and students, capitalizing on the students' experiential information and reminding them "of what they do know." Nahl-Jakobovits (1985) urges librarians to affirm the experiential knowledge of students, their "micro-information environment," and to recognize that affective skills such as comfort in the environment, a sense of acceptance, and absence of fear must be present before learning can happen. Sheridan (1986) concludes that many such collaborative principles, theories, and methods work effectively with adults; thus, traditional hierarchical structures of doing bibliographic instruction must be rejected.

Often, however, showing relevance of the learning and the use of collaborative principles are inadequate in teaching the application of advanced technology. Litzinger and Osif (1983) point out that teaching library patrons to easily access electronic information sources, such as the on-line catalog, poses several challenges. The successful use of this electronic technology relies heavily on the user's ability to create a mental model of the information system. This mental model contains the user's perception of how a system works and what kinds of data it contains, and it enables the user to judge whether a particular system is the best match for his or her information needs. The process of creating this mental model involves cognitive activity, which includes the ability to perceive, conceptualize, and analyze diverse pieces of information. The development of this ability is enhanced when instructional programs provide opportunities that complement the individual learning styles of library patrons.

In the early 1970's, David Kolb, a management expert from Case Western Reserve University, developed an experiential learning model in which he identified two major dimensions of learning, perception and processing. He suggested that learning is influenced by the way people perceive their environment and then process what they perceive. He described a continuum of experience for both processes. At one end of the perception continuum are people who perceive through concrete experience, and at the other extreme are people who perceive through abstract conceptualization.

Using the work of David Kolb, John Dewey, Carl Jung and others and that of scientists who found that the right and left hemispheres of the brain specialize in certain kinds of tasks, Bernice McCarthy (1987) developed The 4MAT®System to describe learning style differences and how the differences combined, create a natural, active learning cycle.

## THE 4MAT® SYSTEM

According to Bernice McCarthy, the 4MAT® System (see Illustration 1) was developed in 1972 to "help teachers organize their teaching based on differences in the way people learn" (October 1990). This eight-step cycle of instruction is based on individual learning styles and information processing preferences as determined by brain dominance. 4MAT® helps teachers understand why some things work with some of their students, while other techniques do not. The 4MAT® System is rooted theoretically in the work of David Kolb. One of his major findings is that people perceive reality differently. When confronted with new situations, some people respond primarily by sensing and feeling their way; others think things through. The feeling/sensing types project themselves into the reality of the moment; they immerse themselves into the actual experience; they perceive through their senses. Conversely, those who think through new experiences are more focused on the abstract nature of reality. They analyze what is happening, appraise situations intellectually, and approach circumstances logically. Both Kolb (1985) and McCarthy (1990) point out that though the two kinds of perception are different, they complement rather than exclude each other. Both are equally valuable, and both have their strengths and weaknesses. Most importantly, every learner needs both types of perception in order to gain the fullest possible understanding of experience.

The second theoretical axiom is that people differ in how they process experiences and information, and subsequently how they make new things part of themselves. Some people prefer to watch first, reflecting on new things, filtering them through their own experiences in order to create meaning that is significant for them. This is a slow, deliberate way of processing information. Other people act on information immediately. They are doers, who need to project themselves into the situation in order to make it theirs. Again, both methods of processing information have strengths and weaknesses, but both are equally viable ways of learning. Information processing is a continuum that moves from the need to internalize to the need to act. McCarthy (1990) asserts that "watchers need to refine their reflective gifts while developing the courage to experiment and try. And doers need to refine their experimenting gifts while developing the patience to watch reflectively."

The 4MAT® System views learning as a natural sequence which progresses sequentially from Quadrant one through Quadrant four experiences. If an instructor includes all types of learning in the classroom, then each student has a better chance of comprehending the material. Movement around the circle is a natural learning progression. Humans sense and feel; they experience, they watch; they reflect, then they think; they develop theories, then they try out theories; they experiment. Finally, they evaluate and synthesize what they have learned in order to apply it to their next similar experience. Based on the McCarthy model, a librarian seeking to develop materials and processes for teaching patrons to use electronic resources should seek to accommodate the needs of diverse learning styles.

Teaching strategies based on the 4MAT® Learning Styles are highly endorsed in education literature. The four major learners (imaginative, analytic, common sense, and dynamic) can use 4MAT® to engage their whole brain. Learners use their most comfortable style while being challenged to function in less comfortable modes (McCarthy, 1990).

In an interview with Susan Leflar (1983), McCarthy emphasizes that the purpose of The 4MAT® System is to help the teacher become more skilled in the use of multiple methods of instruction which increase his/her skill and reach students more effectively. In other words, the intent is "to teach to all learning styles, not to test and label and group students. Whatever the learning style or brain dominance of the student, 4MAT® provides opportunities for each student to do all things relatively well."

Another important aspect of the 4MAT® model, continues McCarthy, is to follow the natural cyclical progression through all four learning styles as devised by Kolb. Each learner has a quadrant or place on the theoretical circle where learning comes more easily. *Imaginative Learners*, those who fall in quadrant one, prefer to learn through a combination of sensing, or feeling, or watching. They like to see all sides, a factor which impedes the decision-making process. In the effort to find personal meaning, they often ask the question "Why?" These learners must understand how learning relates to their values; thus, they seek meaning and clarity. *Analytic Learners*, those who fall in quadrant two, prefer to learn through a combination of watching and developing theories and concepts. For them, the most important question is "What?" Their right hemisphere seeks to integrate new experiences with what they already know, while their left hemisphere seeks that new knowledge. Quadrant two learners respond to new information by organizing it into concepts and theories. They prefer sequential thinking and copious details. They tend to be thorough and industrious, enjoy traditional teaching methods, and find ideas intriguing. Their primary motivation is to identify everything that can be known about a topic, and they have tremendous respect for those experts who can provide that knowledge. *Common Sense Learners*, those who fall in quadrant three, prefer to learn by thinking through concepts and trying things out for themselves, by doing. For these learners, the most important question is "How does it work?" Their right hemisphere seeks applications for what they learn, while their left hemisphere asks the more general "What have other people done?" question. These learners want to

ILLUSTRATION 1

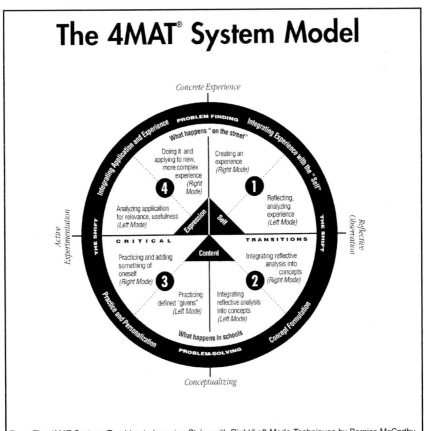

immediately "practice" their knowledge. They are problem-solvers who prefer to experiment and tinker with things because they need to know how things work. This involvement with learning helps them to develop clear, useful understandings that have practical applications. *Dynamic Learners*, those who fall in quadrant four, prefer to learn best by doing and sensing and feeling. These learners ask the question "If"? Their right hemisphere develops extensions of their learning while their left hemisphere seeks to analyze learning for relevance and significance. Quadrant four learners want to see relationships and connections between things, and they synthesize this knowledge into something that creates new experiences for themselves and others.

The role of the teacher changes as he/she teaches "around the circle." In quadrant two, for example, the teacher's role is quite traditional-as Information Giver. In contrast, in quadrant four, the teacher becomes the Evaluator/Remediator, creating a climate of freedom to discover by doing and challenging students to observe, analyze, and share, in addition to helping students who need more direction. So through the progression of the model, the teacher uses a broad knowledge of learning styles and specific methods to teach. In other words, the model provides a vehicle for utilizing the varying instructional modes that the Sheridan article espouses.

The following teaching unit illustrates how The 4MAT® System of Learning can be used to introduce adult learners to the Web.

## USING THE WEB FOR RESEARCH

### Teaching Unit

### Based on Bernice McCarthy's 4MAT® System of Learning

OBJECTIVE: To foster appreciation and develop skills for the Web as part of a continuum of information resources for research rather than as a replacement for traditional resources.

### Quadrant One: Experiencing to Reflecting–Connections

Right Mode: Connect

Objective: To connect with students' personal life research experiences.

To foster group interaction skills.

Activity: Brainstorm–Students share their experiences with research–real life or library–such as buying a car, selecting a movie, determining eligibility for this program/contest/loan/etc., class papers, projects. Students also make a list of the kinds of research.

Assessment: Students' participation in activity.

Left Mode: Examine

Objective: To have students reflect on the experience.

Activity: Discussion of brainstorming activity. Instructor leads class discussion, helping students recognize their concerns and discover that they are not alone in their confusion about the research process. This step provides an opportunity for students to respond to questions such as the following:

- What does organization look like to you?

- How important is organization to you?

- Does it makes a difference in your life?

- What is research to you?

- What kinds of anxieties do you experience when doing research?

- What are the positive things you remember about conducting research in the library?

- Negative things?

- What word describes your initial reaction to doing a research project?

Assessment: Students' participation and contribution to group dialog.

## *Quadrant Two: Reflecting to Conceptualizing–Concepts*

Right Mode: Image

Objective: To extend the experience of research into their own personal experience by seeing not only the whole, but also various combinations of parts.

Activity: "Hidden Square." Students are provided with a visual drawing of a large square, divided into a number of smaller squares. They are then directed to quickly count the total number of squares seen, and report that number orally. How is this problem similar to doing research? What can we learn from this illustration that can be applied to research?

Assessment: Students' success in finding the correct answer. Quality of student engagement in the activity.

Left Mode: Define

Objective: To become more knowledgeable about how the Web enhances the scope of research.

Activity: Instructor provides descriptive information on the Web and its search tools using a PowerPoint® presentation. Students are required to take notes.

Assessment: Understanding of the concepts involved: oral review of information provided. Quality of students' understanding: participation.

### *Quadrant Three: Conceptualizing to Doing–Applications*

Left Mode: Try

Objective: To provide guided practice on Web via Netscape Browser.

Activity: Students complete worksheets and hands-on computer application exercises on searching the World Wide Web. Use textbook practice exercises.

Assessment: Understanding of the concepts involved: students hand in their worksheets. Discover if any concepts must be retaught.

Right Mode: Extend

Objective: To give students the opportunity to personalize the learned material by doing a collaborative project.

Activity: Match pairs of students based on research topic selected from list of topics provided. Students are to find ten sites for researching the topic. Describe each source and evaluate its usefulness for their topic.

Assessment: This is a major performance assessment. Completion of the project congruent with format created by teacher and students prior to the assignment. Students' skill level in finding appropriate resources.

### Quadrant Four: Doing Experiencing–Creation

Left Mode: Refine

Objective: To provide guidance and feedback on students' projects; to encourage students; to polish the project.

Activity: Students complete projects. They analyze their research strategy and its usefulness for future projects. Finally, students individually choose a topic for one class assignment and begin the research process.

Assessment: Evaluation of project usefulness. Ability of students to explore and expand their research strategies to chosen individual topics.

Right Mode: Integrate

Objective: To allow students to share what they learned and to evaluate the learning.

Activity: Partners share the challenges of researching their topic and search strategies with the entire class.

Assessment: Quality of finished project. Quality of student engagement in the activity.

## CONCLUSION

The great value for librarians in using 4MAT® is that one does not have to decide what the individual's learning style is, but rather the system can help librarians become more skilled in the use of multiple methods of instruction which increase the librarian's skills and reach students more effectively. In other words, the emphasis is to teach to all learning styles. As a learner-focused model for adapting curriculum and instruction to the diverse needs of students, 4MAT® benefits teachers/librarians by giving them a framework to design learning activities in a systematic cycle.

In summary, 4MAT® offers a way to accommodate, as well as challenge, all types of learners, by appealing to their accustomed learning styles while stretching them to function in less comfortable modes.

## REFERENCES

Boren, Susan et al. (March 1987). The Higher Educational Amendments of 1985 (P.L. 99-498): A Summary of Provisions. Washington, DC Congressional Research Service, p. CRS-6.

Carr, David. (Spring 1983). "The Agent and the Learner." Public Library Quarterly 2, 3-19.

Council on the Continuing Education Unit. (1984). Principles of Good Practice in Continuing Education. Silver Spring, MD.

Huston, Mary. (Fall 1983). "Rethinking Our Approach for Research Instruction." Research Strategies 4 (2), 185-187.

Knowles, Malcolm S. (1978). The Adult Learner: A Neglected Species. 2nd ed. Houston: Gulf.

Kolb, David. (1985). The Learning Style Inventory. Boston, MA: McBerand Co.

Leflar, S. (1983). "The 4MAT® System: An Interview with Bernice McCarthy." Journal of Development & Remedial Education 6 (2), 4-7.

Lifzinger, Mary Ellen and Osif, Bonnie. (1993). "Accommodating Diverse Learning Styles: Designing Instruction for Electronic Information Sources." In National LOEX Library Instruction Conference: What Is Good Instruction NOW? Library Instruction for the 90s. Ann Arbor, MI: Pierian Press.

McCarthy, Bernice. (1996). About Learning. Oak Brook, IL: Excel.

McCarthy, Bernice. (1987). The 4MAT® System: Teaching to Learning Styles With Right/Left Model Techniques. Oak Brook, IL: Excel.

McCarthy, Bernice. (Oct 1990). "Using the 4MAT® System to Bring Learning Styles to Schools." Educational Leadership, 31-37.

Nahl-Jakobovits, Dian and Leon. (Winter 1985). "Managing the Affective Micro-Information." Research Strategies 3, 17-28.

Oberman, Cerise. (Winter 1983). "Question Analysis and the Learning Cycle." Research Strategies 1, 22.

Sheridan, Jean. (Fall 1986). "Andragogy: A New Concept for Academic Librarians." Research Strategies 4, 156-167.

United States Statutes at Large. 99th Congress, 2nd Session 1986, vol. 100, part 2, pp. 1141-1846, Public Laws.

Vakili, Mary Jane. (1993). "Revamping a Required BI Course for Adult Students." Research Strategies 11 (1), 24-32.

# Delphi Method in Web Site Selection: Using the Experts

## Julian W. Green

**SUMMARY.** The development of Web sites is proceeding at an ever-quickening pace. Adult learners can benefit from the wealth of information accessible in both new sites and changing older sites. However, that excitement is tempered by frustration in following blind leads or encountering questionable quality. One approach is to stay abreast of the latest material by attempting to look at and read every new and modified site. However, time is finite, and many of our students have lives filled with conflicting needs. The Delphi method, a sociological research technique first developed in defense research, is used to elicit expert opinion as a short cut to evaluating Web sites. A specific example with business-related sites is presented as a test case in developing and applying the methodology. The use of Delphi, an oracle-based technique, seems quite appropriate as we assist our adult students to allocate their time wisely. *[Article copies available for a fee from The Haworth Document Delivery Service: 1-800-342-9678. E-mail address: <getinfo@haworthpressinc.com> Website: <http://www.haworthpressinc.com>]*

**KEYWORDS.** World Wide Web, WWW, Delphi, site selection

## *INTRODUCTION*

As information specialists it is important to know, not just what is out there, but how to find it efficiently. The Internet provides rapidly expanding

---

Julian W. Green is Information Specialist and Coordinator of Library Instruction, Library, University of South Carolina at Spartanburg, Spartanburg, SC 29303 (E-mail: jgreen@gw.uscs.edu).

[Haworth co-indexing entry note]: "Delphi Method in Web Site Selection: Using the Experts." Green, Julian W. Co-published simultaneously in *The Reference Librarian* (The Haworth Information Press, an imprint of The Haworth Press, Inc.) No. 69/70, 2000, pp. 299-310; and: *Reference Services for the Adult Learner: Challenging Issues for the Traditional and Technological Era* (ed: Kwasi Sarkodie-Mensah) The Haworth Information Press, an imprint of The Haworth Press, Inc., 2000, pp. 299-310. Single or multiple copies of this article are available for a fee from The Haworth Document Delivery Service [1-800-342-9678, 9:00 a.m. - 5:00 p.m. (EST). E-mail address: getinfo@haworthpressinc.com].

information of varying degrees of value. It is one more world of information that we must incorporate into our knowledge base, and mine for value. We race, as we always have, to assist the users of our libraries, feeling inundated by the immense wave of information available. Any reasonable method that might save us time, energy, and frustration is worthy of our attention.

The university where I work is a good example of an adult constituency and their needs. This regional campus of a state university has as our primary users 3416 undergraduate students, 291 graduate students and 157 faculty, including a relatively large number (33%) of non-traditional students or adult learners (Trail, pers. comm.). These are students whose lives are full, and who look to optimizing their time allocation. They have a very real need for efficiently accessed information, wherever it is located. They are, indeed, affected by a communication revolution which demands our attention (Johnson, 1994).

Informal surveys of Internet usage find our traditional students much more likely to "play" on the Web as contrasted with their non-traditional counterparts. Adult learners, on the other hand, need to do their research and then get back to the rest of their lives as quickly as possible (e.g., Non-Traditional Students to Class, 1997). The enormous amount of information on the Web may be counter-productive for adult students. This extra information takes more time to process and use than less information. Tenopir (1998) stated the issues well: "Of course, it may not always be a good thing to retrieve easily lots of information at the library, home, or on the road. Several database providers predict that finding solutions to information overload will be a major trend." It is, in fact, a problem in information transfer. The increased amount of information is merely one more way of choking the pipeline. We want to decrease the restrictions placed on information by access difficulties–and in this case, access to too much unevaluated material is one of the potential restrictions (Green, 1991; Martin, 1995).

As librarians in active libraries, we know how to find information, even in the rapidly changing world of the Web. But, how many sites there are, and how many more there will be even before finishing the typing of this sentence (e.g., Horwitt, 1997; MacMillan, 1996; Schatz, 1997; Schwarzwalder, 1995, 1996). Given the shortness of life, and the time constraints in the lives of our adult learners, it is highly desirable to be able to predict the usefulness of sites, known and unknown, before spending time with them. We need the help of experts who have the knowledge and time to be able to look at, evaluate, and select sites. We would want to go to a specialist who would be able to predict the potential usefulness of those sites. We would want to go to the oracle.

## DELPHI TECHNIQUE

Delphi as a research method first surfaced in the literature from work at the RAND Corporation in the 1960s (Brown, Cochran, and Dalkey, 1969; Dalkey, 1967; Dalkey and Helmer, 1963; Gordon and Helmer, 1964; Helmer, 1967). The focus was to predict the future, or more exactly, to give study of the future in specific areas more meaningful input. Born in defense research, it is not surprising that the first Delphi study was the application of "expert opinion to the selection, from the point of view of a Soviet strategic planner, of an optimal U.S. industrial target system and to the estimation of the number of A-bombs required to reduce the munitions output by a prescribed amount" (Dalkey and Helmer, 1963). Certainly, it had a powerful, terrifying beginning. However, since then Delphi has evolved; and it has been used in numerous disciplines (e.g., Linstone and Turoff, 1975; Sproull, 1988; Van Dijk, 1989). Librarianship has been among those disciplines with uses ranging from general overviews of the possibilities of using Delphi (Buckley, 1995, 1994) to a specific study asking experts to predict the use and extent of information technology (Koskiala and Huhtanen, 1989). There are even numerous examples of the employment of a Delphi-like method without actually using the name (e.g., Tenopir, 1998), but the basic technique was there with supporting rationale.

Linstone and Turoff (1975) see the Delphi method as a communication process:

> It is not, however, the explicit nature of the application which determines the appropriateness of utilizing Delphi: rather, it is the particular circumstances surrounding the necessarily associated group communication process: 'Who is it that should communicate about the problems, or what alternative mechanisms are available for that communication, and what can we expect to obtain with these alternatives?' (Linstone and Turoff, 1975, p. 4)

They go on to give seven properties of potential applications that "lead to need for employing Delphi." Of those properties, the first five are directly relevant to using Delphi to select Web sites. One would hope that one of the properties, the sixth property, "severe or politically unpalatable disagreements," never comes up in a library setting. The properties of potential applications of Delphi are:

1. The problem does not lend itself to precise analytical techniques but can benefit from subjective judgements on a collective basis;
2. The individuals needed to contribute to the examination of a broad or complex problem have no history of adequate communication and may represent diverse background with respect to experience or expertise;

3. More individuals are needed than can effectively interact in a face-to-face exchange;
4. Time and cost make frequent group meetings infeasible;
5. The efficiency of face-to-face meetings can be increased by a supplemental group communication process;
6. Disagreements among individuals are so severe or politically unpalatable that the communication process must be refereed and/or anonymity assured;
7. The heterogeneity of the participants must be preserved to assure validity of the results, i.e., avoidance of domination by quantity or by strength of personality ("bandwagon effect") (Linstone and Turoff, 1975, p. 4).

Delphi is, then, a predictive method harnessing expert opinion as input, often with iterative feedback to the experts, and requiring the recipients of the input to analyze, interpret, and then apply the input. The opportunity to obtain expert opinion, while at the same time being able to save time, is quite appealing, and would have a tremendous impact on the quality of library services in this area of Web site selection.

## DELPHI METHOD IN CHOOSING WEB SITES

Based on other uses of Delphi and the kinds of applications where it has been helpful, it seems obvious that applying it to the problem of Web site selection is appropriate. Many of the properties that Linstone and Turoff suggest are relevant. The first property, lack of precise analytical techniques, fits our problem of Web site selection. Though there is some work attempting to have Web sites selected more automatically, such as the research of Kleinberg and Raghavan where text-based searching is refined by links in Web sites in hopes of developing more precise searching (Peterson, 1998), this is far from being a precise analytical technique, and is merely one way of attempting to refine results from some of the search engines. Even if those techniques are developed someday, it is a real question as to whether training in such techniques is a worthwhile application of resources or of the adult learner's time.

The second property, that the individuals do not have a history of communicating, is certainly obvious. The adult learner does not spend time with other adult students nor with the Web site developers. As Knowles (1970) points out, adult learners are self-directed, focused on immediate application of knowledge. This need for immediate application compresses the calendar with which the non-traditional students are working. The unique needs and styles of adult learners are well documented (e.g., Boyd, 1980; Knowles,

1984; Harriger, 1994; Hofmann, 1994; Maciuika, 1994), and lead us to search for ways of selecting sites that might better respond to their characteristics and needs.

The third property mentioned by Linstone and Turoff–needing more individuals for the task than those that can interact face-to-face–describes the problem of the massive volume of potential Web sites to assess. The latest estimate of Web sites is over 320 million pages, and with estimated growth at 1000% over the next few years (Lawrence and Giles, 1998). The fourth and fifth properties–excessive time and cost of meeting face-to-face, and the efficiency of other methods–fall naturally from the first three properties. Certainly, the need for time and cost management speaks directly to the needs of our adult learners (Smith, 1995).

Let us expand our consideration of what sort of time we are using, when we contemplate staying abreast of new Web sites. As we all know, the Web is used, and certainly talked about in our profession. Its impact was quick and tremendous (Martin, 1990; Duffy, 1996; Schatz, 1997; Gray, 1997; Lawrence and Giles, 1998; Center for Next Generation Internet, 1998; CyberAtlas, 1998). The existence of approximately 320 million Web pages (Lawrence and Giles, 1998) certainly should give us pause. As we try to deal with what is out there, we have to spend time with the Web, building our understanding and expertise (e.g., Eustace, 1996; Messing, 1996; Solomon, 1997). This often takes the form of deciding to develop our own home page as the way to help our users and us get through the mass of information (e.g., Clyde, 1996). We might think of it as a parallel to having a local library help the public get through the mass of printed information that is/was available–by selection of materials by information professionals. The next step may well go in concert with building subject specific guides to the Web. One example is in the work of Morville and Wickhorst (1996) where they visit virtual libraries to help them build their sites–a Delphi-like technique. Yet, we still need ways to assess what is out there (e.g., Johnson, 1996; Symons, 1996, 1997). Specific examples of evaluation and organization of knowledge abound for both the information professional and the user (e.g., Johnson, 1996; Morville and Wickhorst, 1996; Remeikis and Koska, 1996). So what to do?

As stated above, using the Delphi method in Web site selection is entirely appropriate. In fact, from experience we know that this is not particularly new or unusual; it is what we do often–we ask colleagues and read reviews–that is, we go to the experts. Going to an authority to "predict" potential usefulness of Web sites is not only what many of us do, but actually is preferable as a beginning point for our adult students and our other users as well. It allows us to save our time, the library users' time, and produce a quality product while doing so.

## GOING TO THE ORACLE:
## AN EXAMPLE

Let us, then, go to the oracle. As argued above, this should pull together the opinions of various experts, improving the ultimate product as well as saving time and energy. As an example we will look at business resources on the Web. The opportunity to pull highly relevant information off the Web in this field is tremendous. As we all know, sites of corporations, libraries, universities, vendors, countries, chambers of commerce, and government agencies exist that fit the needs of our adult business students, and of course, of the library's business information specialist. There are a myriad of resources on the net (e.g., MacMillan, 1996), and, therefore, we need to find our oracle.

How then to find the oracle? Each of us may define our oracles differently, depending on our home organization or on the focus of our needs. In the specific case of my home institution, the University of South Carolina at Spartanburg, working in an academic institution with only undergraduate programs in business has us define our oracles with that bias. Using the Delphi method, as a starting point a decision was made to define experts (oracles) as the top-ranked business schools in the country. It was possible, then, to approach any number of evaluations and rankings of business schools such as *Business Week, U.S. News & World Report,* as well as other independent studies, such as the controversial *Gourman Report* (e.g., Reingold, 1997; Tracy and Waldfogel, 1997; Schools of Business, 1998; Specialties, 1998; Gourman, 1997). Each one has its own approach, and each has its advantages and disadvantages (e.g., Schatz, 1993). The goal was to select a number of names of highly respected (i.e., expert) institutions. The next step was to take the top five schools listed for each of the above-mentioned rankings. Once eliminating the overlap (schools that occurred on more than one list) then the names of eight institutions remained. Those schools were Harvard University, Massachusetts Institute of Technology, Northwestern University, Stanford University, University of Chicago, University of Michigan, University of Pennsylvania, and University of Virginia given in alphabetical order. Thus, we had a list of experts. The oracles were ready.

The next step was to visit the selected Web sites, and then to evaluate the relevance of those sites to the particular needs of the home institution and its students. Other important considerations included the accessibility, the organization, the manner of linking, and, of course, the percentage of relevant sites. A quick look at these sites, or specifically, the business "information center" at each, provided choices from which a librarian could select links. Those then could be annotated and provided to the library users through the home institution's Web page. Of these eight sites a range of issues were encountered including the following: (1) some were set up so that the outside user keeps running into areas that are only available to the local community; (2) some had limited breakdown by subject categories; (3) some were significantly slower than others; (4) some had dated material; and, of course, as expected from oracles (5) some provided particularly useful and unanticipated links. For our students and faculty, today, we would select the University of Michigan or the University of Chicago sites as oracles. Naturally, following a choice one would have to monitor regularly for both quality and appropriateness to local curriculum needs.

The students with tight schedules, particularly our adult students, can then access these points without losing time searching for business information resources on the Web. We have developed our collection by adding links to experts. We have used the experts at the University of Chicago and the University of Michigan, in a sense, to predict the future usefulness of sites. Those chosen sites are listed below with relevant annotations describing why we decided to use or not to use.

### SITES–SOURCES FOR ORACLES

Harvard Business School–Baker Library.
*http://library.hbs.edu/*

> Some very nice links, however the many sites that are available only to Harvard students are mixed in, and some sites are out-of-date (e.g., Fortune 500 from 1996). Does contain online versions of bibliographies.

MIT Libraries Virtual Reference Desk.
*http://libraries.mit.edu/services/virtualref.html*

> Direct link to Dewey Library (Management) refers back to Virtual Reference Desk. Alphabetic list of subject areas with very limited business coverage. Too focused for our needs.

Northwestern University Library.
*http://www.library.nwu.edu/reference/business/*

> Some good sites. A number of excellent links to "Super Sites." One such link is to a foreign school with up-to-date useful links (http://www.dis.strath.ac.uk/business/index.html). Includes online research guides.

Stanford University Libraries.
   *http://www-sul.stanford.edu/depts/ssrg/econ/econ1.html*

> Very good links, but focused on economics. One particularly useful site deals with social sciences data with an effective search engine (http://odwin.ucsd.edu/idata/).

University of Chicago Library Resources.
   *http://www.lib.uchicago.edu/LibInfo/SourcesBySubject/BusinessAndEconomics/ connectto.html*

> Good range of links broken into sub-categories. Has some links others do not have. Noteworthy is the UNC Charlotte international business site (http://www.uncc.edu/lis/library/reference/intbus/vibehome.htm).

University of Michigan. Michigan Electronic Library.
   *http://mel.lib.mi.us/business/business-index.html*

> Hundreds of links. Divided by subject, with broad range of topics. Very few annotations.

University of Pennsylvania. Wharton School. Lippincott Library.
   *http://www.library.upenn.edu/resources/business/business.html*

> Good links, and kept to a manageable number. Divided by general category, and then subject listing within category. Some categories are very limited. Up to date.

University of Virginia. Darden Graduate School of Business Admin. The Camp Library.
   *http://www.darden.virginia.edu/library/default.htm*

> Many links. Divided by logical categories, and then by subject. Some dead end paths and others open only to UVa users mixed in with others.

## CONCLUSION

We all need ways to minimize the impact of the information access explosion on both our staff and our users. Not only has the amount of accessible information increased, but also knowledge about the existence of information has done the same. Our adult learners expect quality information in a limited time frame. Potential for frustration is high as the student becomes aware of the wealth of information available, and the lack of typical "selection" or "collection development" carried out in relation to the millions of sites. Our adult student needs assistance from the best librarians available. Fortunately, there is help available from those experts, what I refer to as our Delphi oracles. Careful identification of and use of the expert sites provide us with the help we need. Consultations in ancient Greece with Apollo at Delphi were normally restricted to the 7th day of the Delphic month, Apollo's birthday. Fortunately, given computers and the World Wide Web, we can consult our own oracles more often, and receive counsel on our own wars–our battles to find the right information in a timely fashion, our attempts to properly serve our students.

## REFERENCES

Boyd, Robert and Jerold Apps (eds.). (1980). *Redefining the Discipline of Adult Education.* San Francisco: Jossey-Bass.

Brown, B., S. Cochran and N. Dalkey. (1969). *The Delphi Method, II: Structure of Experiments.* Santa Monica, CA: Rand Corporation, RM-5957-PR.

Buckely, Christopher. (1995). Delphi: A Methodology for Preferences More than Predictors. *Library Management,* 16 (7): 16-19.

Buckley, Christopher C. (1994). Delphi Technique Supplies the Classic Result? *Australian Library Journal,* 43: 158-164.

Center for Next Generation Internet. (1998). Internet Survey Reaches 30 Million Internet Host Level: New Survey Method Implemented. *Biannual Strategic Note.* 15 Feb. 1998. Online. Available: ftp://ftp.genmagic.com/pub/internet/TrendsPR9802. txt. 12 June, 1998.

Clyde, Laurel. (1996). The Library as Information Provider: The Home Page. *The Electronic Librar,.* 14 (6): 549-558.

CyberAtlas. (1998). Who's on the Net in the U.S.? *Market Demographics.* Online. Available: http://www.cyberatlas.com/market/demographics/index.html. 12 June, 1998.

Dalkey, Norman. (1967). *Delphi.* Santa Monica, CA: Rand Corporation, P-3702.

Dalkey, Norman and Olaf Helmer. (1963). An Experimental Application of the Delphi Method to the Use of Experts. *Management Science,* 9: 458-467.

Duffy, Bob and Jenny Yacovissi. (1996). Seven Self-Contradicting Reasons Why the Worldwide Web is Such a Big Deal. *National Online Meeting Proceedings–1996. Information Today.* 17: 81-90.

Eustace, Ken. (1996). Going My Way? Beyond the WEB and the MOO in the Library. *Australian Library Review,* 13 (1): 44-53.

Gordon, T.J. and Olaf Helmer. (1964). *Report on a Long-Range Forecasting Study.* Santa Monica, CA: Rand Corporation, P-2982.

Gourman, Jack. (1997). *The Gourman Report.* New York: Random House.

Gray, Matthew. (1997). Internet Growth Summary. *Web Growth Summary.* Online.

Available: http://www.mit.edu/people/mkgray/net/web-growth-summary.html. 8 December, 1997.

Green, Julian W. (1991). Information Transfer Across Political Boundaries. *Geoscience Information Society, Proceedings,* 22: 97-115.

Harriger, Carolyn. (1994). Adults in College. *Interdisciplinary Handbook of Adult Lifespan Learning.* Ed. Jan Sinnott. Westport, CT: Greenwood Press. 171-185.

Harvard Business School–Baker Library. (1998). http://library.hbs.edu/. 21 June, 1998.

Helmer, Olaf. (1967). *Analysis of the Future: The Delphi Method.* Santa Monica, CA: Rand Corporation, P-3558.

Hofmann, Joan M., Catherine Posteraro, and Helen A. Presz. (1994). *Adult Learners: Why Were They Successful? Lessons Learned via an Adult Learner Task Force.* Paper presented at the Adult Learner Conference, Columbia, SC, 1994. ERIC Document No. ED 375 269.

Horwitt, Elisabeth. (1997). Global Warming to the 'Net. *Computerworld.* 1997 Sep. 29. Online. Ovid. http://www.uscs.edu/ovidweb/ovidweb.cgi. Periodical Abstracts. 03415030.

Imel, Susan. (1994). Guidelines for Working with Adult Learners. *ERIC Digest, no. 154.*

Johnson, Julie. (1996). Government Web Pages: The Lights are on but Nobody is Home. *The Electronic Library,* 14 (2): 149-156.

Johnson, Lynn. (1994). The Future Impact of the Communication Revolution. *Interdisciplinary Handbook of Adult Lifespan Learning.* Ed. Jan Sinnott. Westport, CT: Greenwood Press. 22-30.

Knowles, Malcolm (ed.). (1984). *Andragogy in Action.* San Francisco: Jossey-Bass.

Knowles, Malcolm Shepherd. (1970). *The Modern Practice of Adult Education; Adragogy versus Pedagogy.* NY: Association Press.

Knox, Alan B. (1986). *Helping Adults Learn.* San Francisco: Jossey-Bass.

Koskiala, Sinnikka and Anni Huhtanen. (1989). The Finnish Delphi Study: Forecasting the Extent of Information Technology Use in Libraries in 1996 and 2010. *The Electronic Library,* 7 (3): 170-175.

Lawrence, S. and C.L. Giles. (1998). Searching the World Wide Web. *Science,* 280 (5360): 98-100.

Linstone, Harold A. and Murray Turoff (eds.) (1975). *The Delphi Method: Techniques and Applications.* Reading, MA: Columbia University Press.

MacMillan, Don. (1996). Business Research on the Net: Pros and Cons. *Feliciter,* 42: 50-53.

Maciuika, Laura V., Michael Basseches, and Abigail Lipson. (1994). Exploring Adult Learning from Learners' Perspectives. *Interdisciplinary Handbook of Adult Lifespan Learning.* Ed. Jan Sinnott. Westport, CT: Greenwood Press. 249-269.

Martin, Murray S. (1995). Problems in information transfer in the age of the computer. *Information Technology & Libraries,* 14 (4): 243-246.

Martin, Rebecca. (1990). The Paradox of Public Service: Where Do We Draw the Line? *College & Research Libraries,* 5: 20-26.

Messing, John. (1996). Multimedia, Hypermedia and the Internet: Educational

Technologies for the Twenty-First Century. *Australian Library Review,* 13 (1): 11-17.

MIT Libraries Virtual Reference Desk. (1998). http://libraries.mit.edu/services/virtualref. html. 26 June, 1998.

Morville, Peter and Susan Wickhorst. (1996). Building Subject-Specific Guides to Internet Resources. *Internet Research: Electronic Networking Applications and Policy* 6 (4): 27-32.

Non-Traditional Students to Class. *Horizons.* South Carolina Educational Television. WETV. 21 March, 1997.

Northwestern University Library. (1998). http://www.library.nwu.edu/reference/ business/. 26 June, 1998.

Peterson, I. (1998). Sifting through the Web's Data Jumble. *Science News,* 153 (18): 278.

Reingold, Jennifer. (1997). Corporate America Goes to School. *Business Week,* (3549): 66-72.

Remeikis, Lois and Elizabeth Koska. (1996). Organizing for Knowledge: Developing a Knowledge Management System. *National Oline Meeting Proceedings–1996. Information Today,* 17: 315-318.

Schatz, Bruce. (1997). Information Retrieval in Digital Libraries: Bringing Search to the Net. *Science,* 275: 327-334.

Schools of Business: The Top Schools. (1998). *U.S. News & World Report,* 124 (8): 73.

Schwarzwalder, Robert. (1995). Annual Review of Technology Online. *Database,* 18 (6): 80-82.

Schwarzwalder, Robert. (1996). Technology Online in 1996: Explosive Growth of Sci/tech. On the Web. *Database,* 19 (6): 71-74.

Smith, Laurence N. and Timothy L. Walter. (1995). *The Adult Learner's Guide to College Success.* Belmont, CA: Wadsworth Publishing.

Solomon, Marc. (1997). Retooling the Information Professional. *Searcher,* 5: 10-14.

Specialties: Programs Ranked Best by Business School Deans and M.B.A. Program Heads. (1998). *U.S. News & World Report,* 124 (8): 76.

Sproull, Natalie L. (1988). *Handbook of Research Methods.* Metuchen, NJ: Scarecrow Press.

Stanford University Libraries. (1998). http://www-sul.stanford.edu/depts/ssrg/econ/ econ1.html. 26 June, 1998.

Symons, Ann. (1996). Intelligent Life on the Web: How to Find It. *School Library Journal,* 42 (3): 106-109.

Symons, Ann. (1997). Sizing Up Sites. *School Library Journal,* 43 (4): 22-25.

Tenopir, Carol. (1998). Expert Views on the Future. *Library Journal,* 123 (10): 33-34.

Tracy, Joseph and Joel Waldfogel. (1997). The Best Business Schools: A Market-Based Approach, 70 (1): 1-31.

Trail, Jonathan. (1998). Personal Communication with Jonathan Trail, Coordinator of Institutional Research, University of South Carolina at Spartanburg. May, 1998.

University of Chicago Library Resources. (1998). http://www.lib.uchicago.edu/LibInfo/ SourcesBySubject/BusinessAndEconomics/connectto.html. 26 June, 1998.

University of Michigan. Michigan Electronic Library. (1998). http://mel.lib.mi.us/business/business-index.html. 26 June, 1998.

University of Pennsylvania Library. (1998). http://www.library.upenn.edu/resources/business/business.html. 26 June, 1998.

University of Virginia. Darden Graduate School of Business Admin. The Camp Library. (1998). http://www.darden.virginia.edu/library/default.htm. 26 June, 1998.

Van Dijk, Jan. 1989. Developing an Instrument to Control Technological Change for Employees. *Quality & Quantity,* 23: 189-203.

# SECTION 6:
# SERVING DIVERSE POPULATIONS: DISABLED PATRONS AND INTERNATIONAL STUDENTS

# Reference Services for All:
# How to Support Reference Service
# to Clients with Disabilities

Katherine J. Miller-Gatenby
Michele Chittenden

**SUMMARY.** Ideally, when clients come in to the library, reference staff should be able to focus on their information needs and not be distracted by the disability. Questions like "How will he get into the building?", "How can she use the catalogue?" and others, become important because they indicate barriers to the use of the library by persons with disabilities. If these are not addressed on an organizational level, they affect the individual with the disability, the service provider, i.e., the reference librarian, and the quality of the service provided.

The premise of this article is that the library has a responsibility to address barriers to service for persons with disabilities, and to support reference staff so that they can concentrate on the information need and not be distracted by the client's disability. The kinds of barriers will be addressed based on where they occur: in signage throughout the library, in the reference area including the reference desk, in the collection and in services offered, which includes web sites and bibliographic instruction. A list of electronic and print resources is included. *[Article copies*

Katherine J. Miller-Gatenby is Library Development Officer, National Library of Canada, 395 Wellington Street, Ottawa, Ontario Canada K1A 0N4 (E-mail: katherine. miller@nlc-bnc.ca). Michele Chittenden is Coordinator for Special Readers' Services, Queen's University Libraries, Kingston, Ontario Canada K7L 5C4 (E-mail: CHITTEND@STAUFFER.QUEENSU.CA).

[Haworth co-indexing entry note]: "Reference Services for All: How to Support Reference Service to Clients with Disabilities." Miller-Gatenby, Katherine J., and Michele Chittenden. Co-published simultaneously in *The Reference Librarian* (The Haworth Information Press, an imprint of The Haworth Press, Inc.) No. 69/70, 2000, pp. 313-326; and: *Reference Services for the Adult Learner: Challenging Issues for the Traditional and Technological Era* (ed: Kwasi Sarkodie-Mensah) The Haworth Information Press, an imprint of The Haworth Press, Inc., 2000, pp. 313-326. Single or multiple copies of this article are available for a fee from The Haworth Document Delivery Service [1-800-342-9678, 9:00 a.m. - 5:00 p.m. (EST). E-mail address: getinfo@haworthpressinc.com].

*available for a fee from The Haworth Document Delivery Service: 1-800-342-9678. E-mail address: <getinfo@haworthpressinc.com> Website: <http://www. haworthpressinc.com>]*

**KEYWORDS.** Accessibility, access to libraries, disabled patrons, library service to handicapped, physically handicapped

## INTRODUCTION:
## WHO ARE YOUR PATRONS WITH DISABILITIES?

In both Canada and the United States, around 20% of the population is identified as having a disability. According to Statistics Canada's Health and Activity Limitations Survey, 1991, Canada has an adult disability rate of 17.7% (Statistics Canada 1992). The U.S. Bureau of the Census indicated, in December 1997, that "About 1 in 5 Americans have some kind of disability, and 1 in 10 have a severe disability" (United States, 1997).

The definitions of disability used by the two census bureaus are similar. Statistics Canada's is based on the International Classification of Impairment, Disability and Handicap model developed by the World Health Organization "... a disability is any restriction or lack (resulting from an impairment) of ability to perform an activity in the manner or within the range considered normal for a human being" (Statistics Canada, 1992). The U.S. Bureau of the Census states "A person is considered to have a disability if he or she has difficulty performing certain functions or has difficulty performing activities of daily living, or has difficulty with certain social roles" (United States, 1997).

Both the U.S. Bureau of the Census and Statistics Canada have identified the following possible characteristics of disability: impaired vision, hearing, agility, mobility and speech. Also included are difficulties performing certain social roles, i.e., doing schoolwork for children and working at a job and around the house for adults. This includes children or adults with learning or intellectual disabilities or psychiatric conditions.

Another way of classifying disability has been proposed to the World Health Organization to update the ICIDH (ICIDH, 1998). This classification incorporates two interacting elements to define a "handicap situation": the characteristics of the person and the physical and socio-cultural environment. One of the characteristics of the person may be an impairment, but it is the interaction of that impairment with the environment that produces the handicap situation. This means that impaired mobility requiring the use of a wheelchair is not necessarily a handicap until the wheelchair user encounters stairs at the entrance to your library. Blindness is not necessarily a handicap for a student until the information he/she needs to have to use the library is only available in print. Impaired agility of the hand is not necessarily a handicap until a library patron needs to turn a door knob to open the door to the library's washroom.

As these examples illustrate, your library, as part of the physical and socio-cultural environment, can contribute to creating a handicap situation and that handicap situation may prevent an individual from being able to use your library and your services.

Libraries usually consist of a building or buildings, the collection and access to it (for example, catalogues, finding aids, bibliographies), furniture, equipment, services and staff. As well, an increasing number of libraries use web sites to offer service to their clients. Each of these variables can pose barriers to persons with disabilities. As with most public buildings, access to the library starts with the parking lot and entrances and includes washrooms, doors, elevators, lighting, alarm systems and signs. Barriers in any of these may prevent patrons with disabilities from using the library. Inappropriately designed furniture, book stacks, service desks and study areas can deter persons with disabilities from using basic library service and finding and using the information they need. Public use computers without adaptive technologies for access to the library's catalogue or the internet prevent some library patrons from autonomous use of these tools. Web sites and other services that are designed without considering the needs of persons with disabilities serve to isolate that segment of the population and may prevent them from using the library to its full potential. And finally, inadequately trained staff may feel uncomfortable serving persons with disabilities and consequently offer them a different standard of service.

Reference is frequently where the initial contact between the patron and the library occurs. What would that contact be like for a disabled patron in your library? Would he/she be served as well as other patrons? Would he/she encounter any barriers? Would they be insurmountable? How can you ensure that the encounter would be positive, that there would be no barriers? The best way to answer these questions is to examine the component parts of reference service, starting with the physical space; which includes signage, the reference area and the reference desk and then look at the collection, staff, bibliographic instruction and, finally, the library web site.

(Note: All the dimensions cited are taken from both the *Accessibility Guidelines for Buildings and Facilities* by the United States Architectural and Transportation Barriers Compliance Board and from *The Accessible Canadian Library II: A Resource Tool for Libraries Serving Persons with Disabilities,* published by the National Library of Canada.)

## SIGNAGE

Signs in libraries are used for two main purposes, for direction finding and for instructional purposes. Direction finding signs provide an indication of the overall organization of the library which enables patrons to orient themselves in unfamiliar surroundings. This kind of sign includes those that point the way to a specific library service or site and those that identify the service or site, for example, Reference Desk, Official Publications. Call number labels on items in the collection and shelf labels are further examples of this kind of sign. Instructional signs give directions on the use of library resources. They guide patrons on how to use material, equipment and services and inform them of special conditions, restrictions, and procedures, for example, hours of service, borrowing privileges, use of photocopiers, to name a few.

### Barriers

Barriers to the information provided by signs prevent easy reading. These barriers may be in the material used to make the sign, for example, glare producing plastic or in the design where letters may be too small or the contrast between the background color and letters may be insufficient. As well, the content of the sign may be confusing, with ambiguous information or unclear symbols.

### Recommendations

Effective signs in libraries will take into account the needs of persons with disabilities and follow design principles that will make them readable by, and thus useful for, a wide range of people. Key issues to consider when designing signs are content, readability and placement.

To ensure that the content of the sign is useful, keep in mind what the sign is intended to do, i.e., if it is for direction finding, site identification or instruction, and ensure that it includes only the minimum content necessary. Directional signs in particular should be brief so that they can be read and understood in passing. Use symbols, for example, arrows, International Symbol of Accessibility, washrooms, when possible as these are understood faster and may be more easily read by patrons with visual impairment, learning disabilities or intellectual disabilities. If the information cannot be reduced to sign size, consider other options like pamphlets and guides to the library in print, audio cassette, large print and Braille.

To promote readability, signs should have consistent design throughout the library, i.e., colour, size, shape, pattern, use of punctuation and symbols. They should be well lit (minimum 200 lx), have non-glare finish and characters and symbols should contrast with their background, either dark characters on a light background or light characters on a dark background. The minimum height for characters is 75 mm. (3 in.).

For persons with visual disabilities, signs with raised letters and numerals (a minimum 0.8 mm. or 1/32 in.) and Brailled characters (Grade 2 Braille) and symbols (between 16 mm. or 5/8 in. and 50 mm. or 2 in. high) should be used. These should be mounted on the wall with the centerline at a height of 1500 mm. or 60 in.

Signs should be placed at a consistent level (between 1650 mm. or 66 in. and 3450 mm. or 138 in.) so they can be seen by persons in wheelchairs. Directional signs should be placed with maximum exposure at all decision points along a route and instructional signs should be placed as close as possible to the equipment or item the instructions are intended for. Suspended signs should have 2030 mm. or 80 in. minimum clear head room.

Spine labels on books in the reference collection should be in typeface that is large, dark and easy to read. As well, the shelves holding special format materials, such as talking books, videotapes, audio cassettes and Braille books, as well as items in the collection itself, should have tactile identifiers in addition to print labels.

Signs are an important aspect of communication between library staff and patrons. Consistent, effectively designed and placed signs present a well organized, efficient and accessible library that encourages self sufficient use by all patrons including persons with disabilities.

## REFERENCE AREA

The reference area is usually a high use area of the library. It should be designed to manage the level of traffic and must be accessible to everyone.

### *Barriers*

Poor layout including placement of furniture, shelves and lighting can make the area difficult to navigate for patrons with disabilities. The height of study tables and carrels is typically too low to allow a wheelchair underneath. Lighting can be inadequate for a patron with low vision to read comfortably.

### *Recommendations*

Traffic in the Reference Area should be managed to encourage efficient flow from point to point. Heavy use areas, like service desks and catalogue areas should have adequate space for more than one person to use and for wheelchairs and scooters to negotiate comfortably. The minimum width for a route to be accessible is 915 mm. or 36 in., however, 1065 mm. or 42 in. is preferred as it allows for greater maneuverability. Study the placement of tables, chairs and shelves to ensure that they are not impeding movement.

Tables and work stations should have recessed or removed aprons to accommodate wheelchairs, i.e., between 710 mm. or 28 in. to 865 mm. or 34 in. high and carrels must have an opening width of at least 812 mm. or 32 in. Space behind the table or carrel should allow a wheelchair easy access in and out of the work area. As well, a person in a wheelchair has a reach of about 610 mm. or 24 in. which means that books, computer terminals, and other library tools must be within that range. Facilities or workstations accessible to persons with disabilities should be clearly identified with International Symbols of Accessibility.

## REFERENCE DESK

Frequently, the Reference Desk is the first point of contact for a person using the library. As such, it is important that it be a positive experience, that the focus of service is on the information need expressed by the patron and not the patron's disability. After all, persons with disabilities have the same information needs as other library users, so the reference services your library provides for persons with disabilities should be the same as those you provide for general library users.

### Barriers

The Reference Desk can seem imposing to a person with a disability. Its size, location and layout can pose a number of barriers. These are not insurmountable. They require some thought and planning to address.

### Recommendations

The Reference Desk should be on the main floor of the library. It should be clearly visible and accessible from the library entrance. If there are service desks on other floors, there should be elevator access to those floors and the desks should be visible from the elevator door. The pathway to the desk must be clear and free of obstacles. Move shelving units, waste paper baskets, display cases and book trucks to ensure that individuals who are visually or mobility impaired have a clear path to the desk. All service desks should have rounded corners to prevent persons using walkers, crutches or wheelchairs or persons who are blind from injuring themselves on sharp edges. A chair should be provided for persons who may have difficulty standing for any length of time. The chair should be 475 mm. or 19 in. high with sturdy armrests and should be placed where it will not block wheelchair access.

It is essential that reference staff conduct the reference interview at a face-to-face level with someone in a wheelchair so the desk must be designed so that a person in a wheelchair can roll up to it. This requires a clear space under the desk of at least 725 mm. (29 in.) high and 750 mm. (30 in.) wide. Desks should be equipped with a pen and paper to facilitate conversation with persons who are hard of hearing or deaf.

## COLLECTIONS

### Barriers

The reference stacks can present many barriers to persons with disabilities. Shelves which are too high or too low make it difficult for someone in a wheelchair or on crutches to retrieve a book safely. Generally, the highest and lowest shelves of the stack area will not be accessible to persons in a wheelchair. Narrow aisles prevent individuals in wheelchairs from navigating through the stacks. Poor lighting makes it difficult for patrons who are visually impaired to read call numbers. Heavy, oversize reference books are almost impossible for individuals with chronic pain or limited upper body strength to use.

### Recommendations

Aisles between book stacks should be at least 920 mm. (36 in.) wide to allow a person in a wheelchair or on crutches to successfully navigate through the stacks. Stack aisles should be continuous or provide enough space for a wheelchair to turn around. A minimum turning width of 1500 mm. (60 in.) is required. Reaching from a seated position in a wheelchair is about 610 mm. (24 in.), so shelves should be no higher than 1470 mm. (58 in.) in height and no lower than 400 mm. (16 in.). As well, staff must be available to assist individuals who cannot access the collections themselves.

## STAFF

Technological innovations and removing physical barriers are not enough. Effective library service for persons with disabilities depends on knowledgeable, sensitive staff. It is important to ensure that staff are properly trained and aware of disabilities, both those that are visible and those that are hidden.

## Barriers

Staff members may have preconceptions and misconceptions about persons with certain disabilities and may be unaware that some disabilities are invisible or not readily apparent to others. Without training, they may feel self conscious or uncomfortable serving persons with disabilities and this may lead to a different level of service from what is offered to other patrons.

## Recommendations

All staff should be trained and training should occur on a regular basis. It should address what equitable service and equal access to information mean in the library and should provide guidelines on confidentiality, appropriate behavior, the use of language and how to approach persons with specific disabilities. It should also cover how these guidelines will be enforced.

Sensitivity training too is essential. Attitudinal barriers are often the most difficult to overcome. An effective way to address them is through information sharing and participation in simulation exercises. These exercises increase the staff's knowledge about disabling conditions and how they affect individuals. To be useful, simulation exercises should mimic real life situations at the Reference Desk. Members of local disability organizations should be consulted while developing simulation exercises. It is best if persons with disabilities participate or lead these exercises.

As they are developed, the library's services for persons with disabilities should be mainstreamed into general public service. In addition, however, persons with disabilities may also have specific needs related to their disability. For example, they may require information on programs and services for persons with disabilities. Reference staff should be prepared to respond to these needs as well. Because of this, it is essential to have one staff member whose prime responsibility is service to users with disabilities. This individual would act as liaison with community disability groups; be familiar with adaptive technology and disability issues; and develop specialized services to address specific concerns.

## BIBLIOGRAPHIC INSTRUCTION

The goals of bibliographic instruction are the same for library users with disabilities as they are for other library users: to assist the patron to use library resources effectively and to support present and future learning. To be successful, these programs must provide individuals with the skills needed to conduct library research competently and as independently as possible. Materials, instructional methods and communication strategies will have to be adapted. Adaptive technology provides tools that are very effective to break down barriers and to make library resources accessible. Training to introduce the person with a disability to the relevant technology and special library services and how to use them effectively should be provided.

### Recommendations

The following is a checklist for adapting bibliographic instruction programs for library users with disabilities.

### Materials

Library instruction and promotional aids should:

- Use clear, concise language.
- Be available in alternate formats (Braille, large-print, audio cassette).
- Use different font sizes and styles.
- Combine graphics with written text in order to illustrate important concepts.
- Use colour to highlight directions or instructions.
- Use coloured paper. For example, light blue paper with black lettering is easier for some individuals with low vision to read.

### Instructional Methods

- Ensure that your instruction area is quiet and free of distractions.
- When possible, hold bibliographic instruction classes in an adaptive technology lab or at an adapted workstation.
- Ensure that the size of the instruction group is appropriate to the person's learning needs. Multiple one-on-one sessions work best.
- Indicate concept relationships; for example, say "Therefore . . .", "By contrast . . ."
- Question students during the instruction to determine the level of understanding.
- Focus the bibliographic instruction session on a particular assignment.
- Provide hands-on experience to reinforce the lesson.
- Encourage the student to bring a laptop computer, a tape recorder, or other note-taking devices such as an Alpha Smart Pro or Braille n' Speak to your instruction classes.
- Use multi-modal methods of instruction to present information in multiple ways. Individuals with learning disabilities often learn through a combination of modes: visual, aural, tactile, and kinesthetic.

- Evaluate your instruction program on a regular basis.
- Demonstrate how to use adaptive technology and show how it can be applied in library use. For example, show someone with low vision how to use specialized character-enlarging software to read the information on the library's on-line catalogue. Individuals who are blind should be shown how to use optical character recognition scanner to scan, read and save print material.
- Give users a tour of the library pointing out the resources and services they will need to use. Include the Circulation Desk, the Reference Desk, the photocopiers, the CD ROM stations, the Adaptive Technology Labs(s) or adapted workstation(s), the office of the coordinator of services for persons with disabilities.

### Communication Techniques

- Provide oral as well as written instruction.
- Repeat key points.
- If a person does not understand you, rephrase your sentences or questions using different words. This is particularly important if you are teaching individuals who are deaf or persons with a learning disability or attention deficit disorder.
- Face the individual when you speak, even when interpreters or attendants are present.
- Provide a glossary of library terms. Point out any spelling oddities.
- Explain any unfamiliar or technical words. Libraries are infamous for using words that have little or no meaning to the general population. For example, explain that a monograph is a book and periodical is a library term used for a journal, magazine or a newspaper. Clarification of technical terms is particularly important when instructing persons with learning disabilities, persons who are deaf and persons who are blind.

### LIBRARY WEB SITE

Web sites are an effective tool for libraries to promote and encourage the use of their services and collections. They can also be used to reach people who, for a variety of reasons, are not able to visit the library building, including persons with disabilities. The combination of web technology and adaptive technologies has made equitable access to information a much more real possibility for persons with disabilities. However, because of the tremendous pace of its development since its inception in 1993, the World Wide Web could also increase the inaccessibility of information. It is important therefore to ensure that the library's web site is accessible.

People who are blind, have a visual impairment or a learning disability may use adaptive technology that changes text into either voice or Braille output. These technologies read the text on the screen from left to right and top to bottom. Graphics, because they are not text and frames because it divides the screen into smaller discrete screens are impossible for the technology to decipher, thus losing information. As more and more sites use sound to deliver important information, they can be inaccessible for persons who are deaf or have hearing impairments. As well, the way information is presented on web sites can impede the understanding of that information for persons with intellectual disabilities.

The following are guidelines to follow to ensure that a web site is accessible. For more detailed information about web site accessibility, please see the resource list at the end of this article.

## Pages

Web pages should be created using a consistent style and predictable layout elements, for example, buttons in navigation bars should be in the same location on every page. Use distinguishing information at the beginning of headings, paragraphs, lists, within the text. This allows clients to scan the document quickly to find important information. Punctuation helps structure documents for a screen-reading device, so sentences, paragraphs, headers, titles, list items should use consistent punctuation marks. Do not use blinking text as it can be missed by some screen reading devices. Avoid using background wallpaper unless you provide a simple text description of it.

## Use of Graphics

Graphics in a website can be useful for some clients and can pose serious barriers to the information for other clients. For persons who are blind or visually impaired, the information in graphics is inaccessible. On the other hand, persons with cognitive, learning, or developmental disabilities may find that graphic images or imagemaps help them understand the information better. To meet the needs of both these groups, provide a meaningful text alternative to describe the graphics and make sure that the graphics support the text.

## Navigation

For a web site to be accessible, it should have a consistent navigation structure. Access to the original table of contents, or its equivalent should be provided on every page. Navigation bars make it easy for the user to move quickly around the site. If you use graphical navigational links, they should be concrete and clearly suggestive of their functions. Make sure that you also provide alternatives for users who cannot view graphics. Ensure that the text for each link makes sense when read alone. If you are using text-based links, make sure to use double spacing between items. This makes them easier to read for persons who are visually impaired and easier to use with a mouse, particularly for persons who are mobility impaired.

Imagemaps are images that have active regions, for example, clicking on the region may activate a link. They are helpful for persons who find images easier to understand than text (for instance, persons with cognitive disabilities), however they pose a barrier for persons who cannot use a mouse. To ensure the imagemap is accessible, make sure that any action associated with part of an imagemap can be used without a mouse or other pointing device.

### Use of Frames

HTML frames present a barrier to persons using text only screen readers. If you use frames, provide a link to a page containing similar information or label each frame with title or name, and include a hypertext start-page in NOFRAMES element.

### Audio Clips

Audio clips can enhance sites, however, it is important to provide text versions for persons who are deaf or hearing impaired. Provide captions or transcripts of audio content, and text or audio descriptions of video content.

### Evaluation

Web sites, to remain relevant must be dynamic entities, changing frequently with new information and new technology. It is important therefore to check the accessibility of the web site on a regular basis. Test it with a text-only browser, with no mouse and with multiple graphic browsers.

## CONCLUSION

Both Canada and the United States have legislation that protects the rights of individuals to access to services that are accessible. Canada's Charter of Rights and Freedoms in the Constitution Act of 1982, provincial charters of rights and freedoms and human rights codes and the Americans with Disabilities Act in the United States guarantee access and provide a framework for legal recourse if rights are not respected. However, legal recourse tends to be expensive and time consuming for both the individual and the institution. It is much wiser to address issues and concerns before they become formal complaints and long before they get to the courts.

Addressing accessibility in reference services of an institution as complex as a library may seem daunting. However, as illustrated in this article, many barriers can be readily removed once they are identified, for example, ensuring aisle width is appropriate for wheelchairs and kept clear of obstacles, providing tactile labels for alternative format material, keeping pen and paper at the reference desk to facilitate communication. Furthermore, accessibility can be built in to new services like signs, web sites and bibliographic instruction, as they are developed. The key here is to ensure that the concept of service for all is integrated into the goals and planning processes of the library and of the reference department.

## REFERENCES

Statistics Canada. (1992). "1991 Health and Activity Limitation Survey." *The Daily,* Tuesday, October 13, 1992.

Cantor, Alan (1996). "The ADAPTABLE Approach: A Practical Guide to Planning Accessible Libraries." *Library Hi Tech* Volume 14, Number 1, 41-45.

Draper, James and Brooks, James (1979). *Interior Design for Libraries.* Chicago: American Library Association.

Fawcett, Gail (1996). *Living with Disability in Canada: An Economic Portrait.* Ottawa: Human Resources Development Canada, Office of Disability Issues.

*ICIDH and environmental factors international network.* Canadian Society for the ICIDH Volume 9, Number 2/3, July 1998.

Norton, Melanie J. (1992). "Effective Bibliographic Instruction for Deaf and Hearing-Impaired College Students. " *Library Trends* 41 (1) Summer, 118-150.

Pollet, Dorothy and Haskell, Peter C. (1979). *Sign Systems for Libraries: Solving the Wayfinding Problem,* New York: R.R. Bowker Company.

Reynolds, Linda. (1981). *Signs and Guiding for Libraries.* London: Clive Bingley.

Scott, Wendy (1996). *The Accessible Canadian Library II: A Resource Tool for Libraries Serving Persons with Disabilities,* Rev. ed., Ottawa: National Library of Canada.

United States. Architectural and Transportation Barriers Compliance Board. *Accessibility Guidelines for Buildings and Facilities.* January 1998. Available: http://www.access-board.gov/bfdg/adaag.htm [January 1998].

United States. Bureau of the Census. *Census Brief: Disabilities Affect One-Fifth of All Americans.* CENBR/97-5. December 1997. Available: http://www.census.gov/prod/3/97pubs/cenbr975.pdf

Wright, Keith C. and Davie, Judith F. (1991). *Serving the Disabled: A How-To-Do-It Manual for Librarians.* New York: Neal-Schuman Publishers.

## WEB SOURCES

The Accessible Canadian Library II
   http://www.nlc-bnc.ca/pubs/eacc-can.htm
Accessible Web Page Design
   http://www.ott.igs.net/~starling/acc/actoc.htm
Accessibility Guidelines for Buildings and Facilities
   http://www.access-board.gov/bfdg/adaag.htm
Designing Universal Web Pages
   http://www.psc-cfp.gc.ca/dmd/access/welcome1.htm
EASI: Equal Access to Software and Information
   http://www.rit.edu/~easi/lib.html
Government of Canada Internet Guide
   http://infoservice.gc.ca/programs/guide/main_e.html
Librarians' Connections
   http://www.geocities.com/~drm//DRMlibs.html
Library Services to Persons with Disabilities
   http://www.nlc-bnc.ca/coopprog/edisab.htm
Web Accessibility Initiative (WAI)
   http://www.w3.org/WAI/

# Strategies for Providing Effective Reference Services for International Adult Learners

## Suhasini L. Kumar
## Raghini S. Suresh

**SUMMARY.** In their mission or goals statements, most universities declare their commitment to promoting a multicultural campus. A multicultural campus can only come about with the creation of an environment that provides the support and encouragement that allows for academic growth and success for international students. Reference librarians serve a special role as information providers and can play a significant part in ensuring the academic success of these students. To achieve this, we must first increase our basic understanding of the cultural and economic impact of international students at a national and university level. Further, recognizing the unique pressures under which these international students function will increase awareness and help

Suhasini L. Kumar is Head, Government Documents/Humanities Reference Librarian, Carlson Library, University of Toledo, Toledo, OH 43606 (E-mail: SKUMAR@utnet.utoledo.edu). She works closely with international students and served this past year as Chair of the International Relations Committee of the Cleveland Chapter of the Special Libraries Association. Raghini S. Suresh is Assistant Professor in Libraries and Media Services, Kent State University and Head, Chemistry Physics Library, 312 Williams, Kent State University, Kent, OH 44242 (E-mail: rsuresh@lms.kent.edu). She has served for several years as faculty advisor both to the Indian Students Association and the Executive Council of International Students and is currently Chair of the International Relations Committee of the Cleveland Chapter of the Special Libraries Association.

[Haworth co-indexing entry note]: "Strategies for Providing Effective Reference Services for International Adult Learners." Kumar, Suhasini L., and Raghini S. Suresh. Co-published simultaneously in *The Reference Librarian* (The Haworth Information Press, an imprint of The Haworth Press, Inc.) No. 69/70, 2000, pp. 327-336; and: *Reference Services for the Adult Learner: Challenging Issues for the Traditional and Technological Era* (ed: Kwasi Sarkodie-Mensah) The Haworth Information Press, an imprint of The Haworth Press, Inc., 2000, pp. 327-336. Single or multiple copies of this article are available for a fee from The Haworth Document Delivery Service [1-800-342-9678, 9:00 a.m. - 5:00 p.m. (EST). E-mail address: getinfo@haworthpressinc.com].

*327*

us to position ourselves to effectively meet their information needs. This paper will describe obstacles and problems international students generally deal with in choosing to pursue studies abroad and then suggest practical strategies for overcoming these problems and providing effective reference services. *[Article copies available for a fee from The Haworth Document Delivery Service: 1-800-342-9678. E-mail address: <getinfo @haworthpressinc.com> Website: <http://www.haworthpressinc. com>]*

**KEYWORDS.** Foreign students, reference services, international students, academic success, information needs

## INTRODUCTION

Designing strategies to provide effective reference services for international students requires an investment of thought, time, and effort. At a time when budgets are strained and staff stretched thin, this may appear to be the final straw that could break the camel's back. Efforts on the part of some librarians to develop plans and strategies to serve international students may understandably meet with resistance though not open opposition from others. The bias in this paper is towards Asia/Pacific area students who have to deal with marked differences in the educational and library systems and with significant language issues.

Philosophically, the library community has always been committed to serving the information needs of all patrons and providing the best service possible within our means. However, somewhere in the midst of it all, the international student group enters the scene and as problems are encountered at the service desks, the unspoken questions arise and hang heavy–questions that librarians may wish to ask but never do; questions such as–Why serve the international students–What's in it for us? Why can't the international students be more like "our other students"? If they find it so difficult here why can't they just go back? The international students are a huge drain on our limited resources–aren't they? Confronting these questions and dealing with them may go a long way in removing negative perceptions that cloud the image of international students. Let us first examine the facts regarding the impact of international students in the United States at the national and the university level.

## THE OPEN DOORS 1996/1997 REPORT[1]

The Institute of International Education publishes an annual report called the *Open Doors: Report on International Education Exchange,* which is a comprehensive information resource on international students in the United States from over 200 different countries.

The web site for Open Doors, (http://www.iie.org/opendoors/) describes the Institute of International Education (IIE) as a not for profit educational and cultural exchange organization in the United States with grant support from the Bureau of Educational and Cultural Affairs of the United States Information Agency. Open Doors provides data on national origin, sources of financial support, fields of study, host institutions, academic level, and rates of growth of the international student population in the United States, the economic impact of the international students to the host state and national economies, and several other areas.[2]

The report indicates that the international students attending U.S. colleges and universities increased by only 0.9% this year, which continues a seven year trend in minimal growth. There is apparently an increase in the number of students going to other developed countries. Richard M. Krasno, president and CEO of IIE is quoted in the report as expressing concern regarding this trend. He remarks, "Although the 454,000 international students reported in 1996, make up only slightly more than 3% of the total higher education enrollment in the United States their impact–economic, cultural, and diplomatic–is invaluable, both to our campus communities and to the country."[3] He further states, "Although U.S. colleges and universities are still the most popular choice for international students, we're at risk of losing out to other countries which are aggressively competing for these talented applicants. We need to understand the value of foreign students' participation in U.S. higher education and reach out to protect our 'market share.'"[4]

Another fact that needs to be made clear is the economics of foreign student exchange. The same report states that over two-thirds (67%) of all foreign students receive most of their funding for study in the States from personal and family sources and over 80% receive most of their funding from sources outside the States. The U.S. colleges and universities are the main source of funding for only about 17% of the students and direct U.S. government funds support less than 1% of international graduate students. According to the Institute, international students generate more than $7 billion dollars making them the fifth largest export earner in America.[5] Understanding these facts may help ease the discomfort experienced by staff who regard the international student as depriving the local student of resources.

Now that we have seen some of the facts and figures regarding international students, let us briefly review the literature to identify the main concerns and issues that have been discussed therein. To supplement this literature review, we also conducted personal interviews with international students on the campus of the University of Toledo and at Kent State University. The interviews were to provide us with some personal insights from the perspective of international students. Although we worked from a list of questions, we were particularly interested in having the students express their thoughts and observations within more flexible parameters using open-ended questions and inviting comments and suggestions. The purpose of these interviews was to gather information on what was perceived by them to be the major obstacles for international students in using the libraries in the United States and further to learn from them what they thought would be most helpful in overcoming these obstacles. The interview sampling was intentionally random and not intended by any means to be a scientific survey. It was a search for substantive and qualitative information. The results were not unusual or different from what others have found but we garnered some practical tips from our subjects.

## REVIEW OF THE LITERATURE

There is no question that the library is key to the academic success of these students and that the librarian has a significant role to play in partnering with international students to help them achieve that success. The findings reported in the literature from the studies done on international students and their experiences in the United States seem rather obvious as we read them. Terry Ann Mood, in a study of international students and the academic library, noted that students from Asian countries as opposed to those from Western Europe face more significant language problems and differences between educational and library systems.[6] In a paper presented at an international student conference focusing on the problems of international students in using United States libraries, Dania M. Bilal also noted that the major problems faced by international students had to do with the differences between the educational and library system in their native countries and those in the United States. One recommendation was to increase awareness amongst library science students and librarians of the unique needs of international students.[7] In another significant study, Kwasi Sarkodie-Mensah using an in-depth survey explored the difficulties international students encounter in their use of American academic libraries, and their patterns of library use, and the nature of the libraries in their native countries. He reported that the language of instruction in their native schools had a strong relationship to the difficulties experienced in library use.[8] Other studies have echoed these same findings recommending a variety of library skills training for international students.[9]

A sustained interest in this area has continued to generate articles that have reflected the problems faced by international students in using American libraries and suggested solutions to them.[10] The major focus in several of these articles has been on using library instruction more effectively, improving staff training and communication skills.[11] Mary Beth Allen undertook a study to identify characteristics of the international student and to determine their patterns of library use. She concluded that it was important for the library to identify the characteristics of its user population and develop and implement services to meet the users' needs.[12] In her dissertation, Felicia Lafon, compared library skills of American and international students to determine if separate library instruction programs were necessary for the international students. The study concluded that separate instructional sessions were needed because of differences in language skills, level of familiarity with the library system and with library resources.[13]

Cynthia Mae Helms, in an article on reaching out to the international students, also points out the unique difficulties that international students face particularly in the area of communication, and with the different educational system in the United States.[14] The literature voices an unmistakable need to know the international users and to design specialized instructional sessions for them.[15]

## THE LIBRARIAN'S ROLE

It follows from these reports that what we need is not more studies–but a commitment to doing what every study has reported needs to be done. Some institutions are doing them but it has to become a universal commitment and even more importantly has to become the standard. At the university and departmental level there needs to be a conscious awareness that the international students cannot be expected to succeed if they are not given specialized instruction. There has to be interaction between the international student office and the libraries as they prepare for these library skills workshops. The librarians may choose to take a proactive role in initiating interaction and ongoing communication between the international student office and the library. We have learned that it is important to know our international student population, and therefore it follows that it should be a routine procedure for the international students office to send a list of incoming international students indicating country of origin, and major area of study. Surely, it would make a difference to us and to the shape of our instruction, if we as the reference librarians and the library skills instructors were made aware that 300 Japanese students were coming to our campus this semester to begin their studies in the engineering program.

## COMMITMENT TO MULTICULTURALISM AND CULTURAL DIVERSITY

The mission and goals statements of universities and libraries in the United States, generally tend to include a statement expressing the individual institution's commitment to fostering and promoting multiculturalism and cultural diversity. Several universities invest time and effort in recruiting international students in order to create this culturally rich body of students. As a nation, the United States is open to sharing this beautiful country with peoples of other cultures. Their generosity of spirit towards new immigrants is graciously stated in the Statue of Liberty, in Staten Island, New York:

> Give me your tired, your poor,
> Your huddled masses yearning to breathe free,
> The wretched refuse of your teeming shore.
> Send these, the homeless, tempest-tossed to me.
> I lift my lamp beside the golden door.

Contrast that body of immigrants with the international students we generally encounter at our desks, who are intelligent, generally middle to upper class, yearning to learn and explore new opportunities, the upper crust of the intellectual society in their lands. When they come to us they are full of hope, excitement, dreams and expectation because they see getting here itself as an achievement–they have after all come to the land of opportunity. Will they be disillusioned and disappointed or will their hopes and dreams be fulfilled? What role will we play in enabling them to succeed? At the national and local levels there is a clearly expressed desire to welcome and include the international members within the fabric of our society. This should provide us with not only a context but a motivation that undergirds and inspires our effort to encourage the success of the international students who have come to our institutions.

## UNDERSTANDING THE INTERNATIONAL STUDENTS' NEW WORLD ORDER

International students are eager and motivated to succeed but they initially experience a culture shock that their American counterparts will be unable to comprehend. The initial excitement and euphoria of international students dies down swiftly when they are forced to confront the reality of student life in the United States. International students have to deal with a variety of situations, many of which they may or may not have had to deal with on their own before: finding a place to live, cooking, laundry, rooming with others, a new climate, different food, unfamiliar environment, communication problems, cultural differences, and a significant shift in the educational system. The kaleidoscope of life in America keeps moving. Although the new order is organized and attractive, it is unfamiliar all the same and compels them to make major adjustments in their style of living and working. To help them

achieve academic success in an environment far removed from familiar surroundings, family, and culture calls for understanding on our part and a
genuine interest in their welfare.

## INTERNATIONAL STUDENTS LIBRARY LIAISON

Assigning the role of liaison to international students to one librarian
may help facilitate communication between the library, the international
students, and the other offices on campus that deal with these students and
issues related to them. Having one contact person who attends the orientation for international students and gets introduced to the new students,
hands out business cards, and is perceived as approachable and interested in
them will go a long way towards improving communication, and building a
positive relationship between the library and the international student body.
Only a person who has a keen understanding of international students and a
heart for this type of service should be assigned this role. The role of the
library liaison could be to gather information from the international student
office about incoming international students, their majors and the countries
from which they are coming, and attempting to understand significant cultural differences. Another function could be to keep the reference department informed of these facts. By being involved closely with the international student office and international student orientations the liaison can
establish contact, be accessible and serve to ease the initial communication
barrier and provide the friendly face and bridge to this unfamiliar world of
libraries.

The liaison librarian apart from providing an initial orientation and tour of
the library could enable those students who have more specialized information needs to be introduced to the subject specialists so that the students will
be made aware of ongoing instructional support sessions that are available.
The link that the liaison provides between the international student and the
subject specialist will be particularly important as these students work on
more advanced research projects. Reference by appointment could then be
arranged through the reference office with these subject specialists. What we
heard over and over again in our interviews with the students was their
interest in having instruction in small group sessions. This was preferred by
almost everyone over one on one or large class sessions. Even students who
are proficient in the language may find it difficult to keep up with library
instructional sessions because of the jargon or unfamiliar system.[16] Frustration often comes from trying to follow what the speaker says and from not
being able to understand the simple steps required to understand the Interlibrary Loan system, or using photocopy machines. They may hesitate to ask
for help because of difficulty in expressing themselves. Printed instructions

are very useful because most of them have a much better grasp of the printed over the spoken word. It is also important to keep in mind that when a student encounters difficulties with verbal communication, librarians can ask the student to write down what he or she wants.

To design programs for the international student population as a whole would probably be the simplest and most functional thing libraries can do. However, as far as effectiveness goes this may well end up being wasted time and effort. The international student body is a diverse group that is comprised of students at all levels of language and research skills. It is not possible to draw a simple profile of a typical international student. Factors that would have to be taken into consideration are the country of origin, number of years in this country, language skills, and computer skills.

## OBSTACLES AND PROBLEMS
## INTERNATIONAL STUDENTS ENCOUNTER

The problems international students initially encounter are in many cases easily solved because it may have to do with their being unfamiliar with the library system. Something as mundane as what to do with the back pack when you walk in to the library could cause an anxious moment or two for the student. From our interviews with students we found that the role of the reference librarian is unclear to most of them. Not understanding that reference librarians are there to assist with questions, international students always feel that they are imposing or troubling the librarian with their questions. Knowing the differences between the educational and library systems in their native countries and the United States will allow the librarian to relate more effectively to the experience of the students.[17] Many international students may be coming from systems where they were forced to listen to the instructor and focus solely on class notes. Therefore, these students have had little or no experience in critically evaluating texts or lectures. Copyright laws and plagiarism are other issues that have to be carefully explained. Taking time to explain what is expected, how to use information, analyze it and utilize it responsibly will be of enormous benefit to international students.

Communication barriers are another major obstacle for international students. This may result from the inability of the library staff to understand the student because of variations in pronunciation, intonation, speech patterns, and enunciation.[18] It may also be as a result of the students' inability to clearly express their information need due to their lack of fluency in the language, vocabulary limitations, or a hesitation or timidity in using the language because of lack of confidence in their ability to express themselves adequately. Careful listening and an attempt on the part of the reference librarian to focus on the intent behind the students' words is essential to effective communication. Librarians must guard against ethnocentricity and make every effort to understand the context in which it is being received by the listener. In an article by Cynthia Mae Helms, she opens with this illustration: "An international student, looking through the cards in the print card catalog came across the words 'For holdings see main entry.'" The student walked over to the main entrance of the library, and then came back with a puzzled look that meant: "Where is the main entry? And, what in the world are holdings?"[19] There are situations similar to this that occur frequently in our libraries. It is our responsibility as librarians to have incidents reported to us and then to look beyond the individual situations to the underlying problem to work out a solution.

## *CONCLUSION*

We have to first ask ourselves if we have the desire and the resources to invest time and effort into serving international students. If as an institution our answer is positive, we can move ahead and make a difference. Apart from a genuine interest in and concern for the academic success of the international students, there has to be a university wide effort to increase awareness and understanding of other cultures. International students are disliked or mistrusted oftentimes due to a cultural misunderstanding. Understanding cultural differences will help library personnel cope with the aggressive posture, negative tone or a superior attitude sometimes assumed by international students towards the library staff.[20] We should never forget that our role is to understand the information needs of international students, teach them the necessary skills, and to communicate effectively with them and assist them in achieving their goals. We should not permit surface differences of appearance or speech to distract us so much that we miss the similarities international students have with the typical students that we meet every day.

In today's global economy, where so many business concerns are multinational, our students are increasingly traveling abroad for reasons of study and business. International students provide innumerable opportunities for all of us to learn firsthand about other peoples and cultures. Thus, the presence of international students within our educational system should be regarded as a significant factor in American education, providing us with valuable opportunities to prepare our students to function in a world transformed by the World Wide Web into one devoid of national borders and traditional barriers. It is important for us as librarians to understand the cultural differences of international students who enter our universities, recognize the obstacles and barriers that they encounter, and be prepared to provide effective library instructional programs as we seek to enable them to achieve their dream of academic success.

## REFERENCES

1. "Foreign Students in the U.S." *Open Doors Report 1996-1997,* Institute of International Student Exchange.

2. "Foreign Students in the U.S." *Open Doors Report 1996-1997,* Institute of International Student Exchange.

3. "Foreign Students in the U.S." *Open Doors Report 1996-1997.* Institute of International Student Exchange.

4. "Foreign Students in the U.S." *Open Doors Report 1996-1997.* Institute of International Student Exchange.

5. "The Economics of Foreign Student Exchange." *Open Doors Report 1996-1997.*

6. Mood, Terry Ann "Foreign Students and the Academic Library," RQ 22 (Winter 1982): 177.

7. Bilal, Dania M., "Problems of Foreign Students in Using United States Libraries and the Difficulties of Translating an International Education to Lebanon." in Translating an International Education to a National Environment" Metuchen, NJ: Scarecrow Press, 1990: 26-28.

8. Sarkodie-Mensah, Kwasi. "Foreign Students and U.S. Academic Libraries: A Case Study of Foreign Students in Two Universities in New Orleans, Louisiana" (PhD diss., University of Illinois at Urbana-Champaign), (1988): 2-5.

9. Moeckel, Nancy and Jenny Presnell (1995) " Recognizing, Understanding, and Responding: A Program Model of Library Instruction Services for International Students," The Reference Librarian 51/52: 315-316.

10. Liu, Ziming (1993) "Difficulties and Characteristics of Students from Developing Countries in Using American Libraries," College and Research Libraries 54: 1 (Jan.): 25-31.

11. Kline, Laura S. and Catherine M. Rod (1984) "Library Orientation Programs for Foreign Students: A Survey," RQ 24 (Winter): 210-16.

12. Allen, Mary Beth (1993). "International Students in Academic Libraries: A User Survey," College and Research Libraries 54: 4 (July): 323-333.

13. Lafon, Felicia Suila Kimo, "A Comparative Study and Analysis of the Library Skills of American and Foreign Students at the University of Michigan, Michigan: University of Michigan, 1993.

14. Helms, Cynthia Mae, "Reaching Out to the International Students Through Bibliographic Instruction," The Reference Librarian, NY: The Haworth Press, Inc., No. 51-52 (1995): 296.

15. Osborne, Nancy Seale and Cecilia Poon, "Serving Diverse Library Populations Through the Specialized Instructional Services Concept," The Reference Librarian, NY: The Haworth Press, Inc., No. 51-52 (1995): 285-293.

16. Greenfield, Louise, Susan Johnston and Karen Williams (1986) "Educating the World: Training Library Staff to Communicate Effectively with International Students." Journal of Academic Librarianship 12 (4): 228.

17. Ibid., 229-230.

18. Sarkodie-Mensah, Kwasi (1992) "Dealing with International Students in a Multicultural Era" The Journal of Academic Librarianship, 18 (4): 214-216.

19. Helms, 295.

20. Greenfield, 230.

# Reference Services
# to the International Adult Learner:
# Understanding the Barriers

## Christopher C. Brown

**SUMMARY.** International adult learners include immigrants, nonimmigrants, and foreign-born residents of the United States who are non-native speakers of English and come from a variety of cultures. This population presents a challenge to delivery of reference services, but at the same time is extremely rewarding. Barriers to service are discussed. Linguistic barriers include selection of vocabulary, sentence structure, and various sociolinguistic considerations. The variety of the world's cultures and the impact on reference service are discussed in the context of cultural barriers. Technological barriers include the fast rate in technology change, information literacy, and the impact of the World Wide Web. *[Article copies available for a fee from The Haworth Document Delivery Service: 1-800-342-9678. E-mail address: <getinfo@haworthpressinc. com> Website: <http://www.haworthpressinc.com>]*

**KEYWORDS.** Internationals, culture, language, barriers, technology, foreign-born, immigrants

---

Christopher C. Brown is a member of the Reference Faculty at Penrose Library, University of Denver, 2150 East Evans Avenue, Denver, CO 80208 (E-mail: cbrown@du.edu). He received a BA degree from Moody Bible Institute, Chicago, IL, his MDiv degree from Biola University, did graduate studies in linguistics at Cornell University, and received his MLIS degree from University College, University of Denver in June, 1999.

[Haworth co-indexing entry note]: "Reference Services to the International Adult Learner: Understanding the Barriers." Brown, Christopher C. Co-published simultaneously in *The Reference Librarian* (The Haworth Information Press, an imprint of The Haworth Press, Inc.) No. 69/70, 2000, pp. 337-347; and: *Reference Services for the Adult Learner: Challenging Issues for the Traditional and Technological Era* (ed: Kwasi Sarkodie-Mensah) The Haworth Information Press, an imprint of The Haworth Press, Inc., 2000, pp. 337-347. Single or multiple copies of this article are available for a fee from The Haworth Document Delivery Service [1-800-342-9678, 9:00 a.m. - 5:00 p.m. (EST). E-mail address: getinfo@ haworthpressinc.com].

## INTRODUCTION

Two of the exciting aspects of reference librarianship are the diversity of subject matters we deal with and the diversity of people we help. Work at a reference desk often provides an opportunity to meet people from many walks of life and divergent backgrounds. Among the most interesting are those from other countries. Be they international students, visiting scholars, or learners of English as a foreign language, they enrich our lives and make our work more stimulating. This paper will explore how we can serve this group more effectively.

## INTERNATIONAL ADULT LEARNERS: WHO ARE THEY?

The "foreign-born" in the United States are estimated to be 9.7% of the population or 25.8 million people (Bureau of the Census 1998, Bureau of the Census 1997). It is not possible to make sweeping generalizations about this group, since there are great differences in demographic, social, and economic characteristics. Recent arrivals to the U.S. are likely to be in poverty, yet after around six years here they tend to recover economically. They are not evenly distributed geographically; California, New York, Hawaii, Florida, and New Jersey unsurprisingly have the highest percentage of these internationals. Over 40% of foreign-born persons are of Hispanic origin. While it is true that the majority of the foreign-born in the U.S. are from the Western Hemisphere, it should be remembered that internationals from over 100 countries reside here. In 1996 there were a total of 915,900 immigrants granted admission to the United States. Of these, roughly 65% were family-sponsored preferences (spouses, children, and parents of U.S. citizens), 13% were employment-based preferences, and the rest were other categories such as diversity programs and refugees (Immigration and Naturalization Service 1997) (Figure 1).

Although articles can be found about reference services to immigrant populations (Craver 1991, Marcum and Stone 1991, Ratliff 1990, Somerville 1995), there do not seem to be as many as there are about international students.

A much larger group of internationals that entered the country in 1996 were nonimmigrants. Most of these were tourists or business visitors staying less than three months. A significant segment of this group stays considerably longer and is more likely to show up in front of reference desks needing assistance. These are the international students and visiting scholars. Much has been written about library services to international students. The litera-

FIGURE 1. Immigrants Admitted to U.S., 1996

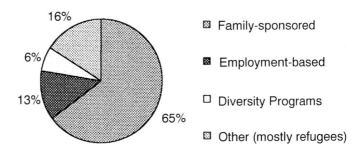

Source: *1996 Statistical Yearbook of the Immigration and Naturalization Service.*

ture falls into several categories. Case studies relating programs and experiences in various libraries seem to be among the most popular (Bryson 1974, Chau and Culbertson 1994, Greenfield, et al. 1986, Hoffman and Popa 1986, Ormondroyd 1989). User surveys seek to find needs of the target audience (Allen 1993, Kline and Rod 1984). Other articles focus on library instruction (Cope and Black 1985, Koehler and Swanson 1988). Articles giving general cultural advice and cultural barriers are most helpful (Ball and Mahony 1987, Macdonald and Sarkodie 1988, Mood 1982, Natowitz 1995). It is also helpful to read a personal testimony of an international (Sarkodie-Mensah 1986).

While much has been written on international students, the international scholar has been generally overlooked (Ball and Mahony 1987). Those particularly interested in providing services to international students or scholars should become familiar with *Open Doors,* published annually by the Institute of International Education (Institute of International Education 1997).

Many of these international adult learners show up in the decennial census as residing in "linguistically isolated households," that is, households where English is neither spoken nor understood (Bureau of Census 1992). Roughly 3.4% of the American population lives in such households. Are these people "hidden" from the help of local libraries? Libraries need to consider ways of reaching out to these people. Some will see the need for literacy programs. Others will acquire foreign language books and serials. Still others may even hire staff who can speak one of the minority languages.

In order to understand the varied circumstances surrounding shifting populations, we can consider the situation of Louisville, Colorado. In November 1996, President Clinton, through Presidential Determination No. 97-8 (61 FR 65147-65148, 11 December 1996), authorized the removal of Iraqi refugees from the area of northern Iraq known as Kurdistan (a project referred to as "Quick Transit I"). After several months of processing on the island of Guam, 56 of these refugees were placed in Louisville, Colorado. At first they went through intensive English classes, secured jobs, and became acclimated to their new country. Within months of arrival some of them made their way to the local public library. This type of situation is not unusual and occurs regularly throughout the States.

To effectively meet the needs of the foreign-born, there is a temptation to polarize the discussion in terms of "us versus them." This approach is rarely helpful, since "they" are not a monolithic group with one way of thinking. Rather than generalizing about all other cultures, the remainder of this paper will focus on barriers to effective communication. To view internationals monolithically is wrong. A better approach is to acknowledge that there are many cultures that greatly differ from our own. Although these cultures may be able to be categorized, classified, and described, it is most helpful to see how we can break down barriers that emanate from our lack of cross-cultural understanding (figure 2).

For purposes of this article, we will use the term "international adult learner" or simply "international" to refer to immigrants, nonimmigrants (including students and scholars), or residents of the United States who were born outside the United States and who have significant linguistic and cultural differences.

## BARRIERS TO EFFECTIVE REFERENCE SERVICES

Let us now explore barriers that would impede effective delivery of reference service. We will examine linguistic, cultural, and technological barriers.

FIGURE 2. 1996 Immigrants and Nonimmigrants Admitted to the U.S.

**Immigrants** . . . . . . . . . . . . . . . . . . . . . . . **915,900**
     Includes family-sponsored immigrants,
     employment-based immigrants, and refugees
**Nonimmigrants** . . . . . . . . . . . . . . . . . . **24,842,503**
     Includes tourists, business travellers,
     government officials, temporary workers
     and their families, and international students
     and their families

Source: *1996 Statistical Yearbook of the Immigration and Naturalization Service.*

### Language Barriers

Language barriers exist on several linguistic levels, and can be addressed in terms of both librarian and user.

*Accent.* Accent is something we recognize is the speech of others, but what we think we ourselves do not have. Accent becomes a barrier to communication if either party has difficulty understanding the other. Many internationals were schooled under British English teachers. They may have difficulty understanding our regional accents. We would do well to remember to enunciate clearly when we speak English. This does not mean that we raise our voices when speaking. This often observed phenomenon is both humiliating and unnecessary.

*Lexicon.* Words are the building blocks of language. Although there are 290,500 entries in the second edition of the Oxford English Dictionary, our daily working vocabulary is actually quite small. Longman, publishers of several dictionaries for learners of English as a second language, utilize the "Longman Defining Vocabulary," a limited vocabulary of only 2,000 words (Procter 1981). We would do well to learn from this and to strive for a less complex lexicon when necessary.

*Syntax.* Another linguistic consideration is syntax or grammar. Non-native English speakers often struggle with our complex sentence structures. When we speak with long sentences containing many embedded phrases and dependent clauses, we often stretch the limits of the hearer. Many people come from cultures where it is not polite to show disagreement and will simply smile as if they understand, when in reality they do not.

*Sociolinguistics.* Sociolinguistics is the study of languages in their social settings. An awareness of the subtleties of cultures in contact can be of value to those who deal with those from other countries. Recalling the Louisville, Colorado refugee project mentioned above, it should be noted that of the 56 refugees who came to Colorado, roughly 1/3 of them are Assyrian, and 2/3 are of Kurdish ancestry. Even though the regional language, Kurdish, is spoken by some of them, Arabic is the *lingua franca* of the region. Yet rivalries going back centuries create a lack of trust that lasts to this day. Sharing language does not always mean sharing ideologies. Librarians sometimes get themselves unintentionally caught up in the middle of these rivalries. It is best to focus on the person at hand and not try to relate the story of "a friend" who may be from the rival group.

*Language as Nationalism.* The reference librarian should be aware of potential rivalries or differences between cultural groups. Just because two people speak the same language does not mean they agree on much else. The case of the Chinese language illustrates this point. Mainland China and the island of Taiwan share the same national language, but for political reasons, call it a different name. What we simply refer to as "Mandarin Chinese" mainland China calls *putonghua*. Taiwan, on the other hand, calls its language *guoyu*. Behind each of these terms lies political connotations. Historically, the various dialects of Chinese have been referred to as "dialects" even though by every linguistic definition they should be referred to as "languages." Someone who only speaks Cantonese cannot understand Mandarin, and vice versa. The reason they are referred to as dialects is that all the linguistic variations are "read" off of the same *hanzi*, or Chinese characters. In October 1957 the mainland Chinese government mandated the use of "simplified" characters throughout the country. Taiwan never adopted this practice.

The wise reference librarian is either well informed concerning politics, or stays out of such conversations.

*Transcription Systems.* To make matters even more complicated for librarians are the different transcription systems that can be used to render Chinese into English. The accepted standard has been the Wade-Giles system, which has also been used by the Taiwanese government. Mainland China uses the *pinyin* transcription, one that is actually preferred by linguists. The reference librarian will need to be aware of these differences when helping users who are Chinese. Use of the *ALA-LC Romanization Tables* (Barry 1997) can be of great help in searching for foreign language materials.

### Cultural Barriers

Besides language there are other cultural barriers as well. The librarian must be aware of these. One can think of culture as an iceberg, with 10% of the iceberg visible, but the rest not visible. Cultural clashes will most likely happen below the surface. A brief survey of some general cultural issues will be followed by library-specific concerns.

*General Cultural Problems.* The need for personal space differs among the world's cultures. South Americans, Southern and Eastern Europeans, and Arabs tend to prefer close personal space, whereas those from Asia, Northern Europe, and North America prefer more of a distance (Sussman and Rosenfeld 1982). What happens, then, when someone tries to come in too close to what we think is a comfortable space? Do we give the same quality of service? Or are we offended when someone invades our space (cf. also Ball, p. 164)?

Another commonly encountered cross-cultural problem is high-context versus low-context communication styles. In high-context communication a high proportion of the message is encoded in the physical context or assumed from existing cultural knowledge. Most Asian cultures such as the Japanese, Chinese, and Koreans utilize this kind of communication. At the other end of the spectrum are low-context cultures. With these, most of the information is expressed explicitly in the language. Typical of these cultures are the Germans, Scandinavians, Swiss, and Americans (Hall 1976). Not surprisingly, those from high-context cultures often have difficulty understanding the cultural cues we take for granted. In reference settings, special care should be taken to be certain that we are perceiving the real question. It is possible that the question was only inferred rather than directly expressed.

The Japanese tend to avoid the direct expression of negative feelings with strangers, not wanting to give offense (Ueda 1974). Awareness of indirect communication, regardless of the culture, can perhaps rescue a reference interview from disaster.

Individualistic cultures focus more on their immediate family and themselves than on larger social groups. In collective cultures the interests of the group take a much higher level of importance, with responsibility and accountability to the collective group (Gudykunst and Ting-Toomey 1988). For example, a husband may not be able to purchase cars without the full consent of his spouse. A business person may not be able to make a decision without meeting with a team. Sensitivity to these differences may play a role in delivery of reference services.

American informality can be confusing to those from other cultures. On the cline of formal cultures on the one hand, and informal ones on the other, the United States generally falls far to the informal side. In other words, most internationals will be more formal in orientation than we are. This formality issue affects everything from the way we are addressed by name and by job title, to attitudes toward age, social status, and gender. It is sometimes helpful to make things easier for your international patron by letting him or her know how you prefer to be addressed. As for age and gender issues, faithful and consistent delivery of reference services goes a long way to breaking down prejudices.

Particularly embarrassing are those times we make friendly conversation to "show how much we know" about another person's country or culture. Unless we really are experts, we shouldn't place ourselves in that position, lest all of our credibility be jeopardized.

Perhaps the most important general cultural factor is that internationals are marginalized in our society. "Marginalization occurs when people are systematically excluded from meaningful participation in economic, social, political, cultural and other forms of human activity in their communities and thus are denied the opportunity to fulfil themselves as human beings" (Fiske 1997). This occurs anywhere in the world when minority cultures interact with the majority. Yet, as providers of reference services, we must ensure that we are not the cause of further disenfranchisement.

*Library-Specific Problems.* Let us now turn to some problems specific to libraries. Some internationals are surprised to learn that most general library collections are open to browsing. They may come from countries with closed stacks and limited collections. They may have little experience with library research. Critical evaluation of texts may be a new concept to them. Some international adult learners may have difficulty accepting the fact that they are ignorant of how to use library resources, and that reference librarians are able to help them (Sarkodie-Mensah 1986).

Another library issue is copyright. Although governed by numerous treaties and international agreements, copyright is often not a concern in some cultures (Greenfield et al. 1986). Published materials are sometimes viewed as community property that can be adapted as needed without attribution. While it is not generally a librarian's duty to enforce Title 17 of the *United States Code,* we should be aware of differences in attitudes toward copyright law and intellectual property rights.

The international's relationship to library staff is also culturally determined. In some countries the professor is the only one who understands research. A student may rely solely on a professor and not approach a librarian for anything. In some countries bureaucracy is so pervasive that people deal with this "red tape" by taking an aggressive stance with officials (Greenfield et al. 1986). Hopefully, after seeing the helpfulness and understanding given them by a reference librarian, they will see us as experts willing to help. When internationals find a sympathetic and helpful librarian, they not only come back for more, they spread the word throughout the community.

### *Technological Barriers*

With technology changing so fast, it's difficult for anyone to keep up, librarian or not (Condic 1995). Reference staff often note the speed with which databases, vendors, access points, and interfaces changes (Sarkodie-Mensah 1997). In an academic setting, someone attending a first-year seminar in how to access materials in his/her field will likely notice significant changes long before the time of graduation. It is difficult to say that adult learners from developed countries have a tremendous advantage over those from less-developed countries, since technologies are changing at record speed.

Information literacy, a challenge generally with library clientele, becomes even more of an issue when we think of our international friends. Cornell University's Mann Library (Kolray et al. 1996) offers an array of workshops to address the topic. Instruction covers library technologies and extends to Internet searching skills as well. Topics include understanding how information is organized, information search and retrieval, evaluation of information, and information management (including bibliographic database management software (Brown 1994) and word processing). Programs such as this can be tailored to the international community in any given library.

We live in exciting times indeed. Nearly monthly there are changes to electronic access in most libraries. What is challenging to librarians is befuddling to users and, even more so, is terrifying to those of international extraction.

The World Wide Web, with all of its shortcomings, has done much to unify technologies and to back the challenge of library instruction easier. Mary Beth Allen's 1993 survey of international student familiarity with online catalogs and computer technologies might yield different results in today's Web-based library environment (Allen 1993).

Perhaps the best approach to this barrier is to focus on generic knowledge rather than on application-specific techniques (Anderson and Bikson 1998). Anderson and Bikson suggest stressing: an accurate model of connectivity (understanding Web browsers and client-server technology, e-mail, and "live" connections such as ftp and telnet); understanding computer logic (how computers are different from us); understanding of the structuring of data and information (data storage, RAM, relational structure); knowledge of generic tools (spelling and grammar checkers, search engines, etc.); understanding of media (not just traditional media, but digital media such as picture formats, sounds, text formats, compression, etc.); and understanding of interfaces (the ways in which people relate to machines).

## SOLUTIONS TO BARRIERS

Having examined some linguistic, cultural, and technological barriers, let us now propose some solutions to these barriers. Suggestions include experiencing some culture shock of your own, perhaps by traveling or immersing yourself in international communities in the U.S.; befriending an international through friendship and hospitality; building and maintaining multilingual collections in our libraries (Somerville 1995); providing staff with a reading list on cross-cultural issues (Mood 1982); offering to proofread a paper; becoming familiar with bibliographic searching in foreign languages, particularly in the languages of the international communities in your area; develop a library vocabulary list (Ormondroyd 1989); provide programs tailored to international students to teach them about libraries (Greenfield et al. 1986); and remember cultural universals: Smile, be approachable.

Library instruction can go a long way to bridging the gap between the needs of the international adult learner and resources available to meet those needs. Internationals may be shy about approaching a stranger with a question. Library instruction sessions can introduce them to a friendly librarian and thus break down barriers (Ball and Mahony 1987). Word-of-mouth can quickly spread throughout ethnic communities as librarians are recognized as helpful and sensitive to internationals.

A reference desk with a helpful librarian may be a foreign concept to some of our international friends, but it should be the place where assistance can be sought on any topic and where no person is made to feel second-class.

## REFERENCES

Allen, Mary Beth. (1993). "International Students in Academic Libraries: A User Survey." *College & Research Libraries* 54 (4): 323-333.

Anderson, Robert H., and Tora K. Bikson. (1998). *Focus on Generic Skills for Information Technology Literacy, Rand Paper Series; P-9018*. Santa Monica, CA: Rand.

Ball, Mary Alice, and Molly Mahony. (1987). "Foreign Students, Libraries, and Culture." *College & Research Libraries* 48: 160-166.

Brown, Christopher C. (1994). "Creating Automated Bibliographies Using Internet-accessible Online Library Catalogs." *Database* 17 (1): 67-71.

Bryson, Montez. (1974). "Libraries Lend Friendship." *International Educational and Cultural Exchange* 10 (2): 29-30.

Bureau of the Census. (1992). *1990 Census of Population and Housing. Guide. Part B, Glossary*. Washington: U.S. Dept. of Commerce, Bureau of the Census.

Bureau of the Census. (1998). *The Foreign-Born Population in the United States: March 1997 (Update), Current Population Reports; P20-507*. Washington: U.S. Dept. of Commerce, Bureau of the Census. Available online from: http://www.census.gov/prod/3/98pubs/p20-507.pdf

Bureau of the Census. (1997). *The Foreign-Born Population: 1996, Current Population Reports; P20-494*. Washington: U.S. Dept. of Commerce, Bureau of the Census. Available online from: http://www.census.gov/prod/2/pop/p20/p20-494.pdf

Chau, May Ying, and Michael R. Culbertson. (1994). "Library Services for International Students: A Study at Colorado State University." *Colorado Libraries* 20 (3): 40-41.

Condic, Kristine S. (1995). *Internet and Academic Librarians: Training, Promotion, and Time, ERIC document; ED387136*.

Cope, Johnnye, and Evelyn Black. (1985). "New Library Orientation for International Students." *College Teaching* 33 (4): 159-162.

Craver, Kathleen W. (1991). "Bridging the Gap: Library Services for Immigrant Populations." *Journal of Youth Services in Libraries* 4 (2): 123-130.

Fiske, Edward B. (1997). *Adult Education in a Polarizing World. Education for All: Status and Trends, ERIC document ED409452:* International Consultative Forum on Education for All. Available online from: http://unesco.uneb.edu/unesco/efa/03july1997.htm

Greenfield, Louise, Susan Johnston, and Karen Williams. (1986). "Educating the World: Training Library Staff to Communicate Effectively with International Students." *Journal of Academic Librarianship* 12 (4): 227-231.

Gudykunst, William B., and Stella Ting-Toomey. (1988). *Culture and Interpersonal Communication.* Newbury Park, CA: Sage Publications.

Hall, E.T. (1976). *Beyond Culture.* New York: Doubleday.

Hoffman, Irene, and Opritsa Popa. (1986). "Library Orientation and Instruction for International Students: The University of California-Davis Experience." *RQ* 25 (3): 356-360.

Immigration and Naturalization Service. (1997). *1996 Statistical Yearbook of the Immigration and Naturalization Service.* Washington: U.S. G.P.O. Available on-line from: http://www.ins.usdoj.gov/statyrbook96/

Institute of International Education. (1997). *Open Doors, 1996-1997: Report on International Education Exchange.* New York: Institute of International Education.

Kline, Laura S., and Catherine M. Rod. (1984). "Library Orientation Programs for Foreign Students: A Survey." *RQ* 24 (2): 210-216.

Koehler, Boyd, and Kathryn Swanson. (1988). "ESL Students and Bibliographic Instruction: Learning Yet Another Language." *Research Strategies* 6 (4): 148-160.

Kolray, Zsuzsa, Ben Trelease, and Philip M. Davis. (1996). "Technologies for Learning: Instructional Support at Cornell's Albert R. Mann Library." *Technologies for Learning* 14 (4): 83-98.

Macdonald, Gina, and Mensah Sarkodie, Elizabeth. (1988). "ESL Students and American Libraries." *College & Research Libraries* 49 (5): 425-431.

Marcum, Deanna B., and Elizabeth W. Stone. (1991). "Literacy: The Library Legacy." *American Libraries* 22 (3): 202-205.

Mood, Terry Ann. (1982). "Foreign Students and the Academic Library." *RQ* 22 (2): 175-180.

Natowitz, Allen. (1995). "International Students in U.S. Academic Libraries: Recent Concerns and Trends." *Research Strategies* 13 (1): 4-16.

Ormondroyd, Joan. (1989). "The International Student and Course-integrated Instruction: The Librarian's Perspective." *Research Strategies* 7 (Fall): 148-158.

Procter, Paul. (1981). *Longman Dictionary of Contemporary English.* Harlow, England: Longman.

Ratliff, Debra D. (1990). "The Refugees in Our Midst." *Colorado Libraries* 16 (3): 18-19.

Sarkodie-Mensah, Kwasi. (1997). "The Human Side of Reference in an Era of Technology." *The Reference Librarian* (59): 131-138.

Sarkodie-Mensah, Kwasi. (1986). "In the Words of a Foreigner." *Research Strategies* 4: 30-31.

Somerville, Mary R. (1995). "Global is Local." *Library Journal* 120 (Feb. 15): 131-133.

Sussman, N., and H. Rosenfeld. (1982). "Influence of Culture, Language and Sex on Conversational Distance." *Journal of Personality and Social Psychology* 42: 66-74.

Ueda, Keiko. (1974). "Sixteen Ways to Avoid Saying "No" in Japan." In *Intercultural Encounters with Japan: Communication-contact and Conflict: Perspectives from the International Conference on Communication Across Cultures Held at International Christian University in Tokyo,* edited by John C. Condon and Mitsuko Saito, 185-192. Tokyo: Simul Press.

# Reference Services:
# Meeting the Needs
# of International Adult Learners

## Calmer D. Chattoo

**SUMMARY.** International adult learners constitute a very large percentage of the international student and scholar population in the United States. The ability of this adult group to use libraries is hampered not only by their language, cultural and educational barriers, but also by librarians' limited understanding of their differences in learning styles. The relationship between learning styles and the methods of instructing them in library use is addressed in this paper. Recommendations for training and instruction of librarians on meeting the needs of this culturally diverse group are also provided. *[Article copies available for a fee from The Haworth Document Delivery Service: 1-800-342-9678. E-mail address: <getinfo@haworthpressinc.com> Website: <http://www.haworthpressinc.com>]*

**KEYWORDS.** Adult learners, comparative librarianship, foreign students, graduate students, international adult learners, international librarianship, international students, library education, learning styles, reference services

## *INTRODUCTION*

A reference librarian, conducting a library orientation, encouraged the students to use the OPAC[1] in order to find out if the library has the informa-

Calmer D. Chattoo is Assistant Librarian, Charles B. Sears Law Library, SUNY at Buffalo, Buffalo, NY 14260-1110 (E-mail: chattoo@acsu.buffalo.edu).

[Haworth co-indexing entry note]: "Reference Services: Meeting the Needs of International Adult Learners." Chattoo, Calmer D. Co-published simultaneously in *The Reference Librarian* (The Haworth Information Press, an imprint of The Haworth Press, Inc.) No. 69/70, 2000, pp. 349-362; and: *Reference Services for the Adult Learner: Challenging Issues for the Traditional and Technological Era* (ed: Kwasi Sarkodie-Mensah) The Haworth Information Press, an imprint of The Haworth Press, Inc., 2000, pp. 349-362. Single or multiple copies of this article are available for a fee from The Haworth Document Delivery Service [1-800-342-9678, 9:00 a.m. - 5:00 p.m. (EST). E-mail address: getinfo@haworthpressinc.com].

tion they need. An international graduate student attending the session, thought that the OPAC was the name of the library's card catalog. Not seeing the catalog cabinets, the student thought that there were so many cabinets, they were kept in a special room called the OPAC. During the tour the student did not notice any area marked "OPAC." The student thought, "Where is the OPAC?" Feeling too embarrassed to ask and for fear of being considered stupid, the student left the library bewildered.

Wanting to find out if the library has information on a certain topic, another international student, in a quiet voice, approached the reference librarian with a request. The reference librarian suggested the student search the online catalog called BISON[2] to find out if the library has books and journals and where they were located. The student was told to note the call number which would indicate exactly where in the stacks the item was located. Being very helpful, the reference librarian demonstrated a search on the staff computer. The student expressed appreciation, and with a puzzled look asked, "What is BISON?" The reference librarian replied, "This is BISON, and you can use the computers over there." In addition to not knowing what BISON meant the student was left to wonder what in the world were call numbers and where were the stacks in that humongous library.

These two scenarios illustrate some of the problems international students face in using American libraries. Problems like these are brought to the fore at the reference desk. Therefore, it is particularly important, that the reference librarian who is placed in a strategic front line position, be prepared to handle the unique differences that international students bring with them to libraries in the United States.

The author's interest in reference services for international adult learners stems from personal experience as an international adult learner in the United States and living with other international adult learners. Her experience as an academic librarian and teacher in the Caribbean has increased her awareness of what the international students, particularly adults, have to grapple with in using American libraries.

## IDENTIFYING THE INTERNATIONAL ADULT LEARNERS WE SERVE

Starting in the 1980's adult education captured the forefront of educational concerns. The literature published on the definition and characteristics of adult learners, and adult learning principles has been tremendous. Library literature provides a myriad of valuable articles on the needs and services of special groups of users such as the handicapped, the disadvantaged, adults and minority groups including international students en bloc. Libraries have developed many innovative ways to successfully cope with the problems of international students. These include tours in the students' native languages (Liestman & Wu, 1990; Lopez, 1983), special library instruction sessions (Goudy & Moushey, 1984), seminars and workshops on cultural differences (Ball & Mahony, 1987; Greenfield et al., 1986). These innovative methods are very helpful but librarians must take a closer look at international students and note that many of them are adults, and because of this unique characteristic, they deserve special attention.

A survey of *Library Literature* and *ERIC Database* from 1980 to 1998 revealed only a handful of articles relating to international adult learners and most of them give peripheral mention of the library's role or the students' experiences in the libraries. This article focuses on the contrasting learning styles of international adult learners and it suggests diverse educational methods which librarians can use to accommodate these learning styles as well as training as the long term objective to solving the students' library problems.

According to the Institute of International Education's annual report for 1996/97, international students studying at the graduate level in the United States make up 42.8% of all international students, recording a slight increase from the previous year (Davis, 1997). The majority of these students receive financial assistance from home governments, institutions and family sources and are the least affected by the financial crisis now facing four of the top ten countries that send students to the United States (Woodard, 1998).

Unlike the number of international undergraduate students which is expected to decline because of the financial crisis (Desruisseaux, 1997), the number of international graduate students is expected to increase (Desruisseaux, 1998). In addition to being able to finance their education through financial assistance, international graduate students continue to come to the United States for other reasons such as, to pursue graduate degrees which are not offered in their home countries and to avail themselves of the range of opportunities that are available ( Desruisseaux, 1998).

The Institute also reported on the number of international scholars (non-immigrant teachers and/or researchers who are not enrolled as students). In 1996/97 the number of these scholars totaled 62,354 and recorded an increase of 5% after three years of little or no growth (Open Doors 1996/97, 1997).

In spite of the growing number of international graduate students and scholars in the United States, interest among librarians in this segment of the international students population is scattered. Sincere efforts in helping them develop the skills necessary for effective, efficient and independent library use begin with librarians recognizing that these students constitute a diverse group of people and taking into consideration their characteristics, needs and learning styles.

## LEARNING STYLES

The role of the librarian today is similar to that of the teaching faculty, in that library use is increasingly discipline-based and instructional. The librarian acts as a teacher and gives instruction either on a one-to-one basis or in a classroom setting. In either setting, ultimately the job of the librarian is to facilitate learning, that is, to get a concept across and to expect the student to remember it. This calls for interaction since teaching is an interactive process (Tennant & Pogson, 1995). However each individual has preferred ways of organizing and transforming what they see, hear, remember, and think about into useful knowledge. These preferred ways are labeled "learning styles" and they can be unique and specific to a cultural group. It simply means that not every nationality learns alike.

### *Change versus Stability*

Personal effort or external circumstances may cause an adult to experience substantial changes in behavior (Knox, 1977), which may facilitate, precipitate, force or frustrate learning. The effectiveness of adult learning may therefore vary greatly in the mix of skill, attitude and knowledge change. The librarian should expect this kind of variety among international adult learners who represent more than 180 different countries (Davis, 1997). Their approaches to learning may reflect previous experience such as extent and type of formal education, recent use of learning procedures and current circumstances that give rise to the need for increased knowledge. One aspect of previous experience that affects international adult learners is the method of formal education in their own countries. Instruction there is encouraged through imitation, memorization and group work (Wayman, 1984), as opposed to the American assertive, verbal, inductive reasoning and independent style.

A 1986 study conducted to determine the learning styles of adults revealed that "learning styles are not congenital, rather, styles develop over time, can change slowly and reflect other characteristics of the person" (Conti & Welborn, 1986). Sonia Bodi agrees that though learning style tends to be stable throughout life, it can change as circumstances demand (Bodi, 1990). Naturally, changes in the educational environment of international adult learners may cause them to alter their learning styles. They may become more aggressive and assume an active as opposed to a passive learning style. This change may result from the fact that they have additional concerns other than acquiring credentials or a diploma. Adjusting to the American academic environment and to life in a new land where they are confronted by strange foods, different mores and separation from family and friends are concerns they likely have to deal with while studying. They also have to cope with studying advanced level courses in a second language.

The aggressive, active learning style of international adult learners is noticeable from their determination to understand the topic at hand. They can be very quick to ask questions about a strange word or expression, like the student in the introduction, and may unashamedly demand clarification of a poorly explained concept. Many times, because of the intricacies and inconsistencies of basic English that they must now learn, they are more intense in their request for explanation than the American students.

### Group Participation

The majority of these learners are reared in a society that encourages strong family ties and they tend to have a preference for group discussion as a learning procedure. They regard the group's success as more important than individual identity and accomplishments (Wayman, 1984). Arriving in a new country where they have limited personal and social contact, these students form close-knit groups and rely heavily on each other for support. Librarians who are alert to this cooperative, collaborative attitude can provide orientation and assistance in getting them started in the use of the library. There is even more reason to believe that involving students in the learning process can enhance learning and stimulate personal development. Conti and Welborn used this method of involving students in the learning process in their study with adult learners. They referred to this as the "student-centered approach" (Conti & Welborn, 1986). Activities such as encouraging students to take responsibility for their own learning, personalizing instruction, and fostering flexibility in the classroom were those favored by teachers using the student-centered approach. Dorsey and Pierson also found that adults profit more from a student-centered approach to learning. Their study revealed that adults learn better by doing, and especially at age thirty-three they possess a greater need for self-actualization and are sensitive towards what is considered essential and beneficial to learn to improve their career (Dorsey & Pierson, 1984).

### Observation

Another learning preference of international adult learners is observation. This method of instruction is heavily steeped in the Chinese, Japanese, and Middle Eastern cultures and is continued in an educational setting (Wayman, 1984). An adult typically approaches a learning activity with expectations and understandings that will likely influence the effectiveness of learning. These expectations and understandings can be clarified through the observation of examples or models of what they should know or be able to do. In a search demonstration this mode is especially helpful if it is personalized by peers who are already competent at performing the activity. Seeing someone like themselves who has recently learned to do a bibliographic search, to read a citation, or to operate a microfiche machine, provides both a role model and a source of encouragement. Special hands-on workshops should be held to teach international adult learners about the Library of Congress (LC) Classi-fication and subject headings, online catalogs and library facilities such as inter-library loan (ILL). This is a direct and effective method of overcoming communication barriers. A nonverbal communication such as a nod from an international adult learner should not be interpreted as a sign that the student understands. Observing them in practice will give the librarian an opportuni-ty to find out for sure if key concepts and methods are understood and the timid ones will have a chance to prove to themselves that they do understand.

## Reading

Reading is another learning procedure preferred by adults (Knox, 1977). International adult learners usually understand better by reading than by listening (Wayman, 1984). The differences and varieties of American English speech patterns make reading a preference for them and their expectations about the learning activity can be further clarified by written descriptions as well. A handout giving an outline guide to the presentation with key concepts and terms with explanations is very helpful, especially when samples are also handed out for examination, and the procedures are walked through during the presentation. This will also help them to understand what many of the teachers, librarians and students say since most Americans do not speak standard English but speak with local dialects and intersperse their lectures or presentations with American slang.

## Previous Experience

Usually when adults set out to learn something, this act is related to a large amount of experience and information that they possess (Tennant, 1995). They are now moving to understand and using the interrelationship of infor-mation and experience as opposed to their younger counterparts who only use structure of content to facilitate retention. Though perhaps unfamiliar with the technological advances in bibliographic access, and services offered by large academic libraries in the United States, international adult learners are typically students with advanced knowledge of the literature in their field. They may be limited in their library experiences due to differences in struc-ture, organization and availability of libraries in their own countries (Kalin,

1992), but many are recognized professors in their own countries, or Fulbright scholars, and are highly motivated, eager to learn and serious of purpose.

The fact that teaching style can make a significant difference in adult learning achievement emphasizes the need for librarians to take a second look at themselves and their actions. There is a greater guarantee of adult learning if the librarian acts as a facilitator and a mentor, rather than a prescriber.

## INNOVATIVE WAYS
## TO INSTRUCT INTERNATIONAL ADULT LEARNERS

The erroneous idea that it is difficult to teach adults is reflected in the saying, "You cannot teach an old dog new tricks." Almost any adult is able to learn almost any subject given sufficient time and attention along with persistence. Throughout life people remember, think and solve problems and studies have shown that the ways adults do this, gradually change due to many factors. Addressing learning styles may not make our library services to international adults perfect, but teaching to a diversity of learning styles may help us to properly instruct them to find and manipulate information in order to improve their performance and to keep up to date in their field.

It is not easy to make concise recommendations for instructing international adult learners en masse in the use of academic libraries in the United States. The range of students' experiences and expectations is vast. They have different cultural backgrounds and each has well defined opinions of the other. There are, however, many simple methods, specifically for international adult learners that can be applied. The next section provides such methods.

### Avoid Using Approaches Used for Teaching Children

Although the approach must be as simple as possible, the librarian must not address international adult learners or the material as they would children. Though code-switching (the adjustment of language to accommodate the needs of the listener), is sometimes necessary to accommodate the needs of this adult group, the librarian must realize that he/she is dealing with adults who are neither childlike nor poorly educated. The librarian who "baby talks" will often realize with embarrassment, that the level of intelligence of these students is higher than his/her approach implies (McDonald & Sarkodie-Mensah, 1988).

### Do Not Isolate Vocabulary

Introduce the vocabulary in context by emphasizing the word, pronouncing it several times to insure the correct pronunciation and introducing it in a complete sentence. Librarians are given to the creation of neologisms and acronyms and take it for granted that the student is in full command of this when that is not the case. Acronyms such as OCLC (Online Computer Library Center), OPAC (Online Public Access Catalog), and LC (Library of Congress), are quite likely not familiar to the students and they probably have never heard these terms before. The students are hard pressed to keep up with this alphabet medley. Shortened titles are also second nature to librarians, for example "fiche" for microfiche. This is not to suggest that librarians avoid the familiar shortened forms, but that their appearance should be followed with a brief explanation of what they signify. Librarians can also provide a multilingual glossary of library terms, and a list of jargon, especially homonyms (e.g., serial, not cereal). This instructional aid can go a long way to overcoming language difficulties or confusion due to library jargon.

### Encourage Discussion

International adult learners may be timid about using the English language or of revealing their different speech patterns. Help them to build confidence with language by being patient and positive. Errors in pronunciation and grammar should not be corrected while the student is speaking. Take mental or written notes of these and individually discuss them afterwards.

### Provide a Relaxed Atmosphere

Learning should be fun and enjoyable. Keep criticism at a minimum. Each student's strengths and special skills should be highlighted and what is needed to correct any weaknesses should be provided.

### Be Creative, Flexible and Resourceful–Use the Interactive Approach

Begin by asking questions to motivate interest and encourage dialogue and discussion. Encourage the students to ask questions. This will help them to practice their oral communication skills and eliminate shyness and hesitancy to approach librarians for help.

### Allow Students to Help Each Other by Encouraging Them to Work in Groups

International adult learners have special experiences and abilities that can enhance the learning situation, so they should be allowed to collaborate during the learning experience. Assistance in bridging the communication gap between international adult learners and American students can be provided by international students who have mastered the use of American libraries. Several studies recommend doing so (Lopez, 1983; Wayman, 1984). American students majoring in foreign languages, such as Chinese, Japanese, Spanish, French, and Korean, should also help lead library tours.

### Be a Good Role Model or Provide One for Them

The librarian or the role model provided should know the content of his/her presentation and effectively demonstrate the skills the students should eventually possess.

### Always Think Positively

Project a confident attitude that these students will achieve the goals that they have set and help convince them that they can learn.

### Use Sophisticated Graphic Aids

The library is a complicated system and the use of illustrations, through the effective use of posters, handouts and notice-board displays, will help the students to learn to understand it. Make using the library fun and enjoyable.

## NEED FOR STAFF TRAINING

Given the difficulties presented in learning styles due to language, culture, and educational customs, librarians need greater access to research on the topic as well as better training to enable them to meet the needs of international adult learners. Jurow agrees that, "well-conceived programs, and well-designed structures will be needed to improve . . . staff skills" (Jurow, 1992), relevant to the specific needs of these students. Though Jacobson does not give any details, she also agrees that a strong staff development program is critical to the success of library instruction for international students (Jacobson, 1988). In discussing a one-day workshop developed at the University of Arizona, Greenfield says, "There was a need to develop instructional techniques and programs to effectively teach international students and underlying this, before we could achieve that goal, we had to prepare our staff to communicate effectively with international students" (Greenfield, 1988). She emphasizes the point that if librarians are to teach international students they must first be taught how to do so.

### Staff Development

For libraries with a large population of international adult learners and the desire and budget to develop programs for them, several things come to mind. These include purchase and promotion of materials about the students' home countries, grouping of Fulbright scholars by field of study and planning specialized library instruction programs for them, and appointing a staff member as liaison to the international community. The liaison librarian can provide outreach by attending international students club meetings, lecturing to English as a Second Language classes, providing signage in languages other than English, establishing and maintaining contact with community groups and organizations.

Terry Ann Mood discusses the importance of staff development especially for libraries lacking the staff and budget for time-consuming and specialized library instruction for these students (Mood, 1982). She suggests providing reading lists of articles concerning international students' experiences in the United States libraries for staff use, a lecture series by international students or international students officers at staff meetings, encouraging staff attendance at international students' meetings and offering the library as a site for their meetings.

Workshops are ideal for briefing librarians on special needs of international students (Robertson, 1992). Greenfield, Johnson and Williams discuss the inclusion of videos and exercises in their workshop as effective training tools, assuming that sensitizing staff to the needs of international students requires more than generalized advice (Greenfield et al., 1986).

### Library Staff and Networking

There are also opportunities for all staff to participate in networking methods which can provide staff development and education on the subject of library instruction for international adult learners. These include:

- *E-mail.* Through the use of e-mail staff can contact and exchange information with colleagues, friends, strangers in the same library, the other library/libraries on campus, the other state libraries, library associations, or libraries across the globe. The use of this method of networking can result in obtaining products, procedures, recommendations, evaluations and a large amount of library-oriented problem resolution possibilities.
- *Listservs.* These are electronic discussion groups to which staff can subscribe. LIBREF-L (Discussion of Library Reference Issues) and BI-L (Bibliographic Instruction Discussion Group) are two listservs that specialize in reference and library instruction. Discussions on these listservs take place among a diverse and knowledgeable membership.
- *Conferences, Workshops and Seminars.* Attending a library or library instruction-oriented conference or workshop such as those organized by the instruction section of the Association of College and Research

Libraries (ACRL) is an excellent networking opportunity for librarians. Conference papers and personal contact can be valuable resources for generating creative ideas for library instruction.

### Formal Training

Formal education can be an effective and reassuring way to learn about the languages, cultures and educational customs of other groups of people. After the 1960's the study of international/comparative librarianship for librarians declined from many library school programs in the United States making room for new courses in information science, media and technology. Aman and Aman note the reasons given for the decline but point out that those reasons run diametrically opposed to the argument that librarianship is an international field (Aman & Aman, 1987). The need to integrate international aspects of library and information science into library education has been raised by a number of library science educators. According to Martha Boaz, most internationalists would recommend the inclusion of a course or two in international and comparative librarianship (Boaz, 1977).

International/comparative librarianship should be added as a requirement for graduation in all library and information science programs. These components should be added to the library schools' reference curriculum and could also become a fundamental part of the program incorporating opportunities for students to study or work in major foreign libraries for credit. The enrollment of international students in library and information science programs provides a unique opportunity for instructors to capitalize on the experiences and intellect of these students. In a reference course, for example, these students can present for discussion and evaluation reference tools commonly used in their native countries. These tools should be made available in the libraries which service the library and information science programs.

Faculty can also seize the opportunities available to study, teach and engage in research in foreign libraries and library schools so as to further enrich the library and information science programs. Without the development of an international perspective in the training and instruction of librarians no national thrust to help international adult learners successfully use American libraries can reach its full potential.

### CONCLUSIONS

Higher education is reported as one of the United States most valuable exports (Open Doors: 1996/97, 1997), and libraries as the centers of universities (Ball and Mahony, 1987). As librarians we need to recognize that we have a part to play in protecting this valuable export. If we are not going to take responsibility for helping international adult learners to overcome their frustrations and anxiety in finding their information needs, eventually the United States will lose them as the chief component of one of its most valuable exports–American higher education. In summarizing the report of Open Doors 1996/97, Richard M. Krasno, president of the Institute of International Education reports that other countries are aggressively competing for these talented applicants and therefore "we need to understand the value of foreign students participation in United States higher education and reach out to protect our 'market share'" (Open Doors: 1996/97, 1997). Our positive response to fulfilling the students' academic needs could be our contribution to protecting the 'market share' of the United States economy.

For the most part, international adult learners are an interesting group with which to work, particularly because of their sense of humor, their unique set of functional skills, attitudes and values that they bring to the campus. They rate knowledge of library use as a contributory factor to their overall academic integration and are rarely bored by the idea of libraries or research (O'Hara, 1984). They are just as curious about libraries as they are about the society in general. Some are cocky, terrified, totally frustrated, or fiercely independent and insist on trying to solve their own problems even when they cannot, but they are usually highly motivated and eager to learn. What they need to know is the same for all other students. It is only how we teach them that may differ because of their different backgrounds and stage of life. We must be more sensitive to their need to access information. Librarians must dispel the negative assumptions and focus on real issues, differences, problems and contrasting learning styles and be flexible. This attitude will go a long way in helping us to better deal with international adult learners.

## NOTES

1. Acronym for **O**nline **P**ublic **A**ccess Catalog.
2. **B**uffalo **I**nformation **S**ystem **O**nline is the University at Buffalo Libraries computerized system which provides quick access to the Library's collections and other library catalogs.

## REFERENCES

Aman, Mohammed A. and Mary Jo Aman. "Reference services and global awareness," *The Reference Librarian* 17 (Spring 1987): 45-50.
Ball, Mary Alice and Molly Mahony. "Foreign students, libraries and culture." *College and Research Libraries* 28 (March 1987): 160-166.
Boaz, Martha. "The comparative and international library science course in Ameri-

can library schools," in *Comparative and international library science.* John F. Harvey, editor. Metuchen, NJ: Scarecrow Press, 1977.

Bodi, Sonia. "Teaching effectiveness and BI: The relevance of learning styles." *College and Research Libraries* 51 (March 1990): 113-119.

Conti, Gary G. and Ruth B. Welborn. "Teaching-learning styles and the adult learner," *Lifelong learning: An omnibus of practice and research 9* (June 1986): 20-23.

Davis, Todd M., ed. *Open Doors, 1996/97: Report on International Education Exchange.* New York: Institute of International Education, 1997.

Desruisseaux, Paul. "Foreign enrollment rises slightly at colleges in the United States," *The Chronicle of Higher Education* (December 12, 1997): A42-A43.

Desruisseaux, Paul. "Economic crisis in Asia; The impact on enrollment in four countries," *The Chronicle of Higher Education* 44 (March 27, 1998): A52-A53.

Desruisseaux, Paul. "Competition intensifies for Asian students," *The Chronicle of Higher Education* 44 (May 29, 1998): A48-A49.

Dorsey, Oscar L. and Michael J. Pierson. "A descriptive study of adult learning styles in a non-traditional education program," *Lifelong learning: An omnibus of practice and research* 7 (June 1984): 10-11.

Goudy, Frank W. and Eugene Moushey. "Library instruction and foreign students: A survey of practices among selected libraries," *The Reference Librarian* 10 (Spring/Summer 1984): 215-226.

Greenfield, Louise, Susan Johnston and Karen Williams. "Educating the world: Training library staff to communicate effectively with international students," *Journal of Academic Librarianship* 12 (September 1986): 227-231.

Greenfield, Louise W. "Training library staff to reach and teach international students," in *Reaching and teaching diverse library user groups. Papers presented at the 16th National LOEX Library Instruction Conference.* Bowling Green: Bowling Green State University. Teresa B. Mensching, editor. Ann Arbor: Pierian Press, 1989.

Jacobson, Frances. "Bibliographic instruction and international students," *Illinois Libraries,* 70 (1988): 628-633.

Jurow, Susan. "Preparing academic and research library staff for the 1990's and beyond," *Journal of Library Administration* 17 (1992): 5-17.

Kalin, S.G. "The international student in the American academic library," in *The role of the American library in international programs.* B.D. Bonita and J.G. Neal, editors. London: JAI Press, Inc., 1992.

Knox, Alan B. *Adult learning and development.* San Francisco: Jossey-Bass, 1977.

Liestman, Daniel and Connie Wu. "Library orientation for international students in their native language," *Research Strategies* 8 (Fall 1990): 191-196.

Lopez, Manuel D. "Chinese spoken here; Foreign student library orientation tours," *College and Research Library News* 8 (September 1983): 256-369.

McDonald, Gina and Elizabeth Sarkodie-Mensah. "ESL students and American libraries," *College and Research Libraries* 49 (September 1988): 427-429.

Mood, Terry Ann. "Foreign students and the academic library," *RQ 22* (Winter 1982): 175-180.

O'Hara, Molly. "Bibliographic instruction for foreign students," in *Academic li-*

braries: Myths and realities. Suzanne C. Dobson and Gary L. Menges, editors. Chicago: Association of College and Research Libraries, 1984.

Open Doors: 1996/97. December 8, 1997. Institute of International Education. April 1998. <http://www.iie.org/opendoors/intro.htm>

Open Doors: 1996/97. December 8, 1997. Institute of International Education. April 1998. <http://www.iie.org/opendoors/forstud8.htm>

Robertson, Joan E. "User education for overseas students in higher education in Scotland," Journal of Librarianship and Information Science 24 (March 1992): 44.

Tennant, Mark and Philip Pogson. Learning and change in the adult years: A developmental perspective. San Francisco: Jossey-Bass, 1995.

Wayman, Sally, G. "The international student in the academic library," Journal of Academic Librarianship 9 (January 1984): 336-341.

Woodard, Colin. "Economic crisis forces Korean students to study at home," The Chronicle of Higher Education 44 (April 1998): A56.

# Reference Services
## and the International Adult Learner

### Daniel Liestman

**SUMMARY.** International adult learners are a growing patron constituency. They share a number of common characteristics, notably their unfamiliarity with many library services. In addition, barriers such as language and communication differences as well as functional issues present challenges to effective service. Libraries can better meet the needs of International Adult Learners by determining what their needs are. In so doing they will be able to provide better programming and improve library instruction. In addition, libraries can partner with other community agencies and institutions to improve service for International Adult Learners. Staff training should also be undertaken to improve the ability of library personnel to interact with this particular user group. *[Article copies available for a fee from The Haworth Document Delivery Service: 1-800-342-9678. E-mail address: <getinfo@haworthpressinc.com> Website: <http://www.haworthpressinc.com>]*

**KEYWORDS.** International students, adult students, reference services, andragogy

## INTRODUCTION

International adult learners represent two strands of special needs users woven together to become an increasingly significant part of the service

Daniel Liestman received his MSLS from the University of Tennessee. He also has an MA in History and a bachelor's degree in History and Mass Communications. He is currently Chair of the Social Sciences and Humanities Libraries, Kansas State University, 209 Hale Library, Kansas State University, Manhattan, KS 66506 (E-mail: dliest@ksu.edu).

[Haworth co-indexing entry note]: "Reference Services and the International Adult Learner." Liestman, Daniel. Co-published simultaneously in *The Reference Librarian* (The Haworth Information Press, an imprint of The Haworth Press, Inc.) No. 69/70, 2000, pp. 363-378; and: *Reference Services for the Adult Learner: Challenging Issues for the Traditional and Technological Era* (ed: Kwasi Sarkodie-Mensah) The Haworth Information Press, an imprint of The Haworth Press, Inc., 2000, pp. 363-378. Single or multiple copies of this article are available for a fee from The Haworth Document Delivery Service [1-800-342-9678, 9:00 a.m. - 5:00 p.m. (EST). E-mail address: getinfo@haworthpressinc.com].

fabric primarily of both academic and public libraries. International adult learners are non-natives twenty-five or more years old engaged in formal or non-formal study programs. They range from highly skilled professionals pursuing advanced graduate education to refugees seeking essential survival skills. Indications are that their numbers are growing. While there are no statistics on this group *per se,* enrollment of non-resident aliens continues to steadily increase at four year colleges and universities. At the same time, the number of students thirty-five years and over involved in formal education programs is projected to increase by half a million from what it was less than five years ago. Within this group, the number of female international adult learners is growing steadily too.[1]

## CHARACTERISTICS OF INTERNATIONAL ADULT LEARNERS

International adult learners share a number of characteristics. They differ from regular adult library users in that they are engaged in systematic learning, often as part of a formalized education program.[2] Like all users, if they are library-oriented to begin with, they are influenced by their past concepts and experiences of libraries and librarians. However, the nature of their experience differs markedly from others. They are frequently in a transitional stage in their lives and differ from traditional eighteen to twenty-four year old students in their life stages, value systems, outside responsibilities, and learning modalities. A significant number are part-time students balancing studies with full-time employment, marriage, family responsibilities, as well as other obligations.[3]

Other traits of international adult learners are less obvious, but just as significant. Most are learning not just for the sake of learning. Instead, they are often strongly goal oriented and are usually seeking to improve their own employment and career circumstances by keeping up with advances in technology and business. As such they are typically highly motivated to succeed and are further driven by a feeling of needing to compete against younger classmates and co-workers.[4] If English is not their native tongue they frequently are insecure about their language abilities. Thus, they come to the library motivated and with a heightened state of readiness for information seeking as well as attendant insecurities. Still, in one university-based study, for example, international learners perceived knowledge of the library as a contributing factor to their success and overall academic integration.[5] Libraries need to be prepared to meet the needs of this distinctive group of users in public services, particularly reference, instruction, and programming by paying particular attention to institutional and situational issues. Beyond this, libraries also need to consider interlacing community activities and staff training in their pattern of service for this growing group of users.

## INTERNATIONAL ADULT LEARNERS
## AND THE REFERENCE INTERFACE

In public services, the reference interface is often the first encounter many international adult learners have with a library. At this critical juncture there begins a strand which will be woven throughout their entire learning experience. It is at this point where they begin to not only master a particular corpus of knowledge but embark on a lifelong process of becoming active researchers in a new culture, and information environment. It is essential therefore that the reference encounter not just seek to emphasize isolated facts or mastery of simple computer skills, such as which button to push. Instead such technical skills need to be combined with critical thinking and strategies for information retrieval to create an information skill set which will enable these learners to effectively and efficiently identify, retrieve, and evaluate information coupled with the knowledge of specific tools and resources.[6]

The challenge, however, is that many international adult learners are entering *terra incognita* when they walk through the doors of a library. While there are many threads in the service fabric, two are of principal importance. First, there are institutional issues which are centered around the organization and the sources and services of the library. Secondly, there are those which are situational—arising from one's situation in life. These center around attitudes and self perceptions about the learner's self and are largely based in cultural as well as linguistic differences.[7]

## GENERAL DIFFERENCES IN LIBRARIES

The institutional aspects of North American libraries often differ from those of the international adult learners' home countries. Libraries in developing nations are often relatively small and contain many outdated books. Users may even be charged a fee to borrow from their own college libraries. Often librarians are not considered professionals and the library administrator is frequently a male faculty member with little or no training in the profession. The differences can be quite striking. Among some Middle Eastern libraries, for example, there are frequently few Arabic language books in the collection to begin with and the limited titles a library owns may be kept for preservation purposes rather than any other use. Other differences may be even more pronounced. In Saudi Arabian university libraries separate facilities are maintained, one for men and the other for women.[8] Too frequently in many less developed countries, public libraries are nonexistent and academic libraries may be little more than textbook repositories where clerks retrieve materials from closed stacks. Such differences are reflective of educational systems based on memorization and use of a single text. Consequently many international adult learners have limited library experience.[9]

Now add automation to a library which already differs significantly from what the international adult learner is familiar and the contrasts become even more pronounced and any pattern of familiarity is seemingly lost. Automation is the most dramatic institutional change in American libraries in the past ten to fifteen years. While its impact on international adult learners is difficult to gauge, the common assumption is that as such learners come from less developed countries and it may be inferred that they do not have the computer expertise of their American counterparts. Indeed a study at Kent State University found a majority of international learners lacked any experience using electronic databases. However, a University of Illinois study suggests a significant number of foreign student learners enjoy equivalent computer experience with their American classmates. In this latter study, however, subjects were among the elites in their home country who would be expected to enjoy such advantages. At the same time, some research suggests older learners tend to have less ability with computers, even though they are the most appreciative of the speed they provide to the research process–as opposed to using paper indexes or the card catalog. But a study of adult learners at Wayne State University indicated that most prefer computer to print indexes indicating no fear of computer searching.[10] The bottom line is that there is no way to generalize the level of expertise or comfort an international adult learner will bring to computer searching. Therefore it is incumbent upon the librarian to avoid stereotyping and be sensitive to the needs of the individual international adult learner regarding automation.

Self service has a longer history in libraries than automation, but may be even more of an institutional challenge for international adult learners. Indeed some of high social status may find the idea to be anathema as they are accustomed to lower classes doing their bidding and librarians may be among those expected to meet their needs. Beyond this, open stacks may present a challenge to a number of adult international users. A study at the University of California–Berkeley, found that forty percent of foreign students were unfamiliar with open stacks. On the other hand, only twelve percent of international learners in a University of Illinois survey reported open stacks were new to them.[11] Even if a learner is familiar with the idea of open stacks, the challenge of alphanumeric call number systems often proves daunting. Other self service functionalities in the public services arena may be new and different too. The open availability to government information is new for many, let alone a whole department devoted to government publications. Inter-library loan, document delivery, and microforms are also potential new areas of discovery.[12] While assisting international adult learners overcome institutional challenges may provide librarians with that teachable moment in working with international adult learners, situational matters are not always so easily overcome.

Situational issues are interwoven between culture and function. The cultural warp consists of behaviors and ideas specific to native cultures such as non-verbal cues and communication styles. Issues which inhibit basic library navigation such as underdeveloped critical thinking skills, differences in educational background, problems with expectations of libraries, and language are the functional weft of situational issues.[13]

Reference service is both an institutional and situational issue. In an institutional context, reference is a service not provided in many libraries world wide. International adult learners are frequently unfamiliar with the concept and may not avail themselves of a opportunity to use it as they are simply not aware of it. At the same time, other international adult learners may be reluctant to approach anyone to admit to a deficiency about a skill with which they feel they should already be familiar. In some cultures, to show ignorance is a shameful thing and is avoided, particularly as they may be mature responsible individuals of position and clout in their home country and to ask a simple question is seen as demeaning. As a result international adult learners often go without needed assistance out of ignorance or shame.[14]

## *LANGUAGE AND COMMUNICATION AS SITUATIONAL BARRIERS*

Language, however, is the most obvious situational barrier for international adult learners particularly among those new to this country. Yet, many may not even realize the limits of their language abilities or inabilities. Japanese students, for example, typically have six years of English training, but what they are taught is impractical save for passing college entrance exams. Translating English literature, such as Shakespeare, into Japanese and learning grammatical terms are the two main activities of Japanese English classes as test scores depend on these skills rather than conversational abilities.[15]

As much of the reference exchange is conducted verbally, that will be the focus of attention here. However, many of the same principles can be applied to written communication too. Communication should be delivered in ways which enhance comprehension, such as: speaking slowly, enunciating, keeping complex sentences to a minimum, defining major terms, and using synonyms and analogies to explain concepts.[16] Using at least some library jargon is probably inevitable, but should be kept to a minimum as such terminology is both unfamiliar and confusing. Witness the perplexed international learner who was told to look for microfiche and went asking for small fish. Using lay terms and providing definitions whenever possible is advisable.

It is also important not to assume that lack of language fluency connotes a lack of intelligence on the part of the international adult learner.[17] Such an assumption ignores the fact that often international adult learners are widely recognized in their own countries as professionals and some are even members of the ruling elite. Others have less standing, but are highly motivated and bright. What is needed is service based on an assumption of competence and explanations given in clear not condescending terms.[18]

Even successful conversation in English is far from a guarantee of cultural understanding or even good communication. In all communication there are basic assumptions, beyond the topic at hand, which are culturally-based. These must be realized in order for successful inter-cultural interaction to occur. For example, in some cultures conformity and uniformity are stressed. Among the Japanese the axiom that "the nail that sticks out will be pounded down" exemplifies this.[19] In their culture, the psycho-social cost of drawing undo attention to one's self or making any error is high and can bring shame not only to the individual but to one's family as well. Consequently, a reticence to ask questions may not just reflect a lack of ability with English, but may instead be grounded in cultural reasons.

Cultural background affects how international adult learners communicate and interact with library personnel in other ways too. In some cultures, women are regarded as being neither as important nor as educated as men. Male members of such a culture, consequently, may not give a female librarian the respect she deserves, or even believe her when she answers a question. At the same time, men from other cultures which are maternally dominant may readily follow a woman librarian's word. Moreover, social standing and the accompanying expectation of deference is a concept with which many Americans are both unaccustomed and uncomfortable. Some international adult learners of high social standing in their home countries have come to anticipate special honor and courtesy. Such expectations, however, can also lead to awkward encounters in the library.[20]

Apart from social issues, nonverbal communication or body language is an important situational component of the inter-cultural communication process. A female librarian who looks at a male from another culture in the eye may be perceived as defiant or being too familiar when all she wants to do is appear attentive. Americans consider a firm handshake as a sign of confidence, while others may consider it to be disrespectful. North Americans nod up and down to mean yes but in some cultures this is a negative signal. Others may couple a positive and negative statement with the nod of the head: "Yes I don't understand." While saying "hi" to strangers may be friendly, it is seen as rude in other cultures. How one stands, walks, gestures, or how closely one stands to another may have meaning which was never intended. North Americans feel comfortable with conversational distance of five feet; while others are used to two feet. Failure to understand these cultural differences can lead to misunderstanding and mild embarrassment. Extreme norm violations are opportunities to explain that Americans are uncomfortable with closeness or touching, for example.[21]

## FUNCTIONAL ISSUES AND INTERNATIONAL ADULT LEARNERS

Beyond the challenges of effective communication, functional issues also loom large in the provision of effective library service. Topic selection can be a case in point. International adult learners frequently have a particular interest in doing research on their home countries, as that is what they are most familiar with. The appropriateness of such research topics is open for discussion, but will not be discussed here. Suffice it to say that if such topics are selected, the international adult learner must be instructed that not everything will be found under the name of their country in the online catalog and that country names can also be used as subheadings; e.g., Art and Education–Mexico.[22] Teaching the intricacies of database searching can be a particularly difficult issue as it may involve explaining concepts with which the international adult learner is unfamiliar. While free text and natural language searching have ameliorated this to some degree, the use of Boolean operators or the unfamiliar hierarchical approach to LCSH subject headings can be still be challenging. The use of synonyms should also be encouraged as should thesauri. Meeting functional issues with international adult learners are among the more intensive activities in which they can be engaged, but among the most rewarding for all parties involved.

## DETERMINING THE NEEDS
## OF INTERNATIONAL ADULT LEARNERS

Meeting the institutional and situational issues of international adult learners is still essentially a reactive process. In order to best serve this unique user group, their perceived and real needs need to be determined and met proactively. To date, libraries have done little to systematically ascertain what are the needs of international adult learners. Perceived needs could include the more obvious ones, such as overcoming cultural-linguistic barriers and unfamiliarity with library services. Real needs are less obvious to both the librarian and the international adult learner, but could include issues of time management or even overcoming presumed but erroneous competency in information seeking skills.

Determining such needs can be accomplished through a variety of means, but is frequently done via a needs survey or through focus groups. Either approach can cover a number of areas. A survey at Arizona State University-West (ASU-W) found, among other things, that international learners felt pressed for time when they came to the library though they did not indicate they were under any greater stress than traditional students. At the same time, although many of the respondents owned a computer and a modem, few used it to search the library catalog from home in order to save time, even though they are highly motivated to do so.[23] A good instrument, such as was used at ASU-W, will get respondents to go beyond perceived needs and reveal real needs. Another approach is focus groups. Although not limited to international adult users, a focus group at SUNY-Oswego found many expressed feelings of intimidation in their attempts to utilize library technology such as CD ROM databases and the new OPAC even though many were comfortable with computers. Discovery of real needs often make new demands on staff time and require rethinking former patterns of service provision.[24]

Surveys, interviews, and focus groups are among the ways in which needs can be determined. Once such data are gathered and analyzed, librarians need to develop appropriate cost/effective measures to address these matters. The possibilities are as limitless as the needs and might include: specialized reference, or instruction involving small groups, native language user instruction, or peer based assistance as was suggested by international learners in a University of Hawaii study.[25] Alternative means of delivering reference services and sources, such as through the WWW may need to be considered too, as should reference consultations at off hours.

## PROGRAMMING OPPORTUNITIES
## FOR INTERNATIONAL ADULT LEARNERS

Whether studies of international adult learners' needs are undertaken or not, there are numerous programming opportunities which can be targeted for this group of users. Such activities can focus on improving their skills and efficiency as well as confidence in accessing and utilizing information. These needs can be met with workshops on different topics arranged to meet the time schedules of international adult users in late afternoons, early evenings, or Saturday mornings. Such workshops can focus on overcoming library anxiety as well as improving information seeking and utilization skills. These users can also be taught how to use their research time more efficiently. Emphasizing things which can be done away from the library such as topic selection, search strategy creation, remote searching, phone/e-mail reference, and access of WWW-based resources should be emphasized.[26] Other specific time needs might be met by programs which provide rapid document delivery service or a photocopy service, which would pull and copy for a nominal fee. Extended library hours are another possibility. Some research indicates international adult learners are studying more hours per week than traditional learners. But, it is unclear if they are less efficient in the use of their time, taking longer to comprehend the material, or really are more diligent.[27] Any library would have to consider the cost and benefits of providing such programming before undertaking such a venture.

## INSTRUCTING INTERNATIONAL ADULT LEARNERS TO BECOME INFORMATION LITERATE

Instruction is a function which needs to be addressed apart from programming. What international adult learners do not need is the traditional dose of library instruction. Their time constraints and focused objectives, combined with the immediate nature of their research questions make the case for more immediate instruction. International adult learners prefer to receive instruction at both point of need and point of use rather than commit additional time to an extra class on the library. Such reference and instructional exchanges should remain brief and relevant enough to convey what is needed, but not overload the international adult learner.[28] As Nicholas G. Tomaiuolo suggests, "Err on the side of providing less information . . . the patron can always come back and ask for more." He adds, "having once considered this axiom antithetical to good library service, I now realize that to provide more information than is necessary, particularly with respect to reentry students is gratuitous pedantics."[29]

## ANDRAGOGY AND INTERNATIONAL ADULT LEARNERS

Although less may be seen as more, such an abbreviated approach to instruction is insufficient. There are some notable education philosophical underpinnings, notably andragogy, to consider in developing instruction for international adult learners. Andragogy derives from the Greek, "andros" meaning grown up or adult, and "agogoos," meaning one who leads.[30] Andragogy seeks to help the adult become competent and is based on adult-to-adult relationships. It is predicated on four assumptions: growth–the learner seeks to move from dependency to autonomy/self direction; cumulative life experience or knowledge is its own resource; the individual's social role is the principle motivation in seeking further education; and learning is centered on problem solving rather than being subject centered.[31] Malcolm Knowles, a leader in the field of adult learning puts it more succinctly. He says adult learning falls into four categories: "what people want to gain, hope to be, wish to do, and want to save."[32] Andragogical library user education for international adult learners is collaborative. It seeks the active participation of the international adult learner and works to overcome hesitancies they may have about becoming involved. As they become involved in the learning process, the learners are provided with feedback which supports them and works to reinforce basic skills. As these are mastered, more complex matters are addressed. All of this works together to equip the learner to apply new knowledge and skills beyond the immediate library environment and to develop them for life-long learning.

There are numerous approaches to library andragogy for international adult learners which the librarian can employ. First, librarians need to acknowledge and affirm the rich experiential knowledge international adult learners bring with them, especially the differences they present from the typical library user. Moreover affective issues such as stress and anxiety about using the library need to be addressed before learning can occur.[33] In group settings a pre-test can be an effective tool for both the librarian and the learners in determining what is already known and not known in order to demonstrate need for instruction. The results of such an exercise can be insightful. In a University of Evansville class of thirty-one adult college students, for example, none scored above sixty percent and a majority of the class was below forty percent. Pre-tests are effective tools in helping learners realize the practical application of user education.[34]

## OTHER LEARNING TOOLS
## FOR INTERNATIONAL ADULT LEARNERS

There are other tools which can assist these learners. Handouts are important for international adult learners as they can be referred to for future reference. This is particularly significant as a common complaint among international learners is that they cannot understand what is said during library orientation tours and they are often reluctant to ask for help. Handouts should summarize major points and might also include a glossary of terms, a map of the library, or whatever else seems appropriate. Another teaching tool is analogy. Analogies are important as they help link ideas together and help learners to grasp concepts of increasing complexity. On the other hand, while humor can be engaging and effective in illustrating a point, it does not always translate well, especially when norms and idioms are involved. Puns in particularly are lost on non-native speakers. However, humor based on exaggeration or universal human attributes may be effective if used sparingly.[35]

Native language and/or peer-based instruction may also be appropriate. While research indicates international learners are just as likely to ask a peer as a librarian a question, most find instruction in their own language more effective than in English. However, with native language instruction, there are other philosophical issues at stake. Some librarians and educators main-tain that the overriding objective of library instruction should be to get inter-national adult learners functioning in English as much as possible and that polyglot library instruction and reference should be eschewed. While this essay is hardly the forum for such a discussion, it is an issue libraries will need to address based on their educational philosophy and the needs of users.[36]

## PARTNERING WITH OTHER ORGANIZATIONS TO ASSIST INTERNATIONAL ADULT LEARNERS

While there are a number of ways in which libraries may interact directly with international adult learners, it is important to remember they exist in a broader context–as do libraries. Collaborating with other community agencies and organizations which also interact with international adult learners is an important way of providing a stronger support system for them and integrating the library further in their lives. In addition, partnering with corporations, public institutions, public schools, or campus advisors and organizations could provide other means of supporting programming such as access to computers and other technology. Interaction with other agencies and organizations also assists libraries in identifying international adult learners. Once they are identi-fied, library services can be promoted through mailing, flyers, posters, list-serves, and word of mouth. Some libraries find it useful to have one staff member devoted to such activities as it makes that person instantly recogniz-able to international adult learners and others. Meanwhile other libraries rely on a committee for activities. No one approach is clearly superior over another, whatever methods are used; networking with adult international learners and outside organizations will help the library to become a recognizable entity for information seeking international adult learners in a broader context.

## STAFF TRAINING ISSUES

David Carr notes that, "however important the information given" to international adult learners, "it is no more important than the quality of the giving."[37] Improving the quality of that giving can be addressed through developing staff awareness and training. Recognizing and understanding the unique needs of this special class of users is essential to the success of any program involved with these learners. Library personnel need to know how to interact in ways which are both positive and effective. A particularly important element of such training is helping staff overcome stereotyping, which places a person in "a category that singles out an individual as sharing assumed characteristics as the basis of this group membership."[38] As a result, staff react to the stereotype rather than the individual which is inherently unfair for both parties involved.[39] Indeed some have opined that "some patrons may be difficult as individuals for which their cultural group is not to blame."[40] However droll this comment may be, it does underscore an important point in helping staff to overcome pre-judging and be equipped to treat each user as an individual and not as a member of a particular class.

There are numerous options for staff training. A needs assessment will aid in determining the nature of the training to be provided. Once needs are determined, goals and objectives for staff training should be established. Such goals might include learning to differentiate between culture and individual behavior; heightening sensitivity to problems facing internationals; or learning to communicate more effectively with them.[41] The University of Arizona conducted such workshops with the goals of having participants experience some of the pressures inherent in trying to understand concepts and words in a second language, feel some of the emotions of culture shock, be aware of their own cultural assumptions and interpretations, and effectively handle inter-cultural communication.[42] Videotape presentations, cross cultural simulations, as well as lectures on cross cultural differences can be used in facilitating such workshops.[43]

In particular, there are certain tools with which staff can be equipped at such training sessions to enhance interactions with international adult learners. *Seeking feedback;* feedback assures that the listener is receiving the message clearly. A survey of University of Pittsburgh international students found one of the things librarians could do to improve communication was to "ask frequently for the person to explain what you have told them to incur they understand, and are not simply agreeing to be polite."[44] *Code switching;* adjusting language to accommodate the needs of listeners, this includes avoidance of slang, careful definition of terms and use of repetition. [45] *Foreign speakers,* again this is a philosophical issue, but some libraries prefer to maintain a list of foreign language speaking staff at public service points who can assist international adult learners in their native tongue. Skits which demonstrate these tools and other issues are an effective way of conveying ideas in a workshop. These and all training activities should seek to impart theory and application. In so doing, staff will be better able to serve and understand international adult learners.

## CONCLUSION

To conclude, there are infinite ways of assisting international adult learners. But, as Carr observes, "We will never find a more important form of life-transforming help than the simplest communicative acts between librarians and learners in the library."[46] These communicative acts, however, are not always easily accomplished. Librarians need to be aware of the diverse users seeking to utilize their sources and services. International adult users, for example, present special opportunities for enhancing a variety of public services, as well as instruction and programming. Beyond this, they also provide an entree for the library to extend itself further in to its community and develop its own personnel. In so doing, a richer tapestry is woven which not only benefits this special class of users, but the community and the library as well.

## REFERENCES

1. Thomas Snyder, Charlene M. Hoffman, and Claire M. Geddes, *Digest of Education Statistics* 1997 (Washington DC: US Department of Education Office of Educational Research and Improvement, 1997): 214-220; *Projections of Education Statistics to 2006,* 25th ed. (Washington DC: US Department of Education Office of Educational Research and Improvement, 1996): 29-31.

2. Technically, such a definition could include those using the library to learn English as a second language, though such an endeavor is beyond the scope of this paper.

3. Betsy Hine, Janet Meek, and Ruth Miller, "Bibliographic Instruction for the Adult Student in an Academic Library, *Continuing Higher Education* 37 (Spring 1989): 20; Carol Hammond, "Nontraditional Students and the Library: Opinions, Preferences and Behaviors, *College and Research Libraries* 55 (July 1994): 323-324.

4. Brian H. Nordstrom, "Non-Traditional Students in Transition," 1989, ED 310686, p. 16.

5. Eric Iovacchini, Linda M. Hall and Dennis D. Hengstler, "Going Back to College: Some Differences Between Adult Students and Traditional Students," *College and University* 60 (Spring 1985): 44, 52; Michael Hu, "Determining the Needs and Attitudes of Non-traditional Students," *College and University* 60 (Spring 1985): 204; Jean Sheridan, "Andragogy: A New Concept for Academic Librarians," *Research Strategies* 4 (Fall 1986): 156-67; Andrea Wyman, "Working with Nontraditional Students in the Academic Library," *Journal of Academic Librarianship* 14 (March 1988): 32; Hammond, "Nontraditional Students and the Library: Opinions, Preferences, and Behaviors," pp. 328-329; Mary Genevieve Lewis, "Library Orientation and Asian College Students," *College and Research Libraries* 30 (May 1969): 267-72.

6. Dania M. Bilal, "International Students' Acquisition of Library Research Skills: Relationship with their English Language Proficiency," *Reference Librarian* 24 (1988): 143.

7. Iovacchini, Hall, and Hengstler, "Going Back to College," 53; Nancy Moeckel and Jenny Presnell, "Recognizing, Understanding, and Responding: A Program Model of Library Services for International Students," *Reference Librarian* 51/52 (1995): 309-319.

8. Mary Alice Ball and Molly Mahoney, "Foreign Students, Libraries, and Culture," *College and Research Libraries* 48 (March 1987): 161.

9. Frank W. Goudy and Eugene Moushey, "Library Instruction and Foreign Students: A Survey of Opinions and Practices Among Selected Libraries," *Reference Librarian* 10 (Spring/Summer 1984): 217.

10. Darlene Mckenzie, "Survey of Library and Information Needs of the International Students at Kent State University," May 1995, ED 390 410, pp. 27-29; Irene Hoffman and Opritsa Popa, "Library Orientation: Instruction for International Students: The University of California-Davis Experience," *RQ* 25 (Spring 1986): 358; Mary Beth Allen, "International Students in Academic Libraries: A User Survey," *College and Research Libraries,* 54 (July 1993): 330; Moeckel and Presnell, "Recognizing, Understanding, and Responding," p. 312; Hammond, "Nontraditional Students and the Library," p. 329; Charolette E. Simon, Information Retrieval Techniques: The Differences in Cognitive Strategies and Search Behaviors among Graduate Students in an Academic Library, Ph.D. diss., Wayne State University, 1995, 86.

11. Hoffman and Popa, "Library Orientation: Instruction for International Students," p. 358; Zimming Liu, "Difficulties and Characteristics of Students from Developing Countries in Using American Libraries," *College and Research Libraries* 54 (January 1993): 27; Allen, "International Students in Academic Libraries: A User Survey," p. 330; Moeckel and Presnell, "Recognizing, Understanding, and Responding: A Program Model of Library Services for International Students," p. 312.

12. Sally Wayman, "The International Student in the Academic Library," *Journal of Academic Librarianship 9* (January 1984): 338-339.

13. Moeckel and Presnell, "Recognizing, Understanding, and Responding," pp. 310-311.

14. Cynthia Mae Helms, "Reaching Out to the International Students Through Bibliographic Instruction," *Reference Librarian* 51/52 (1995): 297; Kwasi Sarkodie-Mensah, "In the Words of a Foreigner," *Research Strategies* 4 (Winter 1986): 31.

15. Yoshi Hendricks, "The Japanese as Library Patrons," *College and Research Libraries News* 52 (April 1991): 224.

16. Louise Greenfield, Susan Johnston, and Karen Williams, "Educating the World: Training Library Staff to Communicate Effectively with International Students," *Journal of Academic Librarianship* 12 (September 1986): 227-331.

17. Jacobson, "Bibliographic Instruction and International Students," p. 629.

18. Gina Macdonald and Elizabeth Sarkodie-Mensah, "ESL Students and American Libraries," *College and Research Libraries,* 49 (September 1988): 427-8.

19. Hendricks, "The Japanese as Library Patrons," 222.

20. Wayman, "The International Student in the Academic Library," p. 337.

21. Tesfai Kflu and Mary A. Loomba, "Academic Libraries and the Culturally Diverse Student Population," *College and Research Libraries News* 51 (June 1990): 527; Wayman, "The International Student in the Academic Library," p. 337; Moeckel and Presnell, "Recognizing, Understanding, and Responding: A Program Model of Library Services for International Students," p. 312; Ball and Mahoney, "Foreign Students, Libraries, and Culture," 164.

22. Barbara Brock, "Library Skills for International Students: From Theory to Practice." in *Bibliographic Instruction and the Learning Process: Theory Style and Motivation,* Carolyn Kirkendall, ed. (Ann Arbor: University of Michigan, 1984): 111-117; Wayman, "The International Student in the Academic Library," p. 339.

23. Hammond, "Nontraditional Students and the Library: Opinions, Preferences and Behaviors." pp. 328-329.

24. Nancy Seale Osborne and Cecilia Poon, "Serving Diverse Library Populations Through Specialized Instructional Services Concept," *Reference Librarian* 51/52 (1995): 289-290; John M. Budd and David G. Robinson, "Enrollment and the Future of Academic Libraries," *Library Journal* 111 (Sept. 15, 1986): 45.

25. Lewis, "Library Orientation and Asian College Students," p. 270.

26. Susan Swords Steffen, "Designing Bibliographic Instruction Programs for Adult Students: The Schaffer Library Experience," *Illinois Libraries* 70 (December 1988): 645.

27. Iovacchini, Hall, and Hengstler, "Going Back to College," p. 54.

28. Nicholas G. Tomaiuolo, "Reconsidering Bibliographic Instruction for Adult Reentry Students: Emphasizing the Practical," *Reference Services Review* (Spring 1990): 49-54; Hammond, "Nontraditional Students and the Library," pp. 334-336.

29. Nicholas G. Tomaiuolo, "Reconsidering Bibliographic Instruction for Adult Reentry Students: Emphasizing the Practical," *References Services Review* (Spring 1990): 50. Lori M. Keenan, "Andragogy Off-Campus: The Library's Role," *Reference Librarian* 24 (1988): 147.

30. Lori M. Keenan, "Andragogy Off-Campus: The Library's Role," *Reference Librarian* 24 (1988): 147.

31. Sheridan, "Andragogy: A New Concept for Academic Librarians," p. 159; Keenan, "Andragogy Off-Campus: The Library's Role," p. 149; Robert Carlson, "The Time of Andragogy," *Adult Education* 30 (Fall 1979): 53.

32. Malcolm Knowles, *Modern Practice of Adult Education: From Pedagogy to Andragogy* (New York: Cambridge University Press, 1980) in Sheridan, "Andragogy: A New Concept for Academic Librarians," p. 158.

33. Sheridan, "Andragogy: A New Concept for Academic Librarians," pp. 162-164.

34. Hine, Meek, and Miller, "Bibliographic Instruction for the Adult Student in an Academic Library," pp. 20-21.

35. Macdonald and Sarkodie-Mensah, "ESL Students and American Libraries," p. 429.

36. Liu, "Difficulties and Characteristics of Students from Developing Countries in Using American Libraries," p. 27; Manuel D. Lopez, "Chinese Spoken Here: Foreign Language Library Orientation Tours," *College and Research Libraries News* 44 (September 1983): 268; Johnnye Cope and Evelyn Black, "New Library Orientation for International Students, *College Teaching* 33 (Fall 1985): 160-1; Daniel Liestman and Connie Wu, "Library Orientation for International Students in their Native Language," *Research Strategies* 8 (Fall 1990): 191-196; Allen Natowitz, "International Students in U.S. Academic Libraries: Recent Trends and Concerns," *Research Strategies* 13 (Winter 1995): 9.

37. David Carr, "The Meanings of the Adult Independent Library Learning Project," *Library Trends* 35 (Fall 1986): 332.

38. J.W. VanderZanden, *American Minority Relations: The Sociology of Racial and Ethnic Groups* (New York: Ronald, 1966): in Ball and Mahoney, "Foreign Students, Libraries, and Culture," p. 164.

39. Nelson R. Cauthen, I.E. Robinson, and H.H. Kraus, "Stereotypes: A Review of the Literature," *Journal of Social Psychology* 84: 104 (June 1971): in Ball and Mahoney, "Foreign Students, Libraries, and Culture," p. 164.

40. Ball and Mahoney, "Foreign Students, Libraries, and Culture," p. 164.

41. Ball and Mahoney, "Foreign Students, Libraries, and Culture," pp. 163-5.

42. Greenfield, Johnston, and Williams, "Educating the World: Training Library Staff to Communicate Effectively with International Students," p. 228.

43. Hoffman and Popa, "Library Orientation: Instruction for International Students," p. 357.

44. Colette Wagner and Augusta S. Kappner, "The Academic Library and the Non-traditional Student," Proceedings of the Arden House Symposium, New York, NY, March 15-17, 1987. ED 284589.

45. Macdonald and Sarkodie-Mensah, "ESL Students and America Libraries," pp. 425-31; Natowitz, "International Students in U.S. Academic Libraries," p. 7.

46. Carr, "The Meanings of the Adult Independent Library Learning Project," p. 341.

# SECTION 7:
# FROM THE HORSE'S MOUTH:
# VIEWS FROM FACULTY,
# ADMINISTRATORS,
# LIBRARIANS, AND STUDENTS

# Faculty Expectations and the Adult Learner: Some Implications for Reference

## Barbara Mullins
## Betsy Park

**SUMMARY.** In addition to the normal difficulties encountered when returning to the academic environment, adult students are expected to use a library that may be very different from the one they have used earlier. While some teaching faculty recognize that these students may need additional help to effectively use the library, others do not. This study investigated faculty expectations for adult students and the academic library. The majority of faculty surveyed believe students need instruction to develop familiarity with library resources and technology. Furthermore, the faculty are willing to work with librarians to ensure students gain these skills. *[Article copies available for a fee from The Haworth Document Delivery Service: 1-800-342-9678. E-mail address: <getinfo @haworthpressinc.com> Website: <http://www.haworthpressinc.com>]*

**KEYWORDS.** Academic libraries, adult students, faculty expectations, college and university libraries–services to adults, college and university libraries–relations with faculty and curriculum

## *INTRODUCTION*

Enrollment trends in the United States indicate that the number of students over the age of 25 in higher education increased from 5.2 million in 1988 to

Barbara Mullins is Assistant Professor, Department of Leadership, University of Memphis (E-mail: mullins.barbara@coe.memphis.edu). Betsy Park is Associate Professor, University Libraries, Reference Department, University of Memphis, Memphis, TN 38152 (E-mail: ehpark@memphis.edu).

[Haworth co-indexing entry note]: "Faculty Expectations and the Adult Learner: Some Implications for Reference." Mullins, Barbara, and Betsy Park. Co-published simultaneously in *The Reference Librarian* (The Haworth Information Press, an imprint of The Haworth Press, Inc.) No. 69/70, 2000, pp. 381-393; and: *Reference Services for the Adult Learner: Challenging Issues for the Traditional and Technological Era* (ed: Kwasi Sarkodie-Mensah) The Haworth Information Press, an imprint of The Haworth Press, Inc., 2000, pp. 381-393. Single or multiple copies of this article are available for a fee from The Haworth Document Delivery Service [1-800-342-9678, 9:00 a.m. - 5:00 p.m. (EST). E-mail address: getinfo@haworthpressinc. com].

6.24 million in 1996–an increase of over 20% (National Center for Educational Statistics, 1998). The College Board (1998) reports that students over the age of 25 make up half of all college enrollments in the U.S. In a survey of adults who had returned to undergraduate and graduate programs, the College Board (1998) found:

- The single most important reason for returning to college relates to the adult's job or career. Adults want new competencies to enter, change or advance their careers.
- There is a trigger life event (divorce, loss of job, children leaving the household) that prompts the return to school.
- Seventy percent of adults are seeking a degree.
- The typical adult student is employed full time.

The University of Memphis, located in an urban setting, has close to 20,000 students of whom 46% are over the age of 25 (Fall 1997 statistics). Returning students typically face the normal difficulties encountered when returning to the academic environment, including the admission process, registering for classes, and preparing class assignments. In addition, many adult students are returning to school with previous library experience in print, rather than electronic, resources. Faculty themselves are often unfamiliar with the new technologies. An understanding of the faculty, their relations with students, and the library will help promote effective library use for these students.

## LITERATURE REVIEW

### Adult Learners

Two areas of literature inform this study, adult learners and faculty/student use of library resources. Andragogy has been alternately described as theory, practical guidelines, and simply assumptions about adult learners (Knowles, 1980; Elias, 1979; Cross, 1981; Brookfield, 1986). Andragogy identifies four characteristics of adult learners: (1) adults wish to be self-directed; (2) adults bring life experiences to the classroom; (3) adults want information that is practical; and (4) adults want to be able to use that information immediately (Knowles, 1980). Additional research on andragogy (Flannery, 1994; Caffarella, 1992; Belenky, Clinchy, Goldberg, and Tarule, 1986) has raised questions about the universality of self-directed learning, particularly in women and minorities. Some research (Grow, 1991) suggests that the characteristic of being self-directed is not an all or nothing concept. Instead it appears in stages among students. At stage 1 students are at a low level of self-direction and need an authority figure to tell them what to do. At stage 4 learners have a high level of self-direction and are both willing and able to plan, execute and evaluate their own learning with or without the help of an expert. Thus, it would be a mistake to assume that all adult students are at the higher stage.

### Faculty and Student Library Use

To date there has been no study of adult students and what faculty expect of them in the library. There have, however, been studies which explore faculty and student library use in general. Students use the library as a function of faculty expectations, assignments and recommendations. Baker's (1997) research of community college faculty indicated that faculty value library use as it relates to a particular discipline and design library assignments to promote student familiarity with the literature of a specific discipline. Sellen and Jirouch (1984) surveyed faculty and students to find that faculty expectations of student library use differed from the students' perceptions of their actual library use. When left on their own, students made very little use of library resources and only did so when there was direct external direction and motivation, usually from faculty and librarians.

Other studies investigate the faculty's perception of their role in ensuring that students have the necessary skills to use a library. Thomas (1984) asked teaching faculty to describe how their students learned to use the library. Approximately one-third of these reported that students consult individually with a librarian, while another third said students developed these skills on their own. When this study was repeated 10 years later, the figures were similar with 28.3% choosing "informal consultation" and 28.3% choosing "on their own" (Thomas, 1994). Amstutz and Whitson (1997) investigated faculty use of new technologies and found that faculty most heavily engaged in research used electronic resources and considered these to be important resources for students. Over half of these respondents placed the responsibility for developing these skills on the students themselves.

Many faculty assume that students will ask questions and learn to use the library on their own. Mellon (1989) quotes faculty, "Why don't the students tell us they don't know how to use the library?" She notes, however, that non-traditional students may be ashamed of their inability to use the library and try to conceal this fact (p. 78). Burrell et al. (1997) surveyed professors who taught core classes at the University of Georgia and found that the majority of professors expected students to ask questions. Only one-third believed students do not ask questions when they are lost. Many professors in this study reported that they do not assign library research because many students have trouble doing research. This decision could be related to what Baker (1997) describes as a perception among faculty that they lack support in helping students with poor writing and study skills in the context of the library assignment. Miritello (1996) found that assumptions of freshman writing students do not fit returning adults. On the surface students appear confident, while underneath many feel uncertain. She, like those in Burrell's group, found that many students are hesitant to seek assistance and have difficulty identifying precisely what it is they are struggling with.

Research on adult learners is not necessarily common knowledge among faculty. Galerstein and Chandler (1982) surveyed faculty at the University of Texas at Dallas and concluded that the best way to handle adult students is to treat them the same way as everyone else in the classroom. They emphasize that adult students must be recognized as a heterogeneous group. Good faculty, they believe, are sensitive to the individuality of all their students regardless of age. Kasworm (1990) found that community college faculty perceived the commitment to completing educational goals to be more tenuous among their students than did 4-year college faculty. In addition there was a clear perception among faculty at both types of institutions that women students have more difficulty completing their educational goals than do male students.

### Characteristics That Lead to Success

Other studies investigated what faculty believed were student characteristics and circumstances that led to success in adult learners. Tesch (1984) categorized these as the ability to be organized, to think clearly, abstractly, logically, and to be intellectually curious. Students who were self-directed and able to use resources usually fared better, as did those who were professionally competent.

Groves and Groves (1980) surveyed faculty at a state university and found that faculty perceived adult students to be highly motivated; to have well focused career goals; to participate actively in class; to be open to new ideas; to relate comfortably to younger students; and to be conscientious regarding completing assignments.

Faculty surveyed by Burrell et al. (1997) believed characteristics that lead to success included the ability to write and think beyond memorization or reporting of facts. They wanted students who could analyze, synthesize, problem-solve, apply, argue persuasively, and critique. Students who were self-motivated, committed to scholarship and independent learners were more likely to be successful.

In a library context Wagner (1988) notes that students who experience the highest degree of success are articulate, at ease in the library, have the self-confidence to approach a librarian, ask questions, reveal their information need, and follow directions (pp. 47-48). For example, the success of the reference interview depends on the interaction between the librarian and the student and is most successful with students with these characteristics.

There is still a good deal to learn about the interaction of faculty, adult students, and the library. Because faculty have sustained contact with these students, they are an important channel of communication for students and librarians alike. An understanding of this relationship will help reference librarians better collaborate with faculty to help adult students.

## METHODOLOGY

A survey containing 50 items was developed based on a review of the scholarly literature. The survey was pilot tested during the 1998 summer session. It was intended to be used as an exploratory tool to investigate trends that could be addressed in a larger study. Four-hundred-seventeen surveys were distributed to faculty teaching courses during the summer session; 57 responses were returned for a return rate of 13%. The largest number (42.1%) of returned surveys came from full professors. Of the faculty who responded, 19.3% teach undergraduate students, 14% teach graduate students, and 59% teach both levels.

Questions on the Likert-scaled survey were grouped into five topical areas: (1) students' ability to conduct library research; (2) factors affecting student use of the library; (3) beliefs about adults students and technology, (4) ways faculty believe students should learn to conduct library research; and (5) perceptions of characteristics of adult students. Responses ranged from 1, "strongly disagree" to 5, "strongly agree." Faculty were also encouraged to write open-ended comments. The data were analyzed by frequency distribution to obtain a preliminary indication of trends. For the purposes of discussion, responses "strongly agree" and "agree" were grouped together as were "strongly disagree" and "disagree." A Pearson correlation was used to examine relationships between faculty perceptions of characteristics of adult students and of adult students' use of library resources. Finally, a content analysis was conducted to identify patterns and themes in the open-ended comments.

## FINDINGS AND DISCUSSION

Figure 1 lists in order of popularity, the library resources that faculty expect students to use. It was surprising that so many faculty send students to use the Internet, because there are only a few terminals in the library with Internet access.

One set of questions asked about faculty perceptions of students' ability to conduct library research for their assignments. Less than half agreed with the

FIGURE 1. Resources Students Are Expected to Use

|  | % |
| --- | --- |
| Discipline specific reference books | 77.2 |
| Internet | 71.9 |
| Card catalog, indexes, bibliographies | 66.7 |
| General reference books | 64.9 |
| Computer databases | 59.6 |
| Reserve readings | 50.9 |
| Readings not on reserve | 47.4 |

following statements: Students' ability to conduct research was adequate; students were familiar with a variety of resources; students used a variety of resources; students had adequate experience for library research; and students were knowledgeable about library technology. Faculty in general recognize that students do not make full use of the library and its resources (see also Baker, 1997; Sellen and Jirouch, 1997). However, 71.1% believed that adult students had enough time to conduct research for assignments and therefore did not consider time as a factor inhibiting student research (Figure 2).

Another set of questions explored factors that faculty perceived to affect student use of the library (Figure 3). Parking was identified as a problem by 64.8% and library resources by 51.9% of respondents. Library resources are a continual problem, one that has been exacerbated by recent budget cuts. Parking may be beyond the direct control of the library. However, its importance should not be overlooked, since it is an issue for adult students who attend part-time and use the library in the evenings. Students are inconvenienced by long walks and may have legitimate concerns for safety at night.

The next questions focused on adult students and technology. Faculty agreed that students needed instruction on library computers (84.3%), with 67.9% believing that students would ask for help. This perception contrasts with the literature that students do not ask for help (Burrell et al., 1997; Miritello, 1996). Faculty were somewhat mixed in their reactions to questions about students' comfort, knowledge, anxiety, and use of computers, but their responses tended to indicate they felt students had prior computer experience, albeit not computers in the library (Figure 4). The faculty perception contrasts with anecdotal evidence from public service staff at the University who indicate that many students are, at least initially, uncomfortable with the computers in general.

FIGURE 2. Adult Students' Ability to Conduct Library Research

|  | % Agree | % Disagree | % No Opinion | Valid Sample Number |
|---|---|---|---|---|
| Adequate | 37.8 | 56.6 | 5.7 | 53 |
| Familiar with resources | 24.6 | 64.1 | 11.3 | 53 |
| Use variety of resources | 32.1 | 54.7 | 13.2 | 53 |
| Adequate time | 71.7 | 18.9 | 9.4 | 53 |
| Understand library terminology | 61.2 | 16.7 | 22.2 | 54 |
| Adequate experience for library research | 16.7 | 66.7 | 16.7 | 54 |
| Knowledgeable about library technology | 20.8 | 58.5 | 20.8 | 53 |

FIGURE 3. Factors Affecting Adult Students' Use of the Library

|  | % Agree | % Disagree | % No Opinion | Valid Sample Number |
|---|---|---|---|---|
| Convenient library hours | 63.0 | 27.8 | 9.3 | 54 |
| Resources appropriate to need | 42.6 | 51.9 | 5.6 | 54 |
| Convenient library parking | 11.1 | 64.8 | 24.1 | 54 |
| Affordable cost of copies | 46.3 | 20.4 | 33.3 | 54 |
| Convenient interlibrary loan process | 61.1 | 20.4 | 18.5 | 54 |

The next set of questions asked faculty how they believed students should learn to conduct library research (Figure 5). Only 7.1% thought students already had the necessary skills. Overwhelmingly the majority of faculty reported that the responsibility for instructing students in the library should be shared by faculty and librarians. Almost 60% agreed that students should attend a formal class lecture conducted by a librarian and the same number agreed that students should attend a required course taught by the faculty members' department. When asked how students should learn research skills, only 22.3% reported that students should develop skills independently. However, exactly how they should learn was not limited to a single option.

The final section of the survey asked faculty to rank various characteristics

FIGURE 4. Adult Students and Library Technology

| | % Agree | % Disagree | % No Opinion | Valid Sample Number |
|---|---|---|---|---|
| Comfortable using computers | 46.1 | 36.5 | 17.3 | 52 |
| Knowledgeable about computers | 38.4 | 40.4 | 21.2 | 52 |
| Ask for help | 67.9 | 17.0 | 15.1 | 53 |
| Anxious about using computers | 32.1 | 50.9 | 17.0 | 53 |
| Do not use computers | 13.5 | 52.0 | 34.6 | 52 |
| Need computer instruction | 84.4 | 07.8 | 07.8 | 51 |

FIGURE 5. How Should Students Learn to Conduct Library Research?

| | % Agree | % Disagree | % No Opinion | Valid Sample Number |
|---|---|---|---|---|
| Already have requisite skills | 07.5 | 87.0 | 05.6 | 54 |
| Develop skills independently | 22.3 | 66.6 | 11.1 | 54 |
| Attend formal class lecture conducted by librarian | 59.3 | 24.1 | 16.7 | 54 |
| Attend required course taught by department | 59.3 | 29.6 | 11.1 | 54 |
| Attend required basic introductory course | 27.8 | 40.8 | 31.5 | 54 |
| Learn from faculty members | 81.5 | 13.0 | 05.6 | 54 |
| Learn from librarians | 81.5 | 14.9 | 03.7 | 54 |

of their adult students (Figure 6). Overall, faculty think highly of adult students. Almost 84% state that students are motivated and committed to completing their education. It is of interest, however, that over 20% of the faculty marked "no opinion" for a number of characteristics. The questions were developed following an extensive review of the literature and the characteristics represent those frequently mentioned in the literature of adult learners (Burrell et al., 1997; Groves and Groves, 1980; Tesch, 1984). Twenty percent of faculty selected "no opinion" to the question of the ability of students to grasp new theories, which suggests that faculty may not use theories in their instruction or faculty themselves are more practice oriented. Forty percent either had no opinion or disagreed when asked if they felt students were able

FIGURE 6. Characteristics of Adult Students

| | % Agree | % Disagree | % No Opinion | Valid Sample Number |
|---|---|---|---|---|
| Motivated and committed | 83.6 | 7.2 | 9.1 | 55 |
| Organized | 70.9 | 7.3 | 21.8 | 55 |
| Think clearly | 70.9 | 10.9 | 18.2 | 54 |
| Think abstractly | 61.1 | 7.4 | 31.5 | 55 |
| Intellectually curious | 65.5 | 14.5 | 20.0 | 53 |
| Professionally competent | 60.4 | 13.2 | 26.4 | 55 |
| Self-directed | 78.1 | 5.4 | 16.4 | 55 |
| Willing to ask for help | 70.9 | 14.5 | 14.5 | 55 |
| Accept constructive feedback | 65.5 | 14.5 | 20.0 | 55 |
| Accept responsibility for learning | 69.1 | 9.1 | 21.8 | 55 |
| Are practical, apply new knowledge | 74.5 | 7.3 | 18.2 | 55 |
| Grasp new theories | 67.3 | 9.1 | 23.6 | 55 |
| Able to concentrate on task at hand | 46.3 | 16.7 | 37.0 | 54 |
| Follow instructions | 38.2 | 27.3 | 34.5 | 55 |
| Turn in assignments on time | 63.1 | 12.3 | 21.1 | 55 |
| Self-starters, can work alone | 15.8 | 36.8 | 47.4 | 55 |
| Able to deal with obstacles | 76.4 | 7.3 | 16.4 | 55 |

to accept constructive feedback. Part of the reason faculty may have no opinion on this question is that their assessment techniques may be limited to multiple choice exams scored by machine. Interestingly, a full 35% believe that students feel that the responsibility for learning lies with someone other than themselves. Thirty-seven percent had no opinion on the question of students' ability to concentrate on tasks at hand without being distracted by personal life circumstances. One can speculate that the number of "no opinion" means that faculty really do not know these students very well or may be unfamiliar with the literature of the adult learner.

The Pearson correlation coefficient was used to assess associations between adult characteristics and other factors. Only correlation significant at the .05 level are discussed here. A number of library variables correlated significantly with characteristics of adult students. There was a positive relationship between statements that adult students have "enough time to complete library assignments" and adult students were "intellectually curious" ($r = .324$, $p = .018$) and "grasp new theories" ($r = .334$, $p = .014$). Students who are intellectually curious and able to grasp new theories tend to spend more time conducting research and visa versa. Since adult students frequently have additional commitments (family, work, or other), they may have less time to spend in the library. One author states that "non-traditional students come to the academic library and play a dangerous survival game in which time is the critical factor" (Wagner, 1988, p. 45). It is interesting to speculate on why faculty did not perceive time as a deterrent. Although no causality can be attributed, it may be that faculty who perceive adult students as being intellectually curious and able to grasp new theories also perceive them as being more able to budget their time for library research. On the other hand, it may be that faculty consciously or unconsciously give assignments that do not require much time in the library.

Students who have adequate experience using the library for research are more likely to be self-directed and able to work independently ($r = .271$, $p = .047$). They are also more likely to be able to concentrate on the task at hand without being distracted by personal life circumstances ($r = .355$, $p = .009$). This suggests that there may be a certain skill involved in putting aside, at least temporarily, family and work situations in order to focus on research.

There was a negative correlation between the statement that "library resources were appropriate for student needs" and four characteristics of adult students. The lower the level of agreement to the statement on appropriate library resources, the higher the level of agreement that students accept "responsibility for their own learning" ($r = -.273$, $p = .048$); are "willing to accept constructive feedback" ($r = -.293$, $p = .033$); are "practical and able to apply new knowledge" ($r = -.363$, $p = .007$); and are "able to deal with obstacles" ($r = -.280$, $p = .042$). The lack of appropriate resources at the library may be a motivating factor in getting students to be responsible for their own learning, to be resourceful, to locate needed resources elsewhere. Or it may be that the skills and abilities associated with an independent, self-directed learner are best revealed when the library does not have the appropriate resources. Conversely, when appropriate resources are available at the library, it may be that students look no further.

A common theme noted by faculty who responded in open-ended comments was the diversity among adult students. They hesitated to make statements about adults as a single, homogeneous, group. They noted the similarity of adult students to traditional age students in that both groups were highly diverse. Although the survey specified that the population of interest was students over the age of 25, a number of faculty seemed uncomfortable with that definition. Several respondents indicated that it was difficult to generalize about adult students and that they considered all students to be adult.

## CONCLUSIONS

What do the faculty tell us about adult students and the library? Faculty expect students to use the university library and emphasize resources in a subject discipline and use of the Internet. There is a very clear message that faculty recognize that students need instruction to develop familiarity with library resources and technology and want to work with librarians to ensure students gain these skills. Communication between faculty and librarians is important. Faculty influence and often determine students' use of an academic library. Librarians can make sure that faculty are fully aware of library services and programs for adult students so that these faculty can relate this information to the students. Teaching faculty are important channels of communication with all students about university services and particularly with adult students who may be on campus part-time and evenings.

Faculty perceive adult students to be a diverse group of individuals. Therefore, a number of different strategies should be available to teach research skills. There should be instruction available for those who are willing, able, and prefer to be self-directed. In addition, there should be instruction available for those who prefer to have a structured program led by a librarian or faculty member with expertise in research skills.

Of all the factors that affect student use of the library, parking was identified as number one. Although librarians have no direct control over campus parking, they may want to be members of campus-wide committees and lobby for better parking and/or better access to the library. They can also provide faculty and students with information on parking, directions to the library, information on safety patrols, and the like.

This number of "no opinion" responses of this study suggests that faculty are not aware of the literature of adult learners. This may also be true for librarians. Both groups might benefit from programs and workshops on the adult learner. Concerned faculty and librarians could work together to develop such programs.

This study was preliminary, but suggests several areas for future research. Studies might investigate perceptions of library use by students, faculty, and librarians and analyze the discrepancies between these perceptions. In addition, research could examine the roles and responsibilities of faculty and librarians in instruction to determine how many in each group feel equipped to instruct in the various areas. There is indication that faculty believe that students have adequate time to complete their library research assignments. Further research should investigate students' perception of time to determine if they indeed do have enough time. Then faculty and librarians could work to develop strategies to help students who feel time constraints. It may be that librarians could offer additional services such as individual consultation or research services that would benefit these students. Further research should be conducted on characteristics of adult students, faculty perceptions of how all these interact for success in the complex library/information environment we all now face. In doing so, collaboration between librarians and faculty is essential. Librarians cannot do this without the support of faculty and faculty cannot maximize the students' library experience without the support of library staff.

## REFERENCES

Amstutz, D. and D. Whitson. (1997) University faculty and information literacy: Who teaches the students? *Research Strategies 15 (1)*, 18-25.

Baker, R. (1997, May). Faculty perceptions towards student library use in a large urban community college. *The Journal of Academic Librarianship, 23*, 177-182.

Burrell, K., Tao, L., Simpson, M. and Mendez-Berrueta, H. (1997). How do we know what we are preparing our students for? A reality check of one university's academic literacy demands. *Research and Teaching in Developmental Education, 13 (2)*, 55-70.

Caffarella, R. (1992). *Psychosocial development of women: Linkages to teaching and leadership in adult education.* Information Series No. 350. ERIC Document Reproduction Services, ED 354 386.

College Board (1998). <www.collegeboard.org>

Flannery, D. (1994). Changing dominant understandings of adults as learners. *New Directions for Adult and Continuing Education, No. 61.* San Francisco: Jossey-Bass.

Galerstein, C. & Chandler, J. (1982). Faculty attitudes toward adult students. *Improving College and University Teaching, 30 (3)*, 133-137.

Groves, S. & Groves, D. (1980). The faculty's perception of the mature adult: A case study. *Alternative Higher Education, 5 (2)*, 106-111.

Grow, G.O. (1991). Teaching learners to be self-directed. *Adult Education Quarterly, 14 (3)*, 125-149.

Kasworm, C. (1990). Adult students in higher education: Myths and realities. *Community/Junior College, 14*, 155-175.

Knowles, M. (1980). *The modern practice of adult education: From pedagogy to andragogy.* (2nd. ed.). New York: Cambridge Press.

Lauber, J. (1995). *Adult returning students and their library needs.* Master's Thesis, Graduate School of Library and Information Science, Chapel Hill, North Carolina.

Mellon, C.A. (1989). Library anxiety and the non-traditional student. In T.B. Mensching (Ed.), *Reaching and teaching diverse user groups: 16th National LOEX Library Instruction Conference.* (pp. 77-81). Ann Arbor: Pierian Press.

Miritello, M. (1996). Teaching writing to adults: Examining assumptions and revising expectations for adult learners in the writing class. *Composition Chronicle, 9*, 6-9.

National Center for Educational Statistics (1998). <nces.ed.gov/pubs98/pj2008/p98c02.html.>

Sellen, M.K. and Jirouch, J. (1984, July). Perceptions of library use by faculty and students: A comparison. *College & Research Libraries, 45,* 259-266.

Tesch, R. (1984). *Adult learners as perceived by their faculty.* Paper presented at the Annual Meeting of the California Educational Research Association, Los Angeles, CA: November. ERIC Document Reproduction Service, ED 240 957.

Thomas, J. (1984, Summer). The university faculty and library instruction. *RQ, 23,* 431-437.

Thomas, J. (1994). Faculty attitudes and habits concerning library instruction: How much has changed since 1982? *Research Strategies, 12 (4),* 209-223.

Wagner, C.A. and Kappner, A.S. (1988). The academic library and the non-traditional student. In P.S. Breivik and R. Wedgeworth (Eds.), *Libraries and the search for academic excellence.* (pp. 43-57). Metuchen, NJ: Scarecrow Press.

# Providing Quality Library Service to the Adult Learner: Views of Students, Faculty, and Administrators

## Patience L. Simmonds

**SUMMARY.** The adult learner in the academic environment faces some unique problems and challenges. Balancing work, family, and a job are just a few examples. Technological changes in information retrieval and research, and in the use of the library can also magnify the adult learner's problems.

The study targets adult learners at Penn State Erie, The Behrend College. Focus groups and questionnaires are used to gather information from both active and non library users among the adult population: their views about the library environment, library resources, service, instruction, other traditional students, and staff. Perceptions about the adult learner are also obtained through face to face interviews with teaching faculty and administrators. Findings from the study will assist librarians to better understand the needs and expectations of the adult learner, and plan accordingly to meet these demands. *[Article copies available for a fee from The Haworth Document Delivery Service: 1-800-342- 9678. E-mail address: <getinfo@haworthpressinc.com> Website: <http://www. haworthpressinc.com>]*

**KEYWORDS.** Adult learners, academic libraries, quality service, Penn State Erie–The Behrend College, needs and expectations, faculty and administrators, perceptions and views, characteristics

Patience L. Simmonds is Assistant Librarian, Pennsylvania State University, Erie, The Behrend College: The Behrend College Library, Station Road, Erie, PA 16563 (E-mail: Pls@psulias.psu.edu).

[Haworth co-indexing entry note]: "Providing Quality Library Service to the Adult Learner: Views of Students, Faculty, and Administrators." Simmonds, Patience L. Co-published simultaneously in *The Reference Librarian* (The Haworth Information Press, an imprint of The Haworth Press, Inc.) No. 69/70, 2000, pp. 395-406; and: *Reference Services for the Adult Learner: Challenging Issues for the Traditional and Technological Era* (ed: Kwasi Sarkodie-Mensah) The Haworth Information Press, an imprint of The Haworth Press, Inc., 2000, pp. 395-406. Single or multiple copies of this article are available for a fee from The Haworth Document Delivery Service [1-800-342-9678, 9:00 a.m. - 5:00 p.m. (EST). E-mail address: getinfo@haworthpressinc.com].

The adult learner in the academic environment faces certain unique problems and challenges: balancing college, work, family, a job, and managing time in general are just a few examples. Technological changes in information retrieval and research, and in the use of library resources, can also magnify the adult learners' academic problems. The number of adult students seeking degrees in higher education has increased dramatically. Merriam and Caffarella attribute the influx of older students to higher education to demographic, economic, and technological development (see Merriam and Caffarella, 1991, chapter 1).[1] The adult learner is now a visible presence on campuses of many academic institutions.

If the predictions of educators come true, more and more colleges and universities will see more adult students in various programs in higher education. Different departments in academic institutions have programs that are aimed at helping adult students make smooth transitions into higher education. The academic library is no exception. Who is the adult learner, and what are some of the characteristics that differentiate him from the traditional 18-24 year old traditional college student? Scholars and librarians in higher education use certain terms to define and discuss adult students. Common among these labels are *"nontraditional students," "adult students," "adult learners," and "older adult students."* Many writers also define the *"adult"* learner in many different ways.

One of such definitions comes from Britton and Baxter: "They are more diverse than the younger students in their motivation, needs, expectation, and experiences of higher education" (Britton & Baxter, 1994).[2]

Most of the literature portrays the adult student as a 24 year old or older, who attends an academic institution part-time and has major life responsibilities in addition to the pursuit of education (Raven & Jimmerson).[3] Most adult learners have made a conscious and focused decision to seek post-secondary education. Despite certain societal obstacles, they still pursue their educational goals. Most adult learners know exactly what they want out of their college experience. They want to utilize their time optimally and complete their education, and do not have the time to fool around with issues not related to their educational pursuit.

From this author's observation, many adult learners make trips to their campuses only to attend classes, making infrequent trips to the library to study or complete assignments. Some adult learners do not use the library at all throughout their college careers.

## THE ADULT LEARNER IN THE LIBRARY: SOME CHARACTERISTICS

What is the relationship of the adult learner to the library? How does he perceive the library within the framework of his academic career? Adult learners have a history of varying degrees and levels of library use. Some adult learners have been out of school for so long that they have not yet learned how to use any of the new electronic resources. Instead of an online catalog, they expect to see a card catalog, and are thus overwhelmed by the numerous databases available. The new ways of searching, the immense capabilities of the systems, and the ability to connect to other resources can discourage them, and make them feel inadequate in the library. A general type of adult learner already knows the basic commands of the on-line catalog, but has to be introduced to the more complex techniques of finding periodical articles, searching print and electronic indexes and abstracts, and effectively researching materials on the Web. Another type of the adult learner is computer literate and knows how to use most of the library resources, especially those on the Web. However, he still needs to learn how to familiarize himself with the local catalog and the other databases. The final type of adult learner thinks that he knows everything about the library and does not need to know more. He refuses to utilize a library's resources and boasts about this lack of utilization. These different types of learners know when they get good service, and they expect good quality service from their library. "If customers say there is quality service, then there is. If they do not, there is not. It does not matter what an organization believes its level of service"(Hernon & Altman, p. 6).[4]

All students have certain expectations of their home library. They expect the library to provide the necessary resources and staff expertise necessary for them to complete their academic requirements. They expect the best quality of service from their library. All students believe that it is their academic right because they pay tuition and are affiliated with an academic institution, to get the best possible service from all departments particularly the library. When students do not receive the service they expect at their college/university library, they go elsewhere. Some will go through their college career not utilizing the libraries' resources, and therefore they do not achieve their full research potential. Some students show a marked dislike for the library and its staff and go throwing around typical expressions like *"this library stinks."* These students prefer the libraries of nearby academic institutions and refuse to use the resources of their own college/university library. What role does the library play in the academic life of the adult learner? What exactly do these adult learners think about their library? Amongst the number of students on college campuses, adult students though numerous, sometimes maintain a certain level of anonymity. They rarely mingle with the younger students and visit the library only when necessary. However, they impact the library in ways that differentiate them from the traditional students. Many adult learners are apologetic about the fact that they have been out of school for a long time and are therefore unfamiliar with the new technologies currently available. This study is undertaken with the notion that adult learners are important and that though they may at this time be a minority on the Behrend College campus, their needs and expectations are equally important to the library staff and therefore worth meeting. The study will seek the students out to find out exactly in their own words what they think about the library, its services, resources, quality service, staff, and what they expect the library to do about it. The views of faculty and administrators will also shed light on the needs and expectations of the adult learner.

## REVIEW OF THE LITERATURE

Higher education literature has covered in great detail, the subject of the nontraditional adult student in the academic environment, and has also dealt with various issues such as time management, stress and traditional/nontraditional programs which confront the *"nontraditional, older adult"* student. Spanard discusses in great detail, various issues, including *"adult students reentering college to complete their degrees,"* and factors which motivate adult learners to reenter college (Spanard, p. 321, 1990).[5] Richardson and King, in their article *"Adult Students in Higher Education: Burden or Boon?"* describe the influx of adult students into higher education and the impact of this change. They state that "in comparison with the 'traditional' student population, the body of adult students does include disproportionate numbers of women and members of ethnic minorities . . . " (Richardson & King, 1998).[6] The National Board of Employment Education and Training in its 1990 report states among other things "that the library's role is to provide its users with the fullest possible knowledge of the material available" (NBEET, 1990:66).[7]

Many librarians have examined some of the issues in higher education and related them to the library and information science environment. Since Sheridan wrote her article "Andragogy: A New Concept for Academic Librarian" (Sheridan, 1986),[8] many librarians have conducted studies, and written extensively about the adult student and the academic library. One of the most important sources consulted for this paper, was Carol Hammond's article which discusses "nontraditional students and the library: opinions, preferences, and behaviors" (Hammond, 1994).[9] In Hammond's study, students were surveyed, and their opinions and views were sought on various issues amongst such as time management, needs, bibliographic instruction, and attitudes regarding library use (Hammond, 1994).[10]

Most of the literature reviewed has dealt with various aspects of the academic library as it pertains to the adult, nontraditional learner (Hammond, 1994).[11] Hammond focuses on the nontraditional students' use of the library, when they want to use the library, what services they consider important, and how they evaluate library services (Hammond, 1994).[12] Leverence concentrates on the nontraditional adult students' perceptions of their library research skills in an automated environment (Leverence, 1997).[13] Andaleeb and Simmonds suggest that users expect the library staff to attend to their needs quickly and efficiently. Promptness is also critical to users' perceptions of responsiveness (Andaleeb & Simmonds, 1998).[14]

## *INSTITUTION CHARACTERISTICS: BACKGROUND OF THE COLLEGE AND LIBRARY*

Penn State Erie, The Behrend College, a college campus within the Pennsylvania State University system, enrolls approximately 3,500 full-time and part-time students. The College comprises four schools: Humanities and Social Sciences, Science, Business and Engineering and Engineering Technology. The College offers four-year degree programs and an MBA. At the time of the study in the fall of 1998, there were approximately seven hundred and forty-two adult learners. Four hundred and sixteen of these students were enrolled as undergraduate students in baccalaureate degree programs, one hundred and seventy-nine of these were enrolled in non-degreed programs, and one hundred and forty-seven were part-time students in the MBA program. Contrary to many academic studies' results indicating that the majority of students enrolled at colleges and universities within the United States are female, Penn State, Erie statistics reveal the exact opposite to be true. Among the adult learner population, there is a 2-to-1 ratio, with male students maintaining the majority. Penn State Erie adult students range in age from 24 to 65. The adult learners are enrolled in all subject areas; however, the majority is in business, management information systems, engineering, and engineering technology and computer science. About five years ago, a new library building was erected on the Penn State, Erie campus. Students at all locations within the Penn State system benefit from the extensive resources available within the Libraries' network.

## *RESOURCES AND SERVICES AVAILABLE TO STUDENTS*

All Penn State, Erie students have access to all resources currently found in LIAS (Library Information Access System). LIAS includes the CAT (Penn State's on-line catalog), informational databases, indexes, abstracts, CD-ROMS, and a plethora of Web resources including full text and full-image articles. Currently, there are about one hundred and fifty databases. LIAS may be accessed from workstations in the library, campus computer centers, as well as remote locations from work or home. The adult learners also have access to CD-ROM databases located in the library. Expanding the abundance of resources of all to all users, and especially adult learners who do not come regularly to the campus is Penn State's association with the Big Ten Libraries. On campus, librarians provide both course-related and course integrated instruction to students at the request of the faculty.

## *METHODOLOGY*

Eighty-five adult students from Penn State, Erie, The Behrend College participated in this study. There were three sessions comprising between eight to ten adult learners in each session. Some of the adult students were solicited as they visited the library, and some of these students in turn recruited their friends and classmates and encouraged them to participate in the discussion. The participants were also given copies of the 25 typed-written questions with enough space for them to answer questions in more detail if they chose to do so. These focus group discussions were audio taped with the consent of the participants. The adult learners introduced themselves to the other group members, and were asked a series of questions. These questions may be found in the appendix of this paper. The students were told that the library staff was interested in providing quality library service and wanted to find out what they thought about the library and the service it provided. The writer used this avenue to give them opportunity to air their satisfaction or dissatisfaction and provide recommendations for future improvement.

Some adult students who could not participate in the organized focus group sessions were targeted in classes that included both large numbers of adult learners and some traditional undergraduate students. All these students were presented with the same 25 typed-written questions presented to the adults in the focus group sessions. The questionnaires were distributed to the students at the end of the semesters immediately after they had completed their semester reviews. The rationale behind this decision was to get a more complete and accurate picture of the adult population. If the views of only the students who visit the library had been solicited, the study would have missed the opinions and recommendations of the adult non-library users. A more accurate picture of adult learners' relationship with the library can also be assessed if the views and opinions of adult students who visit the library are combined with those who did not. Questionnaires obtained in the classrooms from students under 24 years old were discarded. Some of the questionnaires were also distributed to some adult learners enrolled in the MBA program. Face to face interviews and telephone interviews with adult students who had expressed an interest in the study but could not participate in the focus group discussions were also included in the study. Input from faculty who teach adult students was solicited via face-to-face interviews and these were also audio taped.

## FINDINGS

### Adult Learners

During the focus group sessions, adult learners met in a room within the library. They were informed that participation in the study was voluntary. They expressed genuine interest in participating in this study, and hoped that through participation, their presence in the library would become more apparent. Also, they hoped to improve library services for all students. Some of the students had utilized the library for study in the past. The questions asked of the adult students may be found at the end of this article. More adult learner respondents expressed concerns regarding the following issues: library hours, reference service, instruction, library resources, library staff attitudes, traditional student attitudes, remote access to library resources and overall library service. Expanding on the above issues, the students expressed a desire to have librarians provide structured orientation sessions specifically targeted towards adult student needs. Orientation sessions, which they say, should be better advertised since some of them do not visit the campus and the library on a regular basis. These sessions should also be offered at times convenient to adult students. Instruction during these sessions should include information on library resources, research and database searching techniques.

Due to their attendance in English composition classes, many of the adult learners are familiar with just the basics of the library and its resources. Some had not followed up on their own to become more familiar with the resources. Transfer students were even in a worse situation because they had never had any introduction to the library. Most respondents indicated that they appreciated the quiet atmosphere, the spaciousness, and the ample seating availability. However, excessive noise, created by younger students who used the library for social rather than study purposes bothered some adult learners. About 25% of the respondents whose opinions were solicited outside of the library had negative feelings about the library. They did not see the need to use the library and complained about everything from the lack of new books to the dearth of other resources in the library. The majority of the nonusers did not know much about the services or resources the library provides for its users.

Because most adult learners are part-time students and visit the library in the evenings and on the weekends, library hours concerned them greatly. Adult learners aired a preference that the library be open earlier on weekends and closed some time after 1:00 a.m. on weekdays and Sundays. The library currently opens Monday-Thursday 8 a.m.-12 midnight, closing at 6 p.m. on Fridays. On Saturdays, the library opens 12:00 noon-8 p.m., and 1:00 p.m.-midnight on Sundays.

Even though the respondents were satisfied with the quality of reference service received during the day, and some evening hours when librarians were available, they expressed concern when reference librarians were not available to assist them. They felt that when the library was open, it should be continuously staffed by knowledgeable library personnel. They also wanted student assistants in the library to be able to help them more in the evenings and on weekends.

In addition to more books and periodicals in their fields, some adult learners wanted more resources to initiate them to their future careers. They also emphasized the importance of access to library resources at Behrend, the Penn State Libraries System and beyond. The participants were most pleased that the vast array of resources through LIAS could be accessed remotely anywhere. All the adult learner respondents would like the library staff to treat them with respect. They asked that the staff treat them like "customers," and not singled out and treated differently because of their age. Some of them did not have any problems interacting with the traditional students, and had established friendships with some of the younger students based on mutual respect. Others did not want to mix with the traditional students because they considered them abrasive and disrespectful.

### Faculty and Administrators

Input from faculty members was solicited via face-to-face interviews. Provision of quality library service to all students is important to the administrators at Penn State Erie, The Behrend College. Faculty and administrators discussed issues pertaining to both undergraduate students and graduate students enrolled in the MBA program. Some of the topics discussed with the faculty and administrators included unique characteristics of the adult learner; the role the library and the faculty should play in the life of the adult; what services the library should provide for the older nontraditional adult learner, and the administrative perception of the adult learner balancing work and study.

According to the administrators interviewed for this paper, the adult learner sees the library not only as the *"information hub"* for students, but also as a quiet place to study, do research and escape work and family responsibilities temporarily. They grouped undergraduate adult students into three groups regarding library skills: those with no library skills; those with some library skills, but need assistance and direction; and those with library and research skills. Teaching faculty perceive the graduate adult learners as young professionals, between 25 and 35 years of age, who have been previously or are currently employed in jobs that they have held for one to five years, and are furthering their education to obtain promotion or assume managerial positions. Faculty members indicated that they frequently encouraged adult learners to use the library, or assign projects requiring them to use the library. In addition, they mentioned making every effort they could to include a library component in their syllabi, giving extra credit to students using library and Internet resources. Thus for students seeking extra points, using the library becomes a necessity. Some faculty members felt that many students refused to use the library as a result of their unawareness of the available resources and services. Since faculty members would only encourage students to use other libraries in the community in extreme emergencies, it became absolutely necessary for the library to provide at the beginning of each academic year a comprehensive descriptive list of resources within the libraries system, through interlibrary loan, and other member libraries whose services were available to the students. Another observation from those faculty members who consented to the interview suggested that more faculty members give library-related assignments to all students to provide an opportunity for better exposure to library resources. While they agreed that instruction for the adult learner was necessary and beneficial for the adult learner, exempting adults with vast library experience and expertise would prove more beneficial. The efforts of faculty and librarians could then be focused on the needy adult learner.

## DISCUSSION AND CONCLUSION

If librarians want to better help adult students, it is imperative for them to be aware of the unique needs of this special population. Zeithaml, Parasuraman, and Berry state that "knowing what customers expect is the first and possibly most critical step in delivering customer service" (Zeithaml, Parasuraman, & Berry, p. 51).[15]

All students have different needs, and one way to ensure that the needs of the various segments in the academic community are met is to acknowledge the existence of those concerns, examine them, and deal with them by finding workable solutions. Librarians and educators cannot ignore the needs and expectations of the adult learners. Because more adult students are pursuing higher education, and because technology brings certain constraints to the library and information environment, it is important to work together to integrate the information and research needs of all students, especially the needs of the adult learner. It was clear from this study that the adult learners wanted a peaceful environment to study, approachable and knowledgeable library staff who understood the needs of the students, and would not treat them with disrespect and jest even if they asked obvious questions. It was also obvious that the students wanted library staff to be proactive, seeking out the students rather than the other way around. This finding reflects what Andaleeb and Simmonds had found in an earlier study: Students believe that "academic librarians can actually play a proactive role" (Andaleeb & Simmonds, 1998).[16]

Also paramount to the students was immediate and efficient service. There are vast resources available to the students, faculty, and staff, and the adult students would use these resources more with more instruction. More instruction specifically tailored to the adult learner, broken down into manageable sections and made relevant to topics being covered by students by the faculty would be beneficial for adult students. Initial introduction to the library resources and services including local, libraries-wide, and outside the Penn State system will be useful for the students. This information, supplemented with a list of all available resources, should be made available as soon as students start classes. In their spare time they can fall on the list and become familiar with the wealth of resources, including databases, CD-ROM, on site and remote access to various types of information. The study, which was undertaken with the adult learners, the faculty, and the administrators, indicated that the adult learners are indeed an important component of the academic community. They do indeed have needs and expectations which should be met by the library staff and others on campus. There should be a continuous effort on the part of faculty, administrators, and librarians to make sure that the college years of the adult learner become a lifelong learning experience, especially where the library and research needs are concerned.

## REFERENCES

1. Mirriam, Sharon B. and Caffarella, Rosemary S. (1991) " Learning in Adulthood: A Comprehensive Guide" San Francisco: Jossey-Bass.

2. Britton, C. and Baxter, A. "Mature Students Route into Higher Education" *Journal of Access Studies 9* (1994): 215-228.

3. Marieluise Frei Raven and Ronald M. Jimmerson "Perceptions of Nontraditional Students, Teaching and Learning Held by Faculty and Students" *Continuing and Higher Education Review* 56 (Fall 1992) : 137-154.

4. Peter Hernon and Ellen Altman, *Service Quality in Academic Libraries* (Norwood, NJ: Ablex, Publishing Co., 1996).

5. Jan Marie Spanard "Beyond Intent: Reentering College to Complete the Degree" *Review of Educational Research* 60 (3) (Fall 1990): 309-344.

6. John T.E. Richardson and Estelle King "Adult Students in Higher Education: Burden or Boon? *The Journal of Higher Education* 68 (1) (Jan/Feb. 1998): 65-88.

7. National Board of Employment Educational Training (December, 1990) Library Provision in Higher Education Institutions: Commission Report no. 7. Canberra: Australian Government Publishing Service.

8. Jean Sheridan "Andragogy: A New Concept for Academic Librarians." *Research Strategies* 4 (4) (Fall 1986) 156-67.

9. Carol Hammond "Nontraditional Students and the Library: Opinions, Preferences, and Behaviors" *College & Research Libraries* (July 1994) 323-341.

10. Ibid, p. 323-341.

11. Ibid, p. 323-341.

12. Ibid, p. 323-341.

13. Mari Ellen Quirk Leverence "A Study of the Nontraditional Students' Perception of their Library Research Skills." *The Reference Librarian* 58 (1997): 143-161.

14. Syed Saad Andaleeb and Patience L. Simmonds "Explaining User Satisfaction with Academic Strategic Implications" *College and Research Libraries* (March 1998) 156-167.

15. Valarie A. Zeithaml, A. Parasuraman, and Leonard L. Berry. *Delivering Quality Service: Balancing Customer Perceptions and Expectations* (New York: The Free Press. 1990): 51.

16. Syed Saad Andaleeb and Patience L. Simmonds "Explaining User Satisfaction with Academic Libraries: Strategic Implications" *College and Research Libraries* (March 1998) 156-167.

# APPENDIX

## Adult Student Focus Group Questions

1.  How often do you visit the Library?

2.  When do you visit the Library?

3.  What do you think of the Library?

4.  What library services and resources are you familiar with?

5.  How did you find out about the library services and resources?

6.  How does the Library help you in your academic life?

7.  What do you think the Library should be doing to help you?

8.  Do you feel comfortable in the Library?

9.  How well do you interact with the Library Staff/younger students?

10. How effective is the library staff in helping you use/find resources in the library?

11. What kind of problems do you have using the Behrend library?

12. Do you use other nearby libraries in addition to the Behrend Library?

13. Do you prefer other nearby libraries to the Behrend Library? Why?

14a. What are some of the things you like about the Behrend Library?

14b. What are some of the things you dislike about the Library?

## APPENDIX (continued)

15a. What are some of the services/resources you would add?

15b. What are some of the services/resources you would eliminate?

16.  Would you like the library staff to make special concessions for you because of your special circumstances?

17.  How would you like the library staff to treat you as an adult learner?

18.  Do you think the staff provides the best quality service for you?

19.  Name at least five services you would library to add.

20.  Name at least five services you would demand that the library provide for the students.

21.  Why did you decide to continue your education now?

22.  What is your major?

23.  Age (optional).

24.  What recommendations do you have for the improvement of the library services?

# Towards an Integrative Literature Search: Reflections of a 'Wild' Adult Learner

## Robert M. Fisher

**SUMMARY.** An integral learning approach involves principles beyond andragogy, a "new pedagogy," transformative learning, feminist, or postmodernist perspectives and the "integrative knowing" in adult education theory. Drawing on a radical conflict transformation model of eldership, the author presents personal reflections on his own evolution as a library researcher and adult learner for the past 25 years. Skills and metaskills for the reference librarian are included. The traditional helping role and identity of librarians is challenged to become a 'guide' for the hunt, whereby the process of the search is valued as much as the end result. *[Article copies available for a fee from The Haworth Document Delivery Service: 1-800-342-9678. E-mail address: <getinfo@haworthpressinc. com> Website: <http://www.haworthpressinc.com>]*

**KEYWORDS.** Andragogy, adult learning, reference service and the adult learner

### LOSS OF LIFE-SPIRIT:
### FROM 'NATURAL' TO 'SCIENTIFIC' WAYS

Over 25 years ago, in a technical college working on my first wildlife biology paper, I learned to appreciate the kind assistance of the reference

---

Robert M. Fisher is an artist, writer, educator, and counselor in Calgary, Alberta, Canada. He is soon to begin a graduate program in Adult Education at the University of British Columbia.

Address correspondence to: Robert M. Fisher, #400, 2725 Melfa Road; Vancouver, BC V6TIN4 (E-mail: rmfisher@interchange.ubc.ca).

[Haworth co-indexing entry note]: "Towards an Integrative Literature Search: Reflections of a 'Wild' Adult Learner." Fisher, Robert M. Co-published simultaneously in *The Reference Librarian* (The Haworth Information Press, an imprint of The Haworth Press, Inc.) No. 69/70, 2000, pp. 407-417; and: *Reference Services for the Adult Learner: Challenging Issues for the Traditional and Technological Era* (ed: Kwasi Sarkodie-Mensah) The Haworth Information Press, an imprint of The Haworth Press, Inc., 2000, pp. 407-417. Single or multiple copies of this article are available for a fee from The Haworth Document Delivery Service [1-800-342-9678, 9:00 a.m. - 5:00 p.m. (EST). E-mail address: getinfo@haworthpressinc.com].

librarian who seemed to know where to find everything on the topic: "Natural History Of The Great Blue Heron." At age 21, the information world housed in that huge library was an amazing jungle that thoroughly intimidated me. I was no academic. Being raised by primary-schooled poor working class parents left me abnormally unskilled and lacking confidence about thinking and organizing my thoughts on paper. By today's standards and obsession with psychiatric DSM-IV diagnoses of anything a little 'wild,' I'd likely have ended up labeled A.D.D. or perhaps one of the latest labels, O.D.D. ("Oppositional Defiant Disorder"). Yup, that was me; either feeling *attention deficit* (lack of loving attention) or typically feeling *odd* in the educational world. I really wasn't a bad kid. But me and authority (should read: "authority and I") never got along. Mostly, I stayed out of their way and didn't respect the "learning" they said they were to provide me. I learned lots in those early years but not much from teachers, and less from any librarian. No one was peddling the new learning research slogan-of-the-day back then. I'd likely have profited greatly had those school people known about "multiple intelligences" (a la Gardner), student-directed learning, inclusive learning environments or individual learning styles.

Libraries were not this warrior's sacred place. In college library the first day, the fear of the unknown seemed to scramble the little intelligence I thought may exist above my neck. I didn't know what "microfiche" was or even what to do with an "index." The librarian's suggestion that we *"must learn how to use library technology"* was about as foreign and repulsive to me as learning "math" or "motor mechanics." I was an artistic organic-type, not a technical-type. The only machines I was comfortable with then were my bicycle and my drum kit and I used both extremely proficiently. Unfortunately, no teachers picked up on my natural competencies and I didn't get a grade for learning what I was good at. Again, the painful memory of feeling alone and not fitting in, arose. Honestly, I must have been living in aboriginal dreamtime when I was in high school, for not a memory of doing library research remains. And I didn't even do drugs! My junior high librarian was a royal "b." She sent me to the office for sticking bubblegum under one of the library chairs. Libraries, in those teen years, left me with a taste of totalitarian inhibition of my "natural impulses" to cause chaos. I just didn't learn by logical sequences, or at least, I knew I wasn't learning much because the logical-linear pursuit of answering the grade nine orientation library worksheet was a super bore. Following others' maps wasn't as appealing as exploring the territory for myself. But of course, with the coming of the "efficiency" and "accountability" generation of library science and technology, my approach of "just go do it by yourself" and "hunt by trial-and-error" seemed out of synch–maybe, anachronistic?

I wasn't turned-on to learning until that day in the college library when I wanted to know everything that existed on the Great Blue Heron. I'd watched these birds for the past year as a naturalist–naive and free-spirited inquiry. 'Love for the subject,' would be an understatement. Later in university I studied ecology and environmental sciences to learn that being a naturalist (biophilic-type, see Wolf 1994) just wasn't cool if you were to do real objective "science" and empirical quantitative rational-logical research–now, known as "the Supremacist White Male way," with some disgust, by ultra-feminists. I just thought this 'hard science' domination was "better" because that's what everyone said. So, library researching became more scientific (narrow and linear) too, but my love for life, 'wildness' and learning wouldn't be completely dampened. No wonder I switched careers to education, psychology and human services in due time. By the way, I collected ten times more than I needed for that Great Blue Heron paper. The librarians didn't help much beyond that initial hand-holding gesture of patience to make sure I had the basics for doing a search. I got my first 'A' ever. I've never stopped reading, researching and writing on just about anything and most of it for pure enjoyment. I was into lifelong learning before it was hip.

## ADULTS AS INTEGRAL LEARNERS

Now that I've introduced myself, the focus of the rest of this paper is on my own experiences learning and researching as a professional counselor and independent scholar of education, philosophy and psychology. My interests are in liberational ways of being and the freeing of the 'spirit' inside each unique individual. Adult educators may call this "agenda" radical/critical theory (Giroux 1983), emancipatory education (Hart 1990), or more commonly, transformative learning (Mezirow 1991) as the genre to which I relate most. I have experienced the grief and seen the losses of life-spirit in a civilization that continues a modernist agenda of technicalizing everything to mechanical efficiency. When nature became science, much was gained but much was lost.

I would not like to see the scientific technician, called "modern librarian," fall into this trap of a dehumanizing paradigm. I want to share my experiences of how the "accidental," "synchronistic," "order out of chaos" and "curiosity" have been the most valuable aspects of my research process in libraries in that past few years. Schwartz and Russek (1997 p. 18), in their own search for an integral medical model, wrote, " . . . *through a combination of intuition and reason. Great discoveries (and great art) often arise from intuitive (integrative) hunches about diverse patterns and orders in nature.*" What we search for in the reference library is 50% of the discovery. The other 50% of the discovery, which makes it "great" learning and creates unpredictable opportunities for growth, comes from the way we search. As I get older, the latter *"way"* of the search seems to have become more important than the *"what"* in library research. The Great Blue Heron research project had a very narrow "funnel" and the reference librarians were helpful to see I got *"what"* I wanted in the technical aspect of my study at college. But what did they and I miss? What skills (and metaskills) of the *"way"* of library research are required to develop an artistic-organic or, just plain 'wild,' approach to hunting in the modern library? Is there a way to integrate the organic (intuitive) and mechanical (reason-able) ways of knowing and doing research in libraries? Does the seasoned adult learner have a few tips on "hunting" to teach the modern reference librarian? These are a few of the questions I'll explore below. The *integrative paradigm* is a holistic approach to knowledge and experience presented later in this paper. It provides an alternative, or adjunctive route, to the narrow "funneling" and specialization of modern research assumptions and methods.

Changing careers seven times in 25 years apparently is not unusual these days in a rapidly changing world. Adult learners like myself, have lots of experiences we bring to the library search. 'Diversity' is the key word to remember in teaching adult learners. We've been around. It's not all good. It doesn't mean we've learned effectively from the life changes either. The sad truth is, there is no guarantee that we adults actually learn from our experiences. At least that is the criticism I hear from many of the young Generation Xers (who are a category of adult learners, born between 1961-81, completely distinct and unique (Brown 1997) from myself as a babyboomer). But adult learners have the potential to draw on vast experiences from many places like jobs, relationships, roles as parents, and diverse career tracks. We've had more time to practice integral learning. That is, we have lots of information and experiences to integrate new knowledge with a diverse and lengthy past. Simply, adult learners have a "stronger" foundation of diverse knowledge and experiences to work with than younger learners. This is a blessing and a curse. It is however, a key factor, I believe, that makes us naturally integral learners. It also makes us potentially powerful hunters and discoverers, as we'll see later in this paper.

## INTEGRAL LEARNING: INTEGRAL KNOWLEDGE

The adult educational literature generally supports the idea that teaching adults [born before 1961] *"should be approached in a different way"* than teaching younger students (Imel 1995). However, there is little agreement in the literature of how teaching adults is so different, and the assumptions of andragogy (a la Knowles) are highly questionable (Pratt 1993) and under researched (Imel 1995). The term "new pedagogy" (Taylor and Marineau 1995, cited in Imel 1995a) certainly applies to creating inclusive learning environments that meet the needs of most adult learners: *"(1) the validity of the student's experiences as well as support for the emerging self as a focus of education, (2) the contextual nature of knowledge, including the relationship between the learner and his or her knowledge base, and (3) the notion that learning can be a transformative process."* Although transformative learning is most closely associated with adult learning, according to Mezirow, these labels do not adequately fit the challenge appropriate to the reference librarian, nor do they exactly support the case I want to make in this paper. Even the postmodern critique of some adult educators, though generally appealing to my own "way" of learning and living, does not go far enough. The postmodernist view (Kirka 1997), like most feminist views, at least challenges the domination of rational, scientific, and objective reality as the only confident way to knowledge and progress.

It seems that an integrative approach to learning supports what I'm calling for. Wilber (1997) has the most in-depth description of integrative theory. Schwartz and Russek (1997) include "integrative diversity" as one of the most important of the eight world hypotheses (worldviews) for creating an integration of the wealth of data and theories in the health field. Generally, these theorists, outside of adult education per se, are attempting to find a comprehensive model/theory *" . . . that integrates the wealth of seemingly disparate data and theories of health and illness into an organized whole"* (Schwartz and Russek 1997 p. 7). Integral method/theory, like integral practice of learning, involves the learner in an extended processes of synthesis, whereby nothing (at least theoretically) is left out of the quest to know. There is an underlying assumption in the integral approach which respects *diversity and complexity* of nature/reality (as ecologists have repeatedly emphasized). The recent growth of the new sciences of complexity are a sign of a greater appreciation that "everything" is connected in vast complex systems and traditional mechanical ways of knowing are not appropriate to the challenge of knowing in the new systems or holistic paradigm. A new methodology is required to understand complex systems and truths. My concern is well expressed by Wolf (1994 p. 37, cited in Loughlin 1996),

> *Is an innate human fascination with the complexity of life being subverted by a fascination with the complexity of technology? And, if so, are we breaking the band* [sic?] *that keeps us and other species alive?*

A library search on a topic of interest, using an integral approach, is always multi-disciplinary, contextual, and broad with a wide "funnel"–i.e., integral. This does not mean general and shallow, but actually it creates knowledge that is very rich and deep–with possibilities for entirely new emergent discoveries because what was thought to be irrelevant or entirely disparate information, turns out in some cases to be the source, via integration, of a creative quantum leap in knowledge. The new physics, for e.g., made great strides once the traditional "wave" and "particle" division of light was integrated into a whole theory of the "wavicle" phenomenon. The literature on creativity abounds to support the integral approach but that is beyond the scope of this paper.

Loughlin (1996), an adult educator, summarized much of the literature on what she called "integrated knowing." She basically calls for a "learning to change" model, in the transformative learning genre. She argues for *"an integration of rational and non-rational* [feeling, intuitive, relational/con-textual–more feminine] *ways of knowing"* that link directly to a *"value of human care as important dimensions of the learning process"* (p. 7). Reference librarians are no doubt being challenged today to not only be up-to-date on the technology of information but to provide quality care and service to each client and their needs. A large task indeed. They may not have known that this direction of their work in human care is part of an ongoing trend of recognizing the value of holistic approaches and integral methods. However, none of the above models fully validates or supports the approach to hunting down a topic that I have learned best suits me as a 'wild' adult learner.

## SITTING IN THE 'FIRE'

As I have matured, my research approach transformed. I transformed as I became an adult learner. Searching out a specific topic in a large library shifted from a technical quick-fix solution (i.e., finding the key references and quotes as soon as possible) *to* enjoying the hunt (the process) without all the rush and focus on the end-game (the content). More often than not, my search for something I knew, led me to find something unexpected that I didn't know–the latter, far more valuable to me than the former. I'll explain with an example below shortly. I seem to be forgetting all the logical, system-atic and linear ways I was taught to do library research. Upon reflection, it is evident that I had not asked a librarian a single question, nor sought out their guidance for a search in years. The changing computer technology for searches at the local university library is enough to drive me mad. So I let it. I get so mad, I rarely attempt to use it. I keep feeling guilty for not being up-to-date on all the sophisticated ways of doing library searches. The feeling comes from comparing because I feel I cannot keep up with the young aggressive learners in university today. Actually, I find the line-ups and sign-ups more than unbearable and my instincts tell me there are other *ways* to find out what I want in the library. I desire to hunt for what my curiosity is burning with next. I must have lost faith that reference librarians have the skills of 'guidance' for the kind of learning I find best. To others, my best *way,* may be too 'wild.'

Despite what the mainstream thinks, I have found validation for my approach to learning and knowledge in the work of psychotherapists Dr. Arnold and Amy Mindell (of the Process Oriented Psychology Institute, Portland, Oregon). Their expertise is in radical conflict resolution/transformation. I've been teaching their work and my own practices of conflict work for the past few years. There seem a number of skills and metaskills that come out of this work that 'fit' the integral paradigm of library research and knowing generally. In this short article I touch on only a few. Amy's latest book *Sitting in the fire; Large group transformation and using conflict and diversity* (1995) speaks to my warrior soul and echoes my experiences of learning as an adult–one who is endlessly 'pushing the envelope' of discovery.

## DISTINGUISHING SKILLS AND METASKILLS

Earlier I spoke of the *"way"* of doing research, having grown to be more valuable to me than the *"what."* Mindell (1995 p. 43) wrote what was most important in their worldwork, *"Not what you do, but how you do it."* Mindell (1993 p. 85) clarified, *"Not only are the skills and techniques important, but the feelings with which you use the techniques–what Amy calls metaskills–are also crucial."* He wrote,

> *Over and above information and awareness, worldworkers* [conflict resolution workers] *need 'metaskills.' They are crucial. Your work succeeds not because of what you know or do, but because of how you do it. Worldwork springs from your interest in other people and love for them. You care about who they are and what is happening to them. Eldership is an important feeling skill.* (Mindell 1995 p. 43)

"Eldership" is the adult educator/facilitator and learner all under a dignified label–not unlike aboriginal peoples' respect for the adult learner/elder. The concept of "feeling skill" is far too complex to elaborate here. Rather, I'll give an example based on my experiences of library research in recent years. I was searching for recent papers by Ken Wilber in *Psychological Abstracts* (index). I accidentally found my eye catching another name as I was flipping pages by hand rather recklessly. He was an author who had stuck with me for some time as important, although I had rarely thought of his name consciously. I read his book nearly eight years earlier and not another piece since. I looked at his recent article title, forgetting about Wilber, and tracked it down. After reading barely a few paragraphs of this paper I was filled with feelings of joy, verging on awesome excitement. At the back of his paper I saw where he worked and lived–Bath, England. Immediately, I had a 'rush' go through me and a knowing that I was to meet this man. I copied his e-mail down and began correspondence, followed by an application to do graduate work with him. While searching for Wilber (or whatever else popped up to catch my attention), I'd kept an open wide "funnel" for a "felt resonance" (see Heron, 1992) with anything during the search. I was fixed on Wilber but not totally. My 'hunter' was flexible and available to be side-tracked for perhaps better game.

In retrospect, I had an underlying agenda of searching for a new career path, or even a mentor–something that would get me out of the stuck place I felt I was in my life at that time. This was the unconscious "secondary process" (according to Mindell) that was actually more important than the "primary process" of my library search. After communicating with this professor in Bath, I found out he knew and worked with another scholar who I had been trying to track down for a year or so. One thing "synchronistically" (a la Jung) led to another, although the grad program didn't work out. I've made a very important life-long connection with a soul-mentor in Italy from that 'side-track.' Was it accident? I don't know but I don't think so, for I've had many experiences like this in libraries. Some of the best discoveries have come from wandering around the book shelves where I've never been before. Leaving enough of a wide "funnel" in my search left my secondary process available to hunt for what it (I) needed, which I mostly was denying was very important at the time. Eventually, I got back to my Wilber search when I was ready.

The chaos approach to flipping through a huge index almost at random, allowed for this discovery. I was willing to change course in mid-stream. A specific CD-ROM search or linear approach on the computer terminal would leave out so much. The organic 'hands-on' search still seems best for me. The computer design/program is not controlling what I pick up or pass by on my way to the specific term. There is little room for the full instincts of the hunter/elder with sophisticated technology, nor is there room when one doesn't allow, or know, that there are other ways of learning besides the direct efficient, scientific, and logical search approaches taught by librarians. I allowed the process to carry me rather than the end content. This was a skill. It is a skill of the elder to stay wide open at all times. Mindell (1995 p. 43) said,

> *The elder keeps an eye on your internal process while also recognizing the language and body signals of other individuals in the group. The elder monitors the group's 'primary' and 'secondary' processes and knows that your process contributes to the make-up of the field.*

Awareness of the "field" is a complex topic related to the new physics (Arnold Mindell is a trained physicist from M.I.T. as well as Jungian analyst). Basically, when I was looking for Wilber, I was also tuning-in to a "field" of connections and information that is not rational or logically perceptible through normal thinking. Call my "attunement" *intuition* if you wish.

The principle of this integral way of searching is based upon acknowledging "fields" of highly *diverse* information that are very subtle and often are only picked up by body-felt experiences (maybe dreams–night or day), or what some call intuition. There is a purpose in every interaction and "field" I inhabit. The older I am, the more "fields" I'm creating with. Adult learners therefore require the widest "funnel" and guidance from the reference librarian. Every action is important and meaningful, despite how random, accidental or chaotic its surface/apparent occurrence. Everything, 'outside' of me and 'inside' of me is part of the "field" and its dynamics of unfolding. Sounds all pretty 'wild' huh? Well, it is. But it's the healthiest 'wild' madness I know, and it's brought great gifts to me when I could not predict the outcome. I just sat in the 'fire' of the chaos and was willing to not know exactly the "right" way to learn. Let the learning come to you–that, is the wisdom I've gleaned. Fear will be your first enemy and barrier to doing this. That is likely, the fundamental practice of integral learning. And of course, it may not be for everyone in all situations because sitting in the 'fire' isn't always comfortable.

## A FEW SKILLS FOR THE REFERENCE LIBRARIAN: SITTING IN THE 'FIRE'

The modeling of these skills (an art and science) is the best teaching for the adult learners you serve.

1. *Chaos*–make it OK for yourself or your client to "not know" the "right" way to learn (or overpredict what is "best" to learn) in a library search. Value the *'way'* as much as the *'what.'* Be humble and acknowledge your fear head-on and get to know that fear well.
2. *Integral Learning*–provide the widest "funnel" for the search; let the adult choose to narrow it as part of their own learning process. Respect the "field" and one's intuition ("feeling skills") as an equally important 'teacher' as the rational.
3. *Self-knowledge*–understand that all searches are as much about learning about yourself, and finding yourself (and losing yourself) as they are conscious efforts to know more.

## A KEY METASKILL FOR THE REFERENCE LIBRARIAN

There are many metaskills in integral learning. They often emerge as part of the evolution and practice of the skills above. However, the Mindells' point repeatedly to the most basic and important metaskill for this work. It is a form of heartfulness, otherwise known as "compassion." Mindell (1993 p. 85) said,

> *I have no idea how to learn or teach this feeling* [compassion], *though I know that it is more important than any of the other paraphernalia or skills. This detached heartfulness is powerful in your dealing with the most seductive of all trance states: ordinary* ['normal'] *reality.*

The artistic-organic *'way'* of learning never leaves out diversity and depth of experience, that the normal and ordinary world of reality so often occludes. I can think of nothing more destructive than occlusion of non-ordinary experiences (consciousness) in educational practices. William James, the American father of psychology, pointed out, *"Our normal waking consciousness is but one special type. . . . No account of the universe in its totality can be final which leaves these other forms of consciousness quite disregarded . . . "* (cited in Wilber 1977/82 p. 15). Simply, the pure "love" of your work, of learning, of the unordinary, of people and their processes, is a good start to compassion. However, if you let your fear and mistrust of the non-ordinary and 'wild' ways of doing research create a narrow "funnel," then compassion remains hidden. It is difficult to watch one in pain and fear, in suffering and anger when they don't catch their "game" right away. Being able to sit in the 'fire' of all their uncomfortable experiences (and your own) is a sacred act in the preparation to meet the 'teacher' of the unknown. The reference librarian's role and identity is up for renewal as we move into an ever more complex world. I trust this reflection of my own learning and healing journey is of value to you. May you find your eldership and pass it on.

## REFERENCES

Brown, L. Bettina. 1997. "New learning strategies for Generation X." ERIC Digest No. 184. Columbus, OH: ERIC Clearinghouse on Adult, Career, and Vocational Education.

Giroux, Henry A. 1983. *Theory and resistance in education; A pedagogy for the oppressed.* South Hadley, MA: Bergin and Garvey.

Hart, M. 1990. "Critical theory and beyond: Further perspectives on emancipatory education." *Adult Education Quarterly, 40 (2):* 125-138.

Heron, John. 1992. *Feeling and personhood; Psychology in a new key.* London: Sage.

Imel, Susan. 1995. "Teaching adults: Is it different?" ERIC Myths and Realities. Columbus, OH: ERIC Clearinghouse on Adult, Career, and Vocational Education (internet website).

Imel, Susan. 1995a. "Inclusive adult learning environments." ERIC Digest No. 62. Columbus, OH: ERIC Clearinghouse on Adult, Career and Vocational Education.

Kirka, Sandra. 1997. "Postmodernizm and adult education." ERIC Alert On Issues. Columbus, OH: ERIC Clearinghouse on Adult, Career, and Vocational Education (internet website).

Loughlin, Kathleen. 1996. "Learning to change: New directions." *Australian Journal of Adult and Community Education, 36 (1):* 54-61.

Mezirow, J. 1991. *Transformative dimensions of adult learning.* San Francisco, CA: Jossey-Bass.

Mindell, Arnold. 1995. *Sitting in the fire; Large group transformation using conflict and diversity.* Portland, OR: Lao Tse Press.

Mindell, Arnold. 1993. *The shaman's body.* NY: HarperSanFrancisco.

Pratt, D.D. 1993. "Andragogy after twenty-five years." In *An Update on Adult Learning Theory. New Directions for Adult and Continuing Education No. 57,* edited by S.B. Mirriam. San Francisco, CA: Jossey-Bass.

Schwartz, Gary E. and Linda G. Russek. 1997. "The challenge of one medicine: Theories of health and eight 'world hypotheses'." *Advances: The Journal of Mind-Body Health, 13 (3):* 7-23.

Taylor, K. and C. Marineau. (eds.) 1995. *Learning environments for women's adult development: Bridges toward change.* New Directions for Adult and Continuing Education. San Francisco, CA: Jossey-Bass.

Wilber, Ken. 1997. *The eye of Spirit: An integral vision of a world gone slightly mad.* Boston, MA: Shambhala.

Wilber, Ken. 1977/82. *Spectrum of consciousness.* Wheaton, IL: Theosophical Publishing House.

Wolf, E.C. 1994. "What is biophilia?" *Worldwatch, 7 (4):* 37-38.

# Index

A *Nation at Risk*, 225
Academia, adult learners in, reference
    services for, continuing
    implications for, 5-17
Academic librarians, in adult learning
    facilitation, 219-231. *See*
    *also* Adult learning,
    facilitation of, academic
    librarian's role in
Academic libraries
    for adult learners, technological
    considerations in, 9-11
    corporate model for, 171-179. *See*
    *also* Interactive reference, for
    distance learners
    "traditional student" discourse and,
    89
*ACRL Guidelines for Extended*
    *Campus Library Services*,
    114
"Administration, Management and
    Policy," 196
Adult(s), defined, 20,115
Adult basic education, reference
    provision in, unusual model
    of, 181-192. *See also* Adult
    Education Resource and
    Information Service (ARIS)
    aims of, 182
    clients of, 182-183
    effectiveness of, factors
    influencing, 186-190
    introduction to, 182-184
Adult community education, reference
    provision in, unusual model
    of, 181-192. *See also* Adult
    basic education, reference
    provision in, unusual model
    of
"Adult Education," 114-115

"Adult Education and the Public
    Library," 152
Adult Education Resource and
    Information Service (ARIS),
    182
    activities of, 183-184
    aims of, 182
    clients of, 182-183
    effectiveness of, factors
    influencing, 186-190
    reference services of, 184-186
    resource collection, 184-185
    staff of, responsibilities of, 184
Adult learners
    in academia, reference services for
    continuing implications for,
    5-17
    technological considerations in,
    9-11
Adult learners information literacy for,
    lecture and online
    demonstrations, 263-264
    androgogy, 105-106
    attributes of, 8
    challenges facing, 396
    challenges posed by, 9-10
    characteristics of, 8-9,20-21,207,
    255-256,364
    library services directed toward,
    113-118
    andragogy and, 114-115
    proximity of, 114
    reference interview, 116-117
    computer phobia of, elimination of,
    71-72
    concerns of, library services
    directed toward, 113-118
    constructing new identities in
    traditional university setting
    for, 79-93

    *419*

**TO ORDER: CALL: 1-800-429-6784 / FAX: 1-800-895-0582** [Outside US/Canada: + 607-771-0012] / **E-MAIL: getinfo@haworthpressinc.com**

□ YES, please send me Concise Encyclopedia of Chronic Fatigue Syndrome

_____ in hard at $69.95 ISBN: 0-7890-0922-6. (Outside US/Canada/Mexico: $84.00)

_____ in soft at $24.95 ISBN: 0-7890-0923-4. (Outside US/Canada/Mexico: $30.00)

- Individual orders outside US, Canada, and Mexico must be prepaid by check or credit card.
- Discounts are not available on 5+ text prices and not available in conjunction with any other discount.
- Discount not applicable on books priced under $15.00.
- 5+ text prices are not available for jobbers and wholesalers.
- Postage & handling: In US: $4.00 for first book; $1.50 for each additional book. Outside US: $5.00 for first book; $2.00 for each additional book.
- NY, MN, and OH residents: please add appropriate sales tax after postage & handling.
- Canadian residents: please add 7% GST after postage & handling.
- Payment in UNESCO coupons welcome.
- If paying in Canadian dollars, use current exchange rate to convert to US dollars.
- Please allow 3-4 weeks for delivery after publication.
- Prices and discounts subject to change without notice.

Signature _____

□ BILL ME LATER($5 service charge will be added).

(Not available for individuals outside US/Canada/Mexico. Service charge is waived for/jobbers/wholesalers/booksellers.)

□ Check here if billing address is different from shipping address and attach purchase order and billing address information.

□ **PAYMENT ENCLOSED $** _____

(Payment must be in US or Canadian dollars by check or money order drawn on a US or Canadian bank.)

□ **PLEASE BILL MY CREDIT CARD:**

□ AmEx □ Diners Club □ Discover □ Eurocard □ JCB □ Master Card □ Visa

Account Number _____

Expiration Date _____

Signature _____

May we open a confidential credit card account for you for possible future purchases? ( ) Yes ( ) No

**THE HAWORTH PRESS, INC., 10 Alice Street, Binghamton, NY 13904-1580 USA**

---

Please complete the information below or tape your business card in this area.

NAME _____

INSTITUTION _____

ADDRESS _____

CITY _____

STATE _____ ZIP _____

COUNTRY _____

COUNTY (NY residents only) _____

E-MAIL _____

May we use your e-mail address for confirmations and other types of information? ( ) Yes ( ) No. We appreciate receiving your e-mail address and fax number. Haworth would like to e-mail or fax special discount offers to you, as a preferred customer. We will never share, rent, or exchange your e-mail address or fax number. We regard such actions as an invasion of your privacy.

□ YES, please send me Concise Encyclopedia of Chronic Fatigue Syndrome (ISBN: 0-7890-0923-4) to consider on a 60-day no risk examination basis. I understand that ( ) Yes ( ) No. I will receive an invoice payable within 60 days, or that if I decide to adopt the book, my invoice will be cancelled. I understand that I will be billed at the lowest price. (Offer available only to teaching faculty in US, Canada, and Mexico.)

Signature _____

Course Title(s) _____

Current Text(s) _____

Enrollment _____

Semester _____

Office Tel _____ Hours _____

Decision Date _____

(09) (26) 05/00   BIC00